Get the eBook FREE!

(PDF, ePub, Kindle, and liveBook all included)

We believe that once you buy a book from us, you should be able to read it in any format we have available. To get electronic versions of this book at no additional cost to you, purchase and then register this book at the Manning website.

Go to https://www.manning.com/freebook and follow the instructions to complete your pBook registration.

That's it!
Thanks from Manning!

T0100103

Azure Security

Azure Security

BOJAN MAGUŠIĆ

MANNING
SHELTER ISLAND

Manning Publications Co.
20 Baldwin Road
PO Box 761
Shelter Island, NY 11964

Development editor:	Toni Arritola
Review editor:	Aleksandar Dragosavljević
Production editor:	Keri Hales
Copy editor:	Alisa Larson
Proofreader:	Melody Dolab
Technical proofreader:	Karsten Strøbæk
Typesetter and cover designer:	Marija Tudor

ISBN 9781633438811
Printed in the United States of America

To my loving wife, parents, and sister.

brief contents

contents

preface

This book delves into the infinite game of cybersecurity and the ethos of sharing knowledge within this realm. My career at Microsoft has equipped me with invaluable skills and experiences, for which I'm immensely grateful. I owe a debt of gratitude to the brilliant minds who've influenced my journey, many of whom are instrumental in developing and advancing Azure security services that are the focus of this book. Their generosity in sharing knowledge and expertise has been pivotal. My application of their teachings in securing Azure environments for Fortune 500 companies has provided practical insights that I aim to distill in this book.

Rather than encompassing the entire spectrum of Azure's security services, this book offers a deliberate selection of services for effectively securing your Azure environment. While some of these services have broader applications, the primary emphasis is on Azure security. Most tools discussed here are inherent to Azure and seamlessly integrate with the services featured in this book.

The time has come for me to pay forward this knowledge. Security holds immense significance, especially given the frequency of new attacks—occurring every few minutes—and their impact on companies, regardless of size. The shortage of cybersecurity professionals is a pressing issue likely to persist. Security concerns everyone, prompting me to write this book. I'm eager to share insights you can use to better secure your Azure environments. Our collective future hinges on this imperative!

acknowledgments

When I started this project, I hadn't the foggiest idea of the assistance I would receive throughout this process. I'm so grateful for the support of an extraordinary group of people who were patient, forgiving, and generous with their time as well as their advice.

Thank you to my amazing family—my parents Radmila and Franjo Magušić and sister Radmila Magušić—for their unconditional love and support. Throughout my life, you have been and continue to be my biggest champions. Without your support and sacrifices, I wouldn't get to live my dreams.

To the love of my life, Dolores, thank you so much for your love, support, and patience while I wrote this book. Throughout this whole process, you supported me the most and continue to be my biggest advocate.

My development editor, Toni Arritola, served as an exceptional guide on this adventure. Toni, thank you for your patience and guidance and for showing me the ropes of how to write a technical book for Manning. It's because of you that I feel my technical writing has improved, and I will always cherish our chats. Thank you to Rebecca Rinehart for connecting me with Toni, and to Erik Pillar and Brian Sawyer for helping me find my way to Manning. Thank you to Marjan Bace for being my publisher. And, finally, thanks to the whole production staff at Manning, who helped this book come to fruition. I could not have asked for a more extraordinary publishing team.

I'm also incredibly grateful to the many friends and colleagues at Microsoft who took time out of their busy schedules to share their vast knowledge of Azure security with me. Throughout my career at Microsoft, you have been my guiding light and have helped me learn something new each day. Thanks to Shay Amar for partnering with me on a large number of projects and initiatives related to Azure security. Shay, you supported me unconditionally at every step along the way, and I learned so much from you. Your friendship and generosity with both your time and experience have been invaluable to me while I was writing this book. I will always remember our learnings from securing Kubernetes deployments. Tom Janetschek let me stand on his shoulders every day. Tom, your vast technical knowledge is only matched by the kindness of your heart. You have a rare ability to simplify complex topics and make them easier to understand. It's something I strived to replicate while breaking down complex topics in this book. Thank you for generously taking time for our chats and helping me further my understanding of Azure and security in general. I learned more from our chats than you will ever know. Yuri Diogenes inspired me to be the best version of myself each day. Yuri, your coaching and support have been invaluable to me over the past two years. I have learned so much from you, be it from your books, podcasts, or our conversations. You helped me better understand how to achieve high performance without sacrificing work-life balance, which is something both I and my family will be forever grateful to you for. Thank you for writing a cover quote for this book. Mike Martin reviewed chapter 11 and helped me further my understanding of the Azure platform and its many services. Mike, I'll forever cherish our chats. Since our days in the One Commercial Partner organization, you've been my rock and one of my biggest advocates. Javier Soriano reviewed chapter 8 and shared his vast knowledge of Sentinel with me. Javier, thank you for always finding time for our chats and sharing your vast knowledge with me. And a special thanks to the rest of my team: Alex, Dick, Fernanda, Future, Giulio, Gopal, Lara, Liana, Miri, Safeena, Stan, Pavel, Vasavi, and Yura for your camaraderie and friendship while writing this book. Thank you to Mekonnen Kassa and Sebuh Haileleul for their leadership and for supporting my career at Microsoft. I'd also like to thank everyone else at Microsoft who has affected me along the way, especially John Coyle, for helping me navigate and advance my career successfully at Microsoft. Thank you, John, for always finding time for our chats and helping me enjoy the journey. I've learned so much from you.

I would be remiss if I didn't also thank my many reviewers and everyone else who contributed to this book: Abe Menendez, Bikalpa Timilsina, Brian Liceaga, Carsten Jorgensen, Dave Corun, Des Horsley, Gandhirajan N, Geert Van Laethem, Holger Voges, Jason Content, Jason Taylor, Jonathan Bourbonnais, Kunal Jha, Lukasz Kupka, Mali Gorantla, Marcin Sęk, Markus Wolff, Michael Heil, Michael Langdon, Mike Taylor, Paul Love, Prashant Dwivedi, Ranjit Sahai, Renato Gentile, Richard Vaughan, Roman Levchenko, Sam Wadhwa, Sebastian Rogers, Stanley Anozie, and Steve Goodman. Each of you helped shape this book into what it is today, making sure the best version finds its way to readers.

None of this would be possible without the many clients and organizations I have had the privilege of working with over the years. I'm incredibly grateful to have crossed paths with all of you as you were digitally transforming and securing your environments. So many valuable insights that are part of my journey are contained in this book. It's still humbling to have earned the privilege of being considered a trusted advisor on Azure security by so many of you. This is not something I take lightly, and it fills me with immense pride and accountability. While it wouldn't be appropriate to mention any company names, I hope that as you go through this book, you'll recall some of our many conversations.

Finally, a big thank you to all of you who picked up this book and helped it find a happy home on your digital or physical bookshelf.

about this book

This book is written for cyber-defenders of businesses—cybersecurity professionals of wildly different backgrounds and levels of experience who are passionate about protecting their environments and demonstrate tenacity in the face of what looks like chaos every single day. No two days are the same because the landscape in this space changes so quickly. The topics covered in this book empower you to understand how to use native Azure security services to meaningfully and effectively secure applications and resources in the real world.

Who should read this book

Security engineers with up to two years of experience working with the Azure platform are the people who are going to benefit the most from reading this book, as they will recognize themselves in many of the scenarios. Beginner-level experience using the Azure platform (or any other public cloud platform) will help greatly. You certainly don't need to be familiar with (or an expert in) all of the different public cloud services to get the most out of this book. However, if you have a basic understanding of how the Azure platform works, what an Azure subscription is, and what a tenant is, you'll be off to the races.

Maybe your primary focus is not securing applications and systems but rather developing or deploying applications. If so, this book is for you too. You'll be able to gain a much deeper understanding of what's required to secure applications you have developed. This knowledge helps maintain business continuity and prevents any disruptions due to poor security practices so your users can use the application as you intended.

If you are coming from an on-premises world and are moving workloads to the public cloud, this book is for you too. If you start with chapter 1, you will learn about core concepts around cloud security, the challenges that businesses are facing, and how they are applicable to securing resources in Azure. You can then proceed through the other chapters, which show you how to use various Azure security services to harden Azure resources and apply security best practices to them.

Even if you're an experienced Azure security engineer, this book is still for you. The later chapters might contain some insights and new capabilities you haven't seen before. Chapters 7 and 8 about security monitoring and operations are worth a look. Or you can explore chapter 10 to learn how to shift even further left and manage security as code.

How this book is organized: A road map

The topics in this book are organized into 11 chapters, logically grouped into three parts that cover beginner, intermediate, and advanced concepts. I recommend that you go through the chapters in order, as this allows you to get the most out of the examples and concepts in this book.

Part 1 provides a foundational understanding of core concepts applicable to cloud security in Azure. It then transitions into explaining how identity and access management work in Azure:

- Chapter 1 sets the stage. It answers this question: What's in this book for those reading it? It introduces security concepts that help you understand how Azure security services help businesses improve and maintain their security posture.
- Chapter 2 is all about securing identities in Azure. It introduces authentication and authorization concepts before teaching you how to implement secure access using Microsoft's Identity and Access Management platform—namely, Microsoft Entra ID.

Part 2 describes how to harden the most widely used resource types in Azure. It then builds on that discussion by covering threat detection capabilities:

- Chapter 3 is about network security and how to implement a secure network infrastructure in Azure using a set of services commonly referred to as Azure network security.
- Chapter 4 picks up where the previous chapter ended to discuss securing compute resources used to power applications that run on Azure, such as Azure Virtual Machines, Azure App Service, and Azure Kubernetes Service.
- Chapter 5 tackles securing data resources in Azure, such as storage accounts and Azure Key Vault, and how this is applicable to securing the crown jewels of your organization.
- Chapter 6 covers cloud security hygiene. It explains how to use Microsoft's Defender for Cloud capabilities to detect misconfigurations in your workloads and apply security best practices to harden them.
- Chapter 7 continues from chapter 6 to describe how to implement threat detection capabilities for commonly used Azure resource types with Microsoft Defender for Cloud.

Part 3 covers more advanced concepts such as security monitoring and security operations in depth prior to touching on the importance of managing security as code and DevSecOps:

- Chapter 8 discusses building out next-generation security operations capabilities with Microsoft Sentinel and having end-to-end visibility of your digital estate by ingesting data from different data sources. It also covers how to respond to potential signs of compromise using analytics rules and workflow automation in Microsoft Sentinel.
- Chapter 9 describes the different log types available in Azure and how to use them effectively in combination with Azure Monitor before transitioning to security governance.
- Chapter 10 teaches you how to use Azure Policy and Azure Blueprints to ensure that deployed cloud resources are secure by default and adhere to your organization's business rules.
- Chapter 11 touches on managing security as code using infrastructure as code, GitHub actions, and Microsoft Defender for DevOps and how that ties into DevSecOps.

About the code

To follow along with the code listings and exercises provided in this book, you can use the GitHub repository available at https://github.com/bmagusic/azure-security. I'm a big believer in learning by doing! While it might seem tempting to copy-paste the code you find in the repository, I encourage you to type out the code yourself. This will give you a chance to get more hands-on experience. Even if you misspell something and need to troubleshoot, it will provide a valuable learning experience. If you're unfamiliar with the commands I use throughout the book, I provide additional resources and helpful links. In addition, you can always consult the official documentation and reference lists.

The examples provided in this book have been tested to provide you with accurate and up-to-date results. You can even replicate them in your own testing environment. To further solidify your knowledge, explore the exercises scattered throughout the book. While these additional exercises are not mandatory, they help you further your understanding and practical knowledge of this area.

This book contains many examples of source code both in numbered listings and in line with normal text. In both cases, the source code is formatted in a `fixed-width font like this` to separate it from ordinary text. Sometimes code is also **`in bold`** to highlight code that has changed from previous steps in the chapter, such as when a new feature adds to an existing line of code.

In many cases, the original source code has been reformatted; we've added line breaks and reworked indentation to accommodate the available page space in the book. In rare cases, even this was not enough, and listings include line-continuation markers (➥). Additionally, comments in the source code have often been removed from the listings when the code is described in the text. Code annotations accompany many of the listings, highlighting important concepts.

You can get executable snippets of code from the liveBook (online) version of this book at https://livebook.manning.com/book/azure-security. The complete code for the examples in the book is available for download from the Manning website at https://www.manning.com/books/azure-security and from GitHub at https://github .com/bmagusic/azure-security.

liveBook discussion forum

The purchase of *Azure Security* includes free access to liveBook, Manning's online reading platform. Using liveBook's exclusive discussion features, you can attach comments to the book globally or to specific sections or paragraphs. It's a snap to make notes to yourself, ask and answer technical questions, and receive help from the author and other users. To access the forum, go to https://livebook.manning.com/book/azure-security/discussion. You can also learn more about Manning's forums and the rules of conduct at https://livebook.manning.com/discussion.

Manning's commitment to our readers is to provide a venue where a meaningful dialogue between individual readers and between readers and the author can take place. It is not a commitment to any specific amount of participation on the part of the author, whose contribution to the forum remains voluntary (and unpaid). We suggest you try asking the author some challenging questions lest his interest stray! The forum and the archives of previous discussions will be accessible from the publisher's website as long as the book is in print.

about the author

BOJAN MAGUŠIĆ is a product manager with Microsoft on the Customer Experience Engineering Team. In his current role, he acts as a technology expert for Fortune 500 companies, helping them improve their overall security posture in Azure. Prior to that, he worked as a cloud solution architect focused on security, compliance, and identity within Microsoft's One Commercial Partner organization. There, he worked with Microsoft partners across western Europe to help them build out security practices on top of Microsoft's security stack.

In addition to various technical certifications (18+ Microsoft certifications and counting), he is a Prosci® Certified Change Practitioner and has certifications from ISC(2), INSEAD, and the Kellogg School of Management. He has a strong passion for cybersecurity, advancing opportunities for women in tech, and professional development. He is interested in building partnerships with other companies to learn how they support, advance, and retain their cyber talent. You can follow him on LinkedIn at https://www.linkedin.com/in/bojanmagusic/.

about the cover illustration

The figure on the cover of *Azure Security*, "Le général Guadalupe Victoria" or "General Guadalupe Victoria," is taken from a book by Claudio Linati published in 1828. Linati's book includes hand-colored lithographs depicting a variety of civil, military, and religious costumes of Mexican society at the time.

In those days, it was easy to identify where people lived and what their trade or station in life was just by their dress. Manning celebrates the inventiveness and initiative of the computer business with book covers based on the rich diversity of regional culture centuries ago, brought back to life by pictures from collections such as this one.

Part 1

First steps

This part of the book sets the stage for the infinite game that is cybersecurity and securing your resources in Azure.

Chapter 1 introduces core security concepts that help you understand how Azure security services can be used to secure your Azure environment. In chapter 2, I teach you how to secure the identities used to access Azure resources in your environment.

When you're finished with this part of the book, you'll be ready to embark on the next part of the journey that you're on with respect to Azure security.

About Azure security

This chapter covers

- Cybersecurity as an infinite game
- The shared responsibility model
- Azure security services
- The threat landscape
- Cloud security challenges
- The zero trust security model
- Defense in depth

Security is one of the greatest unsolved problems of our time. This complex problem set spans digital environments, physical infrastructure, businesses, and individuals. Digital services have become an integral part of our lives in finance, health, transportation, our jobs, and even how we connect with each other. With all this, however, we're outstripping our ability to provide security. If you think of the word *security*, by its very definition, it means free of threats or danger. Yet, isn't the reality such that businesses are under constant threat?

This concern is highlighted by daily news headlines about ransomware attacks, fraud, theft, public exposure of private data, espionage, and even attacks against physical infrastructure. James P. Carse, a professor at New York University, came up with an interesting theory of how the world works, which was recently popularized by Simon Sinek. Carse theorized that there are two types of games: finite and infinite.

Finite games have known rules, clearly identified players, and a clear winner in the end. Think about a game like chess. In chess, the rules are well understood, it's played by millions of people around the world, and there is no doubt about what winning a chess game looks like. Infinite games are very different. There are no agreed-upon rules in infinite games. Players can be known or unknown, and winning is about staying in the game. Take finance, for example, where rules vary dramatically from country to country. There are both known and unknown players that influence the game, and their decisions can have a massive effect on everyone involved. Cybersecurity is an infinite game.

1.1 *Cybersecurity as an infinite game*

The cyber bad guys are not playing by any agreed-upon rules. There is no such thing as a level playing field. Today, too many businesses and security teams have a finite mindset. In their mind, security is a winner-take-all game. I believe thinking like this is quite dangerous because the landscape changes dramatically so quickly.

I caution you against having that finite game mindset and falling into the trap of believing that a single security solution can solve this problem. Cybersecurity is not a winner-take-all game. It takes a combination of people working together across the industry in a game with no end. So I encourage you to think differently—especially when it comes to cloud security, where the pace of innovation, agility, and complexity is sometimes breathtaking. In this constantly changing game, cybersecurity requires a fundamental shift of mindset. I believe the future of cloud security is going to be shaped by an infinite mindset. We have to turn this game in our favor.

Unfortunately, a significant number of breaches still happen due to poor cybersecurity practices. Insecure configurations of cloud workloads continue to be one of the top causes of breaches. This has been exacerbated by the conditions created due to the Covid-19 pandemic, when many companies had to accelerate their digital transformation and rush to move their workloads from on-premises to the public cloud without giving much thought to security. Virtual machines (VMs) running on public cloud platforms were left exposed on the internet and subject to attacks. User credentials were leaked and used by attackers to gain unauthorized access to an organization's environment. Secrets were unencrypted and left exposed in source code repositories. These poor practices are representative of common causes of cloud security breaches.

The following list highlights a subset of relevant cloud security threats but is by no means an extensive list, as there are many more:

- Ransomware
- Brute-force attacks
- Supply chain attacks

- Zero-day vulnerabilities
- Common vulnerabilities and exposures
- Misconfigurations
- Unauthorized access
- Denial-of-service attacks
- Insider threats
- Data theft

The question then becomes how you secure your Azure environments against common cloud security incidents and threats to your cloud resources. To make progress on this problem, you can use a set of native security services that are available in Azure, most commonly referred to as *Azure security*. This book teaches you the following Azure security services:

- Microsoft Entra ID
- Azure DDoS Protection Standard
- Azure Firewall Standard
- Azure Firewall Premium
- Azure Web Application Firewall
- Microsoft Sentinel
- Microsoft Defender for Cloud
- Microsoft Defender for DevOps
- Azure Monitor
- Azure Key Vault
- Azure Policy

Because Azure is broad, you might have some exposure to some features of Azure and/or Azure security, which is an à la carte approach. In this book, I'll introduce you to Azure security services so you can use all of them. You will learn more about these services in the following chapters. They can be used to secure Azure environments, big and small, with a variety of resource types. The overarching goal of Azure security is to help you secure your digital estate running on Azure while, at the same time, minimizing the likelihood of breaches.

I encourage you to consider what else you need to secure on top of these services, as there are plenty of other misconfigurations that can happen, such as a lack of encryption. Azure security fundamentally revolves around people, processes, and technologies. Most people appreciate security, but they don't necessarily know how to apply the technology effectively to protect their Azure environments from disruption and potential attacks.

This book teaches you how to better configure and implement Azure security in your environment. As an organization looks to secure its public cloud infrastructure, the public cloud provider shares the burden of security. This is widely referred to as the *shared responsibility model*.

1.2   *Shared responsibility model*

There are tasks that the public cloud provider is responsible for securing, and there are tasks that are your responsibility. Knowing what these are matters greatly. You can imagine them as two pieces of a puzzle that need to fit together perfectly! With regard to Azure, have you ever asked yourself what is taken care of by Microsoft? Microsoft takes care of securing the cloud, which includes physically securing the data centers where compute, storage, and networking resources that run your digital services reside. It also provides security checks and authorized personnel that would make some airport security checks look like a stroll in the park. In addition, Microsoft takes care of hardware failure, alternate power supply, and much more. Essentially, Microsoft ensures that the public cloud runs smoothly without you needing to worry about all the things that could possibly go wrong (natural disasters like earthquakes notwithstanding).

What is your responsibility, then? Your responsibility is the security of your resources inside of the cloud, including data that resides in the cloud and aspects of resources that are deployed, like your VMs. In an on-premises world, everything would be your responsibility to secure. However, with public cloud platforms such as Azure, you offload a part of that burden to the public cloud provider. How much burden you offload comes down to the service model in question. Cloud service models originated from the National Institute of Standards and Technology (NIST), which, with regard to the public cloud, defines three main service models:

- *Software as a service (SaaS)*—Offers cloud-based applications that can be used and accessed over the internet
- *Platform as a service (PaaS)*—Offers resources you can use to develop and deploy everything from simple cloud-based applications to enterprise-ready applications
- *Infrastructure as a service (IaaS)*—Offers core compute, storage, and networking resources on demand

NOTE   See how Microsoft defines service models at http://mng.bz/Pzvv.

Each service model outlines your and the cloud provider's responsibilities. Depending on the service model, these responsibilities vary.

In an IaaS service model, physical data center security, physical networking, and physical hosts are secured by the public cloud provider (in this case, Microsoft). Everything on top of that is your responsibility to secure.

In a PaaS service model, you offload more tasks to Microsoft compared to IaaS. In this model, the public cloud provider is responsible for securing the operating system and its virtualization. However, the network- and application-level controls, as well as parts of identity, are a shared responsibility between you and Microsoft.

In a SaaS service model, you offload even more tasks to the public cloud provider, such as securing the network and application-level controls. As you can see, there are differences between each one of these service models. However, what all of them have in common is that securing accounts, identities, clients, endpoints, information, and data falls under your responsibility. You can secure these using Azure security services.

1.3 *Azure security services*

Now you might be asking yourself why you should care about Azure security. I'd like to offer a perspective. First, by properly configuring Azure security services, you're able to avoid disruption to your business and realize the full value of the Azure platform. If you don't secure your environment correctly, there might be no business at all. Second, Azure security helps manage the increasing complexity of attacks. Attacks are getting more sophisticated by the minute and are increasing in volume, both of which are alarming trends!

> **TIP** This book doesn't cover breach trends in depth. For insights about confirmed breaches around the world, you can consult the most recent edition of the widely known Verizon Data Breach Investigations Report (DBIR), available at http://mng.bz/JgEa.

Even during the writing of this book, there are probably new security services being developed and existing ones refined based on what's working well and what's working less well for organizations. Indeed, security is complex. What I've learned from many organizations is that security is not a problem you solve: it's a problem you manage. This problem is further compounded by the fact that no two organizations are the same. Some have complex requirements and large footprints in Azure. How do you go about managing this problem? Improving an organization's security posture is a journey that resembles an ever-evolving cyclical process (figure 1.1).

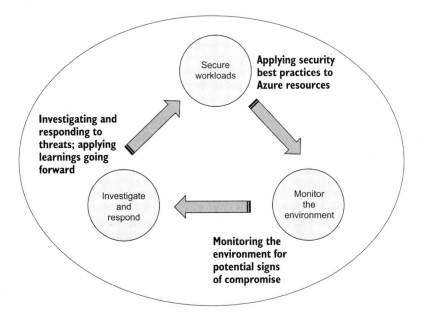

Figure 1.1 Improving an organization's security posture can be seen as an ever-evolving and ever-changing cyclical process.

Improving your organization's security posture is like going to the gym: you need to work consistently to achieve your desired results. When looking holistically at improving an organization's security posture, you can think of it as an iterative process that consists of three phases. The first phase involves securing Azure workloads by ensuring they adhere to security best practices. In the second phase, you monitor the environment for potential signs of compromise and suspicious activity (such as lateral movements). Should there be a potential sign of your environment being compromised, you need to investigate to get a better understanding of what occurred and, if needed, respond accordingly, which is the third phase.

Based on the findings of your investigation, it's of paramount importance that you learn from what has occurred and evolve your thinking to secure your cloud workloads better. Effectively, you should apply what you learn to your security best practices to deploy your Azure resources securely going forward. You should also incorporate learnings from outside of your environment, such as from Azure-specific breaches in other organizations and general security advice from reputable sources. Make this an iterative and ever-evolving process—like going to the gym.

To better understand how to protect your environment from attacks, you first need to get a good understanding of the threat landscape that is affecting organizations.

1.4   *The threat landscape*

New attacks, on average, happen every couple of minutes, affecting companies big and small. They are performed by bad actors (or threat actors, as they're also called)—a person or people who take action to exploit a target system's vulnerability to achieve their goal or objective. These people may be inside your organization (malicious insiders) or outside of it (cyber criminals). From here on, I'll refer to them simply as bad actors.

Bad actors are usually motivated by financial gain, politics, or some other malicious intent. Their attacks are often made possible by vulnerabilities that allow them to take advantage of gaps and weaknesses in the security controls you put in place to safeguard your digital systems. Therefore, it's important to understand how to prevent common vulnerabilities. Vulnerabilities, together with malware and specific groups of bad actors, make up the threat landscape.

Let's return to the analogy of going to the gym: chances are you won't be the only person working out. Other people are probably in the gym, also putting in hard work. If you're brand new to working out, you may ask someone for advice or perhaps observe how others use a particular machine; you may even adopt a part of their workout routine. The same logic can be applied to cybersecurity. By gaining insights into the evolving nature of cyber threats, businesses can better prepare themselves and minimize the likelihood of being compromised. You can try to understand the behavior of bad actors and consider what steps they could take to compromise your environment so that you can protect against them. Bad actors have an intended outcome in mind that they're trying to achieve. In cybersecurity, this intended outcome tends to be called a *goal*. At a high level, the behavior bad actors engage in to achieve their goal is called a *tactic*. A more detailed description of a tactic is referred to as a *technique*. A highly detailed description of a bad actor's technique is called a *procedure*.

TIP See how NIST defines tactics, techniques, and procedures at http://mng.bz/wvza.

Going back to the gym analogy, if your intended outcome (goal) is to lose weight, there are a couple of different ways you can go about achieving this goal. You can adopt a healthier lifestyle (tactic). This tactic may include exercising more, adopting a healthier eating routine, and even tracking your progress weekly by using a scale (techniques). When exercising on a machine, you could look to repeat specific steps required to use that machine in a way that helps you exercise more (procedure).

Together, tactics, techniques, and procedures (or TTPs, as they're commonly referred to in the cybersecurity field) tend to paint a picture of the complexity of cyber threats and help decipher the behavior of bad actors. They can also help demonstrate the evolving nature of the threat landscape. The more you know about the bad actors' behavior, the better prepared you are to preempt it.

Cybercrime is a thriving industry. Solving the problem of cybercrime is similar to solving the problem of "ordinary" crime in the sense that it's a very difficult (if not impossible) task to accomplish. The number of daily pieces of malware continues to rise, which is alarming! However, a significant number of breaches happen due to poor security practices.

Let's take an example of a bad actor trying to compromise your Azure environment's resources for financial gain (goal). First, they attempt to gain a foothold in your environment (tactic). To accomplish this task, bad actors can launch a remote desktop protocol (RDP) brute-force attack (technique). Bad actors will try to guess the RDP password over and over again (typically within a short period of time) until they guess it correctly.

Unfortunately, humans are not great at dealing with passwords. They tend to reuse them, keep them simple, and not use strong factors, such as multifactor authentication (MFA). Weak passwords are common and increase the likelihood of bad actors succeeding in these kinds of attacks. Procedures contain details about the techniques used to achieve the objective. In this context, procedures can be details about the infrastructure bad actors use to perform the attack, who the bad actors are targeting, and more.

As you can imagine, bad actors don't want to get caught perpetrating cybercrime (for obvious reasons), which is why they will put in considerable effort not to get detected while still striving to accomplish their goal. At the same time, bad actors tend to stick to what works well. Vulnerabilities and poor security practices facilitate bad actors' ability to compromise your environment. However, when your security posture increases, the likelihood of bad actors breaching your environment decreases. That is, it becomes harder for bad actors to be successful in their attacks. They must adapt—

and they do! Therefore, the tactics, techniques, and procedures they use change over time. They evolve!

The reality is that the tactics bad actors use today may look very different tomorrow. What they do tomorrow may look very different next week, and so on. Therefore, you need to be consistently improving and maintaining the security posture of your environment. The more you exercise and train, the more your muscles grow and get stronger. These muscles can be seen as your security posture.

1.5   *Cloud security challenges*

Now, let's say that due to advances in technology, new types of machines have been invented that are 10 times better for gym-goers, and your gym has them installed. However, there is a slight challenge: these machines are brand new, and the way they operate is different from the previous ones you've used. Now, you (and everyone else) need to learn how to operate them (to achieve your goal). The same principle applies to implementing security best practices to public cloud resources. Traditional on-premises security controls differ from security controls in the public cloud. Knowing how they differ is key to understanding how to get your desired results. In just the past 10 years, the pace of technical innovation with regard to the public cloud has been staggering. And, just as businesses have taken advantage of these technical innovations, so have bad actors in their attack campaigns. There is a clear need to evolve from constantly catching up to finding a way to be consistently ahead of bad actors.

Thinking about how breaches may occur can help you implement security controls to prevent them. Resources deployed in the public cloud (among other tasks) need to be remotely accessible for management purposes. This accessibility over the internet opens up the possibility of those resources being breached by bad actors.

After gaining access to your environment, bad actors might look to compromise an account and then use that account to gain unauthorized access to more of your environment's resources. They can even spread to other resource types, like databases, storage, IoT devices, and more. This is commonly referred to as *lateral movement*: the bad actors will try to gain access to as many resources as possible by moving between different resource types. Once they've established control over the environment, bad actors will try to accomplish their goal. For example, they may attempt financial gain by holding the organization's environment hostage and asking for a ransom payment, known as a ransomware attack.

Sadly, there are many more types of attacks out there. How breaches occur and what steps bad actors might take to attempt to compromise your public cloud environment is often referred to as the *kill chain model*. A kill chain model consists of five steps: exposure, access, lateral movement, actions on objective, and goal. A simplified version of the model in the context of cloud security is shown in figure 1.2.

You might be asking yourself whether these attacks actually happen in the real world. Unfortunately, they do. To make this palpable, I provide a concrete example in figure 1.3. Other examples can be found by simply searching for the latest cyberattacks on the web.

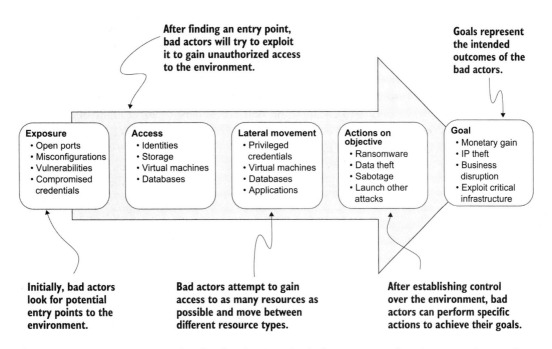

Figure 1.2   **The kill chain model helps visualize the steps that bad actors may perform to compromise your Azure environment.**

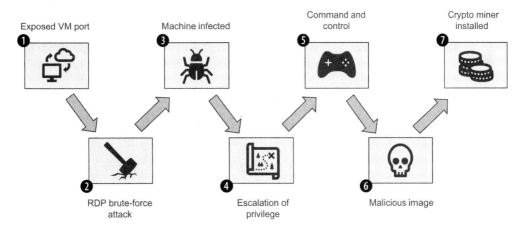

Figure 1.3   **Example of an attack against a public cloud infrastructure in which bad actors use an open VM port to install a crypto miner**

Let's say a VM is deployed in the public cloud and is not adhering to any security best practices. What could possibly go wrong? Well, if that VM's ports are publicly accessible from the internet, bad actors might try to guess the username and password of the account that has access to that VM (remember what this type of attack is called?).

If the VM account is compromised, bad actors will have access to that VM and, in turn, unauthorized access to the environment. With this access, they can deploy malware on the VM to exploit vulnerable applications or systems. They can then spread inside of the environment laterally by compromising even more resources, even spanning different resource types such as Kubernetes clusters.

After gaining access to clusters, the bad actors can deploy a malicious container image to the compromised cluster. This container image, in turn, could be used to run a crypto miner, which incurs financial costs to the unsuspecting owner of the Azure environment while providing financial gain to the bad actors.

Thus, a VM left with an open port, exposed to the internet, could open the door to crypto miners being installed on your Azure compute resources (or worse). Using crypto-mining–specific software has been a successful strategy for bad actors to deliver malware/ransomware in the recent past.

1.6 Digital medievalism

It used to be that you could block or allow access at the perimeter of your corporate network. Company resources and applications that users needed to get their job done were, after all, inside the corporate network, guarded by the defenses you put up to safeguard against threats from outside. Everything inside your defenses was considered trusted, whereas everything outside them was considered untrusted.

A term that I believe best describes this is *digital medievalism*, where organizations and individuals each depend on the walls of their castles and the strength of their citizens against bad actors who can simply retreat to their own castle with the spoils of an attack. However, with the rapid adoption of cloud services, users now need to access a variety of different applications to get their job done. These applications can be accessed from a variety of devices—for example, a mobile phone, tablet, or personal laptop.

This has fundamentally changed the security perimeter, as many applications (like Microsoft 365 and Salesforce CRM) don't reside inside of your corporate network and behind the walls of the castles you've built. They reside outside them, and if they're outside your walls, how can you ever trust that they're safe?

Blocking or allowing access no longer happens at the perimeter of your corporate network. Therefore, the traditional security model of digital medievalism is no longer sufficient. Now we need a perimeter-less security approach, where instead of trusting that resources are safe because they are located behind the walls of your castle, you always need to verify. This concept of never implicitly trusting that resources are safe and always verifying is the cornerstone of what is commonly referred to as the *zero trust* security model.

1.7 The zero trust security model

The premise behind zero trust is that requests made to public cloud resources shouldn't be trusted by default. Instead, they should be verified. This holds true even if these resources are located behind your castle's walls and inside your corporate network. Remember the legend of the Trojan horse?! In it, soldiers were able to capture the city of Troy by hiding inside a wooden horse to get past the city's walls.

Instead of assuming that everything inside your corporate network is secure, the zero trust model assumes a breach and verifies each request as though it originated from outside your castle's walls (or from an untrusted location). This assumed-breach mindset also helps minimize the potential effect of bad actors gaining access to your Azure environment by helping you to respond and fix the problem more quickly.

The three widely referenced principles of the zero trust security model are as follows:

- *Verify explicitly*—Always authenticate and authorize based on all available data points, including identity, device, location, service, and unusual behavior.
- *Use least-privileged access*—Give just enough access and permissions for the task at hand and only when needed.
- *Assume breach*—Improve defenses by minimizing the blast radius, and actively monitor the environment for potentially suspicious activities and signs of compromise.

Zero trust is not a specific product or service but rather an approach to designing and implementing the three cornerstone principles of the zero trust security model. Instead of shying away from using services that are outside your corporate network, this security model allows you to adapt to them and manage their complexity. Given that most of your services and apps are outside your corporate network, zero trust is a valuable multidimensional approach to security.

There is no silver bullet when it comes to security. Therefore, it's prudent to apply several layers of security. This pattern is commonly referred to as *defense in depth*.

1.8 *Defense in depth*

Defense in depth helps you to reduce the overall likelihood of a successful breach by putting several layers of security together. To explain this concept, I'll use an example from sports. Let's say that you're playing soccer and you are a bad actor: your objective is to score a goal. The goalkeeper stands in your way; therefore, you only need to get past that one person to achieve your objective.

Now, what if another player, who is also attempting to thwart your efforts, is standing between you and the goalkeeper? Would it be more difficult to achieve your objective? Yes, it would—you would need to get past that player and the goalkeeper. What happens when yet another player is added? You quickly realize that with each additional player added between you and the goalkeeper, it becomes that much more difficult for you to achieve your objective.

The same logic can be applied to securing your Azure environment. By adding more layers of security, you're effectively making it harder for bad actors to get past your security controls and be successful in their attacks. Also, by having more layers of security, if one layer fails (say one of the players between you and the goalkeeper gets injured), the other layers are still there to secure the underlying resources in Azure.

It's time to combine the idea that improving an organization's security posture resembles a journey that consists of three phases—secure workloads, monitor and detect threats, and investigate and respond—with what you know about defense in depth. That is, you need to add more than one security control to each of the three phases by using more than one Azure security service. These layers of security need to take into account and protect against the steps bad actors could take to compromise your environment (as visualized in the kill chain model).

You need to consider the steps of the cloud kill chain model because an attack might not start with bad actors trying to gain access to your Azure environment. Bad actors might have already gained access to your environment and be looking to achieve their goal—for example, launching a ransomware attack to hold your Azure resources hostage for a ransom payment. Therefore, you need to add several Azure security services to each step of the kill chain model.

You may wonder how you go about doing that. You start by identifying the resources that you need to secure. Azure environments tend to include a vast number of different resource types. For the sake of simplicity, I'll group these different types into five categories: identities, data, applications, infrastructure, and networking resources (figure 1.4). Therefore, you need to look at securing each one of these

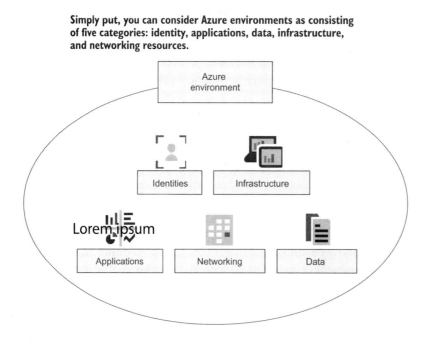

Figure 1.4 Azure environments usually include different resource types.

categories by applying several Azure security services—both across the steps of the kill chain model and mapped to the three stages of improving an organization's security posture (securing workloads, monitoring and detecting threats, and investigating and responding).

Because users are able to access cloud services from any location and any device, identity has turned itself into the primary security perimeter. Bad actors are adapting their attack campaigns to focus on the human layer of an organization's cyber defense. And because identities are used to access cloud services and perform specific actions over resources, they become an ideal entry point if they're not kept secure.

1.8.1   Securing identities

Let's begin with identities (you learn more about identities in the next chapter). Using the kill chain model, start by looking at what steps bad actors could take to find an entry point to your environment and exploit any weaknesses and vulnerabilities to gain unauthorized access. Then, apply more than one Azure security service to prevent them from achieving their goal.

Bad actors could use a brute-force attack to compromise a user's identity and breach your environment. In the secure workloads stage, you need to protect against these attacks. Therefore, you need to be able to detect a suspicious login and respond to it—for example, by prompting the user to authenticate with an MFA.

You can use Microsoft Entra ID to both detect suspicious login and enforce MFA. However, as I previously mentioned, there is no silver bullet when it comes to security, and an attack might start by using an already compromised identity to gain access to even more resources (lateral movement). Therefore, you also need to apply several Azure security services to the other steps of the kill chain model.

You can use Microsoft Entra ID to secure identities that have privileged permissions, like user admins, from being compromised. If Microsoft Entra ID's identity protection capability detects identities potentially being compromised, you can enforce additional controls, like requiring the user to change their password.

However, bad actors might have already compromised the identity of users with privileged permissions and may be attempting to use them to compromise even more identities by launching a phishing campaign. You can use Microsoft Sentinel to detect this suspicious behavior and contain it via an automated response. Figure 1.5 depicts an example of an attack and the steps bad actors might take to achieve their goal. In parallel, it shows the Azure security services you can use to secure the identities in your environment.

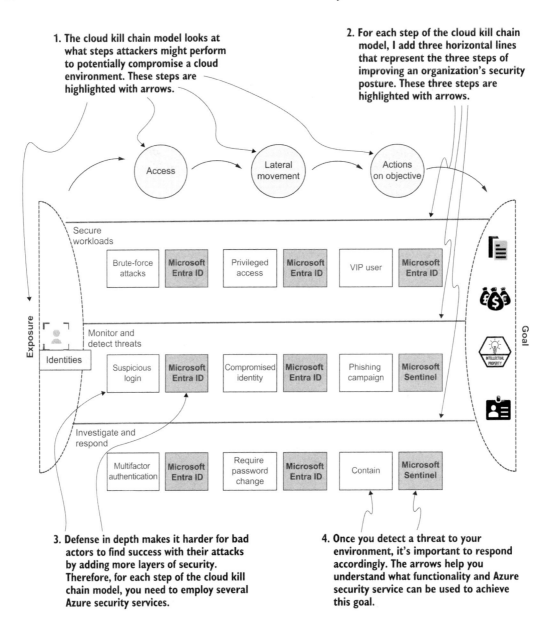

1. The cloud kill chain model looks at what steps attackers might perform to potentially compromise a cloud environment. These steps are highlighted with arrows.

2. For each step of the cloud kill chain model, I add three horizontal lines that represent the three steps of improving an organization's security posture. These three steps are highlighted with arrows.

3. Defense in depth makes it harder for bad actors to find success with their attacks by adding more layers of security. Therefore, for each step of the cloud kill chain model, you need to employ several Azure security services.

4. Once you detect a threat to your environment, it's important to respond accordingly. The arrows help you understand what functionality and Azure security service can be used to achieve this goal.

Figure 1.5 Azure security services that can be used to secure identities in your Azure environment

1.8.2 *Securing infrastructure and networking resources*

Securing identities is important, especially because they're used to manage infrastructure and networking resources. You shouldn't rely on any single security control (defense in depth, remember?). However, if your identities are compromised, you need to secure other Azure resource types of your environment, like infrastructure and networking resources (figure 1.6). For simplicity, I'll cover these categories together (don't worry; chapters 3 and 4 cover each category separately and in more detail).

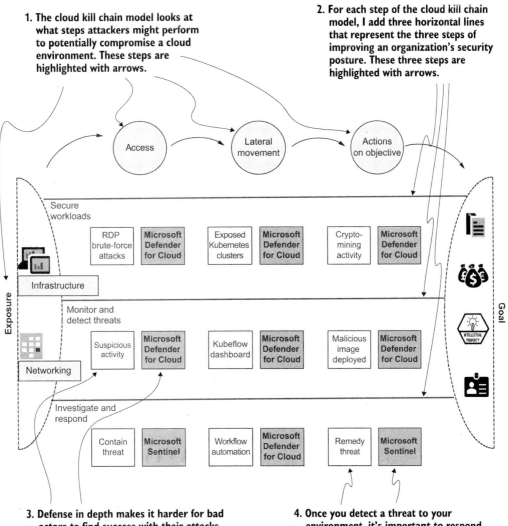

1. The cloud kill chain model looks at what steps attackers might perform to potentially compromise a cloud environment. These steps are highlighted with arrows.

2. For each step of the cloud kill chain model, I add three horizontal lines that represent the three steps of improving an organization's security posture. These three steps are highlighted with arrows.

3. Defense in depth makes it harder for bad actors to find success with their attacks by adding more layers of security. Therefore, for each step of the cloud kill chain model, you need to employ several Azure security services.

4. Once you detect a threat to your environment, it's important to respond accordingly. The arrows help you understand what functionality and Azure security service can be used to achieve this goal.

Figure 1.6 Azure security services that can be used to secure infrastructure and network resources in your Azure environment

To prevent bad actors from finding weaknesses or vulnerabilities they can use to breach your environment, you can follow security best practice guidance provided by Microsoft Defender for Cloud to help harden your Azure resources' defense. It can also be used to monitor those resources (for example, VMs) and detect potential attacks, such as RDP brute-force attacks. You can then investigate this security incident further with Microsoft Sentinel and even trigger an automated response.

Following these steps, you also need to prevent bad actors from spreading laterally inside your environment. Imagine that in your Kubernetes deployment, a privileged service is left exposed, like the Kubeflow dashboard. By gaining access to Kubeflow, bad actors can deploy a malicious crypto-mining image. Microsoft Defender for Cloud can detect exposure of sensitive interfaces, including Kubeflow, as well as crypto-mining activity on the nodes themselves; trigger a response using workflow automation (discussed in chapters 6 and 7); and alert you to the deployment of the malicious image via Microsoft Sentinel.

You can then use Microsoft Sentinel to resolve the threat (figure 1.6) by triggering an automated response. Infrastructure resources typically have applications running on them. Additionally, data can be stored in those applications as well as on the infrastructure resources themselves. Therefore, you need to secure applications and data too!

1.8.3   *Securing applications and data*

Securing data and applications is as important as securing other resource types in your Azure environment. You can use Azure Policy to employ guardrails and ensure deployed resources adhere to security best practices and your organization's business rules. Microsoft Defender for Cloud is able to detect whether deployed resources adhere to security best practices. For certain scenarios, it even offers the capability to automatically fix misconfiguration of your resources, improving your organization's security posture. If bad actors move laterally and compromise more resources, such as storage accounts that hold sensitive information, Microsoft Defender for Cloud and Microsoft Sentinel can be used to detect these suspicious activities and respond to them. Figure 1.7 depicts these Azure security services as well as the relevant threats.

Using multiple Azure security services adds more layers of security by applying a defense-in-depth mindset. This mindset minimizes the likelihood that bad actors will succeed in their attacks. Having several layers of security protects against attacks that attempt to compromise the identities, data, applications, infrastructure, and network resources of your Azure environment.

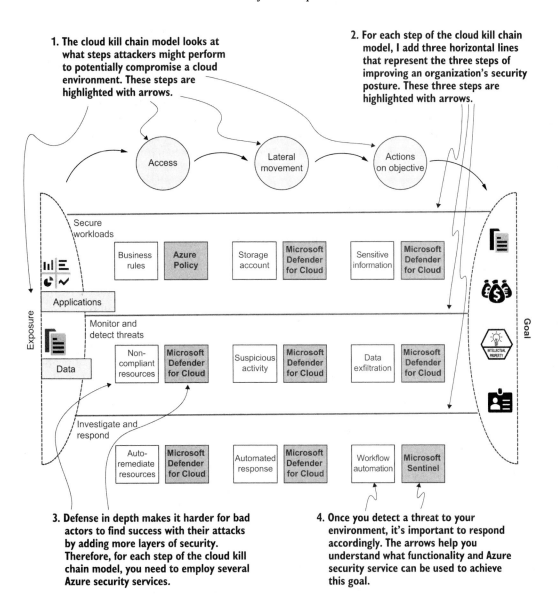

1. The cloud kill chain model looks at what steps attackers might perform to potentially compromise a cloud environment. These steps are highlighted with arrows.

2. For each step of the cloud kill chain model, I add three horizontal lines that represent the three steps of improving an organization's security posture. These three steps are highlighted with arrows.

3. Defense in depth makes it harder for bad actors to find success with their attacks by adding more layers of security. Therefore, for each step of the cloud kill chain model, you need to employ several Azure security services.

4. Once you detect a threat to your environment, it's important to respond accordingly. The arrows help you understand what functionality and Azure security service can be used to achieve this goal.

Figure 1.7   Azure security services that can be used to secure data and applications in your Azure environment

1.8.4   Heroes and villains in this book

To make security concepts in this book easier to understand, I'll rely on the help of three fictional characters. Their names are Alice, Bob, and Eve. You might have come across their names before, as they're commonly used, especially when talking about cryptography and protocols. These three characters make it easier to read this book, as many of the scenarios in this book revolve around the problems that Alice and Bob have.

Alice and Bob are our heroes. Bob is an application developer looking to run his application in Azure, and he often relies on Alice to help him secure his application. Alice is the cyber defender of her organization's Azure environment, looking to secure it against Eve. Eve is a fictional example of a bad actor. She is the villain in this book as she tries to bring chaos to Alice and Bob's day by launching attacks and looking for ways to circumvent the Azure security service they have put in place to compromise their Azure environment.

When I asked myself what I wanted my readers to come away with after reading this book, I considered having Alice and Bob build and secure an application. However, because Azure is very broad, there are way too many different permutations to cover all of them in this book. It would be like a kaleidoscope: when you turn it, the pieces make a different picture.

Security engineers with up to two years of experience working with the Azure platform and application developers looking to secure their applications running on Azure are going to benefit the most from reading this book. They will recognize themselves in many of the scenarios that Alice and Bob face throughout this book. Eve is incredibly shrewd, and the tactics she uses today could look very different tomorrow. The good news is that there are more cyber defenders than bad actors, and Alice and Bob will need to work together to stall Eve's efforts. Cybersecurity is, after all, a team sport. It is built on the foundation of knowing how to secure the identities, applications, data, infrastructure, and networking resources of your Azure environment. This is precisely what this book teaches you to do!

Summary

- Cybersecurity can be seen as an infinite game. The players in this game are not playing by any agreed-upon rules.
- The shared responsibility model gives you a sense of what you are responsible for securing in an Azure environment, compared to what the public cloud provider is responsible for securing.
- Improving an organization's security posture can be seen as an iterative process consisting of several phases. Azure security is a set of security services that you can use to secure identities, data, applications, infrastructure, and networking resources in your Azure environment.
- Understanding how attacks occur is important because it allows you to implement security controls to improve your overall security posture.
- The behaviors of bad actors continue to evolve, as do the tactics, techniques, and procedures used in attacks.
- Adding several layers of security helps to reduce the probability of a breach being successful. This can be achieved by applying more than one Azure security service.

Securing identities in Azure: The four pillars of identity and Azure Active Directory

This chapter covers

- The four pillars of identity
- Authentication
- Authorization
- Custom roles
- Identity governance

NOTE Microsoft has recently renamed Azure Active Directory to Microsoft Entra ID and the Azure Active Directory Premium P2 plan to Microsoft Entra ID P2. See http://mng.bz/yQXB for more information.

Securing identities is a fundamental building block of securing any Azure environment. Yet, many application developers and IT managers I talk to say they often lose track of who has access and to what. This problem is further compounded by the fact that people responsible for giving access to users don't always know what resources users actually need (or don't need) access to. When there is little to no automation, this process can easily become error prone and difficult to manage.

Have you ever found yourself needing to provide secure access to users in your organization? How did you go about doing this? Luckily, you're not alone. Providing secure access to users is exactly what's top of mind for Alice, too. She's one of the fictional characters whose help I rely on (with the occasional guest appearances by Bob and Eve) to make it easier to explain how to provide secure access to users in Azure. Along the way, I'll introduce you to a couple of additional models and concepts, which make it easier to understand how identities are secured in Azure.

> **NOTE** To follow along with the code listings and exercises in this chapter, you can use the GitHub repository (https://github.com/bmagusic/azure-security).

In this chapter, you learn how to distinguish between the four pillars of identity and how to implement them successfully in Azure using Microsoft's Identity and Access Management (IAM) service called *Azure Active Directory (Azure AD)*. IAM is widely understood as a way of enabling the right users to access the right resources at the right time for the right reasons.

> **NOTE** You can see how Gartner defines IAM at http://mng.bz/D4Pw.

IAM services have a lot of capabilities aimed at securing identities. Most of these capabilities can be divided into four main groupings of functionalities. These groupings on which IAM services rely can be mapped to the *four pillars of identity*, as discussed next.

2.1 Four pillars of identity

The four pillars of identity (figure 2.1) can help guide you through the complex world of IAM. They are commonly referred to as the four *As*:

- *Authentication*—Revolves around the questions "Who are you?" and "Are you who you claim to be?"

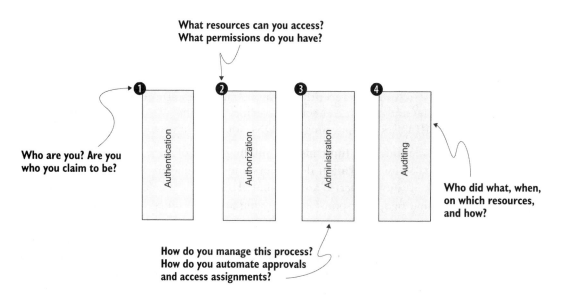

Figure 2.1 Understanding the four pillars of identity on which the IAM system is usually built

- *Authorization*—Revolves around the questions "What can you access?" and "What actions can you perform on specific resources?"
- *Administration*—Revolves around simplified management of identities' automated approvals and access assignment process.
- *Auditing*—Revolves around the question "Who did what, when, on which resources, and how?"

You learn more about each one of these pillars as you go along in this chapter. Remember that they are here to help guide you as you explore how to secure your identities in Azure, using Microsoft's IAM service called *Azure Active Directory.*

2.1.1   *What is Azure Active Directory?*

Azure AD is Microsoft's cloud-based IAM that allows you to provide users access to the right resources at the right time for the right reasons. It's built on the four pillars of identity (the four *As*). Combined with the power of the public cloud, it allows for an IAM service that is fault-tolerant and globally available. This chapter teaches you how to secure the identities of your Azure environment using Azure AD. When you sign up for an Azure subscription, an Azure *tenant* is automatically created for you. An Azure tenant is the representation of your organization in Azure. Each Azure tenant has a dedicated instance of a directory where identity-related information for your users, groups, and applications is stored; it's also used to perform IAM functions for tenant resources.

Azure AD inside your tenant and your Azure subscriptions have a *one-to-many* relationship. You might have a large number of Azure subscriptions in your tenant, and Azure AD can be associated with any number of Azure subscriptions, but each Azure subscription can only be associated with one Azure AD directory. The relationship between Azure AD and Azure subscriptions is depicted in figure 2.2.

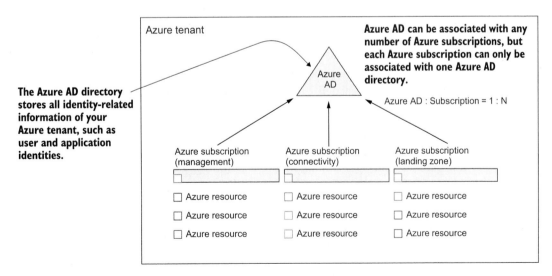

Figure 2.2   The relationship between Azure AD and Azure subscriptions

This one-to-many relationship between Azure AD and Azure subscriptions is convenient because each Azure subscription inside your Azure tenant can use the same identities that are stored in your tenant's directory. This means that when you secure the identities that are stored in the directory, they can be used securely across multiple Azure subscriptions in your tenant.

2.1.2 What is an identity?

As you recall, *identity* is a widely used general term for implementation of users and applications in systems—both of which are commonly discussed in books in relation to identities. Therefore, I will teach you how to secure users and applications against bad actors. I'll also cover managed identities (don't worry; I'll explain what those are soon) using an example.

As previously mentioned, in this chapter, I'll rely on the help of three fictional characters: Alice, Bob, and Eve. Just to remind you, Alice and Bob are cyber-defenders looking to secure their Azure environment against Eve, who is a fictional example of a bad actor. Alice is looking to secure her identity, as well as the identities of other users in her organization, such as Bob. Bob uses Azure to perform a variety of tasks, such as deploying and developing applications, creating and managing resources that applications need to function properly, and implementing security best practices for those resources. However, Bob can't get started until he has a way of accessing Azure as a user. What he needs is an identity! The first step is to create an identity for Bob.

2.1.3 Azure AD user identities in action

Each identity can be seen as a unique identifier, which contains specific attributes, such as a username, password, or PIN. The username identifies the user. In turn, the user can use their username in combination with their credential, such as a password or PIN, to gain access to Azure and perform specific activities.

There are different ways to create identities in Azure, including the Azure portal, Azure PowerShell, and Azure command-line interface (CLI). The Azure portal provides you with an easy-to-understand graphical user interface (GUI), ideal for newcomers to Azure. Large organizations and more experienced Azure users tend to prefer using Azure PowerShell or Azure CLI because they allow them to automate tasks in Azure, including creating identities in bulk.

> **NOTE** Both PowerShell and Azure CLI can be used to create the identity for Bob. I will use Azure CLI because Azure CLI feels more natural than PowerShell, and its syntax is similar to Bash scripting (for those of you who've worked with Linux systems).

You can run Azure CLI either locally on your workstation or in Azure Cloud Shell. Azure Cloud Shell is a browser-based shell environment available through the Azure portal. It's available without any prior installation. If this is the first time you're setting it up, a storage account gets created as part of the setting up process. You access Azure Cloud Shell by opening a browser and going to https://shell.azure.com or, after logging into the Azure portal, selecting the cloud shell icon in the upper-right corner. This opens Azure Cloud Shell, allowing you to choose from two shell environments: Bash and PowerShell. Bash comes preinstalled with Azure CLI. In this book, whenever possible, I'll use the Azure CLI and the Bash environment in Azure Cloud Shell.

> **NOTE** Visit the appendix to install the Azure CLI on your workstation to remotely run commands in this chapter.

To create an identity for Bob using the Azure CLI via Azure Cloud Shell, you need to provide parameters. These parameters include the display name; a username, which needs to be unique; and a password, which should be complex and different from other users' passwords. You should avoid using generic and *weak* passwords that are easily guessable. Listing 2.1 is an example of a *strong* password (don't worry; the user is able to change the password the next time they sign in). Bob uses the combination of his username and password to sign in to Azure. Creating a new user in Azure AD requires a user or global administrator. To create an identity for Bob, run the following command in Azure Cloud Shell.

Listing 2.1   Creating a user identity in Azure AD

Displays the name of the user identity

The password used to sign in. The user can change it the next time they sign in.

```
az ad user create --display-name "Bob Miller"
--password dQ76bmz7rMVs9gSP
--user-principal-name bob@contoso.com
--force-change-password-next-sign-in true
```

The username of the new user, which must contain one of the verified domains for your Azure tenant

Requires the user to change their password the next time they sign in

After this command runs, it creates an identity for Bob, as you can see from the following output:

```
{
    "@odata.context": "https://graph.microsoft.com/v1.0/$metadata#users/$entity",
    "businessPhones": [],
    "displayName": "Bob Miller",
    "givenName": null,
    "id": "6904c116-75bc-4e42-ba8b-5a0d1ac4bec4",
    "jobTitle": null,
    "mail": null,
    "mobilePhone": null,
    "officeLocation": null,
    "preferredLanguage": null,
    "surname": null,
    "userPrincipalName": "bob@contoso.com"
}
```

You can see the username of the user in the `userPrincipalName` field and the unique identifier for this identity in the `id` field.

Exercise 2.1

To help you internalize what you learn in this chapter, create an identity for a fourth fictional character named Charlie. For the purposes of this exercise, make sure you're using a lab environment and not creating identities in your corporate environment. If you need help using the command to create the identity for Charlie, you can start at http://mng.bz/o1My.

When creating identities in Azure AD, you need to provide a username that is unique at that point in time. Usernames used by identities are widely referred to as *user principal names*, and user identities as *user principals*. The username needs to be provided in addition to the user's password and display name, which is typically a combination of the first and last names.

When you create an identity for Bob (and potentially Charlie), it is stored in the directory—the same place where your other users' identities are stored (after you create them). This same directory can also be used to store identities for applications. This is especially useful if you have applications that need to access Azure resources, such as a database running on Azure. To access Azure resources, applications need identities, which are widely referred to as *service principals*.

2.1.4   *Azure AD service principals in action*

Service principals can use different ways to sign in; the most commonly used are passwords and certificates. When creating a service principal in Azure AD, you can choose how you want to configure the access that the service principal has to specific Azure resources. This feature is convenient because it allows you to create the service principal and specify the Azure resources it can access in the same step. I will cover access and permissions to Azure resources later in this chapter.

Start by creating the identity for an application without specifying the Azure resources it can access. You create an identity for an application in the form of a service principal in Azure AD by running the following command in Azure Cloud Shell:

```
az ad sp create-for-rbac -n "MyAmazingApp"
```

◁─┐ **The command used to**
   create a service principal

After this command runs, it creates the identity for an application called MyAmazing-App, as you can see from the following output:

```
The output includes credentials that you must protect. Be sure that you do
not include these credentials in your code or check the credentials into your
source control. For more information, see https://aka.ms/azadsp-cli
{
    "appId": "728cd0c5-8ada-459f-8476-144a003d4857",
    "displayName": ""MyAmazingApp"",
    "password": "2568Q~R0ltg5Q2_R_G-vs5gN6X2pdta",
    "tenant": "00000000-0000-0000-0000-000000000000"
}
```

The display name of your application ┌▷ (points to "displayName" line)

The unique identifier of your application ◁─ (points to "appId" line)

The password used by the application to sign in ◁─┐ (points to "password" line)

WARNING In the output, you see the password used to sign in. Make sure to protect these credentials because anyone who has them could impersonate the identity of the service principal that you created and gain access to your Azure environment.

Exercise 2.2

I believe in learning by doing. To help you internalize what you learn in this chapter, create another service principal. If you need help using the command to create this service principal, you can start at http://mng.bz/6Dvp.

Service principals require a password or certificate to sign in. Both are cumbersome to use because they need to be protected and managed. Additionally, they need to be stored, sometimes on the resources. If you don't want to manage passwords or certificates, you can use a *managed identity* instead of using service principals.

2.1.5 *Managed identity in Azure AD*

Managed identity is a capability of Azure AD that provides you with an identity that your organization can use to access cloud services without needing to manage or store passwords or certificates. Managed identities are best suited when you want to use an Azure resource, such as Azure App Services or Azure virtual machines (VMs), to access services that support Azure AD authentication. I'll cover authentication in more detail shortly. There are two types of managed identities:

- *System-assigned*—Tied to a single Azure resource; used to access cloud services that support managed identities
- *User-assigned*—Created as a standalone Azure resource; used by multiple Azure resources to access cloud services that support managed identities

Imagine you have an Azure resource that needs to perform API calls against Azure services that support Azure AD authentication. Instead of creating a service principal for your Azure resource where you need to manage secrets, you can create a managed identity for it.

2.1.6 *Managed identity in action*

To create a managed identity, start by creating a user-assigned managed identity for an Azure resource. You need to provide a name for the managed identity and the name of the resource group in which it will be created.

NOTE If you don't have or don't want to use an existing resource group, you can create a new one. For help creating a new resource group, you can start at http://mng.bz/nWyV.

Run the following command in Azure Cloud Shell to create your first managed identity:

```
az identity create --name MyManagedIdentity        ◁──┐  The name of the
➥--resource-group MyResourceGroup          ◁──┐      │  managed identity
                                                │
              The resource group name in which  │
              the managed identity is created   │
```

After this command runs, it creates a managed identity for your Azure resource called
MyManagedIdentity, as you can see from the following output:

```
{
  "clientId": "b0f14b46-df49-4172-8325-8f7f6946005a",
  "id": "/subscriptions/00000000-0000-0000-0000-000000000000/resourcegroups
  ➥/chapter2/providers/Microsoft.ManagedIdentity/userAssignedIdentities
  ➥/MyManagedIdentity",
  "location": "northeurope",
  "name": "MyManagedIdentity",
  "principalId": "f3d0581d-d6df-4392-a1f5-69a9f859af5b",
  "resourceGroup": "MyResourceGroup",
  "tags": {},
  "tenantId": "00000000-0000-0000-0000-000000000000",
  "type": "Microsoft.ManagedIdentity/userAssignedIdentities"
}
```

After you create your first managed identity, you can give it permission to access
specific Azure resources (I'll cover permissions later in this chapter). To use managed
identity to access Azure resources, the Azure service needs to support managed
identities.

> **NOTE** Not all Azure services support managed identities. To consult the most
> up-to-date list of Azure services that support managed identities, you can start
> at http://mng.bz/vnGm.

Exercise 2.3

For extra practice, create another user-assigned managed identity. If you need help
with using the command used to create this managed identity, you can start at
http://mng.bz/4Do5.

At this point, you've successfully created identities for your user and application, and
you've even created a managed identity (table 2.1).

Table 2.1 Overview of different identities you created in this chapter

User principal	Service principal	Managed identity
Name: Bob Miller Unique identifier: Bob@contoso.com Password: dQ76bmz7rMVs9gSP	Name; MyAmazingApp Unique identifier: 723cd0c5-8ada -459f-8476-144a003d4587 Password: 2568Q~R0ltg5Q2_R_ G-vs5gN6X2pdta	Name: MyManagedIdentity Unique identifier: b0f14b46-df49 -4172-8325-8f7f6946005a

But before these identities can be used to access Azure resources, they first need to *authenticate.*

2.2 Authentication

Authentication verifies that the identity used is indeed the one that it claims to be. It revolves around questions such as "Who are you?" and "Are you who you claim to be?" I'll explain this using the following analogy. Imagine you are on your way to the airport to go on holiday to a warm and sunny destination. When you arrive, before you're allowed to board the plane, you're required to pass through customs and immigration, where you are asked to provide a form of identification. In Europe, this can be a document such as a passport or an ID card. The document that you hand over is then used to confirm that you are who you say you are. The same principle applies to authentication. It's the process of verifying the identity of a user or application.

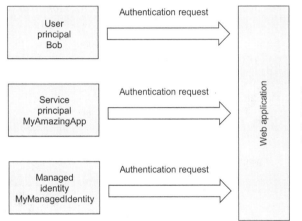

Figure 2.3 Authentication process between identities and resource serving data

As part of the authentication process, the identity of a user or application needs to authenticate, typically against a service serving data—for example, a web application like in figure 2.3. As you recall, the identity of a user or application that is authenticating against the web application is commonly referred to as a principal, and the web application serving data as a resource. The password or certificate that the principal provides to the resource as part of the authentication process is referred to as a *credential.* As a reward for a successful authentication, the principal receives *tokens*—artifacts that convey successful authentication and are used to grant access to a resource, such as the web application serving data.

Credentials, at a point in time, are stored and managed by the resource (such as the web application) on behalf of principals, which is known as *basic authentication.*

Each resource—for example, each web application—needs to store the credentials of the principals that access the web application. The resource storing the credentials of principals, in addition to providing a service to principals, also must secure those credentials against an ever-evolving threat landscape. Microsoft is fading out basic authentication from their products that use them, and so should you.

Passwords are often reused by users across different applications. Therefore, if one web application is breached by a bad actor (like Eve), they could use the stolen credentials to try to authenticate to other web applications on behalf of the principal (like Bob). Assuming Bob uses the same username and password across different web applications, Eve could authenticate as Bob to these web applications. Do you see the problem with this approach? Nowadays, resources are more focused on providing data to principals, and they outsource the task of securing credentials (and other IAM operations) to an *identity provider.*

Using an identity provider as part of the authentication process is known as *modern authentication.* The main idea behind using an identity provider as part of the authentication process is that the principal (user or application) is redirected to the identity provider to authenticate. This implies a *trust relationship* between the identity provider and each resource serving data. If the authentication is successful, the identity provider will redirect the principal to the resource (figure 2.4).

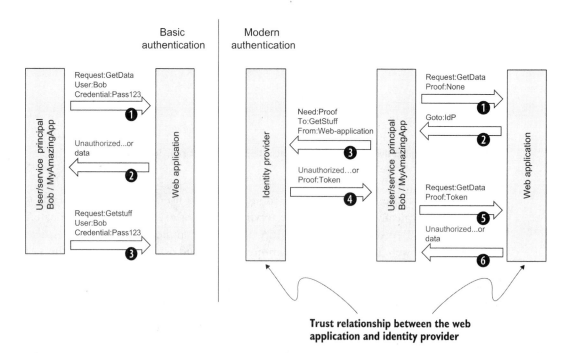

Figure 2.4   A comparison of basic and modern authentication using the identities you created

2.2.1   *Azure AD as an IAM service*

Azure AD can be seen as both the IAM service built into Azure and an identity provider for other platforms and applications. In this chapter, I'll focus on Azure AD as an IAM service that you use to secure the identities of your users and applications. For example, Bob needs to access Azure; he first needs to authenticate with his identity to Azure AD, which is Azure's IAM service. He does so by providing the combination of his username and password to prove that he is indeed who he claims to be (namely, Bob).

Anyone who possesses the combination of his username and password could use it to authenticate to Azure as him. Can you imagine the security implications of this? Therefore, it's paramount to protect and safeguard Bob's credentials that he uses to access Azure. Even if his username and password were disclosed, you need to ensure that Eve isn't able to access the environment. For this, you can use *multifactor authentication (MFA)*.

2.2.2   *Importance of multifactor authentication*

MFA is the process of prompting a user for a second proof of identity to confirm they are who they claim to be during the authentication process. The most widely used second forms of verifying an identity are the following:

- *Something you know*—Usually a password or PIN
- *Something you have*—Usually a mobile phone, ID card, or FIDO2 security key
- *Something you are*—Usually a biometric marker, such as a fingerprint or retinal scan

> **NOTE** FIDO2 security keys are external security keys that can be used as an authentication method. They're based on the Fast Identity Online (FIDO) authentication standard. To learn more about FIDO, you can start at https://fidoalliance.org.

MFA helps protect your users' identities by *hardening* them. Hardening is a way to secure identities and resources by reducing their surface of vulnerability and making it more difficult for bad actors like Eve to compromise them. For identities, this can be done by prompting for a second factor in addition to username and password. Azure AD provides an integrated MFA service into Azure called *Azure MFA*.

2.2.3   *Azure MFA*

Azure MFA supports a variety of verification methods that can be used as a second factor to prove that a user is who they claim to be. For example, Bob receives an automated voice call; he answers the call and presses the # key to authenticate. He is also prompted through a text message sent to his mobile number. It contains a verification code he needs to enter to authenticate again. Another option is for Bob to use a mobile authentication app that prompts him to choose Verify on his mobile phone. Hardware authentication devices such as FIDO2 security keys can be used too. These verification methods, depicted in figure 2.5, are widely used.

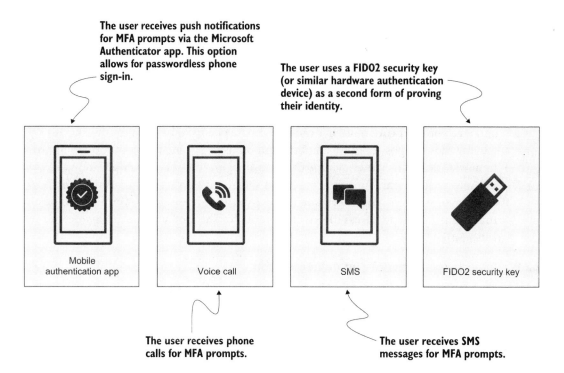

Figure 2.5   **Examples of a second form of authentication used with Azure MFA**

To prompt for a second form of authentication, Azure AD first needs to have information stored detailing the verification method to use. Your users, like Bob, need to register this information and add a verification method to their profile. After users add at least one verification method, they're able to benefit from Azure MFA and are prompted for a second form of identification when authenticating with their credentials.

> **NOTE**   The importance of enabling MFA is highlighted by the results of a study published by Microsoft in September 2019. Microsoft found that your account is more than 99.9% less likely to be compromised if you use MFA. To read the findings of this study, you can start at http://mng.bz/QP41.

Azure MFA is an important step in making your identities more than 99.9% less likely to be compromised. You can access the basic MFA functionality using Azure's *security defaults*.

2.2.4   *Security defaults in Azure AD*

Security defaults are a set of features in Azure AD that provides you with MFA capability for all of your users. Because security defaults come at no additional cost (they are free), there is a tradeoff: all your users must register for MFA using the mobile authentication app Microsoft Authenticator. If your Azure tenant was created after October 22, 2019, security defaults are already enabled in your tenant. If you need to enable security defaults yourself for your tenant, perform the following steps:

1 Navigate to the Azure portal, and select Azure Active Directory.
2 Choose Manage, and then, under Properties, select Manage Security Defaults.
3 Set the Enable Security Defaults toggle to Yes (figure 2.6).

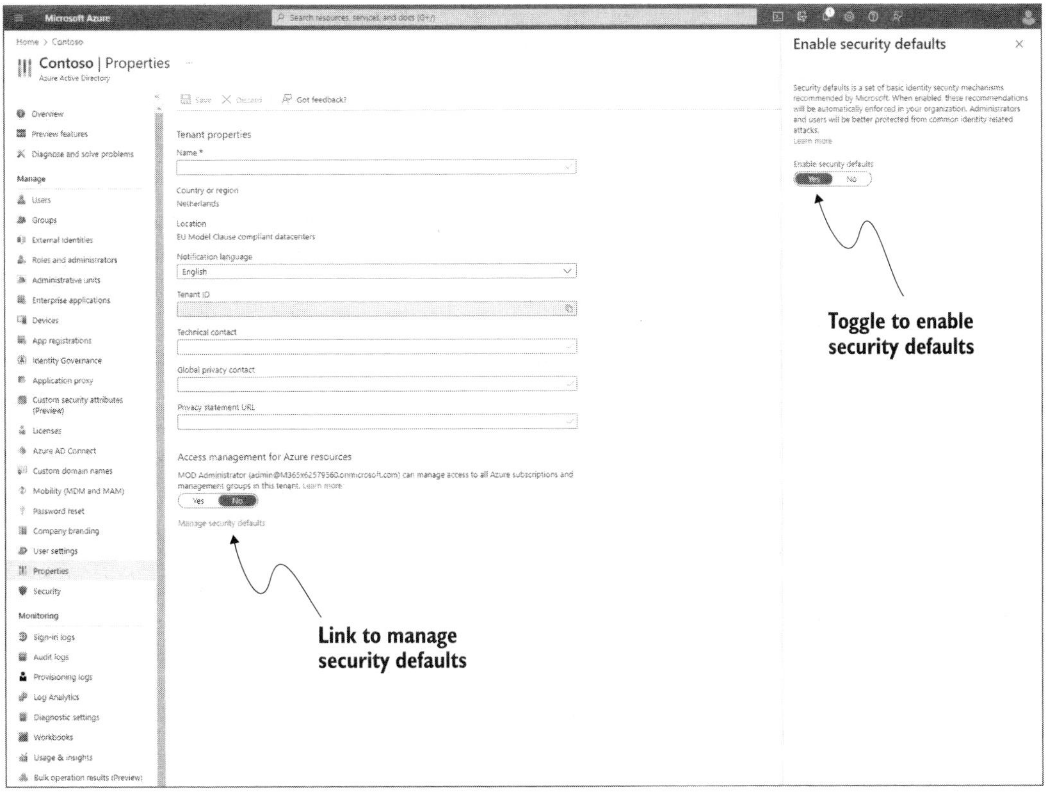

Figure 2.6   Enabling security defaults through the Azure portal

After you've enabled security defaults, all of your users are prompted for MFA via a numeric value in the Microsoft authenticator app. The implication of using security defaults is that your users need to download and set up the Microsoft Authenticator app on their phones (and have mobile phones to begin with). Security defaults provide you with a cost-effective Azure MFA option for all your users. However, security defaults enable MFA across the board, regardless of all available data points, such as anomalous behavior and sign-in risk. That is, security defaults prompt for MFA regardless of the context and can affect the productivity of users. To enforce MFA, depending on whether a sign-in to your Azure environment is deemed risky, you can use a capability called *identity protection.*

2.2.5 *Identity protection*

Do you want to automate the process for detecting suspicious sign-ins to your Azure environment? As you recall, as part of the authentication process, an identity consisting of a username and credential can be used to sign in to Azure. With regard to a potentially compromised sign-in, there are two levels at which risk can be detected: at the identity itself and at the sign-in.

Suppose Bob decides to work remotely from an unfamiliar location (somewhere warm and sunny comes to mind). While working remotely, he needs to access the Azure environment to perform his job, such as when developing and deploying applications in Azure. His attempt to authenticate from an unfamiliar location can be seen as a risk tied to the identity. The unfamiliar location can also be seen as risky as it raises suspicion that the user is not who they claim to be and that their credentials have been compromised. To detect risk at both levels, you can use identity protection. Identity protection uses machine learning algorithms to establish a baseline of the usual user behavior over time and then uses that baseline to distinguish between usual user activities and anomalous behavior. Because identity protection uses machine learning, it's considered a premium capability in Azure AD. To use it, your users need to be covered by an Azure AD Premium P2 license. Examples of detections included in identity protection are shown in table 2.2.

Table 2.2   Examples of identity protection detections in Azure AD

Detection	Description
Anonymous IP address	Tor exit nodes or anonymizer VPNs
Atypical travel	Travel distance too high for travel time
Leaked credentials	Credentials compromised on the web
Malware linked IP address	Botnet linked IP addresses
Unfamiliar sign-in properties	Unfamiliar sign-ins are based on past user activity.
Suspicious browser	Suspicious sign-in activity from the same browser

The benefit of using identity protection is that it allows you to automate the process of detecting risk both at the identity level (like the user Bob) and sign-in level (such as the user Bob accessing Azure resources from an unfamiliar location). You can also use identity protection for other scenarios, for example, to ring-fence users who shouldn't be working outside of a particular geographical location due to a specific requirement, such as working on sensitive government projects. The way you configure identity protection to automate risk detection at both levels is through policies.

2.2.6 *Identity protection in action*

Before configuring identity protection policies, there are three main parameters you need to be aware of:

- *Users*—Specifies the identities this policy applies to
- *Sign-in risk*—Specifies from what risk level this policy becomes applicable
- *Access*—Specifies whether access is blocked or allowed (with the possibility to enforce a control)

AUTOMATE RISK DETECTION AT THE USER LEVEL

When automating risk detection at the identity (user) level, the control that can be optionally enforced is to require a password change. This differs from automating detection at the sign-in level, as the control that can be enforced there is to require MFA. These policies are straightforward to configure. I'll start by teaching you how to configure the policy of automatically detecting risk at the identity level. For the purposes of this example, use the identity you created earlier for Bob.

> **NOTE** Assigning the users you're going to need for this example requires an Azure AD Premium license. More information about signing up for an Azure AD Premium license is available at http://mng.bz/XNel.

The following process solves the requirement for detecting risk when Bob signs in, but it can also be applied to other users. To configure an identity protection policy for Bob's user, follow these steps:

1. Navigate to the Azure portal with the global administrator or security administrator role assigned.
2. Select Azure Active Directory, and then, under Manage, click Security.
3. On the left side, under Protect, select Identity Protection, and click User Risk Policy.
4. Choose Bob (or Alice) as the identity to which this policy applies (figure 2.7).
5. In the User Risk Section, select High from the following options:
   - High
   - Medium and Above
   - Low and Above

   Each option specifies from what risk level this policy will begin to be applied. Selecting High implies that you want to automate detections that have a high level only.
6. Choose Access, where you are presented with the following options:
   - Block Access
   - Allow Access (and Optionally Require Password Change)

   These options allow you to specify whether access should be blocked or granted (with an option to enforce a control).

7 Click Allow Access, and then select Require Password Change.
8 Don't forget to select On at the bottom of the page where it says Enforce Policy.

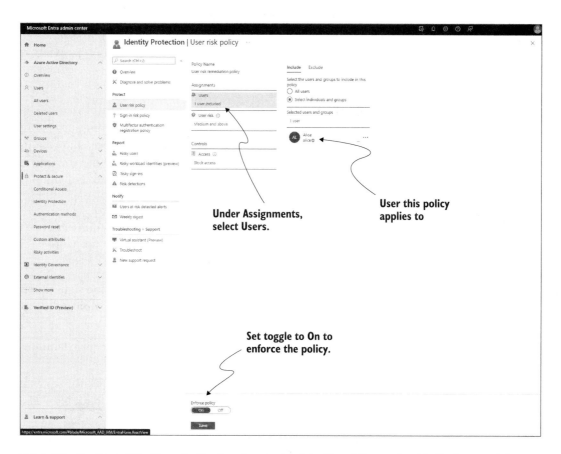

Figure 2.7   **Configuring identity protection to automate risk detection at the user level in the Azure portal**

This configuration ensures that when a risk deemed to be high is detected at the user level, Bob is still able to access the Azure environment. However, he needs to perform a password change. Just to remind you, identity protection allows you to automate this process of detecting risk at both the identity level (like the user Bob) and sign-in level (such as the user Bob accessing Azure resources from an unfamiliar location).

AUTOMATE RISK DETECTION AT THE SIGN-IN LEVEL

Configuring identity protection to detect risk at the sign-in level is done by selecting Sign-In Risk Policy and executing a similar sequence of steps as you did when configuring the user risk policy. There are, however, the following two main distinctions:

- The sign-in risk policy is tied to detecting risk at the sign-in level and not at the user level.
- Under Access, you can optionally enforce the control of Require Multifactor Authentication, instead of Require Password Change.

Exercise 2.4

To reinforce what you learn in this section, create a policy that automates risk detection at the sign-in level. If you need help with creating this policy, you can start at http://mng.bz/yQK7.

Identity protection gives you the ability to automate the detection of sign-in risk at both levels—on the identity that is used to perform the sign-in and on the sign-in itself. It applies to all Azure resources and applications. However, with identity protection, you don't have the flexibility to define a multitude of users and sign-in risk policies. When you configure identity protection, whether a user or sign-in risk policy, it applies to all the users and groups that you select. If you require more granularity and flexibility, you can use *conditional access*.

2.2.7 *Conditional access in Azure AD*

Have you ever wanted to block user access from untrusted locations? Conditional access is a capability in Azure AD that gives you the flexibility of enforcing Azure MFA and identity protection at the same time at a more granular level, compared with Azure MFA or identity protection alone. Conditional access uses machine learning and other available data points, such as IP location information, device information, and application-level information, and can calculate real-time risk to detect potentially compromised sign-in attempts to your Azure environment. Conditional access refers to the ability to apply different security policies depending on the scenario. It also allows you to cover additional use cases that are not covered by security defaults, Azure MFA, or identity protection policies, such as the following:

- Requiring MFA for Azure management tasks, such as configuring VMs to turn on or turn off on a predefined schedule
- Blocking access from untrusted locations
- Blocking access to specific applications for risky sign-in behavior
- Requiring all users to register their security information used for MFA

To explain how conditional access policies work, I'll use three building blocks: *assignments*, *conditions*, and *controls*. Assignments specify the identities and applications that the policy applies to. Conditions allow you to select and configure a series of checks that need to be performed and to control access. Finally, controls allow you to block or grant access, with the option to enforce additional safeguards (such as requiring

MFA). Conditional access policies are built on top of these three building blocks (figure 2.8).

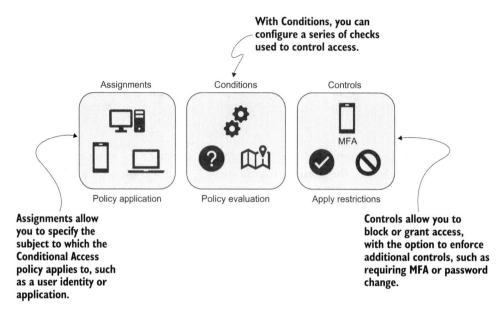

Figure 2.8   A simplified view of how conditional access in Azure AD works

With conditional access policies, you can define key parameters of access (allow, block, or conditions of access). They require capabilities to comply with policies and maintain security of access to your Azure environment. To use conditional access, your users require an Azure AD Premium P1 license. If you would like to use identity protection and risk-based policies in combination with conditional access, your users need to be covered by an Azure AD Premium P2 license. You can configure conditional access policies based on the example of Bob working remotely. When Bob needs to perform Azure management tasks (assignments) from any location other than the corporate offices (conditions), he is prompted for MFA (controls).

> **NOTE**   If you enabled security defaults for your Azure tenant, you need to disable them prior to configuring conditional access.

2.2.8   *Conditional access in action*

Suppose you want to configure conditional access to require MFA for management tasks in Azure. To configure a conditional access policy for Bob's user, perform the following steps:

1 Navigate to the Azure portal with the conditional access administrator role assigned.

2 Select Azure Active Directory, and then, under Manage, click Security.

3 On the left, under Protect, select Conditional Access, and click New Policy.

4 Under Name, click Require MFA for Azure Management Tasks as the policy name (figure 2.9).

5 Under Assignments, click Users or Workload Identities.

6 Choose Select Users and Groups, and then click Users and Groups.

7 From the list of users and groups, select Bob's user, and then click Select.

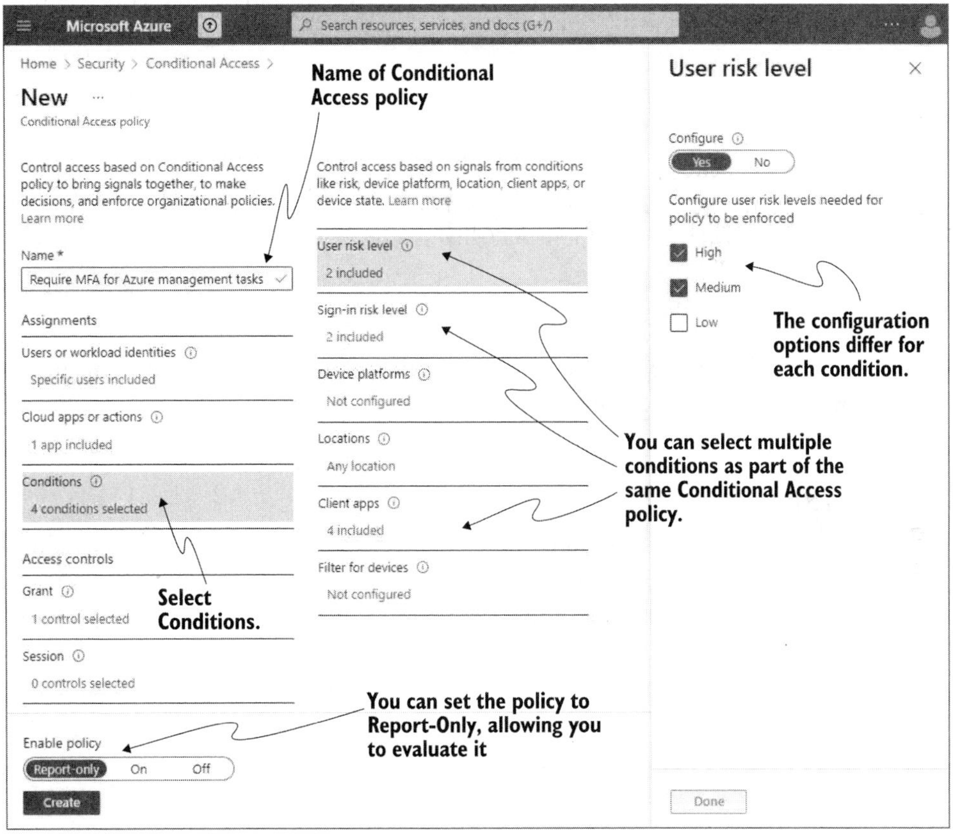

Figure 2.9 Configuring a conditional access policy in the Azure portal

8 Under Assignments, choose Cloud Apps or Actions.

9 Click Select App, and then select None.

10 From the list of applications, select Microsoft Azure Management (you might need to use the search bar and type in the name).

11 Click Select.

12   Select Conditions, and then click Locations.

13   Set the Configure toggle to No.

14   Switch over to the Exclude tab, and select All Trusted Locations. This will ensure that the policy applies only to locations outside those you defined as trusted (for example, your corporate offices). You can specify your corporate offices in Trusted Locations.

15   Under Grant, select Grant Access with Require Multifactor Authentication selected.

16   Finally, set the Enable Policy toggle to Report-Only. This configuration will ensure that the policy is evaluated but not enforced, allowing you to determine the effect of this policy on users before enforcing it. You can then enforce the policy by setting the Enable Policy toggle to On.

Exercise 2.5

To solidify your knowledge of conditional access, create a policy that requires MFA when sign-in risk is medium or high. If you need help creating this policy, you can start at http://mng.bz/MB6E.

If all conditions of this policy are met, Bob will be able to authenticate successfully and get access. Now, the question is, what can he access in Azure? Or what is he authorized to do?

2.3   *Authorization*

The second of the four pillars of identity is *authorization* (remember the four As?). Authorization revolves around the questions "What can you access?" and "What actions can you perform?" once your user or application has been authenticated. It is the process of granting or denying access to a system by verifying whether the identity used has the necessary permissions to perform the requested action. For authorization, you use Azure's authorization mechanism, which authorizes an action based on a role assigned to a user.

Authorization verifies that the user is allowed to perform the actions they're trying to do. To see how this looks, let's return to the hypothetical example of going on holiday. After you hand your passport to the border control agent for inspection and they verify your identity (authentication), depending on the entry requirements of your destination, you are able or unable to continue your journey. For example, do you have the required visa?

This check of what permissions you have and what activities you can perform based on your identity (for example, your ability to enter a specific country) can be seen as authorization. Authorization allows you to provide permissions to individuals/groups, which they can use to perform specific activities, such as their day-to-day activities, inside your Azure environment. To contribute toward achieving business goals, employees need to have permission to do their job effectively by performing specific tasks or activities.

Most companies have many employees with different responsibilities, each needing the right permissions to perform their job effectively. For example, going on holiday may require different types of visas that allow you to enter a certain country, such as a holiday visa or a work visa. Each visa includes its own set of activities you can perform after you enter a certain country. These permissions are standardized based on roles. The same concept can be applied to authorization. Assigning a custom set of permissions to each user is tedious and error prone, especially as the number of users increases. As most organizations have duties aligned to specific roles, it's possible to choose roles containing permissions that can be used to perform specific activities. Luckily, Azure has a built-in authorization system called *Azure role-based access control (RBAC)* that allows you to do exactly that.

2.3.1 *Azure role-based access control*

Azure RBAC is an authorization system built into the Azure platform. Authorization revolves around the questions "What permissions does the identity have, and what can it do?" Azure RBAC helps you specify and manage what actions users (like Bob) can perform on Azure resources.

The following are some examples of what you can do with Azure RBAC:

- Allow a group of administrators to manage VMs within an Azure subscription
- Allow one user to manage VMs and another to manage SQL databases in a subscription
- Allow a group of application developers to deploy and manage all resources within a resource group

Azure RBAC allows for a set of permissions, called *roles*, to be assigned to identities, ensuring they have the right level of permission to perform their job. It allows you to granularly control the level of users' access and includes several built-in roles you can use.

2.3.2 *How does Azure RBAC work?*

Roles are key to understanding how Azure RBAC works. Roles provide identities (*security principal* in Azure RBAC) with a certain set of permissions (*role definition*) over specific resources (*scope*). I'll cover each one of these in more detail, starting with the security principal.

SECURITY PRINCIPAL

The security principal is the subject in the Azure RBAC or the "who" in the authorization process to gain access to certain Azure resources. It can be a user, such as Bob, who needs access to Azure resources. It can also be a group of users—for example, a group of administrators that needs access to all VMs inside the subscription in Azure to manage them. It can also be a service principal, such as an application that needs access to a storage account or a managed identity. Any one of these can be considered a security principal from an Azure RBAC perspective. After you identify the "who," you need to determine the permissions they need. This set of permissions is called *role definitions.*

ROLE DEFINITIONS

If a security principal is seen as the "who" in the Azure RBAC authorization process, role definitions can be seen as the "'what." They both answer this question: What actions can the user or application perform on Azure resources? Role definitions (or roles, as they're commonly referred to) specify the concrete permissions that the security principal can perform on the resources. These permissions could be read, write, or delete. They can be granular and really specific, such as being able to perform write operations on a particular resource inside a resource group. On the other hand, they can be wide and high level, such as being able to perform all operations on a management group and all subscriptions beneath it. However, it would be tedious if you needed to create all these roles from scratch. Because most organizations have a need to perform similar tasks on resources in Azure, you can use out-of-the-box roles in Azure RBAC, called *built-in role definitions* (or roles). These built-in roles provide you with a predefined collection of permissions necessary to perform a specific task effectively. You need to be aware of the following four fundamental built-in roles in Azure RBAC:

- *Owner*—Has full access to all resources, including the right to delegate access to other users
- *Contributor*—Can access and manage all types of resources but can't delegate access to other users
- *Reader*—Can view existing resources
- *User access administrator*—Can manage access to Azure resources

> **NOTE** You can see a list of all available Azure built-in roles here: http://mng.bz/a1jx.

Imagine you need to deploy a VM on Azure. Azure RBAC has a built-in role called a *Virtual Machine Contributor* that gives you the permissions you need to perform that action. It also ensures you're adhering to the least privilege principle (remember the three cornerstone principles of zero trust discussed in section 1.7?) by limiting the permissions to this specific task and resource type only and denying access to perform actions on other resource types, such as storage accounts. The role definition in Azure consists of several properties, which can help you understand the building blocks of the roles. To see the properties for the Virtual Machine Contributor role, you can run the following command in Azure Cloud Shell:

```
az role definition list --name "Virtual Machine Contributor"
```

This command gets the role definitions for the Virtual Machine Contributor, but it can be applied to other roles. After you run the command, it shows the role definitions, as you can see from the following output:

```
[
  {
    "assignableScopes": [
      "/"
    ],
    "description": "Lets you manage virtual machines, but not access to them,
    ➥and not the virtual network or storage account they're connected to.",
    "id": "/subscriptions/00000000-0000-0000-0000-000000000000/providers
    ➥/Microsoft.Authorization/roleDefinitions/9980e02c-c2be-4d73-94e8
    ➥-173b1dc7cf3c",
    "name": "9980e02c-c2be-4d73-94e8-173b1dc7cf3c",
    "permissions": [
      {
        "actions": [
          "Microsoft.Authorization/*/read",
          "Microsoft.Compute/availabilitySets/*",
          "Microsoft.Compute/locations/*",
          "Microsoft.Compute/virtualMachines/*",
          "Microsoft.Compute/virtualMachineScaleSets/*",
          "Microsoft.Compute/cloudServices/*",
          "Microsoft.Compute/disks/write",
          "Microsoft.Compute/disks/read",
          "Microsoft.Compute/disks/delete",
          "Microsoft.DevTestLab/schedules/*",
          "Microsoft.Insights/alertRules/*",
          ...
          "Microsoft.ResourceHealth/availabilityStatuses/read",
          "Microsoft.Resources/deployments/*",
          "Microsoft.Resources/subscriptions/resourceGroups/read",
          "Microsoft.SerialConsole/serialPorts/connect/action",
          "Microsoft.SqlVirtualMachine/*",
          "Microsoft.Storage/storageAccounts/listKeys/action",
          "Microsoft.Storage/storageAccounts/read",
          "Microsoft.Support/*"
        ],
        "dataActions": [],
        "notActions": [],
        "notDataActions": []
      }
    ],
    "roleName": "Virtual Machine Contributor",
    "roleType": "BuiltInRole",
    "type": "Microsoft.Authorization/roleDefinitions"
  }
]
```

As you analyze the role definition output, it's important you understand the difference between the control and data plane.

CONTROL AND DATA PLANE

There are specific resources that contain data, such as storage accounts. You can give a security principal permissions to the resource (such as the storage account) and to the data that resides in the resource (such as the data inside of the storage account). For example, if Bob has the Reader role in the resource group in which the storage account resides, he can view the storage account. However, by default, he can't read the underlying data that is stored on the storage account. These two types of actions are known as *control plane actions* and *data plane actions*. Both are important in Azure RBAC. Control plane actions are added to the `actions` and `notActions` properties, whereas data plane actions are added to the `dataActions` and `notDataActions` properties.

Now that you know the "who" and "what," the outstanding question is "on what?" The set of Azure resources to which roles are applied is called *scope*.

SCOPE

Scope allows you to implement the principle of least privilege by ensuring that the security principal has access only to the Azure resources they need. It is of paramount importance that you ensure identities are not overpermissioned. Should the identity of the security principal be compromised, with scope, you can ensure that the effect of a potential breach is minimized by giving the security principal access only to those resources that they need access to. Fundamentally, in Azure, you can assign role definitions at the following four scopes:

- Resource level
- Resource group level
- Subscription level
- Management group level

The least-specific scope—and the one with the widest reach—is the management group level, as this role applies to all subscriptions, resource groups, and resources in its hierarchy. It has the highest level of privileges, as it applies to all the resources in the management group.

Once you identify the "who," the "what" and "on what?", you can tie these together into a *role assignment*.

2.3.3   Role assignment

In Azure, you give permissions defined in the role definition to a security principal over a set of Azure resources defined in scope by creating a role assignment, which grants access to Azure resources. The implication is that by removing the role assignment, you can effectively remove access to Azure resources. When creating a role assignment, make sure you use a user with owner or user access administrator status, as these two have role assignment write permissions that are needed to create role assignments.

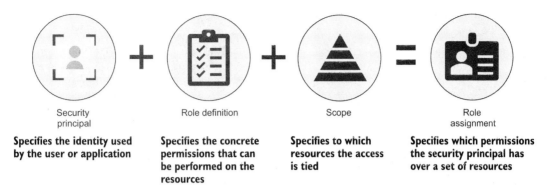

Security principal	Role definition	Scope	Role assignment
Specifies the identity used by the user or application	**Specifies the concrete permissions that can be performed on the resources**	**Specifies to which resources the access is tied**	**Specifies which permissions the security principal has over a set of resources**

Figure 2.10 Core components of role assignments in Azure RBAC

The role assignment process is depicted in figure 2.10. Here, the security principal is Bob, the role definition is the Virtual Machine Contributor role, and the scope is an Azure subscription.

2.3.4 *Azure role-based access control in action*

To assign Bob the Virtual Machine Contributor role at a subscription scope, run the following command in Azure Cloud Shell:

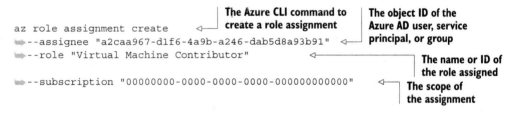

```
az role assignment create
→ --assignee "a2caa967-d1f6-4a9b-a246-dab5d8a93b91"
→ --role "Virtual Machine Contributor"

→ --subscription "00000000-0000-0000-0000-000000000000"
```

This code creates the role assignment, as you can see from the following output:

```
{
  "canDelegate": null,
  "condition": null,
  "conditionVersion": null,
  "description": null,
  "id": "/subscriptions/00000000-0000-0000-0000-000000000000
  →/providers/Microsoft.Authorization/roleAssignments
  →/63dbe701-7bc5-47fd-a765-a730d1fff435",
  "name": "63dbe701-7bc5-47fd-a765-a730d1fff435",
  "principalId": "a2caa967-d1f6-4a9b-a246-dab5d8a93b91",
  "principalType": "User",
  "subscription": "00000000-0000-0000-0000-000000000000",
  "roleDefinitionId": "/subscriptions/00000000-0000-0000-0000-000000000000
  →/providers/Microsoft.Authorization/roleDefinitions
  →/9980e02c-c2be-4d73-94e8-173b1dc7cf3c",
  "scope": "/subscriptions/00000000-0000-0000-0000-000000000000",
  "type": "Microsoft.Authorization/roleAssignments"
}
```

Exercise 2.6

To strengthen your knowledge of this Azure RBAC assignment, assign the Storage Blob Data Contributor role at resource scope to the service principal you created earlier in this chapter. To learn more about the permissions included in this particular role, you can start at http://mng.bz/a1jx. If you need help creating this assignment, you can start at http://mng.bz/gB6Z.

2.4   *Custom roles*

No two organizations are the same, and some have specific requirements. Therefore, it is sometimes necessary to provide specific (and, at times, granular) permissions to a specific set of users. Custom roles can help. They provide you with the ability to assign custom permissions, typically by modifying an existing set of permissions.

Custom roles can be used when you want to create your own set of permissions. An example might be if you want to enable a user to perform the action of restarting VMs but not be able to delete or create new ones. With custom roles in Azure RBAC, you can specify the select set of permissions that your users need and create a custom role for it. The advantage of creating a custom role is that you can group a specific set of permissions into a single role definition; you don't need to assign several built-in role definitions to a user. Assigning multiple role definitions often leads to users being overpermissioned, which is the opposite of the least privilege principle.

2.5   *Custom roles in action*

To create a custom role, you need to specify the required permissions in a JSON file. This JSON file has a predetermined format, where control plane operations are placed in the `Actions` and `NotActions` brackets, and data plane operations, respectively, in the `DataActions` and `NotDataActions` brackets.

NOTE   You can consult a list of available permissions at http://mng.bz/e1aw.

In addition to the specified permissions, you need to determine on which scope the custom role can be used. To do so, place the scope in the `AssignableScopes` brackets. You can use the following JSON file as guidance:

```
{
      "Name": "Restart Virtual Machines",
      "IsCustom": true,
      "Description": "Restart Virtual Machines.",
      "Actions": [
        "Microsoft.Compute/virtualMachines/read",
      "Microsoft.Compute/virtualMachines/start/action",
      "Microsoft.Compute/virtualMachines/restart/action",
      "Microsoft.Resources/subscriptions/resourceGroups/read"
      ],
      "NotActions": [
      ],
      "DataActions": [
```

```
      ],
      "NotDataActions": [
      ],
      "AssignableScopes": [
              "/subscriptions/00000000-0000-0000-0000-000000000000"
      ]
}
```

This JSON file contains permissions for a custom role that allows users to restart a VM at a subscription scope. To create this custom role, if you're using Azure Cloud Shell, you need to upload the JSON file using the Upload/Download option in Cloud Shell, and then select Upload and choose the JSON file. After you upload the JSON file, run the following command in Azure Cloud Shell to create the custom role:

```
az role definition create --role-definition customRoleDefinition.json
```

This command creates the custom role, and your output should look similar to the following:

```
{
  "assignableScopes": [
    "/subscriptions/00000000-0000-0000-0000-000000000000"
  ],
  "description": "Restart Virtual Machines.",
  "id": "/subscriptions/00000000-0000-0000-0000-000000000000/providers
➥/Microsoft.Authorization/roleDefinitions/eccbcf52-253d-4ea9-8498
➥-2f03177ae050",
  "name": "eccbcf52-253d-4ea9-8498-2f03177ae050",
  "permissions": [
    {
      "actions": [
        "Microsoft.Compute/virtualMachines/read",
        "Microsoft.Compute/virtualMachines/start/action",
        "Microsoft.Compute/virtualMachines/restart/action",
        "Microsoft.Resources/subscriptions/resourceGroups/read"
      ],
      "dataActions": [],
      "notActions": [],
      "notDataActions": []
    }
  ],
  "roleName": "Restart Virtual Machines",
  "roleType": "CustomRole",
  "type": "Microsoft.Authorization/roleDefinitions"
}
```

After creating the custom role, you can assign it using the `az role assignment` command. To assign the Restart Virtual Machines role to Bob at a subscription scope, run the following command in Azure Cloud Shell:

```
az role assignment create --assignee "a2caa967-d1f6-4a9b-a246-dab5d8a93b91"
➥--role "Restart Virtual Machines"
➥--subscription  "00000000-0000-0000-0000-000000000000"
```

This returns the following output:

```
{
  "canDelegate": null,
  "condition": null,
  "conditionVersion": null,
  "description": null,
  "id": "/subscriptions/00000000-0000-0000-0000-000000000000/providers
➡/Microsoft.Authorization/roleAssignments/3095197f-a54f-4c2e-a7d5
➡-4935660c1362",
  "name": "3095197f-a54f-4c2e-a7d5-4935660c1362",
  "principalId": "a2caa967-d1f6-4a9b-a246-dab5d8a93b91",
  "principalType": "User",
  "roleDefinitionId": "/subscriptions/00000000-0000-0000-0000-000000000000
➡/providers/Microsoft.Authorization/roleDefinitions
➡/eccbcf52-253d-4ea9-8498-2f03177ae050",
  "scope": "/subscriptions/00000000-0000-0000-0000-000000000000",
  "type": "Microsoft.Authorization/roleAssignments"
}
```

When creating custom roles, as a best practice, specify the `Actions` and `DataActions` permissions. Although custom roles support the wildcard character to define permissions, additional permissions granted in the future might lead to unwanted behavior.

Now that you understand authorization, there are still two identity pillars left to be covered—namely, administration and auditing. Administration revolves around simplifying management, automated approvals, and access assignment process. Auditing addresses the question "Who did what, when, and how?" In Azure AD, both of these pillars of identity are covered by i*dentity governance.*

2.6 *Identity governance*

Identity governance is not one specific feature but rather a set of capabilities that span the administration and auditing pillar of the four pillars of identity (the four *A*s). After a specific activity has been performed, it's important for auditing purposes to be able to document who has done what and when. Also, as time goes by, users' responsibilities might change. Therefore, the permissions they need to perform their job need to change as they need permissions to perform other types of activities or tasks—potentially, even on other Azure resource types. Employees may also leave the company, and others may join. This ongoing process of employees joining the company, moving to other roles within, and leaving the company—referred to as joiners–movers–leavers—highlights the need to be able to track who did what and when.

This is where identity governance comes into play. It allows organizations to achieve their business goals by having a standardized way of auditing who did what and when and managing the complexity around this process. The goal is to have a balance between security and productivity, empowering users to do their work by ensuring that the right controls are in place. The first step is to make sure you minimize the number of people inside your organization who have privileged access. For this, you can use a capability called *privileged identity management (PIM)*.

2.6.1 Privileged identity management

PIM is a capability in Azure AD that allows you to minimize the number of users inside your organization that have privileged access. The reason for doing so is twofold. First, you ensure that users can't mistakenly affect resources to which they shouldn't have access, such as deleting a VM in a production subscription. Second, if a bad actor compromises the identity of your user, you're minimizing the effect of the damage they may do with that identity.

There are valid reasons for certain users to have privileged access. However, instead of having privileged access all the time, it is prudent to have it only when needed to perform tasks that require it. This is known as providing *just-in-time* administrative access. PIM facilitates the management and auditing of admin roles across Azure, allowing you to see which users are assigned privileged roles. You can even set approval flows for privilege escalation and get alerts for administrative access activation.

> **TIP** If you're interested in learning more about how Microsoft implemented PIM, you can learn more about it at https://www.aka.ms/PIMatMS.

You can use PIM to remove users from roles that they aren't using and move them to less privileged roles with the option to be eligible for privileged access.

PIM allows you to manage the following roles and groups:

- *Azure roles*—Azure RBAC roles
- *Azure AD roles*—Roles used to manage Azure AD
- *Privileged access groups*

You can assign them to users or groups. The assignment can be either active or eligible, with the option to set a start and end time for each. *Active* means that it's already in effect, whereas *eligible* means that the user can activate the role that they've been made eligible for when they need to perform tasks that require privileged access.

Now that you understand how to work with PIM, I will show you how to configure it.

2.6.2 PIM in action

As mentioned, you can configure PIM for Azure roles, Azure AD roles, and privileged access groups. Given our example of Bob's activity so far in the chapter, we will focus on configuring PIM for Azure roles, which can be broken down into the following four main steps:

1 Discovery of Azure resources
2 Configuration of Azure role settings
3 Assigning Azure roles
4 Activating assigned Azure roles

DISCOVERY OF AZURE RESOURCES

The first step is to discover Azure resources. This step is all about identifying and specifying which Azure resources you are going to protect with PIM, allowing you to identify privileged administrators. To discover Azure resources, you need to perform the following steps:

1 Navigate to the Azure portal, and sign in with a role such as the owner or user access administrator.

2 Select Azure AD Privileged Identity Management, and then click Azure Roles.

3 Click Discover Resources to launch a page showing you the subscriptions you have to write permissions to.

4 Select the subscription that you'd like to protect with PIM, and click Manage Resource.

5 When shown a prompt to confirm the onboarding, click Yes.

After you specify the resources you're going to protect with PIM, you're ready to move on to the next step of configuring Azure role settings.

CONFIGURATION OF AZURE ROLE SETTINGS

In this step, you will specify the default configuration that is applied to Azure role assignments in PIM. To configure Azure role settings, perform the following steps:

1 Navigate to Azure AD Privileged Identity Management, and select Azure Resources.

2 Select the subscription you used in the previous section, and click Settings.

3 From the long list of Azure roles, select the one you want to configure, such as Virtual Machine Administrator Login, and then click the Edit option.

4 In the Activation tab, select the Assignments tab.

5 Click the Notification tab.

6 Select Update.

You can repeat steps 2 through 7 for other subscriptions and Azure roles for which you'd like to configure Azure role settings. After you configure them, you are ready to assign an Azure role.

ASSIGNING THE AZURE ROLE

Assigning an Azure role allows you to specify the identities that can assume a certain Azure role. At a high level, it allows you to perform a mapping of identities and permissions. These settings can either be permanent (active) or for a certain period of time (eligible) after performing a specific action. By making identities eligible, instead of assigning them permissions permanently, the identities only assume a particular role when they need to perform a specific action. In turn, you can customize this action (by configuring the Azure role settings) to meet your organization's needs. You can, for example, require MFA on activation and approval to activate. To assign Azure roles to identities, follow these steps:

1 Navigate to Azure AD Privileged Identity Management, and choose Azure Resources.

2 Select the subscription you used in the previous section, and click Roles.

3 Click Add Assignments.

4 In the Membership tab, under Select Role, from the long list of Azure roles, select the role you want to assign, such as Virtual Machine Administrator Login.

5 Under Select Member(s), select Bob or the group that you want to assign to the role you selected in the previous step, and click Next.

6 Under Assignment Type, you can choose between Active and Eligible. Select Eligible, as this will ensure that the user needs to perform an action to use this role.

7 Under Assignment Starts and Assignment Ends, specify the time interval for this assignment.

8 Select Assign.

After successfully completing these steps, you should be back to the Roles blade. In this blade, you should see a list of rows, each containing an entry that specifies the Azure role, number of active assignments, and number of eligible assignments. After completing steps 3 to 8, you should see the number of eligible assignments for Virtual Machine Administrator Login incremented by one. This overview of Azure roles, together with eligible and active assignments, is helpful when you want to move users from permanently privileged roles to less privileged roles.

You have specified the Azure resources protected with PIM, the default configuration is applied to Azure role assignments, and identities can assume specific Azure roles. Now, let's examine how identities activate the roles assigned to them.

ACTIVATING ASSIGNED AZURE ROLES

Activating assigned Azure roles allows identities to assume privileged access for a predetermined period of time. To do so, do the following steps:

1 Navigate to Azure AD Privileged Identity Management, and choose My Roles.

2 Choose Azure Resource Roles to open a list of eligible Azure roles that the identity in question can assume.

3 From the list of available Azure roles—for example, Virtual Machine Administrator Login—select Activate.

4 Provide mandatory information, such as duration in hours, justification, and the scope of the resources needed, followed by Activate.

5 If prompted that you need to verify your identity with Azure MFA, choose Verify My Identity.

6 Follow the instructions, and perform the MFA challenge.

7 Once successful, select Activate.

8 If the activation requires approval, you will receive a notification in the upper-right corner, followed by another notification with the resolution of your request (either accepted or denied).

These steps show how you can use PIM to enable on-demand, just-in-time privileged access for your identities. Using PIM, you can even configure approval flows for privilege activation. This, in turn, allows you to get alerts and view the history of privileged activation. After identities are given privileged access—especially if it's active and permanently assigned—it's important to review privileged access on an ongoing basis using *access reviews*.

2.6.3 Access reviews

Access reviews in Azure AD allow you to manage risk associated with identities with any access by auditing and recertifying their access. You can configure the frequency and actions to automate the recertification process. You should use access reviews when you need to recertify access to resources, applications, and even administrative roles across Azure. Another common use case for using access reviews is to remove access from people in your organization who have changed teams or departments. You should also use access reviews to regularly confirm that users need access to critical Azure resources and manage access of users in privileged roles. Access reviews are mostly commonly used to review the following:

- Azure resource roles
- Azure AD roles
- Azure AD group memberships
- Applications integrated with Azure AD
- Access packages (I'll cover these shortly)

As part of the access review creation process, you need to select a reviewer. The reviewer is a person or group of people responsible for reviewing access by identities and deciding whether to remove or keep access. It's typical for a workload owner in Azure to be the reviewer. With this foundational understanding of the access review process, I will now show how you can use access reviews to manage user access to Azure resource roles.

ACCESS REVIEWS IN ACTION

To create access reviews, perform the following actions:

1. Navigate to Identity Governance inside the Azure portal.
2. Choose Azure Resources under Privileged Identity Management.
3. From the list of available subscriptions, select the subscription that you used when configuring PIM.
4. Choose Access Reviews, followed by New, which will open the wizard to create an access review.
5. Enter the name and description for your access review. Make sure they are easy to understand, as both are going to be shown to the reviewers.
6. Specify the date when you'd like the access review to start, and then specify its frequency, which can be one time, weekly, monthly, quarterly, annually, or semi-annually.

7 For Duration, specify the maximum number of days reviewers will have to perform the review.

8 Under End, specify how the recurring access reviews should end: never, by a specific date, or after a certain number of occurrences.

9 For Users Scope, select Users, Groups, or Service Principals that have access to the Azure resource role.

10 Under Review Role Membership, select the privileged Azure resource roles you'd like to review.

11 From the Assignment Type dropdown, select the criteria for choosing assignments.

12 From the Reviewers dropdown, select the reviewers for this access review. You can choose between different options, depending on the choice you made in step 9.

13 Next, specify the configuration options for when an access review finishes. You can configure to automatically remove access for users who were denied by setting the toggle Auto Apply Results to Resource to Enable. Alternatively, you can manually apply the results by setting the toggle to Disable.

14 You can choose which action is taken should the reviewers not complete the review by the end of the review period using With If Reviewers Don't Respond.

15 If you want other stakeholders to be notified, select them under At the End of Review, Send Notification To.

16 If required, expand Advanced Settings and configure additional settings.

After successfully completing these steps, you should be back to the Access Reviews blade and be able to see the access review you created. Next, I'll show you how to perform an access review on the review you just created.

PERFORMING AN ACCESS REVIEW

Access reviews are straightforward to perform. To do so, complete the following steps:

1 Navigate to Access Reviews under Privileged Identity Management.

2 Choose Review Access, which will open a blade with any pending access reviews.

3 Click the review that you created.

4 Select Approve or Deny.

As they move between different projects or departments, access reviews allow you to review access and remove it when not needed. Although access reviews help you to ensure that the users no longer have access to resources from the previous project, they're not helpful in providing users access to new applications or groups or managing the complexity around this process. For those purposes, you can use Azure AD *entitlement management.*

What is entitlement management?

Azure AD entitlement management is a capability of identity governance, allowing you to automate access to groups, applications, and SharePoint sites. The advantage of using entitlement management is that it allows you to create access packages based on your business/project's needs and set expiration dates and approvals to ensure that access to resources is time limited and appropriate. It allows you to monitor what assets users are accessing, how long they have access for, and whether they should be permitted to have access in the first place.

Because Azure AD entitlement management is geared more toward automating access to groups, applications, teams, and SharePoint sites, I won't cover it in more detail. However, I would be doing you a disservice if I didn't mention it, as it's a core capability of identity governance in Azure AD and one that you will likely encounter.

2.7   Answers to exercises

Exercise 2.1

Run the following command in Azure Cloud Shell with the user administrator role assigned:

```
az ad user create --display-name "Charlie Brown"
➥--password bR63bmz53jMVs7d2b
➥--user-principal-name charlie@contoso.com
➥--force-change-password-next-sign-in true
```

Exercise 2.2

```
az ad sp create-for-rbac -n "MySecondAmazingApp"
```

Exercise 2.3

```
az identity create --name SecondManagedIdentity
```

Exercise 2.4

Perform the following actions with the security administrator role assigned:

1   Sign in to the Azure portal, and navigate to Azure Active Directory.
2   Security > Identity Protection > Sign-In Risk Policy.
3   Users > All Users.
4   In the User Risk Section, select High.
5   Click Access, and choose Allow Access.
6   Select Require Multifactor Authentication, and click Done.
7   Under Policy Enforcement, select Enabled.
8   Click Save.

Exercise 2.5

1 Navigate to Azure Active Directory.
2 Security > Conditional Access > +Create New Policy.
3 Under Name, click Require MFA for Elevated Sign-In Risk.
4 Assignments > Users or Workload Identities > Users and Groups > Bob.
5 Cloud Apps or Actions > Include > All Cloud Apps.
6 Access controls > Grant.
7 Select Grant Access and Require Multifactor Authentication.
8 Set Enable Policy to Report-Only.
9 Click Create.

Exercise 2.6

```
az role assignment create
--assignee "723cd0c5-8ada-459f-8476-144a003d4587"
--role "Storage Blob Data Contributor"
--subscription "<subscriptionID>"
```

Summary

- Your identities are the primary security perimeter as they are used to access cloud services and can perform specific actions over resources. They should be verified and monitored and adhere to the least privilege principle.

- While service principals require you to manage and secure credentials, with managed identity, you don't need to manage any credentials. However, not all Azure services support managed identity.

- MFA helps protect your identities by hardening them and making it more difficult for bad actors to compromise them. Hardening is accomplished by prompting for a second factor of authentication in addition to a username and password.

- Conditional access provides you with the greatest flexibility and granularity when it comes to controlling the authentication process.

- Azure RBAC provides you with an authorization mechanism that is built into Azure. It provides you with a variety of built-in roles, and you can create custom roles.

- Identity governance in Azure AD has a lot of capabilities. PIM can be used to minimize the number of roles in your organization that have privileged access and ensure you're meeting the least privilege principle.

- Access reviews allow you to review privileged access on an ongoing basis and remove access when it is no longer required.

Part 2

Securing Azure resources

Now that you know how to secure the identities used to access your Azure resources, you're ready to proceed to the next part of the journey that you're on with respect to Azure security. This part teaches you how to secure commonly used resource types in Azure.

Chapter 3 is all about network security in Azure. It teaches you how to implement a secure network infrastructure in Azure using a set of services commonly referred to as Azure network security. In chapter 4, you learn how to secure compute resources, which are widely used to run applications in Azure, such as VMs, Azure Kubernetes Services, and Azure App Service.

Chapter 5 covers securing data resources in Azure, such as storage accounts and Azure Key Vault, which are commonly used to store data, secrets, and certificates. In chapter 6, I teach you how to use Microsoft Defender for Cloud to continuously assess the configuration of your Azure resources and apply security best practice guidance.

Chapter 7 picks up where the previous chapter left off and teaches you how to enable and apply threat detection capabilities with Defender for Cloud to detect suspicious activities and potential signs of compromise of your Azure environment.

When you're finished with this part of the book, you'll be ready to embark on the next part the journey you're on with respect to Azure security.

Implementing network security in Azure: Firewall, WAF, and DDoS protection

This chapter covers

- Azure network security
- Azure Firewall
- Azure Web Application Firewall
- Mitigating DDoS attacks

Networking continues to be a fundamental building block of any public cloud environment. This chapter teaches you how to implement a secure network infrastructure in Azure. In it, you learn how to differentiate between the various network security services in Azure and implement them effectively.

> **NOTE** To follow along with the exercises in this chapter, you can use the GitHub repository available at https://github.com/bmagusic/azure -security.

Along the way, I'll introduce you to a couple of additional models and concepts that make it easier to understand how to implement network security in Azure. You will learn Azure network security using an example of securing resources in Azure and providing secure access to these resources through the implementation of native network security services. These native network security services are commonly referred to as *Azure network security*.

3.1 Azure network security

Azure network security is a set of Azure services that you can use to implement a secure network infrastructure in Azure. The network security services this chapter teaches you are the following:

- Azure Firewall Standard
- Azure Firewall Premium
- Azure Web Application Firewall
- Azure DDoS Protection Basic
- Azure DDoS Protection Standard

You could also use third-party network security appliances in Azure to provide coverage for more advanced use cases. But you must know how these third-party network security appliances work, and using them usually incurs additional charges in Azure. Therefore, in this chapter, I'll focus solely on the native network security services available in Azure. These services are native to Azure, meaning that they are well-integrated into the Azure platform and provide protection against common attacks.

The services that I will teach you in this chapter protect against attacks that target the network, transport, and application layers. These layers are commonly referred to as layers 3, 4, and 7, respectively.

> **NOTE** Throughout this chapter, I refer to layers 3, 4, and 7. If you're not familiar with these layers from the Open Systems Interconnection (OSI) reference model, you can start at http://mng.bz/qrm6.

If I focused solely on network security in this chapter and left out application security, I would be doing you a disservice. Network and application security are closely coupled, as attacks targeting web applications use the fact that web applications are accessible over the internet. Therefore, I'll cover both network and application security in this chapter to help you add more layers of defense to your network infrastructure in Azure (defense-in-depth, remember?). Before I start teaching you about Azure network security services, I want to touch briefly on network segmentation to remind you of its importance.

3.1.1 The importance of network segmentation

Virtual networks (VNets) are the basic building blocks that you're going to use when implementing network security in Azure. You can think of them as the cloud equivalent to local switches in traditional on-premises networks. They allow you to divide your Azure network infrastructure into segments that align with your organization's applications and Azure resources. Network segmentation is also incredibly useful in preventing lateral movement should a bad actor gain access to your environment.

> **NOTE** To freshen your knowledge of the various Azure networking services that can be used, see http://mng.bz/7D47.

By default, different VNets function as isolated segments. You can connect different VNets into one network using VNet peering. Peering allows Azure resources from one VNet to access resources or platform-as-a-service (PaaS) services from another VNet. To control and filter network traffic between these VNets, you can use network security groups (NSGs). Together, all these services (figure 3.1) facilitate implementing the principle of least privilege that you learned about in the previous chapter, as least privilege can be applied to VNets too.

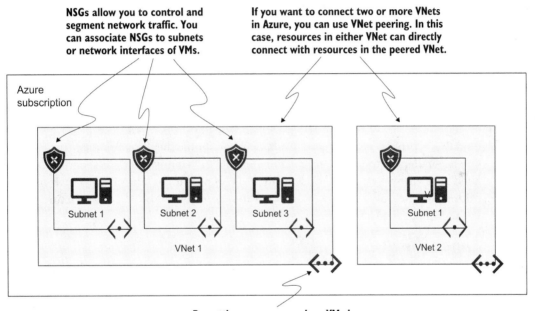

Figure 3.1 The relationship between an Azure subscription, VNets, subnets, and NSGs

Applying the principle of least privilege to VNets means that you give your Azure resources, which are sources of network traffic, access to only those network destinations that they need to perform their intended purpose and deny access to everything else. This is known as the *positive security model*.

3.1.2   *Positive security model*

You can look at the positive security model as having a list of allowed network destinations. All network traffic is denied except the network traffic intended for allowed network destinations. You should strive for the positive security model wherever possible, and instead of denying network traffic to what you consider to be known as malicious, you should look to allow network traffic to only allowed network destinations.

Imagine you had a compute Azure resource in Azure hosting a web application. The compute resource should only need to communicate outbound with a handful of destination IP addresses (unless you have unique requirements, which the majority of organizations don't). Therefore, network traffic should be allowed to only these destination IP addresses. Network traffic to all other network destinations should be blocked.

Another way to look at this model is to consider the scenario in which Eve, the fictional bad actor, has gained unauthorized access to your compute resources in Azure, such as a web application. In the first chapter, you learned how bad actors look to communicate with a command-and-control infrastructure and exfiltrate information from your environment. For this to happen, network traffic must be allowed to the bad actor's IP addresses. By enforcing a positive-security model and allowing network access only to known network destinations, you're able to prevent the bad actor from communicating with their command-and-control infrastructure and exfiltrating data from your environment.

The principle of least privilege, network segmentation, and the positive security model are proven security best practices that should be a mandatory part of your defense-in-depth strategy. There is no silver bullet when it comes to security, and you need to apply several layers of security to keep bad actors out of your environment. Adding another layer of network security to secure your network infrastructure comes in the form of Azure Firewall.

3.2   *Azure Firewall*

Suppose you need to implement a solution that inspects all incoming network traffic. Azure Firewall is a fully managed PaaS offering that allows you to inspect and centrally control your network traffic. It supports both *north–south* and *east–west* network traffic. North–south traffic refers to network traffic that flows between Azure and an outside network destination, such as your on-premises network. East–west traffic refers to network traffic flowing within Azure, such as between different VNets. Instead of imagining Azure Firewall as a single Azure resource, you should picture it as a set of resources that provide a fully managed firewall network service. This set of resources is managed by Microsoft, allowing you to benefit from a fully stateful firewall service that is highly available without needing to manage the underlying set of resources that Azure Firewall uses. Azure Firewall is a paid offering that comes in the form of three SKUs: Basic, Standard, and Premium.

3.2.1 *Azure Firewall Standard vs. Premium*

Azure Firewall Standard allows you to control layers 3, 4, and 7 traffic. Additionally, it's integrated with Microsoft's threat intelligence feeds and can deny network traffic to or from network destinations that are known to be malicious. This threat intelligence feed is kept updated by Microsoft and includes new and emerging threats coming from bad actors.

Azure Firewall Premium offers more advanced capabilities compared to Standard. Its capabilities are aligned to capabilities known as next-generation firewalls and include the following:

- Transport Layer Security (TLS) inspection
- An intrusion detection and prevention system (IDPS)
- URL filtering
- Web categories

NOTE In October 2022, Microsoft introduced the Azure Firewall Basic SKU. To learn more about it, you can start at http://mng.bz/mVXW.

In order for you to benefit from Azure Firewall's capabilities and add them to your defense-in-depth strategy, this chapter teaches you how to deploy and configure Azure Firewall, starting with Azure Firewall Standard.

3.2.2 *Azure Firewall Standard in action*

The set of resources that make up Azure Firewall resides as Azure resources inside a resource group. This resource group resides in an Azure subscription that you choose during deployment. When deploying Azure Firewall Standard, you need to specify the VNet and subnet because this set of resources, which make up Azure Firewall, are going to be deployed. To use an existing VNet, you must have a subnet in the VNet called `AzureFirewallSubnet`. If you select a new VNet, the subnet is created automatically during deployment.

The `AzureFirewallSubnet` subnet is used to deploy the set of resources that make up Azure Firewall and are managed by Microsoft. Therefore, this subnet needs to exist, and it cannot be used by any other Azure resources.

> **Exercise 3.1**
>
> There is a substantial cost involved with running Azure Firewall. For extra practice, create a resource group that will contain all the resources that you're going to deploy in this chapter. That way, when you're done with the chapter and no longer need these resources, you can clean them up by deleting the resource group.

When deploying Azure Firewall, there is also a requirement for a public IP address. Because Azure Firewall is a managed PaaS offering, Microsoft needs a way to communicate with its underlying resources to manage them. This means that even if you're using Azure Firewall to control internal network traffic only, you need to have a public IP address, which Microsoft uses to communicate with the underlying resources.

To deploy Azure Firewall in your environment, you need to perform the following steps in order:

1 Create an Azure Firewall instance.
2 Create a route table to route traffic.
3 Create a route entry in the route table.
4 Associate the route table to the Azure Firewall instance.

3.2.3   *Creating an Azure Firewall instance*

To create an Azure Firewall Standard instance, select the Azure subscription that you're using to deploy Azure Firewall Standard and a VNet with a subnet called `AzureFirewallSubnet`. (For the purposes of this example, I'll use an existing VNet called `myVNet`.) Then, using Azure Cloud Shell, run the following commands in the Azure CLI to create an Azure Firewall instance and a set of its underlying resources.

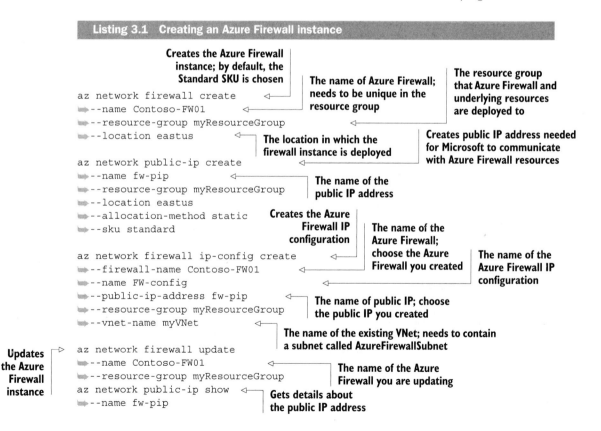

Listing 3.1   Creating an Azure Firewall instance

```
➥--resource-group myResourceGroup
fwprivaddr="$(az network firewall ip-config list -g myResourceGroup
-f Contoso-FW01 --query "[?name=='FW-config'].privateIpAddress"
--output tsv)"
```

If you're using Azure CLI locally, these commands require version 2.15.0 or higher. You also might be prompted to install the Azure CLI extension if this is the first time you're using the `az network firewall` command.

After this command runs, it creates Azure Firewall Standard and the underlying resources, as you can see from the following output:

```
{
  "applicationRuleCollections": [],
  "etag": "W/\"7c7f7863-af05-4114-af77-cbc13635246c\"",
  "firewallPolicy": null,
  "hubIpAddresses": null,
  "id": "/subscriptions/00000000-0000-0000-0000-000000000000/resourceGroups
➥/myResourceGroup/providers/Microsoft.Network/azureFirewalls/Contoso-FW01",
  "ipConfigurations": [],
  "ipGroups": null,
  "location": "eastus",
  "managementIpConfiguration": null,
  "name": "Contoso-FW01",
  "natRuleCollections": [],
  "networkRuleCollections": [],
  "provisioningState": "Succeeded",
  "resourceGroup": "myResourceGroup",
  "sku": {
    "name": "AZFW_VNet",
    "tier": "Standard"
  },
  "tags": {
    "createddate": "08/19/2022",
    "owner": "bmagusic"
  },
  "threatIntelMode": "Alert",
  "type": "Microsoft.Network/azureFirewalls",
  "virtualHub": null,
  "zones": null
...
```

NOTE Take note of the private IP address listed under `ipAddress`. You'll need it for one of the next steps.

After you deploy Azure Firewall, you can start routing traffic to it.

3.2.4 *Routing traffic to Azure Firewall*

After you create an Azure Firewall instance, you need to route traffic to it. You send traffic to Azure Firewall using *route tables*. Route tables contain one or more routes that dictate where traffic is sent. Routes can be applied to all traffic or just a portion of it. You can associate route tables to subnets, which dictate where traffic for that subnet is sent.

To start directing traffic to Azure Firewall, you need to create a route table and then associate it with a subnet. To create a route table, run the following commands in Azure Cloud Shell.

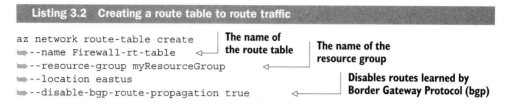

Listing 3.2 **Creating a route table to route traffic**

After this command runs, it creates the route table `Firewall-rt-table`. Your output should look similar to the following:

```
{
  "disableBgpRoutePropagation": true,
  "etag": "W/\"41222efd-c9e3-43de-b1cb-85dac9938abc\"",
  "id": "/subscriptions/00000000-0000-0000-0000-000000000000/resourceGroups
    /myResourceGroups/providers/Microsoft.Network/routeTables/Firewall-rt-table",
  "location": "eastus",
  "name": "Firewall-rt-table",
  "provisioningState": "Succeeded",
  "resourceGroup": "myResourceGroup",
  "resourceGuid": "7aef96d5-fb90-4023-bef3-a5e09aa519e6",
  "routes": [],
  "subnets": null,
  "tags": {
    "createddate": "08/19/2022",
    "owner": "bmagusic"
  },
  "type": "Microsoft.Network/routeTables"
}
```

When you create the route table, it doesn't contain any routes, and it's not associated with any subnet, as seen in the output under `routes` and `subnets`. Next up, you'll add a route to the route table. The route will direct traffic to Azure Firewall.

3.2.5 *Routing to direct traffic*

To create a route, run the following commands in Azure Cloud Shell.

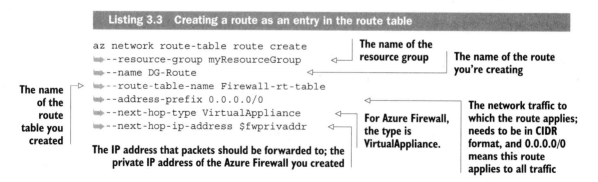

Listing 3.3 **Creating a route as an entry in the route table**

After this command runs, it creates a route `DG-Route`, as you can see from the following output:

```
{
  "addressPrefix": "0.0.0.0/0",
  "etag": "W/\"cc33018b-0d6d-415c-9f47-bfbbbb78ba02\"",
  "hasBgpOverride": false,
  "id": "/subscriptions/00000000-0000-0000-0000-000000000000/resourceGroups
  ➥/myResourceGroup/providers/Microsoft.Network/routeTables
  ➥/Firewall-rt-table/routes/DG-Route",
  "name": "DG-Route",
  "nextHopIpAddress": "10.0.1.4",
  "nextHopType": "VirtualAppliance",
  "provisioningState": "Succeeded",
  "resourceGroup": "myResourceGroup",
  "type": "Microsoft.Network/routeTables/routes"
}
```

Now that you've successfully added the route to the route table, you'll associate the route table to a subnet.

3.2.6 Associating a route table to a subnet

To associate the route table with a subnet, run the following command in Azure Cloud Shell.

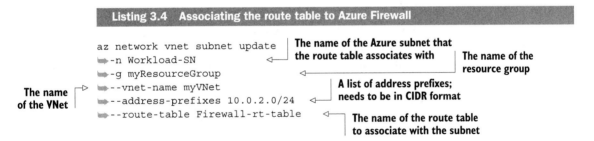

Listing 3.4 Associating the route table to Azure Firewall

After this command runs, it associates the route table `Firewall-rt-table` with subnet `Workload-SN`, as you can see in the following output:

```
{
  "addressPrefix": "10.0.2.0/24",
  "addressPrefixes": null,
  "applicationGatewayIpConfigurations": null,
  "delegations": [],
  "etag": "W/\"4c4201fe-2fd0-4bde-a7cf-97c974263324\"",
  "id": "/subscriptions/00000000-0000-0000-0000-000000000000/resourceGroups
  ➥/myResourceGroup/providers/Microsoft.Network/virtualNetworks/myVNet
  ➥/subnets/Workload-SN",
  "ipAllocations": null,
  "ipConfigurationProfiles": null,
  "ipConfigurations": [
    {
      "etag": null,
```

```
        "id": "/subscriptions/00000000-0000-0000-0000-000000000000
    ➥/resourceGroups/myResourceGroup/providers/Microsoft.Network
    ➥/networkInterfaces/Srv-Work-NIC/ipConfigurations/ipconfig1",
        "name": null,
        "privateIpAddress": null,
        "privateIpAllocationMethod": null,
        "provisioningState": null,
        "publicIpAddress": null,
        "resourceGroup": "myResourceGroup",
        "subnet": null
    }
],
"name": "Workload-SN",
...
```

At this point, your network traffic is directed to the Azure Firewall. By default, Azure Firewall blocks all traffic unless you explicitly create rules to allow traffic.

3.2.7   *Allowing Azure Firewall traffic*

You can create different rule types depending on the traffic you want to allow. The rule types are as follows:

- Destination network address translation (DNAT)
- Network
- Application

Each rule type serves an intended purpose and has a different priority with regard to processing order. All traffic that passes through Azure Firewall is evaluated based on these rules and their priority and is either allowed or blocked. By default, DNAT rules are applied first to traffic routed to Azure Firewall, followed by network rules, and then application rules. If no matches are found in any of these rule types, Azure Firewall reverts to its default behavior of blocking all traffic. I will go over each of the rule types, together with their intended purpose, starting with DNAT rules.

DNAT RULES

Say you need to allow traffic to internal resources to perform management activities. DNAT rules allow or deny inbound traffic to your network. Inbound traffic is sent to Azure Firewall's public IP address, which then, based on DNAT rules, either blocks or allows traffic to pass through to your internal resources in Azure. Typically, DNAT rules are used to facilitate management access to your internal resources in Azure. However, they should be used with caution, as they allow for traffic from outside of your network to be forwarded to inside your network.

Rules are typically organized in rule collections, which contain one or multiple rules. For easier management, rule collections can be further grouped into a rule collection group, which contains one or multiple rule collections. To create a DNAT rule that will be part of a rule collection, run the following command in Azure Cloud Shell.

Listing 3.5   Creating a DNAT rule for Azure Firewall

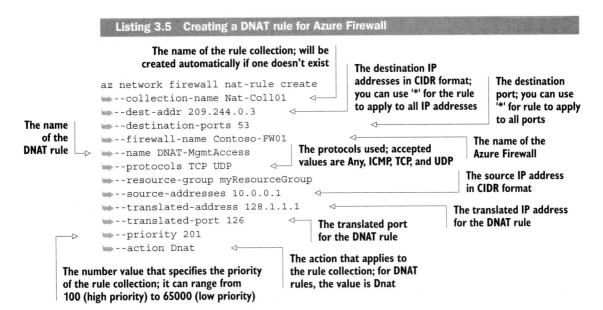

The name of the rule collection; will be created automatically if one doesn't exist

The destination IP addresses in CIDR format; you can use '*' for the rule to apply to all IP addresses

The destination port; you can use '*' for rule to apply to all ports

The name of the DNAT rule

The protocols used; accepted values are Any, ICMP, TCP, and UDP

The name of the Azure Firewall

The source IP address in CIDR format

The translated IP address for the DNAT rule

The translated port for the DNAT rule

The number value that specifies the priority of the rule collection; it can range from 100 (high priority) to 65000 (low priority)

The action that applies to the rule collection; for DNAT rules, the value is Dnat

```
az network firewall nat-rule create
--collection-name Nat-Coll01
--dest-addr 209.244.0.3
--destination-ports 53
--firewall-name Contoso-FW01
--name DNAT-MgmtAccess
--protocols TCP UDP
--resource-group myResourceGroup
--source-addresses 10.0.0.1
--translated-address 128.1.1.1
--translated-port 126
--priority 201
--action Dnat
```

After this command runs, it creates the network rule collection containing the network rule DNAT-MgmtAccess, as you can see from the following output:

```
Creating rule collection 'Net-Coll01'.
{
  "description": null,
  "destinationAddresses": [
    "209.244.0.3"
  ],
  "destinationPorts": [
    "53"
  ],
  "destinationFqdns": [],
  "destinationIpGroups": [],

  "name": "DNAT-MgmtAccess",
  "protocols": [
    "TCP",
    "UDP"
  ],
  "sourceAddresses": [
    "10.0.0.1"
  ],
  "sourceIpGroups": []
}
...
```

Depending on your network architecture, instead of allowing inbound traffic to your internal resources in Azure, you might want to control traffic between peered VNets. For this, you can use network rules.

NETWORK RULES

Network rules allow you to control traffic between your VNets. Similar to DNAT rules, network rules are grouped into network rule collections, which contain one or multiple network rules. To create a network rule that will be part of a network rule collection, run the following command in Azure Cloud Shell.

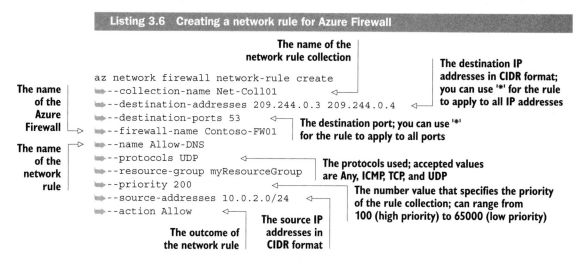

Listing 3.6 Creating a network rule for Azure Firewall

After this command runs, it creates the network rule collection containing the network rule `Allow-DNS`. Your output should look similar to the following:

```
Creating rule collection 'Net-Coll01'.
{
  "description": null,
  "destinationAddresses": [
    "209.244.0.3",
    "209.244.0.4"
  ],
  "destinationFqdns": [],
  "destinationIpGroups": [],
  "destinationPorts": [
    "53"
  ],
  "name": "Allow-DNS",
  "protocols": [
    "UDP"
  ],
  "sourceAddresses": [
    "10.0.2.0/24"
  ],
  "sourceIpGroups": []
}
```

The output contains a section with the network rule that you created. In addition to network rules that are used to control traffic between VNets, organizations also need rules to control outbound traffic. For this, you can create application rules.

APPLICATION RULES

Application rules allow you to control traffic from your network to the internet. Similar to network rules, application rules are grouped into application rule collections, which contain one or multiple application rules. To create an application rule collection containing an application rule, run the following command in Azure Cloud Shell.

Listing 3.7 Creating an application rule for Azure Firewall

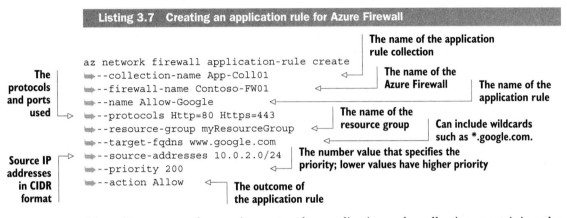

After this command runs, it creates the application rule collection containing the application rule `Allow-Google`, as you can see from the following output:

```
Creating rule collection 'App-Coll01'.
{
  "actions": [],
  "description": null,
  "direction": "Inbound",
  "fqdnTags": [],
  "name": "Allow-Google",
  "priority": 0,
  "protocols": [
    {
      "port": 80,
      "protocolType": "Http"
    },
    {
      "port": 443,
      "protocolType": "Https"
    }
  ],
  "sourceAddresses": [
    "10.0.2.0/24"
  ],
  "sourceIpGroups": [],
  "targetFqdns": [
    "www.google.com"
  ]
}
```

DNAT rules, together with network and application rules, provide a way to allow traffic to pass through Azure Firewall. The combination of these three rule types effectively allows you to mitigate Azure Firewall's default behavior of blocking traffic. Suppose there are instances where after outbound traffic reaches Azure Firewall, you wish to forward it somewhere other than the internet. This case is common for organizations that use another network virtual appliance in combination with Azure Firewall.

Typically, in this scenario, after going through Azure Firewall, outbound traffic is forwarded to the network virtual appliance, such as a third-party firewall, for further inspection. Azure Firewall, by default, forwards outbound traffic it receives to the internet. If you want to forward outbound traffic to a network virtual appliance instead, you need to use *forced tunneling*.

FORCED TUNNELING

Forced tunneling allows you to configure Azure Firewall to route outbound traffic to another network destination rather than the internet. Forced tunneling must be enabled when creating Azure Firewall, and it cannot be enabled after the Azure Firewall instance has been created.

To route traffic to another network destination instead of the internet, you need to add routes to the `AzureFirewallSubnet`. Importantly, to support forced tunneling, Azure Firewall needs an additional subnet called `AzureFirewallManagementSubnet` with its own public IP address.

Some organizations have requirements for more advanced capabilities, beyond controlling traffic, such as traffic inspection. For this, you can use Azure Firewall Premium.

3.2.8   *Azure Firewall Premium*

Both Azure Firewall Premium and Standard are paid SKUs. However, Azure Firewall Premium provides organizations with more advanced capabilities than Azure Firewall Standard. It's suited for environments that need to adhere to certain regulatory standards, such as Payment Card Industry Data Security (PCI DSS). It builds on the set of capabilities available in Standard and provides additional capabilities such as TLS inspection, IDPS, URL filtering, and Web categories.

TLS INSPECTION

TLS is a protocol commonly used to encrypt Hypertext Transfer Protocol (HTTP)-related traffic. Although this encryption provides additional security, it can be misused by bad actors, like Eve, to hide potentially malicious activity in HTTP traffic. The ability to decrypt HTTP-related traffic to inspect it is known as *TLS termination*. Azure Firewall Premium provides the ability to decrypt this traffic, inspect it for signs of malicious activity, and then re-encrypt it before sending it to its intended destination using certificates.

In addition to TLS termination, another common requirement is the ability to detect malicious network activity based on signatures. For this, you can use the IDPS capability of Azure Firewall Premium.

AN INTRUSION DETECTION AND PREVENTION SYSTEM

A network IDPS allows you to monitor traffic on your network for potential signs of malicious activity, which is typically accomplished by using signatures (such as fingerprinting actual malware) or signature-based rules. Azure Firewall Premium provides an IDPS capability that is signature based. These signatures are managed and kept up to date by Microsoft.

> **NOTE** To deploy Azure Firewall Premium, you can use the template available in the GitHub repository (https://github.com/bmagusic/azure-security).

The list of Azure Firewall's capabilities is expected to continue to grow over time. Have you ever wondered how to best configure all these capabilities?! You can configure each capability individually for each Azure firewall instance. However, this method doesn't scale. Instead, you can use the Azure Firewall policy.

3.2.9 *Azure Firewall policy*

The Azure Firewall policy allows you to apply configurations to Azure Firewalls at scale. The idea is that instead of applying configurations to individual Azure Firewall instances, you can create an object, called an Azure Firewall policy, that can be applied to many instances of Azure Firewall. This one-to-many relationship between the Azure Firewall policy and Azure Firewall is suitable for managing and configuring Azure Firewall at scale. The Azure Firewall policy is tightly coupled with *Azure Firewall Manager*.

3.2.10 *Azure Firewall Manager*

Most organizations deploy Azure Firewall inside a central VNet peered with other VNets. This architecture is commonly known as *hub-and-spoke* topology (figure 3.2).

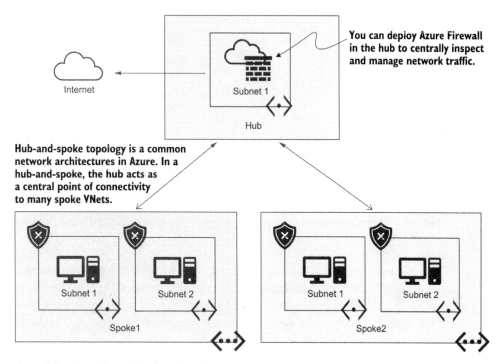

Figure 3.2   Azure Firewall deployed in a hub-and-spoke topology

In this topology, the hub serves as a central point of connection, whereas the spokes can represent different Azure subscriptions or even different business units. The hub allows traffic that traverses it, originating from spokes, to be controlled and inspected before being routed to the internet. It also allows security to be applied centrally in the hub VNet, rather than applying it in every spoke. When you deploy Azure Firewall in a hub VNet, you can use Azure Firewall Manager to centrally manage Azure Firewalls (figure 3.3).

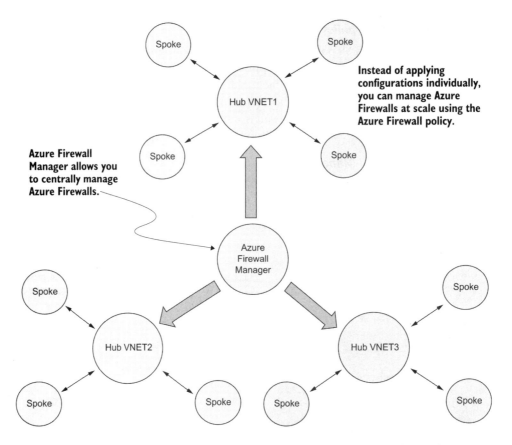

Figure 3.3   Azure Firewall Manager allows you to centrally manage multiple Azure Firewall instances.

While Azure Firewall has layer-7 capabilities, the primary focus of most firewall solutions is providing capabilities that protect against attacks targeting layers 3 and 4. To protect web applications against attacks targeting layer 7, most organizations place a Web Application Firewall (WAF) in front of public-facing web applications. You can implement WAF capabilities in Azure using *Azure Web Application Firewall.*

3.3 *Azure Web Application Firewall*

With new vulnerabilities being discovered daily, it is important to protect your applications running in Azure against web application vulnerabilities and common attacks. Azure WAF inspects inbound traffic destined for the application layer, helping to detect and prevent layer-7 attacks against your web applications.

Instead of considering Azure WAF as a single capability, imagine it as a set of capabilities that, according to the Open Web Application Security Project (OWASP) Foundation, helps protect your web applications against common vulnerabilities and exploits, including SQL injection and cross-site scripting. OWASP shares guidance and practices that help prevent most common web application vulnerabilities. This guidance is widely used in the form of industry best practices called *core rule sets* (CRSs).

Azure WAF rules are based on OWASP CRSs and are preconfigured, managed, and kept updated by Microsoft. Azure WAF can be deployed with Azure Application Gateway, Azure Front Door, and Content Delivery Network (CDN). If you have a frontend for your web application, in most cases, you will configure WAF functionality on either Azure Application Gateway or Azure Front Door. Therefore, my focus is teaching you how to deploy Azure WAF functionalities on these two platforms.

Although deploying WAF on Azure Application Gateway and Azure Front Door has the same overarching goal of preventing attacks against your web application, there are some differences when implementing WAF capabilities. Azure WAF tightly integrates with the Azure service it is attached to. Because differences exist between Azure Application Gateway and Azure Front Door, differences will also exist between the respective WAF capabilities. The main differences between the WAF capabilities of each are in the CRSs and the way rule matching and blocking are handled in Azure Application Gateway and Azure Front Door.

3.3.1 *Azure WAF on Azure Application Gateway in action*

Azure Application Gateway is a layer-7 load-balancing solution that allows you to manage traffic to your web application. It's a regional service that provides load balancing between your compute resources (for example, virtual machines or containers). This makes it suitable for web applications that are deployed inside of a single Azure region. To manage your Application Gateway WAF, you use a WAF policy.

If you're using WAF configuration, I encourage you to adopt a WAF policy because WAF configuration is considered a legacy method for managing Application Gateway WAF. A WAF policy is a separate Azure resource that can be associated with Application Gateway to manage WAF capabilities. A WAF policy can only be associated with Application Gateway v2. If you're using Application Gateway v1, you will need to deploy it as an Application Gateway v2 to use a WAF policy.

> **NOTE** If you need to deploy your Application Gateway v1 as an Application Gateway v2 to be able to use the WAF policy, you can start at http://mng.bz/5wn8.

Most of the permissions that you need to create and associate a WAF policy with an Application Gateway are part of the Network Contributor role.

WAF POLICY FOR APPLICATION GATEWAY

To create the WAF policy, you will again use the Azure CLI. Run the following command in Azure Cloud Shell to create the WAF policy.

> **Listing 3.8   Creating a WAF policy for Application Gateway v2**

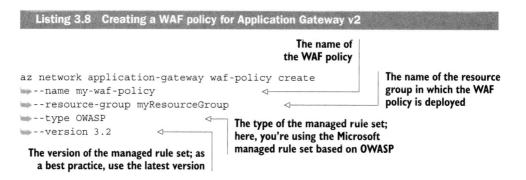

After this command runs, it creates a WAF policy, as you can see from the following output:

```
{
  "applicationGateways": null,
  "customRules": [],
  "httpListeners": null,
  "id": "/subscriptions/00000000-0000-0000-0000-000000000000/resourceGroups
➥/myResourceGroup/providers/Microsoft.Network
➥/ApplicationGatewayWebApplicationFirewallPolicies/my-waf-policy",
  "location": "northeurope",
  "managedRules": {
    "exclusions": [],
    "managedRuleSets": [
      {
        "ruleGroupOverrides": [],
        "ruleSetType": "OWASP",
        "ruleSetVersion": "3.2"
      }
    ]
  },
  "name": "my-waf-policy",
  "pathBasedRules": null,
  "policySettings": {
    "fileUploadLimitInMb": 100,
    "maxRequestBodySizeInKb": 128,
    "mode": "Detection",
    "requestBodyCheck": true,
    "state": "Disabled"
  },
  "provisioningState": "Updating",
  "resourceGroup": "myResourceGroup",
  "resourceState": null,
```

```
  "tags": {
    "createddate": "08/12/2022",
    "owner": "bmagusic"
  },
  "type": "Microsoft.Network
➥/ApplicationGatewayWebApplicationFirewallPolicies"
}
```

In addition to being a preconfigured and Microsoft-managed rule set based on OWASP CRSs, as part of Azure WAF for Application Gateway, you can also enable managed bot protection.

MANAGED BOT PROTECTION FOR APPLICATION GATEWAY

It is important to protect your web applications in Azure against malicious bots. Managed bot protection for Application Gateway comes in the form of a rule set that WAF uses to block or log requests that originate from IP addresses associated with known malicious bots.

To determine which IP addresses are associated with bots known to be malicious, Microsoft uses its vast threat intelligence trove, commonly referred to as the *Microsoft Intelligent Security Graph*. Over time, the IP addresses malicious bots use change, and there's real value in using Microsoft threat intelligence and managed bot protection as part of your Azure WAF. To add managed bot protection to the WAF policy you created, run the following command in Azure Cloud Shell.

Listing 3.9 Adding managed bot protection to a WAF policy for Application Gateway

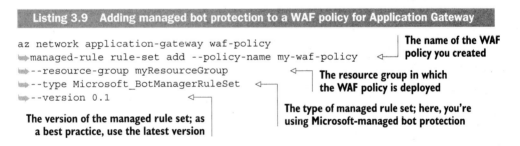

```
az network application-gateway waf-policy
➥managed-rule rule-set add --policy-name my-waf-policy       The name of the WAF
➥--resource-group myResourceGroup                            policy you created
➥--type Microsoft_BotManagerRuleSet
➥--version 0.1
```

The resource group in which the WAF policy is deployed

The type of managed rule set; here, you're using Microsoft-managed bot protection

The version of the managed rule set; as a best practice, use the latest version

After this command runs, it will add managed bot protection to `my-waf-policy`, the WAF policy you created earlier. The output after running the command should look similar to the following:

```
{
  "applicationGateways": null,
  "customRules": [],
  "etag": "W/\"2118c582-9c49-4c09-9aa4-21a0830e0410\"",
  "httpListeners": null,
  "id": "/subscriptions/00000000-0000-0000-0000-000000000000/resourceGroups
➥/myResourceGroup/providers/Microsoft.Network
➥/ApplicationGatewayWebApplicationFirewallPolicies/my-waf-policy",
  "location": "northeurope",
  "managedRules": {
    "exclusions": [],
    "managedRuleSets": [
```

```
    {
      "ruleGroupOverrides": [],
      "ruleSetType": "OWASP",
      "ruleSetVersion": "3.2"
    },
    {
      "ruleGroupOverrides": [],
      "ruleSetType": "Microsoft_BotManagerRuleSet",
      "ruleSetVersion": "0.1"
    }
  ]
},
"name": "my-waf-policy",
...
```

The `managedRuleSets` section should contain `Microsoft_BotManagerRuleSet` as
`ruleSetType`. After creating the WAF policy and adding Microsoft-managed rule sets
to it for OWASP CRSs and bot protection, you can associate the WAF policy when creating a new Application Gateway v2 or use an existing one.

CREATING AN APPLICATION GATEWAY WITH A WAF POLICY

Run the following command in Azure Cloud Shell to create an Application Gateway
v2 and associate the WAF policy you created.

Listing 3.10   Creating an Application Gateway v2 and associating it with a WAF policy

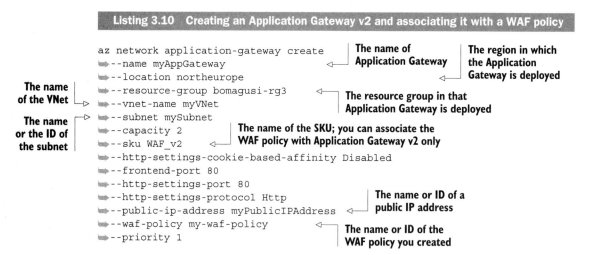

After this command runs, it creates the Application Gateway v2 and associates the
WAF policy `my-waf-policy` with it, as you can see from the following output:

```
{
  "applicationGateway": {
    ...
    ...
    "firewallPolicy": {
      "id": "/subscriptions/00000000-0000-0000-0000-000000000000
        /resourceGroups/myResourceGroup/providers/Microsoft.Network
```

```
⇒/ApplicationGatewayWebApplicationFirewallPolicies/my-waf-policy",
```

. . .

The output shows the name of the WAF policy in the `firewallPolicy` section. After you associate the WAF policy with the Application Gateway, it is disabled and in *detection* mode. The Application Gateway WAF can be configured in two modes:

- *Detection*—Monitors and logs all threat alerts; in this mode, incoming requests that match rule sets are not blocked, only logged
- *Prevention*—Logs all threat alerts; in this mode, incoming requests that match rule sets are blocked

ENABLING A WAF POLICY FOR APPLICATION GATEWAY

You can enable the WAF policy you created and set it to block incoming requests that match the rule sets by switching the mode from detection to prevention. Run the following command in Azure Cloud Shell.

> **Listing 3.11 Enabling a WAF policy for Application Gateway: Prevention mode**

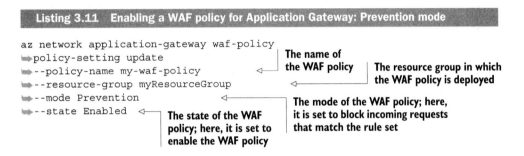

Running this command ensures that incoming requests are evaluated based on the managed rule sets for OWASP CRSs and bot protection. All incoming requests that match the rule sets are blocked because the WAF policy is enabled and set to prevention mode.

When evaluating whether to block incoming requests that match rule sets, Azure WAF on Application Gateway uses *anomaly scoring*.

ANOMALY SCORING

Anomaly scoring assigns a certain severity and score to rules. The possible severities and scores are shown in table 3.1.

Table 3.1 Possible values of severities and scores used in anomaly scoring

Severity	Score
Critical	5
Error	4
Warning	3
Notice	2

When in prevention mode, the WAF Policy blocks incoming requests that have an anomaly score equal to or greater than 5. The score is cumulative—that is, if an incoming request matches two rules, one with an anomaly score of 3 and the other with a score of 2, the combined score is 5, and the incoming request is blocked. Anomaly scoring is unique to Azure WAF on Application Gateway and is not used on Azure WAF on Azure Front Door.

3.3.2   *Azure WAF on Azure Front Door in action*

If your web application needs to be available in different regions, in most cases, you'll use Azure Front Door. Azure Front Door functions as a layer-7 load-balancing solution that can route your traffic to backends inside and outside of Azure (potentially even to other public cloud providers).

The main difference between Azure Front Door and Application Gateway, also a layer-7 load-balancing solution, is that Azure Front Door is a global load-balancing service. That is, Azure Front Door is not confined to a particular Azure region, making it a global service and suitable for multiregional—and even mulitcloud—deployment of your web applications.

To protect your web applications against attacks, you can enable Azure WAF on Azure Front Door (figure 3.4).

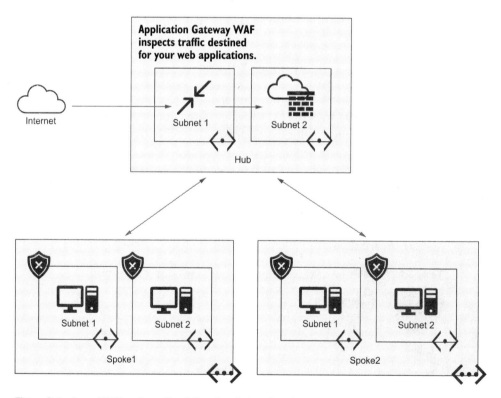

Figure 3.4   Azure WAF on Azure Front Door in a hub-and-spoke topology

To manage WAF capabilities on Azure Front Door, you will continue to use WAF policies. WAF policies in combination with Azure Front Door are similar to WAF policies on Application Gateway. They are separate Azure resources that can be associated with Azure Front Door to manage WAF capabilities. Most of the permissions that you need to create and associate a WAF policy with an Azure Front Door are part of the Network Contributor role.

WAF POLICY FOR AZURE FRONT DOOR

To create a WAF policy for Azure Front Door, run the following command in Azure Cloud Shell.

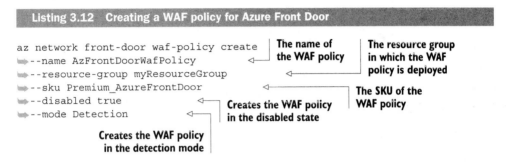

Listing 3.12   Creating a WAF policy for Azure Front Door

After this command runs, it creates the WAF policy for Azure Front Door called `AzFrontDoorWafPolicy`, as you can see from the following output:

```
{
  "customRules": {
    "rules": []
  },
  "etag": null,
  "frontendEndpointLinks": [],
  "id": "/subscriptions/00000000-0000-0000-0000-000000000000/resourceGroups
  /myResourceGroup/providers/Microsoft.Network
  /frontdoorwebapplicationfirewallpolicies/AzFrontDoorWafPolicy",
  "location": "Global",
  "managedRules": {
    "managedRuleSets": []
  },
  "name": "AzFrontDoorWafPolicy",
  "policySettings": {
    "customBlockResponseBody": null,
    "customBlockResponseStatusCode": null,
    "enabledState": "Disabled",
    "mode": "Detection",
    "redirectUrl": null,
    "requestBodyCheck": "Enabled"
  },
  "provisioningState": "Succeeded",
  "resourceGroup": "myResourceGroup",
  "resourceState": "Enabled",
  "routingRuleLinks": [],
```

```
"securityPolicyLinks": [],
"sku": {
  "name": "Premium_AzureFrontDoor"
},
"tags": {
  "createddate": "08/14/2022",
  "owner": "bmagusic"
},
"type": "Microsoft.Network/frontdoorwebapplicationfirewallpolicies"
}
```

The output shows that the WAF policy you associated with Azure Front Door is disabled and in detection mode. WAF on Azure Front Door can be configured in two modes:

- *Detection*—Monitors and logs requests that match WAF rules; when in this mode, requests that match WAF rules are not blocked.
- *Prevention*—Logs all requests; when in this mode, incoming requests that match WAF rules are blocked.

A MANAGED RULE SET FOR AZURE FRONT DOOR

To add a Microsoft-managed rule set based on OWASP CRSs to the WAF policy you created, run the following command in Azure Cloud Shell.

Listing 3.13   Adding a managed rule set to a WAF policy for Azure Front Door

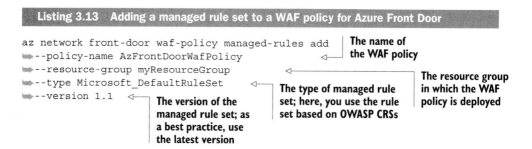

```
az network front-door waf-policy managed-rules add
--policy-name AzFrontDoorWafPolicy
--resource-group myResourceGroup
--type Microsoft_DefaultRuleSet
--version 1.1
```

The name of the WAF policy

The resource group in which the WAF policy is deployed

The type of managed rule set; here, you use the rule set based on OWASP CRSs

The version of the managed rule set; as a best practice, use the latest version

After this command runs, it will add the Microsoft managed rule set based on OWASP CRSs to your WAF Policy `AzFrontDoorWafPolicy`. This rule set is managed and updated to remain current by Microsoft. Your output should look similar to the following:

```
{
  "customRules": {
    "rules": []
  },
  "etag": null,
  "frontendEndpointLinks": [],
  "id":"/subscriptions/00000000-0000-0000-0000-000000000000/resourceGroups
/myResourceGroup/providers/Microsoft.Network
/frontdoorwebapplicationfirewallpolicies/AzFrontDoorWafPolicy",
  "location": "Global",
  "managedRules": {
    "managedRuleSets": [
      {
```

```
        "exclusions": [],
        "ruleGroupOverrides": [],
        "ruleSetAction": null,
        "ruleSetType": "Microsoft_DefaultRuleSet",
        "ruleSetVersion": "1.1"
      }
    ]
  },
  "name": "AzFrontDoorWafPolicy",
  ...
```

The `managedRuleSets` section contains `Microsoft_DeafultRuleSet` as `ruleSetType`.

In addition to a managed rule set based on OWASP CRSs, you can also enable managed bot protection. When you enable managed bot protection on Azure WAF for Front Door, Microsoft uses its vast threat intelligence from the Microsoft Intelligent Security Graph. This threat intelligence data is used to identify IP addresses associated with malicious bots.

Azure WAF on Front Door uses this information to automatically classify bots into good, unknown, and bad. Good bots can be web crawlers used by search engines, whereas bad bots are deemed malicious based on Microsoft's threat intelligence data. Traffic from good bots is not deemed malicious and is allowed, traffic from unknown bots is allowed and logged, and traffic from bad bots is deemed malicious and blocked.

MANAGED BOT PROTECTION FOR AZURE FRONT DOOR

To add managed bot protection to the WAF policy that you created for Azure Front Door, run the following command in Azure Cloud Shell.

Listing 3.14 Adding managed bot protection to a WAF policy for Azure Front Door

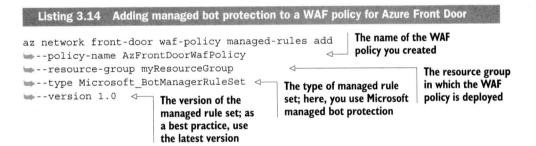

After this command runs, it adds the managed bot protection to the WAF policy `AzFrontDoorWafPolicy`, as you can see from the following output:

```
{
  "customRules": {
    "rules": []
  },
  "etag": null,
  "frontendEndpointLinks": [],
  "id":"/subscriptions/00000000-0000-0000-0000-000000000000/resourceGroups
  /myResourceGroup/providers/Microsoft.Network
  /frontdoorwebapplicationfirewallpolicies/AzFrontDoorWafPolicy",
```

```
    "location": "Global",
    "managedRules": {
      "managedRuleSets": [
        {
          "exclusions": [],
          "ruleGroupOverrides": [],
          "ruleSetAction": null,
          "ruleSetType": "Microsoft_DefaultRuleSet",
          "ruleSetVersion": "1.1"
        },
        {
          "exclusions": [],
          "ruleGroupOverrides": [],
          "ruleSetAction": null,
          "ruleSetType": "Microsoft_BotManagerRuleSet",
          "ruleSetVersion": "1.0"
        }
      ]
    },
    "name": "AzFrontDoorWafPolicy",
    ...
```

The `managedRuleSets` section contains `Microsoft_BotManagerRuleSet` as a `ruleSet-Type`. You've created the WAF policy for Azure Front Door and added a Microsoft-managed rule set with OWASP CRSs and bot protection. Next, you need to associate the WAF policy with an Azure Front Door profile.

SECURITY POLICY FOR AZURE FRONT DOOR

You can add the WAF policy to an Azure Front Door profile by creating a security policy. Run the following command in Azure Cloud Shell to create a security policy and associate the WAF policy you created with the Azure Font Door profile.

Listing 3.15   Creating a security policy to associate a WAF policy with Azure Front Door

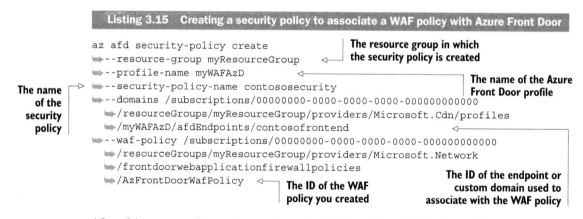

After this command runs, it associates the WAF policy with the Azure Front Door profile, as you can see from the following output:

```
{
    "deploymentStatus": "NotStarted",
    "id":"/subscriptions/00000000-0000-0000-0000-000000000000/resourceGroups
```

```
➥/myResourceGroup/providers/Microsoft.Cdn/profiles/bojanWAFAzD
➥/securitypolicies/contososecurity",
"name": "contososecurity",
"parameters": {
  "associations": [
    {
      "domains": [
        {
          "id":"/subscriptions/00000000-0000-0000-0000-000000000000
          ➥/resourceGroups/myResourceGroup/providers/Microsoft.Cdn
          ➥/profiles/myWAFAzD/afdEndpoints/contosofrontend",
          "isActive": true,
          "resourceGroup": "myResourceGroup"
        }
      ],
      "patternsToMatch": [
        "/*"
      ]
    }
  ],
  "type": "WebApplicationFirewall",
  "wafPolicy": {
    "id":"/subscriptions/00000000-0000-0000-0000-000000000000
    ➥/resourceGroups/myResourceGroup/providers/Microsoft.Network
    ➥/frontdoorwebapplicationfirewallpolicies/AzFrontDoorWafPolicy",
    "resourceGroup": "myResourceGroup"
  }
},
"profileName": null,
"provisioningState": "Succeeded",
"resourceGroup": "myResourceGroup",
"systemData": null,
"type": "Microsoft.Cdn/profiles/securitypolicies"
}
```

You can enable WAF capabilities on Azure Front Door and use either prevention or detection mode. As previously noted, when in detection mode, incoming requests that match WAF rules are not blocked. To block requests that match WAF rules, use prevention mode.

The behavior of WAF on Azure Front Door is different when compared with WAF on Application Gateway because WAF on Azure Front Door does not have anomaly scoring. Switching from detection to prevention can have an effect on incoming requests to your web applications. To prevent legitimate incoming requests from being blocked, you must be sure Azure WAF suits the specific needs of your organization and applications, which is known as *tuning* Azure WAF.

3.3.3 Tuning Azure WAF

Tuning Azure WAF on both Application Gateway and Azure Front Door follows the same overarching logic of ensuring that Azure WAF capabilities suit the specific needs of your organization and applications. After you associate a WAF policy with either Application Gateway or Azure Front Door, you should leave the WAF policy in detection mode as a best practice. Leaving the WAF policy in detection mode allows you to test incoming requests to your application and discover false positives.

During the testing period, you should test the intended features of your application and send only requests to your application you believe are legitimate. This helps you to identify false positives more easily. While in detection mode, Azure WAF will log these requests as WAF logs, and you can investigate them further (I'll cover logging in chapter 9). The information in WAF logs can be incredibly helpful in removing false positives. When you feel confident that false positives have been addressed, you can switch Azure WAF to prevention mode.

When in prevention mode, Azure WAF will block any requests that match its rule set, so it's important to do sufficient testing while Azure WAF is in detection mode. After you switch Azure WAF to prevention mode, you should continue to monitor the Azure WAF logs over time for false positives. Adding new features to your application may result in new, legitimate traffic being blocked because it hasn't been tested. Monitoring over time helps you to discover and correct these new false positives.

Of course, over time, your application may also receive illegitimate requests. Distributed denial of services (DDoS) attacks are an example of illegitimate incoming requests. Mitigating these attacks helps add resiliency to your Azure infrastructure and should be part of your defense-in-depth strategy.

3.4   *Mitigating DDoS attacks*

DDoS attacks take advantage of the fact that your public-facing web applications are accessible over the internet. DDoS attacks are not new, but they are effective, and you need to protect your web applications and Azure resources against them. Bad actors typically launch DDoS attacks from multiple sources to make it more difficult for your web applications to discern between legitimate and malicious traffic.

Imagine you have a web application running on Azure that is used by customers to place orders and purchase items. A DDoS attack could make your application unavailable to customers, and you could incur financial damage equivalent to the profit you missed out on while your application was down—not to mention the reputation damage and cost of getting your web application up and running again after the attack. These attacks could also result in additional damages and lead to unexpected charges.

Suppose you're using cloud-native services as a backend to your web application that scales automatically based on customer demand (such as Application Gateway v2 or Virtual Machine Scale Sets). A DDoS attack can cause these resources to autoscale, resulting in unexpected charges and costs to your Azure bill. Thus, protecting your web applications and resources against DDoS attacks is a crucial step in building a secure networking infrastructure in Azure. You can mitigate DDoS attacks in Azure by using Azure DDoS Protection.

3.4.1   *DDoS Protection in Azure*

Azure DDoS Protection is a DDoS mitigation service available in Azure. Public IP addresses are the entry points to your Azure environment from a network traffic perspective. Therefore, Azure DDoS Protection applies protection to these public IP addresses in Azure. It uses a proprietary technology to determine the difference between legitimate and potential DDoS attacks.

Azure DDoS Protection uses three separate metrics to set a threshold value to differentiate between legitimate and potentially malicious traffic:

- Inbound SYN packets to trigger DDoS mitigation
- Inbound TCP packets to trigger DDoS mitigation
- Inbound UDP packets to trigger DDoS mitigation.

It sets this threshold value above the observed traffic level that is considered usual. Everything equal to or greater than the threshold value is considered to be potentially malicious traffic.

Rather than sending potentially malicious traffic directly to your public IP addresses in Azure, it's first analyzed using proprietary technology to determine whether it's malicious. This proprietary technology looks at various traffic properties of the network and transport layer and applies a number of mitigation techniques to the traffic it inspects.

Traffic that is determined to be malicious is dropped. Traffic that is determined to be legitimate is analyzed and inspected but not dropped. This is important because a legitimate increase in traffic to your web applications can occur, such as an increase in customers visiting your web application during the holiday season.

Azure DDoS Protection comes in the form of two SKUs: Basic and Standard.

AZURE DDoS PROTECTION BASIC

Azure DDoS Protection Basic is available at no additional cost as part of Azure and provides platform-level protection for your Azure resources against DDoS attacks. Basic is built into Azure—you don't need to set anything up. The threshold values are determined based on the average of all aggregated traffic intended for a particular Azure region. This metric tends to translate into threshold values for public IP addresses being higher compared to the Standard version.

Although Basic provides free DDoS mitigation capabilities, most organizations require the more advanced mitigation capabilities provided in Azure DDoS Protection Standard.

AZURE DDoS PROTECTION STANDARD

Azure DDoS Protection Standard is a paid SKU that provides additional benefits compared to Azure DDoS Protection Basic. Azure DDoS Protection Standard offers the following advanced capabilities:

- Always-on traffic monitoring
- Adaptive real-time tuning
- DDoS Protection alerts, monitoring, and telemetry
- Protection planning
- Cost protection
- DDoS rapid response support

With Azure DDoS Protection Standard, the threshold values are set dynamically for each of your public IPs in Azure based on the observed traffic over time, depending on the traffic, for each individual IP address. The Standard version has several other benefits compared with the Basic version, including DDoS Protection metrics that can be used to monitor and visualize the threshold values used to differentiate between malicious and legitimate traffic.

In addition to the metrics and log information, organizations that usually opt for Azure DDoS Protection Standard tend to appreciate the dynamically set thresholds specific to each IP address, as well as cost protection during verified DDoS attacks. Should an organization's cloud-native services (such as Virtual Machine Scale Sets) autoscale due to an increase in traffic during a verified DDoS attack, this cost will be credited back to the organization. Unlike Basic, which requires no configuration, Azure DDoS Protection Standard is applied by creating an Azure DDoS Protection plan.

3.4.2 Creating an Azure DDoS Protection plan

Azure DDoS Protection protects IP addresses that are associated with your VNet. To create a DDoS Protection plan, you need to specify the name of the plan and the resource group in which it's deployed. Run the following command using Azure CLI in Azure Cloud Shell to create an Azure DDoS Protection Standard plan.

Listing 3.16 Creating a plan for Azure DDoS Protection Standard

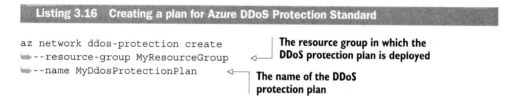

After this command runs, it creates the Azure DDoS Protection plan, as you can see from the following output:

```
{
  "etag": "W/\"df05e2fc-f518-4bbd-8cff-c5967f5b24d5\"",
  "id": "/subscriptions/00000000-0000-0000-0000-000000000000
  /resourceGroups/myResourceGroup/providers/Microsoft.Network
  /ddosProtectionPlans/MyDdosProtectionPlan",
  "location": "northeurope",
  "name": "MyDdosProtectionPlan",
  "provisioningState": "Succeeded",
  "resourceGroup": "myResourceGroup",
  "resourceGuid": null,
  "tags": {
    "createddate": "08/17/2022",
    "owner": "bmagusic"
  },
  "type": "Microsoft.Network/ddosProtectionPlans",
  "virtualNetworks": null
}
```

To apply the Azure DDoS Protection Standard plan you created, you need to associate it with the VNet of the public IP addresses that you want to protect against DDoS attacks.

ASSOCIATING AN AZURE VNET

To associate the DDoS Protection plan to an existing VNet, run the following command in Azure Cloud Shell.

Listing 3.17 Associating the DDoS Protection plan with an existing VNet

```
az network ddos-protection update
➥--resource-group MyResourceGroup        ⭠  The resource group in which the DDoS
                                              Protection plan will be deployed
➥--name MyDdosProtectionPlan             ⭠
➥--vnets MyVnet      ⭠   The names or IDs of the   The name of the DDoS
                         VNets associated with the  Protection plan
                         DDoS Protection plan
```

After this command runs, it associates the Azure DDoS Protection plan you created, as you can see from the following output::

```
{
  "etag": "W/\"df05e2fc-f518-4bbd-8cff-c5967f5b24d5\"",
  "id": "/subscriptions/00000000-0000-0000-0000-000000000000
➥/resourceGroups/myResourceGroup/providers/Microsoft.Network
➥/ddosProtectionPlans/MyDdosProtectionPlan",
  "location": "northeurope",
  "name": "MyDdosProtectionPlan",
  "provisioningState": "Succeeded",
  "resourceGroup": "myResourceGroup",
  "resourceGuid": null,
  "tags": {
    "createddate": "08/17/2022",
    "owner": "bmagusic"
  },
  "type": "Microsoft.Network/ddosProtectionPlans",
  "virtualNetworks": [
    {
      "id": "/ subscriptions/00000000-0000-0000-0000-000000000000
➥/resourceGroups/myResourceGroup/providers/Microsoft.Network
➥/virtualNetworks/myVNet",
      "resourceGroup": "myResourceGroup"
    }
  ]
}
```

The `virtualNetworks` section contains the ID of the VNet that you associated the DDoS Protection plan with.

VALIDATING AZURE DDOS PROTECTION

An important part of finalizing the deployment of Azure DDoS Protection Standard is to validate DDoS Protection to ensure that the IP addresses of your VNet are, indeed, protected from DDoS attacks. To validate the protection plan you created, run the following command in Azure Cloud Shell.

Listing 3.18   Validating Azure DDoS Protection Standard plan deployment

```
az network ddos-protection show
--resource-group MyResourceGroup
--name MyDdosProtectionPlan
```

The output returns the details of the Azure DDoS Protection plan that you associated with the VNet. You can use these details to confirm that the plan does, in fact, cover the public IP addresses that you would like to protect against DDoS attacks.

In addition to running the previous command, you can use the logs and metrics available as part of Azure DDoS Protection Standard. I'll cover logging in chapter 9. However, know that you can use logging information for further analysis of DDoS attacks. The metrics for Azure DDoS Protection Standard provide you with the ability to analyze how the threshold values, which Azure DDoS Protection uses to discern between legitimate and potentially malicious traffic, behave for your public IP addresses. They also provide the ability to analyze the threshold values during potential DDoS attacks.

3.5   Answers to exercises

Exercise 3.1

To create a resource group in the Central US region, run the following command:

```
az group create -l central -n myResourceGroup
```

To delete the resource group, together with all the resources, after you're finished with the chapter, run the following command:

```
az group delete -n myResourceGroup -y
```

Summary

- Azure network security is a set of Azure security services that you can use to build a secure network infrastructure in Azure. It includes Azure Firewall, Azure WAF, and Azure DDoS Protection. These services provide security value on top of your existing network infrastructure.
- Azure Firewall provides a way to control and inspect traffic between VNets and between your network and the internet. Azure Firewall Premium builds on the capabilities in Standard and adds more advanced capabilities such as TLS inspection, Intrusion Detection System and Intrusion Prevention System, and full URL filtering.
- Azure WAF provides a set of capabilities based on OWASP rule sets that are managed and kept updated by Microsoft. In addition, it can provide managed bot protection to help shield your applications from these kinds of attacks.
- Azure DDoS Protection Basic is a free offering that provides platform-level protection, but it lacks advanced visibility and flexibility available in Azure DDoS Protection Standard. When using Standard, the threshold values for your public IP addresses are set dynamically based on the observed traffic pattern for each IP address, whereas in Basic, this is done at the level of the Azure region.

Securing compute resources in Azure: Azure Bastion, Kubernetes, and Azure App Service

This chapter covers

- Azure Bastion
- Securing Kubernetes clusters
- What makes container security different
- Securing Azure App Service

Compute resources are a foundational building block of any public cloud environment. Thus, securing the compute resources in Azure on top of which your applications and digital services run helps avoid unintended disruption to your business by making your services more resilient against cyberattacks—because if you don't secure compute resources from bad actors, you might have no business at all.

4.1 Azure compute resources

Public cloud environments consist of various building blocks that you can use to build applications and digital services in Azure, such as Azure storage, backup, and recovery services (figure 4.1). They run digital services vital to organizations and their businesses by powering your application code; without them, your applications wouldn't run.

Thus, you need to consider how to protect your resources from bad actors as well as from people inside your organization who might expose the services through misconfigurations (or misuse). Understanding how to implement security for compute resources in Azure matters greatly. This chapter teaches you how to differentiate between the various Azure security services that can be used to secure compute resources and implement them effectively.

NOTE   To follow along with the exercises in this chapter, you can use the GitHub repository (https://github.com/bmagusic/azure-security).

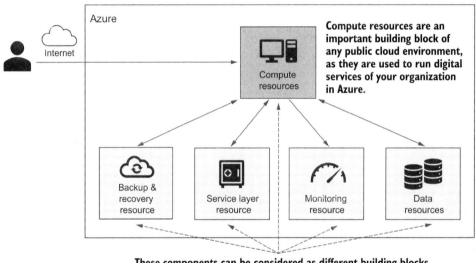

Figure 4.1   Compute resources are one of the main building blocks in Azure.

Azure offers a variety of compute resources, each of which is intended to cover specific use cases when deploying and running digital services. These digital services tend to run on compute workloads such as Azure Virtual Machines (VMs), Azure App Service, and Azure Kubernetes Service (AKS). Although Azure offers additional compute resources, these three workloads are common and can be used to deploy both traditional and cloud-native applications. By learning how to secure them, you'll be able to protect a variety of applications that run digital services.

Much of what you learn in this chapter can be used alongside the concepts you've learned in chapter 3 about Azure network security. As I've mentioned previously, there is no silver bullet when it comes to security. Thus, you should try to complement what you've learned in the previous two chapters with what you'll learn in this chapter to apply a defense-in-depth strategy.

Along the way, I'll introduce you to a couple of additional services and concepts that make it easier to understand how to secure compute resources in Azure, such as Azure Container Registry (ACR). You'll learn this by focusing on an example of securing different aspects of Azure VMs, Azure App Service, and AKS and providing secure access to these resources. We'll begin by looking at how to provide secure access to your VMs through *Azure Bastion*.

4.2   Azure Bastion

Imagine that you have VMs in Azure running business-critical workloads needed for digital services vital to your organization. Therefore, you need to provide secure remote desktop protocol (RDP) or shell (SSH) access to these VMs. In the previous chapter, you learned how Azure network security services can help. In this chapter, you'll learn about an additional service that can be added to your Azure security toolkit—namely, Azure Bastion.

Azure Bastion is a fully managed platform as a service (PaaS) that provides you with secure RDP and SSH access to your Azure VMs without needing to publicly expose the ports on your VMs. This is advantageous because opening RDP or SSH ports on your VMs, even to trusted IP addresses, leaves your VMs open to attacks. To prevent this vulnerability, you can use a *bastion host*, such as Azure Bastion.

Bastion hosts are commonly used to provide secure access to VMs and resources inside of your virtual network (VNet). Another name for bastion hosts is *jump servers*, and both names are widely used to convey the same concept (from here on, I'll use *bastion hosts*). Bastion hosts allow you to avoid exposing VMs inside your VNet directly to the internet, which is ill-advised and carries security risks. Exposed VMs can have their ports scanned by bad actors and are vulnerable to RDP brute-force attacks. By placing a bastion host on the perimeter of your network between your VMs and the internet, you can harden it against attacks. Thus, you can provide secure access to the VMs in your VNet (figure 4.2) by not publicly exposing your RDP and SSH ports.

Because Azure Bastion is a fully managed PaaS service, the hardening of the bastion host and everything that goes with it—such as keeping it up to date against vulnerabilities—is done by the public cloud provider (in this case, Microsoft). Managing a bastion host yourself requires both effort and expertise. With Azure Bastion, you can offload time-consuming management tasks to Microsoft.

The functionalities available in Bastion differ based on the SKU. Azure Bastion supports two SKUs: Basic and Standard.

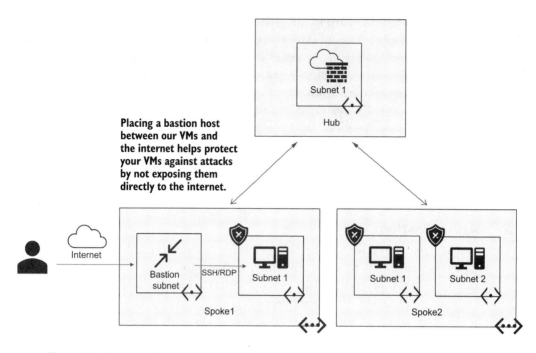

Figure 4.2 Azure Bastion in hub-and-spoke topology

4.2.1 Basic vs. Standard SKU

When implementing Azure Bastion, you need to specify the SKU. *Basic* provides you with the core functionality needed to provide secure RDP and SSH connectivity to your VMs, such as connecting to Linux VMs using SSH and connecting to Windows VMs using RDP. *Standard* provides you with all the same functionalities as Basic, plus some advanced features.

The advanced features provided in Standard include the ability to connect to Linux VMs using RDP and to Windows VMs using SSH. It also allows you to authenticate using a private key stored in Azure Key Vault (I'll cover Azure Key Vault in chapter 5). Other advanced features are the ability to upload and download files and disable copy and paste in web-based clients.

If you want to use the advanced features available in the Standard SKU, you need to specify the SKU using your browser and the Azure portal. Other ways of specifying the SKU, such as using the Azure command-line interface (CLI; I'll cover this shortly) or PowerShell, currently only support the Basic SKU.

4.2.2 Azure Bastion in action

To deploy Azure Bastion, you need to specify the VNet to which the Bastion host gets deployed. You also need to create a dedicated Azure Bastion subnet. It's important to note the following:

- The name of the subnet in which you deploy Azure Bastion must be `Azure-BastionSubnet`.
- The dedicated subnet needs to be in the same VNet and resource group as the Bastion host. The way you connect to client VMs is through an Azure Bastion instance.

An instance is like a special Azure VM that is fully managed by Azure and contains all the processes that Azure Bastion requires to provide you with secure connectivity to your VMs. Instances are created in the `AzureBastionSubnet`:

- The number of instances is dependent on the SKU you specify; it determines the number of concurrent RDP and SSH connections.
- Each instance can support 25 concurrent RDP and 50 concurrent SSH connections for commonly used workloads.
- The Basic SKU provides two instances. The Standard SKU allows you to select the number of instances and thus manage and increase the number of concurrent supported sessions, known as *host scaling*.
- The smallest Azure Bastion subnet you can create is `/26`. If you need to support host scaling, you need to create a subnet of `/26` or larger.
- You can opt to create the Azure Bastion subnet in an existing VNet that contains VMs to which you want to provide secure RDP/SSH access.

To create a new VNet with the Azure Bastion subnet, run the following command in Azure Cloud Shell.

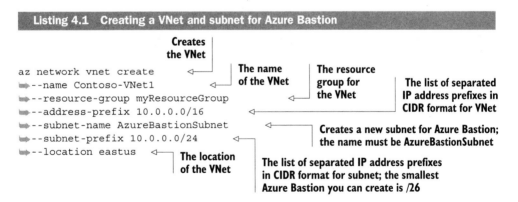

Listing 4.1   Creating a VNet and subnet for Azure Bastion

After this command runs, it creates the VNet with an Azure Bastion subnet, as you can see from the following output:

```
...
    "ipAllocations": null,
    "location": "eastus",
    "name": "Contoso-VNet1",
    "provisioningState": "Succeeded",
    "resourceGroup": " myResourceGroup ",
    "resourceGuid": "8c29674c-dcba-4564-aea2-2af4712be9f1",
```

```
"subnets": [
  {
    "addressPrefix": "10.0.0.0/24",
    "addressPrefixes": null,
    "applicationGatewayIpConfigurations": null,
    "delegations": [],
    "etag": "W/\"bfdb0ac1-9507-44dd-8928-d3271b833acc\"",
    "id": "/subscriptions/00000000-0000-0000-0000-000000000000
    ➥/resourceGroups/bomagusi-rg4/providers/Microsoft.Network
    ➥/virtualNetworks/MyVnet/subnets/AzureBastionSubnet",
    "ipAllocations": null,
    "ipConfigurationProfiles": null,
    "ipConfigurations": null,
    "name": "AzureBastionSubnet",
    "natGateway": null,
    "networkSecurityGroup": null,
    "privateEndpointNetworkPolicies": "Disabled",
    "privateEndpoints": null,
    "privateLinkServiceNetworkPolicies": "Enabled",
    "provisioningState": "Succeeded",
    "purpose": null,
    "resourceGroup": "myResourceGroup",
    "resourceNavigationLinks": null,
    "routeTable": null,
    "serviceAssociationLinks": null,
    "serviceEndpointPolicies": null,
    "serviceEndpoints": null,
    "type": "Microsoft.Network/virtualNetworks/subnets"
  }
. . .
```

NOTE All Azure Bastion resources deployed after November 21, 2021 must have a subnet size of /26 or larger. If you deployed Azure Bastion resources prior to that date, your Azure Bastion resources will continue to work. However, if you would like to use host scaling capability, you need to increase the size of the AzureBastionSubnet to /26 or larger. Keep in mind that the Azure Bastion subnet cannot contain additional resources because Azure uses this subnet to deploy Bastion resources.

When deploying Azure Bastion, you need to specify a public IP address. Bastion uses the public IP address to provide secure RDP/SSH access (over port 443). You can choose to use an existing public IP address as long as it meets the following criteria:

- The IP address is not already in use.
- The IP address needs to be located in the same Azure region as the Azure Bastion resource you're creating.
- The SKU needs to be Standard.
- The allocation method needs to be Static.

If you already have an existing IP address in your environment that fits these criteria, great. Otherwise, you can create a new public IP address by running the following command in Azure Cloud Shell.

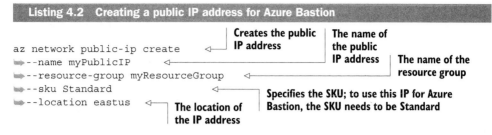

Listing 4.2 Creating a public IP address for Azure Bastion

```
az network public-ip create          ◁──┐ Creates the public │ The name of
                                         │ IP address         │ the public
──▶ --name myPublicIP         ◁──                             │ IP address │ The name of the
──▶ --resource-group myResourceGroup    ◁───────────────────────────────── resource group
──▶ --sku Standard            ◁──────────────┐ Specifies the SKU; to use this IP for Azure
──▶ --location eastus    ◁──┐ The location of │ Bastion, the SKU needs to be Standard
                            │ the IP address
```

After this command runs, it creates the public IP address. Your output should look similar to the following:

```
...
   "ipConfiguration": null,
   "ipTags": [],
   "linkedPublicIpAddress": null,
   "location": "eastus",
   "migrationPhase": null,
   "name": "MyPublicIp",
   "natGateway": null,
   "provisioningState": "Succeeded",
   "publicIpAddressVersion": "IPv4",
   "publicIpAllocationMethod": "Static",
   "publicIpPrefix": null,
   "resourceGroup": "myResourceGroup",
   "resourceGuid": "e3137ca0-8ce1-457f-be16-562d846ee264",
   "servicePublicIpAddress": null,
   "sku": {
     "name": "Standard",
     "tier": "Regional"
   },
...
```

With the Azure portal, you can create a new VNet and public IP address when you create the Bastion resource. However, when using the CLI, the commands are dependent on one another and need to be applied in sequence. After you have a public IP address that meets the criteria for Azure Bastion and have deployed the Azure Bastion subnet, you can then create a new Azure Bastion resource `AzureBastionSubnet` by running the following command in Azure Cloud Shell.

> **CAUTION** You can upgrade from Basic to Standard using your browser and Azure portal. The reverse, however, is not supported: you can't downgrade from the Standard to the Basic SKU. To downgrade from Standard to Basic, you must delete the Azure Bastion host and recreate it specifying the Basic SKU.

Listing 4.3 Creating a new Azure Bastion resource

```
az network bastion create               ◁──┐ Creates the Azure
──▶ --name contosoBastion   ◁──┐ The name of the │ Bastion resource
                               │ Azure Bastion host
```

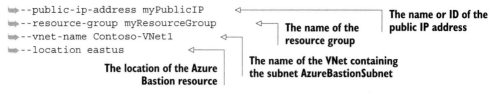

After this command runs, it creates the Azure Bastion resource, as you can see from the following output:

```
{
   "disableCopyPaste": false,
   "dnsName": "bst-cc80ba31-43af-4c7b-8054-0235c21419b6.bastion.azure.com",
   "enableFileCopy": false,
   "enableIpConnect": false,
   "enableShareableLink": false,
   "enableTunneling": false,
   ...
         "resourceGroup": "myResourceGroup"
      },
      "type": "Microsoft.Network/bastionHosts/bastionHostIpConfigurations"
   }
   ],
   "location": "eastus",
   "name": "MyBastion",
   "provisioningState": "Succeeded",
   "resourceGroup": "myResourceGroup",
   "scaleUnits": 2,
   "sku": {
      "name": "Standard"
   },
   "tags": {
      "owner": "bmagusic"
   },
   "type": "Microsoft.Network/bastionHosts"
}
...
```

Now that you've successfully created your Azure Bastion resource, you can connect to an Azure VM. When using Azure Bastion to connect to your VMs, you can choose one of two options: using your browser and the Azure portal or using the native RDP/SSH agent installed on your computer.

4.2.3   *Connecting to Azure Bastion using your browser and Azure portal*

If you don't have an RDP or SSH client installed, you can connect using your browser. Using your browser lets you connect to your Azure VMs directly from the Azure portal over Transport Layer Security (TLS).

> **NOTE**   TLS is a transport layer protocol designed to provide security and is commonly used to secure HTTP traffic.

As a prerequisite to making a connection to Azure Bastion over a browser, you need to have the Reader role assigned on the following resources:

- The Azure Bastion resource
- The VM you're connecting to
- The network interface controller (NIC) with the private IP address of the VM
- The VNet of the VM you're connecting to (if the Bastion deployment is in a peered VNet)

To connect over your browser, perform the following steps:

1 Navigate to the Azure portal with the Reader role assigned on the necessary resources.
2 Choose the VM to which you want to connect.
3 On the left-hand side, under Operations, choose Bastion.
4 The options you can select depend on the Bastion SKU. Unless you're using the Standard SKU, you cannot change the port number and protocol used under Connection Settings (figure 4.2).
5 Specify the port number and protocol to connect to the VM (for example, 3389 and RDP for Windows machines or 22 and SSH for Linux machines).
6 In the Authentication Type, select an option from the dropdown. Figure 4.3 shows Password as the selected option.
7 Based on the option you selected, fill out the required values.
8 Click Connect to establish a connection to the VM.

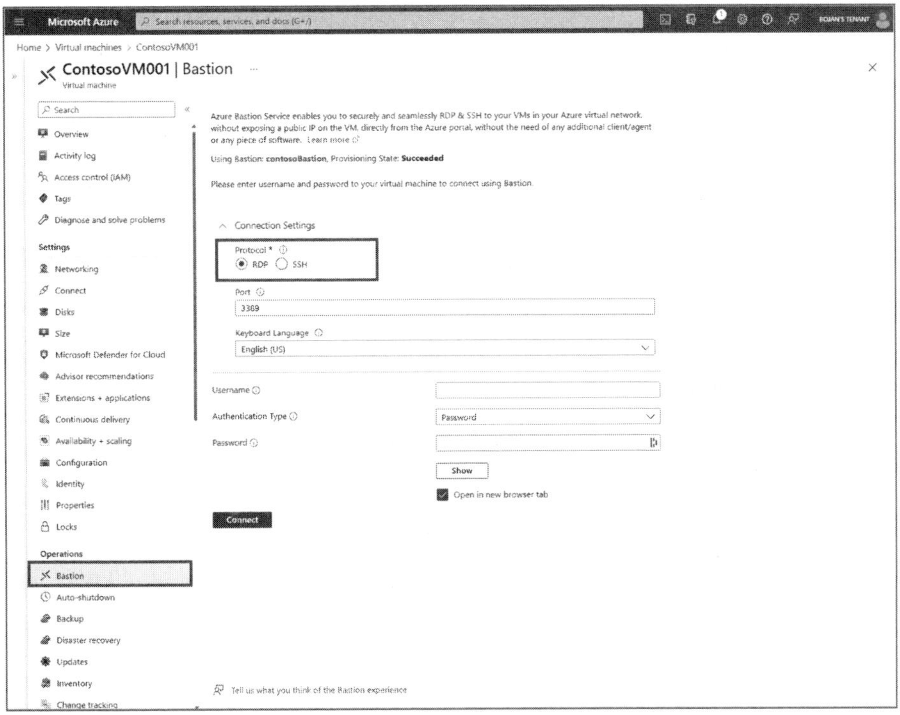

Figure 4.3 Configuration settings for connecting to VMs using a browser and the Azure portal

If you're presented with the option Open in New Browser Tab, leave it selected so the VM session opens in a new tab, similar to figure 4.4. While you might have deployed agents and extensions to your VMs for monitoring or management purposes, Azure Bastion is a completely agentless service and doesn't require any additional agents for RDP/SSH.

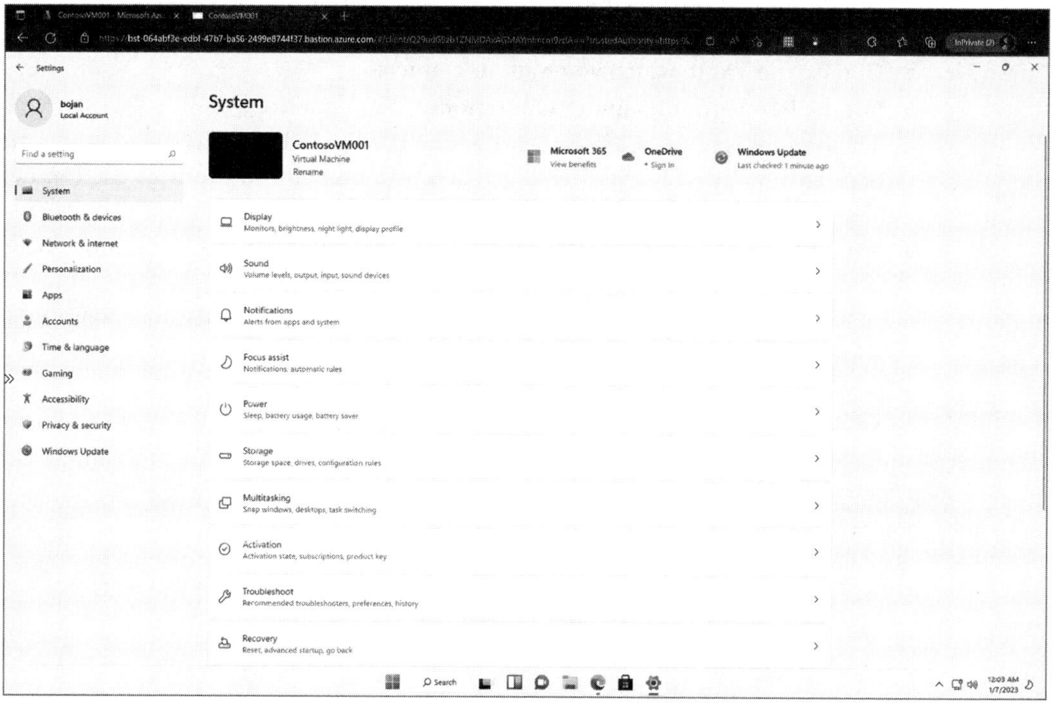

Figure 4.4   A VM session opened in a new tab using Azure Bastion and a browser

Exercise 4.1

After you create an Azure Bastion in your environment using Password as the authentication type, connect to the bastion host using your browser and the Azure portal. For the purposes of this exercise, you can either connect to a Linux or Windows VM.

The browser you use to connect must support HTML 5, such as Microsoft Edge or Google Chrome. Alternatively, if you have an RDP or SSH client installed on your machine, you can use the client to connect to the VM.

4.2.4 *Connecting to Azure Bastion using the native RDP or SSH client*

To connect to a VM using the native RDP or SSH client, you need to use the Azure CLI. There are also two important requirements that need to be fulfilled to connect to VMs using the native RDP/SSH client:

- The Azure Bastion instance or instances need to be deployed using the Standard SKU.
- Native client support needs to be enabled on the Azure Bastion instance.

You can enable native client support when deploying the Azure Bastion instance through the Azure CLI using the `--enable-tunneling` parameter. To enable the native client support on an existing Azure Bastion instance, run the following command in Azure CLI.

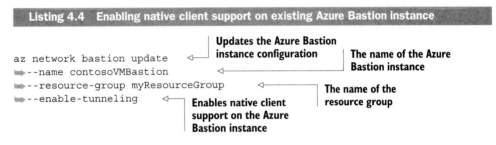

Listing 4.4 Enabling native client support on existing Azure Bastion instance

After this command runs, it enables the native client support on the existing Azure Bastion instance, as you can see from the following output:

```
{
  "disableCopyPaste": false,
  "dnsName": "bst-81101bf4-bedd-48fd-a626-5b02e1e6b7a2.bastion.azure.com",
  "enableFileCopy": false,
  "enableIpConnect": false,
  "enableShareableLink": false,
  "enableTunneling": true,
  "etag": "W/\"22c43b65-fcdd-4b70-8059-5561fe3d649a\"",
  "id": "/subscriptions/00000000-0000-0000-0000-000000000000
  /resourceGroups/myResourceGroup/providers/Microsoft.Network
  /bastionHosts/contosoVMBastion",
...
```

Native client support can also be enabled via a browser and the Azure portal. To enable native client support via a browser, perform the following steps:

1 Navigate to Azure portal, and select the Azure Bastion instance on which you want to enable the native client support.

2 On the left, under Settings, choose Configuration.

3 Ensure the Native Client Support is selected (figure 4.5).

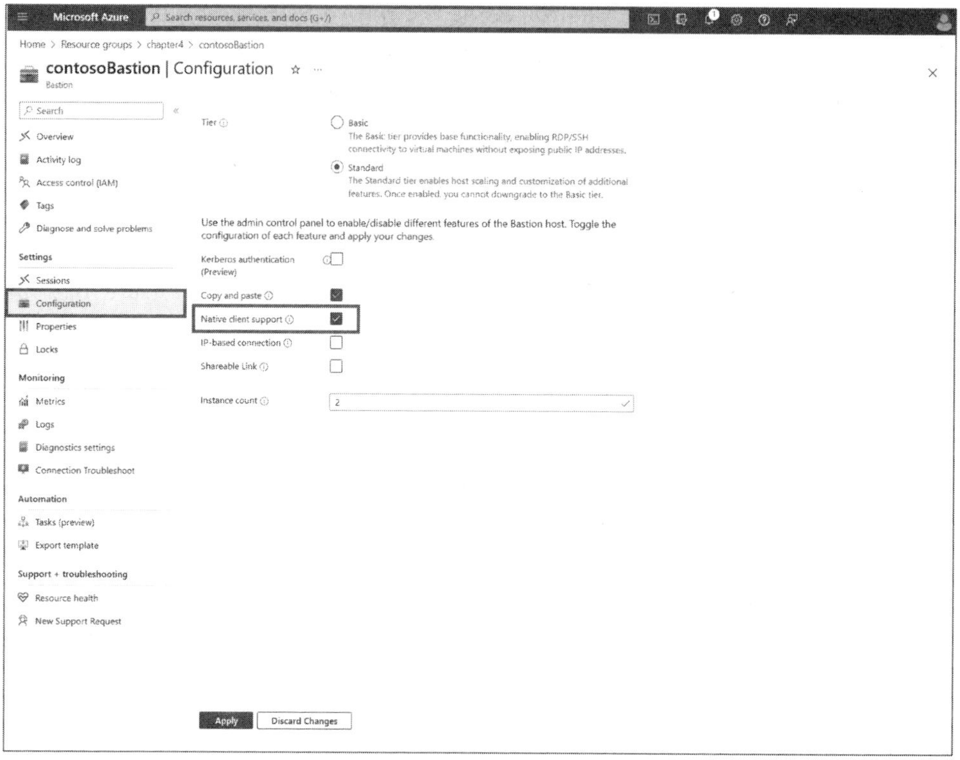

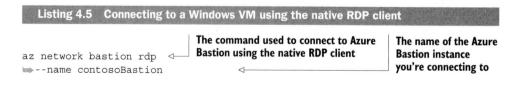

Figure 4.5   Enabling native client support on Azure Bastion via a browser and the Azure portal

To make a connection to Azure Bastion using native client support, you need to have the Reader role assigned to the following resources:

- The Azure Bastion resource
- The VM you're connecting to
- The NIC with the private IP address of the VM

In addition, if you enabled the Microsoft Entra ID login on the VM, you need the Virtual Machine Administrator Login or Virtual Machine User Login role.

> **NOTE**   The inbound port 3389 needs to be open for the connection to the VM to be established.

To connect to a Windows VM using the native RDP client, run the following command.

Listing 4.5   Connecting to a Windows VM using the native RDP client

```
az network bastion rdp       ◁── The command used to connect to Azure
  --name contosoBastion           Bastion using the native RDP client
                            ◁────────────────────────
```

The command used to connect to Azure Bastion using the native RDP client

The name of the Azure Bastion instance you're connecting to

```
➡--resource-group myResourceGroup          ◁─────       The name of the
➡--target-resource-id /subscriptions                    resource group
  ➡/00000000-0000-0000-0000-000000000000/resourceGroups
  ➡/myResourceGroup/providers/Microsoft.Compute          The resource ID of the
  ➡/virtualMachines/ContosoVM001              ◁─────      VM you're connecting to
➡--resource-port "3389"       ◁──    The resource port of the
                                     VM you're connecting to
```

If you want to specify a custom port rather than use port 3389 (the default port for RDP), you must specify the port value using the parameter --resource-port. After the command runs, it prompts you to insert your credentials, after which it will open the session to the target VM.

> **NOTE** The inbound port 22 needs to be open for the connection to the VM to be established.

Connecting to a Windows VM using the native SSH client differs slightly from using the native RDP client. To connect using the native SSH, run the following command.

Listing 4.6 Connecting to a Windows VM using the native SSH client

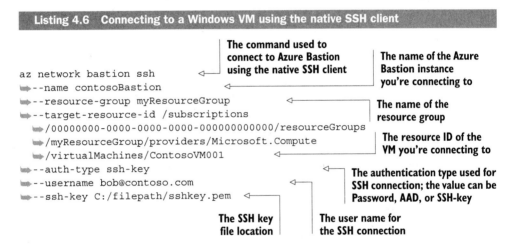

Similarly, when you connect using the RDP client, the inbound port 22 (the default port for SSH) needs to be open. If you want to specify a custom port, you must add the parameter --resource-port and the specific port value to the command.

After the command runs, it prompts you for your credentials. After you provide the credentials, a new session will open on the VM you're connecting to.

Exercise 4.2

To solidify your knowledge of Azure Bastion, complete the following exercise. After you enable the native client support on Azure Bastion via the browser, connect to one of your Linux VMs using the native SSH client.

You are not likely to connect to Azure Bastion using all options. You're probably going to pick the one that suits you best. For future reference, the requirements for each option are aggregated in table 4.1.

Table 4.1 Overview of dependencies/requirements for connecting to Azure Bastion

With a browser and Azure portal	With a native RDP client	With a native SSH client
Reader role on Azure Bastion resource	Reader role on Azure Bastion resource	Reader role on Azure Bastion resource
Reader role on the Azure VM you're connecting to	Reader role on the Azure VM you're connecting to	Reader role on Azure VM you're connecting to
Reader role on NIC with the private IP address of the VM	Reader role on NIC with the private IP address of the VM	Reader role on NIC with the private IP address of the VM
If Bastion deployment is in a peered VNet, Reader role on the VNet of the VM you're connecting to	Azure Bastion deployed using Standard SKU	Azure Bastion deployed using Standard SKU
	Native Client Support enabled on the Bastion instance	Native Client Supports enabled on Bastion instance
	Inbound port 3389 open or custom port (if you're not using port 3389)	Inbound port 22 open or custom port (if you're not using port 22). If you enabled the Microsoft Entra ID login on the VM you're connecting to, Virtual Machine Administrator Login or Virtual Machine User Login role
	If you enabled the Microsoft Entra ID login on the VM you're connecting to, Virtual Machine Administrator Login or Virtual Machine User Login role	

NOTE   To learn more about how Azure Bastion works as part of an enterprise network with Azure Firewall, network security groups (NSGs), and route tables, you can start at http://mng.bz/mV0W.

4.3   Securing Kubernetes clusters

Before going into how to secure Kubernetes, I want to remind you of some key foundational concepts applicable to containers and Kubernetes. It can be challenging to talk about securing Kubernetes if you don't have the foundations in place, starting with what containers are.

4.3.1   What are containers?

Similar to shipping containers used by Maersk and other shipping companies to package goods and transport them to their intended destination, software containers package software to move it reliably from one computing environment to another. Therefore, you can see a container image as an executable unit of software that contains the entire runtime environment. That is, it contains the application and everything that the application needs to run, such as its code, all of its dependencies, and configuration files.

Containers allow you to take all the files and settings required for your application to run and move them from one server to another. That means that a developer can build a container image on their local machine and then move that image to a development, testing, or staging environment where that container image will run as a container. You can understand the container image as a blueprint to create many (even hundreds) of containers. Containers are very resource efficient, and multiple containers can be deployed on a single OS (figure 4.6).

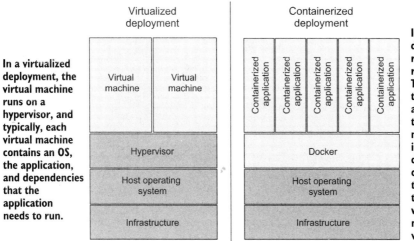

Figure 4.6 Multiple containers can run on a single OS hosted on a virtual machine.

Containers revolutionized how businesses build applications because they're cost-effective, can share the same OS, spin up quickly, and can run anywhere. Their ability to run anywhere allows developers to build container images locally and then deploy them into production with the same runtime environment.

When developers are creating container images, they need some place to save and access them as they're created. This is where a *container registry* comes into play.

4.3.2 What is a container registry?

The container registry serves as a place where developers can store container images. They can then share them by uploading (or *pushing*) images to a container registry or downloading (or *pulling*) them to another system to run as a container, such as a Kubernetes cluster (figure 4.7).

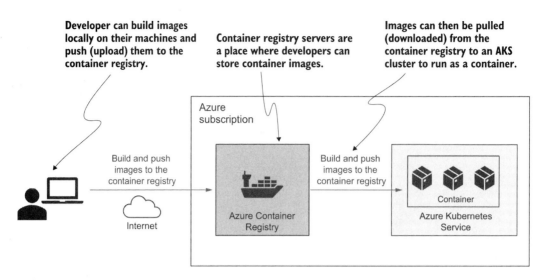

Figure 4.7   Pushing and pulling images from ACR

ACR is an example of a container registry managed by Microsoft.

4.3.3   *What is Kubernetes?*

Even though containers revolutionized how applications are built, they became a headache for infrastructure and networking teams because they needed to manage when and where containers should run. They had to make sure they were load-balancing traffic to containers evenly, even horizontally scaling containers out and back in. In addition, they needed to deploy and orchestrate these containerized applications in production environments. In 2014, Google set out to solve these challenges and came up with Kubernetes, an open source solution that automates containers' deployment, management, and visibility. Kubernetes ensures that containers are running on the VMs you expect them to be running on with the desired configuration and networking controls. Although not the only option, Kubernetes is the most commonly used container orchestration tool.

4.3.4   *How does Kubernetes work?*

When you're working with a Kubernetes cluster, there are two main components: the *control plane* and the *worker nodes*. The control plane hosts the components that are used to manage the Kubernetes cluster. It is where the Kubernetes API server is located, which is the central part of the cluster. You can think of the API server as the brain of the Kubernetes cluster. It's what users interact with when they want to deploy new containers or make any sort of configuration changes. The control plane enforces the desired configuration state on all worker nodes.

Worker nodes can be virtual or physical machines. A single worker node hosts pods that run one or more containers. A *pod* is the basic deployment unit within Kubernetes and typically represents a single instance of your application (although in more advanced scenarios, a pod can contain multiple containers, as depicted in figure 4.8).

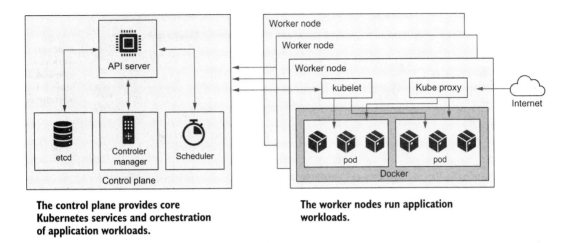

The control plane provides core Kubernetes services and orchestration of application workloads.

The worker nodes run application workloads.

Figure 4.8 Kubernetes cluster architecture is made of the control plane and worker nodes.

Another key term is *service*. A service is the way that Kubernetes configures a proxy to send traffic to a set of pods. Because pods can be short lived, it's not feasible to create networking rules with a static IP address for each pod because that pod eventually is replaced with another pod. Therefore, services provide a layer of abstraction to identify which pods perform similar functions based on different sorts of labels and manual grouping (which can also be dynamically updated).

The service has a single IP address and Domain Name System (DNS) entry that allows access to a logical grouping of pods, regardless of the pod version that is currently running. Through services, worker nodes can be exposed to the outside world, which opens them to potential attacks. If an attacker gets access to one worker node that has permission to communicate with other worker nodes, an attacker can potentially use that to move laterally. Therefore, security and networking teams need to consider strong segmentation controls.

Another important term is *namespaces*. These are virtual clusters within the physical Kubernetes cluster. They're meant to give users, teams, or projects a virtually separated environment to work in and prevent users and teams from getting in each other's way by limiting the Kubernetes objects that each team can see and access (figure 4.9). *Deployments* are how users and teams communicate with Kubernetes to define which images to use for applications, the number of pods that should be running, and how the pod should be updated. Deployments are how users tell Kubernetes what they want their workloads to look like, and the control plane can then enforce the desired state.

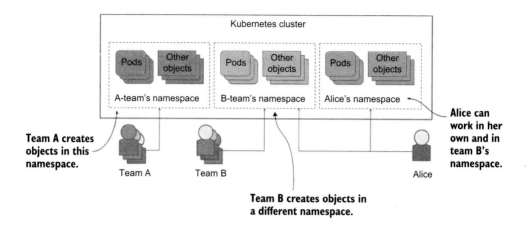

Figure 4.9   Use of namespaces in Kubernetes clusters

Last, there are *DaemonSets*. DaemonSets are a way of ensuring that each node runs a specific application in one of the pods. Because pods are present on each and every worker node within the Kubernetes cluster, DaemonSets are typically used for long-term running services that are required for a Kubernetes cluster, such as maintenance, monitoring, or log forwarding. They can also be used to detect threats to Kubernetes clusters (I'll cover this topic in chapter 7).

When setting up and managing the Kubernetes clusters, you can choose between *managed* and *unmanaged Kubernetes*.

4.3.5   *Managed vs. unmanaged Kubernetes*

Managed Kubernetes implies that installation and management of the Kubernetes cluster is done by someone else, usually the public cloud provider. An example of managed Kubernetes is AKS. AKS is a managed Kubernetes offering available in Azure that allows you to offload many of the Kubernetes-related maintenance and monitoring tasks over to the public cloud provider (in this case, Microsoft).

When you create an AKS cluster, the control plane containing the API servers and other components is automatically created and configured by Azure. As such, you can focus on other tasks, such as developing applications, rather than managing the cluster infrastructure. In AKS, both you and Microsoft share the responsibility when it comes to the worker nodes. Microsoft provides patches and new images for your worker nodes weekly but doesn't automatically apply those patches. Patching the worker nodes' OS and runtime components is your responsibility (figure 4.9). Similarly, as new Kubernetes patches, which can contain security and functional improvements to Kubernetes, become available, it's your responsibility to ensure your clusters' Kubernetes version is kept up to date.

In a managed Kubernetes cluster (such as **AKS**), the control plane is created and configured automatically by the public cloud provider (in this case, by Microsoft).

While the public cloud provider is responsible for the control plane, it's your responsibility to manage the nodes.

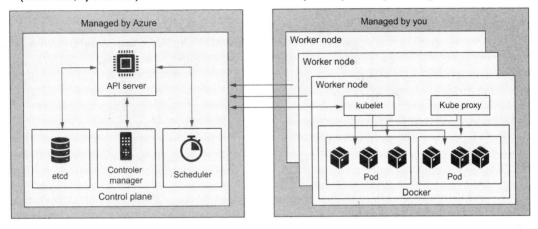

Figure 4.10   In AKS, Microsoft configures and maintains the control plane.

In *unmanaged Kubernetes,* you need to manage all aspects of Kubernetes manually. These tasks include, among others, creating the VMs used by the Kubernetes cluster, creating and configuring the control plane, and installing and configuring all other components required by the Kubernetes cluster. Thus, securing unmanaged and managed Kubernetes clusters is different from securing more traditional compute resources (for example, servers). To better secure your clusters, it's good to understand first what makes securing containers so important.

4.4 *What makes container security different?*

Containers are designed to be lightweight and short lived; they are not meant to be used like servers. They are immutable, which means they can't be modified when they're running in the Kubernetes cluster. You can't update, patch, or make any changes to a running container. If you update the code or apply a patch, you need to rebuild the entire container image and redeploy it. That's different from what security teams looking after more traditional workloads, such as servers, are used to.

With servers, security teams are familiar with remotely connecting and updating the configuration accordingly. With containers, they can't do that. Instead, they need to rebuild and redeploy the container image. Due to the highly dynamic nature of containerized environments, their short-lived nature makes monitoring them increasingly difficult. Therefore, you can't rely on typical monitoring tools used for servers because these tools are not equipped to see which pods are running or which containers are running inside of these pods, much less any problems inside them.

This challenge is further compounded by the lack of professionals who know how to properly secure containerized environments. Thus, next, I'll share some of the challenges that security teams face when securing their Kubernetes clusters.

4.4.1 Typical challenges when securing Kubernetes clusters

Kubernetes creates many identities that are used by in-cluster applications, and securing them is an important aspect of Kubernetes security. One of the challenges with these securing identities is the number and variety of the identities used within the context of a Kubernetes cluster, including the following:

- Identities used by users to authenticate to the cluster
- Identities used within the cluster, such as Kubernetes service accounts
- Identities and applications within the cluster that are used to communicate with resources outside the cluster, such as a SQL database

Securing these different identities is important because if an attacker compromises even one of them, it opens up various lateral-movement opportunities, such as pod escape. Pod escape is a lateral movement technique in which a bad actor uses misconfigurations or vulnerabilities to escape from the container grouping and reach the underlying host machine to access other container groupings running on it.

Another threat area is images with vulnerabilities. If a container with vulnerabilities is running within a service that is exposed to the internet, that vulnerability can be exploited by Eve, our fictional character representing bad actors. Furthermore, if that container has extensive privileges or includes a service account with privileges, Eve could get access to the host OS of one of the worker nodes or access the API servers and start sending some malicious requests to it.

Privileged containers have all the capabilities of the host machine, which removes the typical limitations that containers have. So, if a bad actor gains access to a privileged container, they can take many actions on that host machine. This attack is typically referred to as *escaping to the host* and is commonly used to deploy malware or other malicious payloads on the host machine.

> **NOTE** If you want to learn more about threats facing Kubernetes security, you can start with Kubernetes Goat (https://github.com/madhuakula/kubernetes-goat). Kubernetes Goat is an interactive Kubernetes security-learning playground that has intentionally vulnerable scenarios. The purpose is to teach you about common vulnerabilities and misconfigurations in Kubernetes clusters. It is meant to be used for educational purposes only in a safe and isolated environment.

Our bad actor Eve could also get access to a private registry (such as ACR), which allows access control to images. She could plant a compromised image in the registry and then deploy it to the cluster. This attack is commonly referred to as *backdoor containers* and can be used to run malicious code, such as crypto-mining software. To address these challenges, you need to follow a holistic approach to securing your clusters and container registries.

4.4.2 *Securing Azure Kubernetes Service and Azure Container Registry*

When planning to secure your Kubernetes clusters (such as AKS) and container registries (such as ACR), you need to approach security across the lifecycle of a container. Developers code applications and build container images. The image is then moved (pushed) to a container registry. It is then deployed (pulled) to run inside the Kubernetes cluster.

You should use trusted base images to create your container images. Base images can be seen as the starting point for most container-based workflows. Choosing images randomly is ill advised because they can have malware or other vulnerabilities on them. Scanning images can help because scanning performs a series of security checks on images to detect vulnerabilities. Therefore, while building images, you need to scan them to address any known vulnerabilities before you move them to a container registry, where they will be pulled to run inside a container in a Kubernetes cluster.

When images are in a container registry, you should continue to scan them for any vulnerabilities—specifically for any zero-day vulnerabilities—that may have surfaced since you moved the images to the container registry. In addition to securing container images, you should also secure the registry itself by not allowing public access, ensuring that you're encrypting images at rest, and enforcing role-based access control (RBAC). Public access to container registries allows attackers to push a malicious container image to the registry. With RBAC, you can define who can and can't access the container registry or publish images.

When deploying container images, you should use *Kubernetes admission controllers*. An admission controller allows you to enforce organization-wide policies within Kubernetes. These can range from ensuring you're enforcing least-privilege access controls for containers to ensuring that containers are deployed from only trusted registries and adhere to specific CPU and memory limits, especially in the event of a distributed denial of services attack.

In addition, when using admission controllers, you should limit access to the Kubernetes API server—for example, by placing it in a private VNet and enforcing RBAC. Last, if you discover that an image has vulnerabilities, you should block that image from being deployed to the Kubernetes cluster, especially if it's going to be running in a pod that is exposed to the internet.

4.4.3 *Security monitoring for Azure Kubernetes Service and Azure Container Registry*

When your containers are running, you want to monitor for any suspicious activity using security-monitoring solutions (such as Microsoft Defender for Cloud or Microsoft Sentinel, which are covered in more detail in chapters 7 and 8). These monitoring solutions alert you that crypto-mining processes or fileless attacks are in progress.

Using Microsoft Defender for Cloud and Microsoft Sentinel

Microsoft Defender for Cloud's continuous assessment capabilities can detect misconfigurations in your clusters and provide you with security best-practice guidance on how to fix those misconfigurations. In addition, it provides threat detection capabilities by monitoring your clusters for suspicious activities that may be indicative of an attack. If certainty is high enough that the suspicious activity is, in fact, an attack, it generates a security alert. You can then forward this security alert to Microsoft Sentinel to investigate the incident even further (taking into account data from other sources) and respond accordingly.

Another principle worth adhering to is ensuring that no changes are made to containers while they're running and making sure containers are immutable. If you discover vulnerabilities, patching a running container won't help because the next time the cluster scales out, it will just spin up a new container from the image that was sitting in the container registry that hasn't been patched. Therefore, if someone starts running a process within a production container, that's a suspicious activity that could be an indication of an attack from our bad actor Eve. New vulnerabilities might be discovered after your containers are running, and it's paramount to continuously monitor them for vulnerabilities.

Your goal is to keep your applications secure and running without vulnerabilities. In addition to Kubernetes and VMs, you can use Azure App Service to run your applications in Azure.

4.5   *Securing Azure App Service*

Another commonly used compute resource in Azure is *Azure App Service*. Azure App Service (or App Service, as it's commonly referred to) is an HTTP-based service that allows you to host your web applications, mobile backends, and REST APIs in Azure. It supports both Windows and Linux environments and a variety of programming languages (such as ASP.NET, Python, PHP, Node.js, Ruby, and Java). You can even use it to host containers.

Because Azure App Service is HTTP based, you should always ensure that HTTP traffic is redirected to HTTPS traffic. This increases security by making sure only the user's browser and the Azure App Service resource can decrypt the traffic. Similarly, if your web application hosted on Azure App Service needs to transfer files using File Transfer Protocol (FTP), you should enforce FTPS for additional security.

For enhanced security, it's also recommended that you use managed identities because they eliminate the need to manage credentials and secrets when a web application hosted on Azure App Service needs to access other Azure resources, such as Azure storage. Unfortunately, I still encounter developers that don't use managed identities. Another important aspect when securing Azure App Service revolves around authentication and authorization.

4.5.1 Authentication and authorization

Azure App Service provides you with a built-in authentication and authorization mechanism. As you recall from chapter 2, Microsoft Entra ID can be used both as a service to secure your identities and as an identity provider. Using an identity provider allows you to offload authentication and authorization to a trusted service rather than implementing them yourself.

When used in the context of an identity provider, the capabilities of Microsoft Entra ID are commonly referred to as the *Microsoft identity platform*. It is not the only identity provider that can be used by Azure App Service; you can use Google, Facebook, Twitter, or any OpenID Connect provider. When enabled with any of these identity providers, authentication and authorization run separately from your application code and are configured using app settings.

Another important aspect of securing Azure App Service is blocking and filtering network traffic using access restrictions.

4.5.2 Access restrictions

Access restrictions for your Azure App Services function similarly to network access-control lists. Access restrictions allow you to control inbound access to all your Azure App Service–hosted workloads by creating rules. Access restriction rules can be of the following types:

- *IPv4*—Allows you to specify an IPv4 address block in CIDR notation
- *Ipv6A*—Allows you to specify an IPv6 address block in CIDR notation
- *VNet*—Allows you to specify selected VNet subnets
- *Service tag*—Allows you to specify service tags

Rules are evaluated based on their priority, which you assign when creating an access restriction rule; the rule with the lowest priority takes precedence. To configure access restrictions, you need to have at least the following permissions on the subnet or at a higher level:

- Microsoft.Web/sites/config/read
- Microsoft.Web/sites/config/write
- Microsoft.Network/virtualNetworks/subnets/joinViaServiceEndpoint/action (only needed for VNet-type rules)

> **NOTE** At maximum, you can have 512 access restriction rules. If your organization requires more, you can use Azure App Gateway or Azure Front Door (see chapter 3). Access restrictions apply to inbound traffic only, and they can't be used for traffic entering through a private endpoint. To configure restrictions to private endpoints, you can use NSGs.

If you need to restrict the IP addresses from which your Azure App Service–hosted workloads can be accessed, you can use an IP-based access restriction rule.

IP-BASED ACCESS RESTRICTION RULE

To use IP-based access restriction rules, your app needs to be in an Azure App Service. When a request is made to your Azure App Service–hosted workloads, the originating IP address is checked against the rules you define in your access restriction list. If the IP address matches any of the IP address blocks you defined, then, depending on the action you specify, access is either allowed or denied. Say you have an app Contoso-WebApp001 and that you want to restrict access only to 122.131.144.0/24. To do so, you can create an IP-based access restriction rule by running the following CLI command in Azure Cloud Shell.

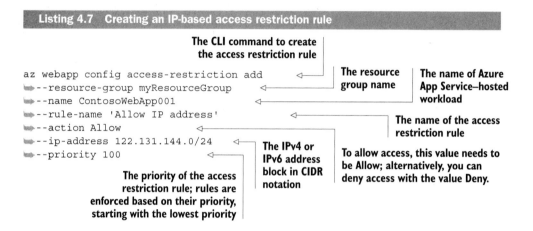

Listing 4.7 Creating an IP-based access restriction rule

After this command runs, it creates an IP-based access restriction rule, as you can see from the following output:

```
...
[
  {
    "action": "Allow",
    "description": null,
    "headers": null,
    "ipAddress": "122.131.144.0/24",
    "name": "Allow IP address",
    "priority": 100,
    "subnetMask": null,
    "subnetTrafficTag": null,
    "tag": "Default",
    "vnetSubnetResourceId": null,
    "vnetTrafficTag": null
  },
  {
    "action": "Deny",
    "description": "Deny all access",
    "headers": null,
    "ipAddress": "Any",
    "name": "Deny all",
```

```
        "priority": 2147483647,
        "subnetMask": null,
        "subnetTrafficTag": null,
        "tag": null,
        "vnetSubnetResourceId": null,
        "vnetTrafficTag": null
    }
]...
```

The output shows that a second rule has been added. After you add an access restriction rule, an implicit rule is added automatically that denies all traffic. This rule has the highest priority and, as such, only comes into effect when no other rules are matched.

IP-based access restriction rules are useful and serve their intended purpose. However, with the proliferation of remote work, IP addresses can change frequently. In addition, you might be using services that typically don't use fixed IP addresses, making IP-based access restriction rules cumbersome to use. Another type of access restriction rule you can create is based on type VNet and is called a service endpoint–based rule.

SERVICE ENDPOINT–BASED ACCESS RESTRICTION RULE

Service endpoint–based rules can restrict inbound access to your Azure App Service–hosted workloads so that the originating IP address is from a VNet subnet you specify. Using service endpoints to restrict access to apps that run in an App Service Environment is not supported. If your app is in an App Service Environment, you can restrict access by creating an IP-based access restriction rule (as discussed in the previous section).

Say that for your app `ContosoWebApp001`, you want to restrict access to subnet `VMSubnet` in `Contoso-VNet1`. To do so, you can create a service endpoint–based access restriction rule by running the following CLI command in Azure Cloud Shell.

> **Listing 4.8 Creating a service endpoint–based access restriction rule**

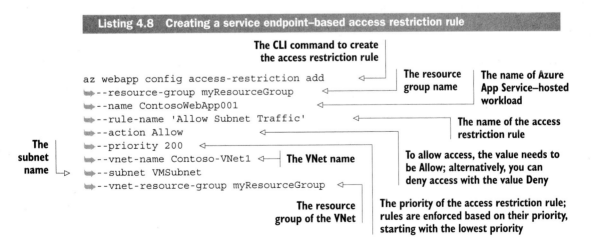

The CLI command to create the access restriction rule

```
az webapp config access-restriction add
  --resource-group myResourceGroup
  --name ContosoWebApp001
  --rule-name 'Allow Subnet Traffic'
  --action Allow
  --priority 200
  --vnet-name Contoso-VNet1
  --subnet VMSubnet
  --vnet-resource-group myResourceGroup
```

The subnet name

The VNet name

The resource group of the VNet

The resource group name

The name of Azure App Service–hosted workload

The name of the access restriction rule

To allow access, the value needs to be Allow; alternatively, you can deny access with the value Deny

The priority of the access restriction rule; rules are enforced based on their priority, starting with the lowest priority

After this command runs, it creates a service endpoint–based access restriction rule. Your output should look similar to the following:

```
...
  {
    "action": "Allow",
    "description": null,
    "headers": null,
    "ipAddress": null,
    "name": "Allow Subnet Traffic",
    "priority": 200,
    "subnetMask": null,
    "subnetTrafficTag": null,
    "tag": "Default",
    "vnetSubnetResourceId": "/subscriptions/00000000-0000-0000-0000
    ➥-000000000000/resourceGroups/myResourceGroup/providers
    ➥/Microsoft.Network/virtualNetworks/Contoso-VNet1/subnets/VMSubnet",
    "vnetTrafficTag": null
  },
...
```

Exercise 4.3

For extra practice, select another VNet in your Azure environment. Then, for an Azure App Service workload, use Azure CLI to restrict inbound access so that the originating IP address is from a VNet subnet you selected. This exercise helps solidify your knowledge of using service endpoint–based access restriction rules.

In addition to IP- and service endpoint–based rules, you can also create rules using Azure service tags.

SERVICE TAG–BASED ACCESS RESTRICTION RULE

With service tag–based rules, you can restrict inbound access to your Azure App Service–hosted workloads so that the originating IP address is from a defined set of IP addresses for Azure services. Effectively, this allows you to filter inbound traffic coming from certain Azure services.

Imagine that for your app `ContosoWebApp001`, you want to restrict access to an Azure Front Door instance and include an HTTP header restriction. Header restrictions can be used for any rule type, and their intended use is to inspect the incoming request and filter based on the HTTP header value. To do so, you can create a service endpoint–based access restriction rule by running the following CLI command in Azure Cloud Shell.

Listing 4.9 Creating a service tag–based access restriction rule

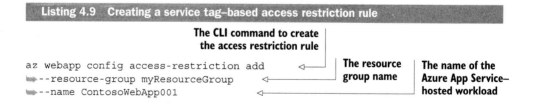

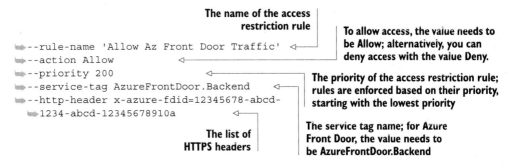

After this command runs, it creates a service tag–based access restriction rule, as you can see from the following output:

```
...
{
    "action": "Allow",
    "description": null,
    "headers": {
      "x-azure-fdid": [
        "12345678-abcd-1234-abcd-12345678910a"
      ]
    },
    "ipAddress": "AzureFrontDoor.Backend",
    "name": "Allow Az Front Door Traffic",
    "priority": 200,
    "subnetMask": null,
    "subnetTrafficTag": null,
    "tag": "ServiceTag",
    "vnetSubnetResourceId": null,
    "vnetTrafficTag": null
},
...
```

In addition to filtering access to your Azure App Service–hosted workloads, another important aspect when securing Azure App Service is preventing *subdomain takeover*.

4.5.3   Subdomain takeover

Subdomain takeover is a serious threat that affects organizations that routinely create and delete many Azure resources. It enables bad actors (like the fictional character Eve) to redirect network traffic intended for your domain to their site, which they can then use to perform malicious activities, including, among others, phishing campaigns and credential harvesting.

Subdomain takeover typically happens when you have a record in your DNS zone that points to an Azure resource that has been deprovisioned. This is commonly referred to as a *dangling DNS*. It provides the bad actor with a window of opportunity to provision an Azure resource with exactly the same fully qualified domain name (FQDN) as the Azure resource you deprovisioned. By doing so, the bad actor uses the fact that the record in your DNS zone wasn't removed and still points to the Azure resource you deprovisioned. If the bad actor creates an Azure resource with the same

FQDN as the Azure resource that you deprovisioned, the record in your DNS zone redirects traffic meant for your domain to the Azure resource that the bad actor created.

SUBDOMAIN TAKEOVER IN ACTION

Imagine the following example. You create an Azure resource to host your web application. When creating this Azure resource, you provision it with the following FQDN: `app-bestwebapp-dev-001.azurewebsites.net`. To redirect users to your web application, you insert a record in your DNS zone with the subdomain `bestwebapp` `.mycompany.com`. This ensures that traffic intended for `bestwebapp.mycompany.com` is routed to your Azure resource hosting the web application.

Now, imagine that for some reason (for example, no longer being needed), the Azure resource that you provisioned is deleted, and the record you created for that resource wasn't removed from your DNS zone. If the record is not removed, it's advertised as still active, even though it doesn't route traffic to an actual Azure resource (because you deleted it). This dangling DNS can be picked up by Eve and other bad actors, who can then take over your DNS subdomain by assigning it to their subscription's Azure resource. Eve can simply provision an Azure resource with the same FQDN you used for the deleted Azure resource (namely, `app-bestwebapp-dev` `-001.azurewebsites.net`). The record in your DNS zone still points to this FQDN and thus allows traffic to be sent to Eve's site, where Eve can use it to perform malicious activities, such as phishing campaigns.

PREVENTING SUBDOMAIN TAKEOVER

To prevent subdomain takeover, you can use Azure App Service's custom domain verification to create a special type of record when creating DNS entries. Creating an `asuid.{subdomain}`record of type TXT with the Domain Verification ID prevents another Azure subscription from taking over your subdomain. In chapter 7, I'll introduce you to Microsoft Defender for App Service, which you can use to detect dangling DNS records and protect your domains.

> ### Using Microsoft Defender for Cloud to monitor Azure App Service
>
> In addition to detecting dangling DNS, Microsoft Defender for Cloud can be used to monitor your Azure App Service resources for suspicious activities indicative of a web application attack. I'll explain Defender for Cloud in greater detail in chapters 6 and 7, where I discuss how you can use its monitoring and continuous assessment capabilities to secure Azure App Service and other Azure resources.

Another important aspect of securing your Azure App Service resources is ensuring they're patched.

4.5.4 *OS and application-stack patching*

It's important to ensure that Azure App Service–hosted workloads you're using are patched and kept up to date. One of the advantages of using Azure App Service is that it's a PaaS service, which means that the public cloud provider (in this case, Microsoft) is responsible for keeping the OS and application stack patched and up to date. Azure manages the patching of both the physical servers and VMs that run the Azure App Service resources. It provides patches on a monthly basis, unless the need for patching is immediate (such as in the case of a zero-day vulnerability), in which case it handles the patching with a higher priority.

As for the patching of the application stack, new stable versions are added periodically. Some versions may overwrite the existing installation, meaning that your application automatically runs on the latest version of the application stack (with no backward-compatibility problems), whereas others might be installed side by side. A side-by-side installation gives you control over when to upgrade your application to the new version, but you need to do it manually by upgrading to the latest version.

> **NOTE** For manually upgrading supported language runtimes (such as Node.js or Python), you can start at http://mng.bz/5wG8.

This chapter is about securing commonly used compute resources in Azure. Compute resources are a foundational building block of any public cloud environment. But they're not alone. Another foundational building block of public cloud environments is data (or Azure services that store data), which I'll teach you how to secure in the next chapter.

4.6   Answers to exercises

Exercise 4.1

To connect to a Linux VM using your browser and the Azure portal, perform the following actions:

1   Navigate to the Azure portal with the Reader role assigned to the necessary resources.
2   Choose the Linux VM to which you want to connect.
3   On the left-hand side, under Operations, choose Bastion.
4   Enter 22 for the port number and select SSH for the protocol to connect to the Linux VM.
5   In the Authentication Type, select Password.
6   Fill out the username and password fields.
7   Click Connect to establish a connection to the Linux VM.

To connect to a Windows VM using your browser and the Azure portal, perform the following actions:

1   Navigate to the Azure portal with the Reader role assigned to the necessary resources.
2   Choose the Linux VM to which you want to connect.
3   On the left-hand side, under Operations, choose Bastion.
4   Enter 3389 for the port number and select RDP for the protocol to connect to the Windows VM.

   5 In the Authentication Type, select Password.

   6 Fill out the username and password fields.

   7 Click Connect to establish a connection to the Linux VM.

Exercise 4.2

```
az network bastion ssh
➥--name contosoBastion
➥--resource-group myResourceGroup
➥--target-resource-id /subscriptions/00000000-0000-0000-0000-000000000000
  ➥/resourceGroups/myResourceGroup/providers/Microsoft.Compute
  ➥/virtualMachines/ContosoVM001
➥--auth-type "password"
➥--username "<Username>"
```

Exercise 4.3

```
az webapp config access-restriction add
➥--resource-group <resourceGroup>
➥--name <AzureAppServiceWorkload>
➥--rule-name 'Allow Subnet Traffic'
➥--action Allow
➥--priority 200
➥--vnet-name <vnet>
➥--subnet <subnet>
➥--vnet-resource-group <vnetResourceGroup>
```

Summary

- By deploying an Azure Bastion instance, you can provision a bastion host, located in front of your Azure VMs, that is managed and hardened by Microsoft. You can then use this Azure Bastion instance to provide secure access to your VMs over TLS without needing to publicly expose RDP or SSH ports on your VMs.
- To connect to Azure Bastion, you can use a variety of options, including the Azure portal, native RDP client, and native SSH client.
- When building container images, you should use trusted base images to create your container images. When images are in a container registry, you should continue to scan them for any vulnerabilities—specifically for any zero-day vulnerabilities—that may have surfaced since you moved the images to the container registry. This capability, as well as monitoring your Kubernetes clusters for threats, are covered in chapter 7.
- Access restrictions allow you to restrict access to your Azure App Service–hosted workloads. Access restrictions are based on rules, which can be of various types. These rules provide you with an effective way to restrict access based on IP addresses originating from specific locations, subnets, or Azure services.
- It's of paramount importance to ensure that you remove records from your DNS zone that point to deleted Azure resources. Not doing so provides bad actors with a window of opportunity to perform a subdomain takeover and redirect traffic meant for your domain to their site in order to use it for malicious activities. Monitoring your Azure App Service–hosted workloads for threats is covered in chapter 7.

Securing data in Azure Storage accounts: Azure Key Vault

This chapter covers

- Securing storage accounts
- Managing storage encryption
- Securing Azure Key Vault

In 2017, *The Economist* published an article (http://mng.bz/6Dzp) that asserted that data, not oil, had risen to become the world's most valuable resource over the previous decade. This notion that data has become the new oil highlights data's importance to businesses. Similar to how oil is used to power the vehicles that you see on roads (unless you live surrounded by electric vehicles), data is used to power better decision-making in organizations.

If data is indeed the new oil, you can consider Azure as the pipeline through which that new oil flows. As you can imagine, securing that pipeline is pretty darn important. Another way of looking at data is to consider it the *crown jewels of an organization*—a commonly used phrase to emphasize the importance of data and to position it as one of the most critical assets a business possesses.

Regardless of whether you consider data the crown jewels or the new oil, both comparisons underscore the intrinsic value that data holds to organizations and its importance to their daily operations. How to secure your crown jewels or your oil pipelines against bad actors and the fictitious character Eve is what this chapter teaches you.

As you can imagine, data comes in different forms and can be stored in different places. Data can range from customer information that your business collects to confidential earnings reports that you keep, intellectual property, medical research, and employee social security numbers. This data can reside in different places. When it comes to Azure, the most commonly used services for data storage are *storage accounts, databases,* and *Azure Key Vault.* I'll cover how to secure databases in chapters 6 and 7. Therefore, to help you keep the crown jewels (or the oil pipelines) of your organization safe, I'll focus on teaching you how to secure various aspects of storage accounts and key vaults in Azure that are used to store your data, starting with storage accounts.

> **NOTE** To follow along with the exercises in this chapter, you can use the GitHub repository (https://github.com/bmagusic/azure-security).

5.1 *Securing storage accounts*

An Azure Storage account is an Azure resource accessible over HTTP or HTTPS that can contain various Azure Storage data objects such as blobs, disks, tables, queues, and files. It can vary in performance tiers (premium or standard), access tiers (hot or cool), and deployment models (Resource Manager or classic). Depending on your scenario, you can choose one of the following Azure Storage accounts:

- Standard general purpose v2—Supports block storage (including Data Lake Storage), queue storage, table storage, and Azure files
- Premium block blobs—Supports block storage (including Data Lake Storage)
- Premium page blobs—Supports page blobs only
- Premium file shares—Supports Azure file shares only

To create a storage account to use throughout this chapter (if you don't already have one), run the command in the following listing.

Listing 5.1 Creating a storage account

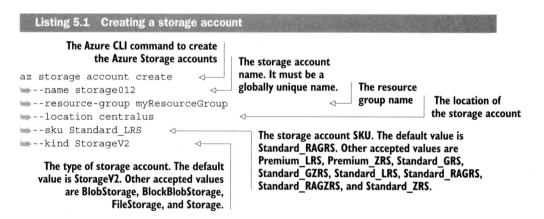

```
az storage account create
    --name storage012
    --resource-group myResourceGroup
    --location centralus
    --sku Standard_LRS
    --kind StorageV2
```

The Azure CLI command to create the Azure Storage accounts

The storage account name. It must be a globally unique name.

The resource group name

The location of the storage account

The type of storage account. The default value is StorageV2. Other accepted values are BlobStorage, BlockBlobStorage, FileStorage, and Storage.

The storage account SKU. The default value is Standard_RAGRS. Other accepted values are Premium_LRS, Premium_ZRS, Standard_GRS, Standard_GZRS, Standard_LRS, Standard_RAGRS, Standard_RAGZRS, and Standard_ZRS.

After this command runs, it creates the storage account. Your output looks similar to the following:

```
...
  "primaryLocation": "centralus",
  "privateEndpointConnections": [],
  "provisioningState": "Succeeded",
  "publicNetworkAccess": null,
  "resourceGroup": "chapter5",
  "routingPreference": null,
  "sasPolicy": null,
  "secondaryEndpoints": {
    "blob": "https://storage012-secondary.blob.core.windows.net/",
    "dfs": "https://storage012-secondary.dfs.core.windows.net/",
    "file": null,
    "internetEndpoints": null,
    "microsoftEndpoints": null,
    "queue": "https://storage012-secondary.queue.core.windows.net/",
    "table": "https://storage012-secondary.table.core.windows.net/",
    "web": "https://storage012-secondary.z19.web.core.windows.net/"
  },
  "secondaryLocation": "eastus2",
  "sku": {
    "name": "Standard_RAGRS",
    "tier": "Standard"
  },
...
```

After you create a storage account, it has a public endpoint accessible via the internet. By default, storage accounts accept connections from clients on any network. An important aspect of securing your storage accounts is blocking and restricting network traffic. For this, you can use Azure Storage firewall.

5.1.1 *Azure Storage firewall*

Azure Storage firewall allows you to block access to your storage accounts or restrict access to requests coming from one or more specified public IP addresses, subnets, or even resource instances of some Azure services. You do this by configuring firewall rules. When you configure firewall rules for your storage accounts, by default, Azure Storage firewall blocks incoming requests for data unless the requests are coming from inside of a virtual network (VNet) or allowed public IP addresses. To secure access to your storage accounts, you should first block requests from all networks on the public endpoint of your storage account. Then you can configure firewall rules that allow access from specified VNETs and one or more trusted public IP addresses. You can combine firewall rules that allow both access from specified VNets and public IP addresses on the same storage account.

ALLOW ACCESS FROM SPECIFIC VNETS

Imagine you want to restrict access to your storage account to a specific VNet in your environment that contains a service that needs to access storage accounts to read data—for example, virtual machines (VMs) running the application that Bob, the fictional character used throughout this book, is building. To configure the Azure Storage firewall to allow traffic from specified VNets, run the following command-line interface (CLI) command in Azure Cloud Shell.

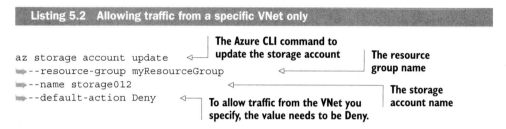

Listing 5.2   Allowing traffic from a specific VNet only

```
az storage account update
--resource-group myResourceGroup
--name storage012
--default-action Deny
```

The Azure CLI command to update the storage account

The resource group name

The storage account name

To allow traffic from the VNet you specify, the value needs to be Deny.

After this command runs, it allows traffic from specific VNets. Your output should look similar to the following:

```
...
  "keyPolicy": null,
  "kind": "StorageV2",
  "largeFileSharesState": null,
  "lastGeoFailoverTime": null,
  "location": "centralus",
  "minimumTlsVersion": "TLS1_0",
  "name": "storage012",
  "networkRuleSet": {
    "bypass": "AzureServices",
    "defaultAction": "Deny",
    "ipRules": [],
    "resourceAccessRules": null,
    "virtualNetworkRules": []
  },
...
```

The VNet and subnet that you want to restrict access to your storage accounts need to have the service endpoint for Azure Storage enabled. To enable it on the existing VNET1 and subnet VMSubnet, run the following CLI command.

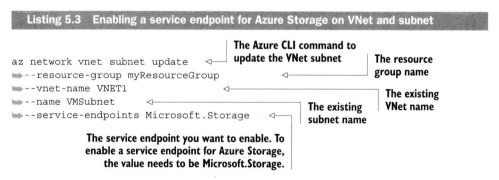

Listing 5.3   Enabling a service endpoint for Azure Storage on VNet and subnet

```
az network vnet subnet update
--resource-group myResourceGroup
--vnet-name VNET1
--name VMSubnet
--service-endpoints Microsoft.Storage
```

The Azure CLI command to update the VNet subnet

The resource group name

The existing VNet name

The existing subnet name

The service endpoint you want to enable. To enable a service endpoint for Azure Storage, the value needs to be Microsoft.Storage.

After this command runs, it enables a service endpoint for Azure Storage on the subnet you specify. Your output should look similar to the following:

```
...
"serviceEndpoints": [
    {
        "locations": [
          "centralus",
          "eastus2"
        ],
        "provisioningState": "Succeeded",
        "service": "Microsoft.Storage"
    }
  ],
...
```

Only after you enable a service endpoint for Azure Storage on the subnet can you add a network rule that restricts access to a VNet and subnet. To do this, run the following CLI command in Azure Cloud Shell.

Listing 5.4 Adding a network rule for a VNet and subnet

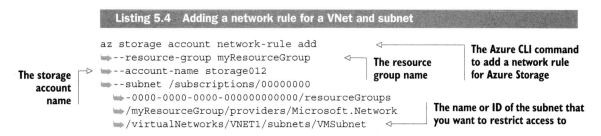

After this command runs, it adds the network rule for the subnet you specify, as you can see from the following output:

```
...
"networkRuleSet": {
    "bypass": "AzureServices",
    "defaultAction": "Deny",
    "ipRules": [],
    "resourceAccessRules": null,
    "virtualNetworkRules": [
      {
        "action": "Allow",
        "state": "Succeeded",
        "virtualNetworkResourceId": "/subscriptions/
        00000000-0000-0000-0000-000000000000/resourceGroups/myResourceGroup
        /providers/Microsoft.Network/virtualNetworks/VNET1/subnets/VMSubnet"
      }
    ]
},...
```

In addition to restricting access to a VNET and subnet (such as one containing your VMs), you can also restrict access to a specific IPv4 address range.

Allowing access from specific IPv4 address ranges

You can restrict access to an IPv4 address range corresponding to your office location by running the following CLI command.

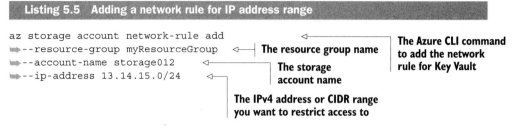

```
az storage account network-rule add
--resource-group myResourceGroup
--account-name storage012
--ip-address 13.14.15.0/24
```

The resource group name

The storage
account name

The IPv4 address or CIDR range
you want to restrict access to

The Azure CLI command
to add the network
rule for Key Vault

After this command runs, it adds the network rule for an IP address range. Your output should look similar to the following:

```
. . .
"networkRuleSet": {
    "bypass": "AzureServices",
    "defaultAction": "Deny",
    "ipRules": [
      {
        "action": "Allow",
        "ipAddressOrRange": "13.14.15.0/24"
      }
    ],
    "resourceAccessRules": null,
    "virtualNetworkRules": [
      {
        "action": "Allow",
        "state": "Succeeded",
        "virtualNetworkResourceId": "/subscriptions
        /00000000-0000-0000-0000-000000000000/resourceGroups/chapter5
        /providers/Microsoft.Network/virtualNetworks/VNET1/subnets/VMSubnet"
      }
    ]
. . .
```

As you can see from the output, you can combine firewall rules that allow both access from specified VNets and public IP addresses on the same storage account.

In addition to restricting access to storage accounts, an important aspect of securing storage accounts is authorizing control and data plane operations. In Azure, operations are divided into two categories: control plane and data plane operations. For example, you can manage resources in your subscription, such as by creating and deleting a storage account, through the control plane. On the other hand, you use the data plane to read and write data to the storage account. An important aspect of securing your storage accounts is to provide authorization for both, starting with *authorizing control plane operations.*

5.1.2   *Authorizing control plane operations*

You can restrict who can delete and manage storage accounts in your Azure environment. Azure Storage supports using Azure role-based access control (RBAC) to authorize control plane operations. You can choose from various built-in roles that grant permissions to invoke control plane operations (such as creating and deleting storage accounts). The built-in RBAC roles specific to control plane operations in Azure Storage are the following:

- *Owner*—Has full access to all storage resources, including the right to delegate access to other users
- *Contributor*—Can access and manage all types of storage resources but can't delegate access to other users
- *Reader*—Can view information about existing storage resources but cannot view the account keys
- *Storage Account Contributor*—Can manage storage resources and create and manage subscription resource group deployments
- *User Access Administrator*—Can manage access to storage resources and assign any permissions to themselves and others
- *Virtual Machine Contributor*—Can manage VMs but not the storage resources to which the VMs are connected

NOTE You can see a list of all available Azure built-in roles here: http://mng.bz/o19y.

These Azure RBAC roles are specifically designed to be used with the Azure Storage resource provider. You can assign these (as well as other) Azure RBAC roles at various scopes. For control plane operations, you can assign a role at the management group, subscription, resource group, or storage account level. When determining the scope, as a best practice, you should adhere to the principle of least privilege (see chapter 2) and only grant the narrowest possible scope. The narrowest possible scope in the case of control plane operations for Azure Storage is assigning roles at the storage account level, whereas the broadest is at the management group level.

Control plane operations on Azure Storage resources don't include permissions to access data stored in storage resources. However, if the Azure RBAC role supports the `Microsoft.Storage/storageAccounts/listkeys/action`, you can list storage account keys to access data stored in storage resources. Therefore, you can consider account access keys as the admin password for your storage resources. Of the built-in RBAC roles specific to control plane operations in Azure Storage I listed previously, only the Reader role doesn't have access to account keys. To control permissions to access data stored in Azure Storage resources, you can authorize data plane operations.

5.1.3 *Authorizing data plane operations*

Say you want to allow someone to manage configurations on your storage accounts but not be able to read data stored inside of those accounts. Azure Storage provides a variety of options for authorizing data plane operations, including the following:

- *Microsoft Entra ID integration*—Supports Azure blobs, queues, and table resources
- *Shared access signature*—Supports Azure blobs, files (REST), queues, and table resources

- *Storage account key*—Supports Azure blobs, files (Server Message Block and REST), queues, and table resources

Other options include on-premise Active Directory Domain Services and Azure AD Domain Services. However, I'll cover the following authorization options because they're widely used: Microsoft Entra ID integration, shared access signatures (SAS), and storage account key.

MICROSOFT ENTRA ID INTEGRATION

To authorize data plane operations, such as creating a container or getting properties from an existing container, you can use Microsoft Entra ID. This is the recommended approach for authorizing data plane operations because Microsoft Entra ID provides authorized access using Azure RBAC. To create a container using Microsoft Entra ID integration, run the following command.

Listing 5.6   Authorizing data plane operations using Microsoft Entra ID

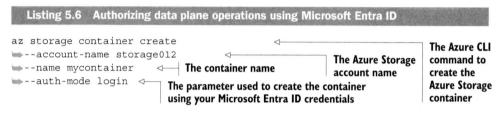

After this command runs, it creates the container using your Microsoft Entra ID credentials. Your output should look similar to the following:

```
{
  "accessTier": "Hot",
  "allowBlobPublicAccess": true,
  "allowCrossTenantReplication": null,
  "allowSharedKeyAccess": null,
  "allowedCopyScope": null,
  "azureFilesIdentityBasedAuthentication": null,
  "blobRestoreStatus": null,
  "creationTime": "2022-12-03T21:56:18.466263+00:00",
  "customDomain": null,
  "defaultToOAuthAuthentication": null,
  "dnsEndpointType": null,
  "enableHttpsTrafficOnly": true,
  "enableNfsV3": null,
  "encryption": {
    "encryptionIdentity": null,
    "keySource": "Microsoft.Storage",
    "keyVaultProperties": null,
    "requireInfrastructureEncryption": true,
    "services": {
      "blob": {
        "enabled": true,
        "keyType": "Account",
        "lastEnabledTime": "2022-12-03T21:56:18.606901+00:00"
      },
```

```
      "file": {
        "enabled": true,
        "keyType": "Account",
        "lastEnabledTime": "2022-12-03T21:56:18.606901+00:00"
      },
      "queue": null,
      "table": null
  }
...
```

With Microsoft Entra ID integration, you can scope access at the following scopes:

- *Management group*—Access applies to all subscriptions > resource groups > storage accounts > containers > blobs.
- *Subscription*—Access applies to all resource groups > storage accounts > containers > blobs.
- *Resource group*—Access applies to all storage accounts > containers > blobs.
- *Individual storage account*—Access applies to all containers > blobs.
- *Individual container*—Access applies to all blobs in a container.

When determining at what scope to assign permissions, you should adhere to the principle of least privilege and assign the narrowest possible scope.

SAS

An SAS is another way to authorize data plane operations in Azure Storage resources. By using an SAS, you can perform the data plane operations that are permitted by the SAS. Imagine you want to provide one of your partner organizations with restricted access to an individual container called mycontainer. With an SAS, you can provide them with access to the individual container for a specific period of time with a set of permissions you specify. To create a container using an SAS, run the following command.

Listing 5.7 Authorizing data plane operations using an SAS token

After this command runs, it creates the container using your SAS token. Your output should look similar to the following:

```
{
  "accessTier": "Hot",
  "allowBlobPublicAccess": true,
  "allowCrossTenantReplication": null,
  "allowSharedKeyAccess": null,
  "allowedCopyScope": null,
  "azureFilesIdentityBasedAuthentication": null,
  "blobRestoreStatus": null,
```

```
"creationTime": "2022-12-03T21:56:18.466263+00:00",
"customDomain": null,
"defaultToOAuthAuthentication": null,
"dnsEndpointType": null,
"enableHttpsTrafficOnly": true,
"enableNfsV3": null,
"encryption": {
  "encryptionIdentity": null,
  "keySource": "Microsoft.Storage",
  "keyVaultProperties": null,
  "requireInfrastructureEncryption": true,
  "services": {
    "blob": {
      "enabled": true,
      "keyType": "Account",
      "lastEnabledTime": "2022-12-03T21:56:18.606901+00:00"
    },
    "file": {
      "enabled": true,
      "keyType": "Account",
      "lastEnabledTime": "2022-12-03T21:56:18.606901+00:00"
    },
    "queue": null,
    "table": null
  }
...
```

Another way of authorizing data plane operations is by using storage account keys.

STORAGE ACCOUNT KEYS

Storage account keys, also known as storage access keys, are a less secure option than Microsoft Entra ID integration and SAS for authorizing data plane operations to Azure Storage resources. Storage account keys provide more permissions than, for example, SAS, and they provide complete access to your storage accounts, including to the data stored in those storage accounts. Therefore, the recommendation is to use Microsoft Entra ID integration or SAS whenever possible rather than storage account keys for authorization of data plane operations.

Each storage account has two account keys. Should either key be disclosed or get compromised, all data in your storage account is at risk of being compromised. Therefore, if you're using storage account keys, such as for an application that is running in Azure, the recommendation is to rotate the keys periodically. This limits the effects should either of the keys be compromised.

To authorize data plane operations using a storage account key, run the following command.

Listing 5.8 Authorizing data plane operations using a storage account key

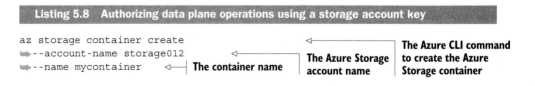

```
➡--account-key 2015-02-21&st=2015-07...        ◁──┐ The storage
➡--auth-mode key   ◁──┐ You need to use the key       │ account key
                      │ parameter for authorization   ⌐
                      │ via the storage account key.
```

After this command runs, it creates the container using your storage account key. Your output should look similar to the following:

```json
{
  "accessTier": "Hot",
  "allowBlobPublicAccess": true,
  "allowCrossTenantReplication": null,
  "allowSharedKeyAccess": null,
  "allowedCopyScope": null,
  "azureFilesIdentityBasedAuthentication": null,
  "blobRestoreStatus": null,
  "creationTime": "2022-12-03T21:56:18.466263+00:00",
  "customDomain": null,
  "defaultToOAuthAuthentication": null,
  "dnsEndpointType": null,
  "enableHttpsTrafficOnly": true,
  "enableNfsV3": null,
  "encryption": {
    "encryptionIdentity": null,
    "keySource": "Microsoft.Storage",
    "keyVaultProperties": null,
    "requireInfrastructureEncryption": true,
    "services": {
      "blob": {
        "enabled": true,
        "keyType": "Account",
        "lastEnabledTime": "2022-12-03T21:56:18.606901+00:00"
      },
      "file": {
        "enabled": true,
        "keyType": "Account",
        "lastEnabledTime": "2022-12-03T21:56:18.606901+00:00"
      },
      "queue": null,
      "table": null
    }
  }
...
```

In addition to authorization of control and data plane operations, other important aspects of securing Azure Storage resources (and the data that resides in them) are encryption and using service-side encryption (SSE).

5.1.4 SSE

SSE is used by Azure Storage to encrypt your data in Azure automatically at no additional cost. Data is encrypted using 256-bit Advanced Encryption Standard (AES) encryption, one of the strongest block ciphers out there. SSE is applied regardless of the deployment model (Resource Manager or classic), performance tier (premium or standard), or access tier (hot or cool) of your Azure Storage accounts. It encrypts all Azure Storage data objects, such as blobs, disks, tables, queues, and files, including encrypting all object metadata. If your blob was created after October 20, 2017, it is encrypted by default using SSE. Blobs created before that date continue to be encrypted by Microsoft through a background process. To determine whether your blob is encrypted with SSE, you can check the value of the created property (which will tell you when it was created) or by running the following command.

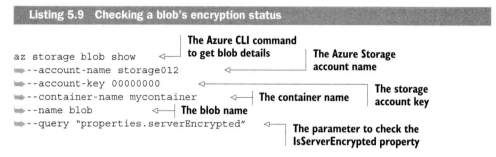

Listing 5.9   Checking a blob's encryption status

After this command runs, the value returned is `true` for encrypted blobs. If your blob was created before October 20, 2017, and isn't encrypted, you can force encryption by downloading and re-uploading the blob (for example, with the help of AzCopy). By default, data in storage accounts is encrypted using Microsoft-managed encryption keys. Alternatively, you can encrypt data in storage accounts using your own encryption key, which is discussed next.

5.1.5   Encryption key management

When managing encryption using your own keys, you can choose from the following options:

- *Customer-managed key with Azure Key Vault*—This option allows you to use your own encryption key to encrypt and decrypt data in Blob Storage and Azure Files. The key needs to be stored either in Azure Key Vault or Azure Key Vault Managed Hardware Security Model (HSM).
- *Customer-provided key on Blob Storage operations*—This option allows a client to provide an encryption key when making requests against Azure Blob storage. The keys can be stored in Azure Key Vault or in an alternative key store.

Using a customer-managed key with Azure Key Vault is widely done, and it's something you might also encounter. Therefore, to teach you how to manage encryption using your own (customer-managed) key, I'll choose this option.

5.1.6   Encryption using a customer-managed key

Using your own encryption key allows you to specify a customer-managed key that controls access to the key that encrypts your data. This key can be stored in Azure Key Vault or Azure Key Vault Managed HSM. The Key Vault can be in a different tenant, region, and subscription compared to the storage account. When deciding to use customer-managed keys, you can either create your own keys or use the Azure Key Vault APIs to generate keys. Regardless of which one of these two options you choose, you need an Azure Key Vault admin role to grant permissions to the encryption key for a managed identity. The managed identity can be either one that you manage (user assigned) or a managed identity associated with the storage account itself (system managed).

To access a customer-managed key in Azure Key Vault, the managed identity you use needs to have at least the following permissions: `get`, `wrapkey`, and `unwrapkey`. When an Azure Storage admin configures encryption with a customer-managed key, the storage account uses the managed identity (either user or system assigned) to which the Azure Key Vault admin has granted permissions to authenticate access to Azure Key Vault using Microsoft Entra ID as the identity provider. Then, Azure Storage wraps the account encryption key with the customer-managed key in Azure Key Vault and sends requests to Azure Key Vault to unwrap the account encryption key for encryption and decryption purposes. Figure 5.1 depicts this process.

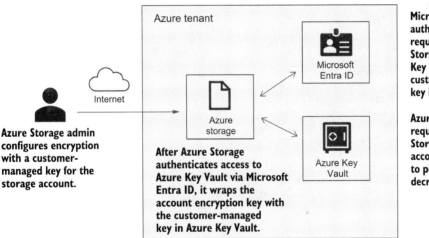

Figure 5.1 Azure Storage encryption using a customer-managed key

To encrypt data stored in Queue and Table storage using a customer-managed key, you need to include the `--encryption-key-type-for-queue` and `--encryption-key-type-for-table` parameters, respectively, with the value `Account` when creating the storage account (listing 5.1). This ensures these services are included in the customer-managed key protection, as the protection of data stored in Queue and Table storage isn't automatically enabled when customer-managed keys are enabled for the storage account.

5.1.7   *Encryption using a customer-managed key in action*

To enable encryption to use customer-managed keys, you need to have either an Azure Key Vault or Azure Key Vault Managed HSM to store the encryption key. If you need to create a new Azure Key Vault, run the following command.

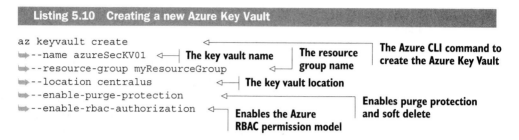

Listing 5.10   Creating a new Azure Key Vault

After this command runs, it creates the key vault, as you can see from the following output:

```
{
  "id": "/subscriptions/00000000-0000-0000-0000-000000000000/resourceGroups
    /chapter5/providers/Microsoft.KeyVault/vaults/azureSecKV01",
  "location": "centralus",
  "name": "azureSecKV01",
  "properties": {
    "accessPolicies": [],
    "createMode": null,
    "enablePurgeProtection": true,
    "enableRbacAuthorization": true,
    "enableSoftDelete": true,
    "enabledForDeployment": false,
    "enabledForDiskEncryption": null,
    "enabledForTemplateDeployment": null,
    "hsmPoolResourceId": null,
    "networkAcls": null,
    "privateEndpointConnections": null,
    "provisioningState": "Succeeded",
    "publicNetworkAccess": "Enabled",
    "sku": {
      "family": "A",
      "name": "standard"
    },
    "softDeleteRetentionInDays": 90,
    "tenantId": "00000000-0000-0000-0000-000000000000",
    "vaultUri": "https://azureseckv01.vault.azure.net/"
  },
  ...
```

To create an encryption key in the key vault, you need to have the Key Vault Crypto Officer role (you don't need more information about this role here, but I provide it later in this chapter). To assign this role to a user, such as Bob, one of the fictional characters in this book, run the following command.

Listing 5.11 Assigning the Key Vault Crypto Officer role

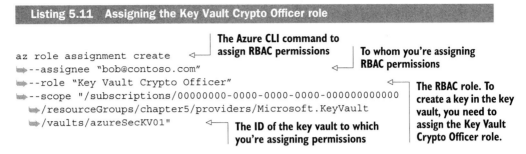

```
az role assignment create
--assignee "bob@contoso.com"
--role "Key Vault Crypto Officer"
--scope "/subscriptions/00000000-0000-0000-0000-000000000000
/resourceGroups/chapter5/providers/Microsoft.KeyVault
/vaults/azureSecKV01"
```

The Azure CLI command to assign RBAC permissions

To whom you're assigning RBAC permissions

The RBAC role. To create a key in the key vault, you need to assign the Key Vault Crypto Officer role.

The ID of the key vault to which you're assigning permissions

After this command runs, it assigns the Key Vault Crypto Officer role. Your output should look similar to the following:

```
{
  "canDelegate": null,
  "condition": null,
  "conditionVersion": null,
  "description": null,
  "id": "/subscriptions/00000000-0000-0000-0000-000000000000/resourceGroups
  /chapter5/providers/Microsoft.KeyVault/vaults/azureSecKV01/providers
  /Microsoft.Authorization/roleAssignments
  /97cba6d2-2597-4e68-92e3-20cf509b9003",
  "name": "97cba6d2-2597-4e68-92e3-20cf509b9003",
  "principalId": "a2caa967-d1f6-4a9b-a246-dab5d8a93b91",
  "principalType": "User",
  "resourceGroup": "chapter5",
  "roleDefinitionId": "/subscriptions/00000000-0000-0000-0000-000000000000
  /providers/Microsoft.Authorization/roleDefinitions
  /14b46e9e-c2b7-41b4-b07b-48a6ebf60603",
  "scope": "/subscriptions/00000000-0000-0000-0000-000000000000/resourceGroups
  /chapter5/providers/Microsoft.KeyVault/vaults/azureSecKV01",
  "type": "Microsoft.Authorization/roleAssignments"
}
...
```

After you have assigned your user the Key Vault Crypto Office role, you can proceed with adding a key to the key vault. To add a key to the key vault, run the following command.

Listing 5.12 Adding a key to the key vault

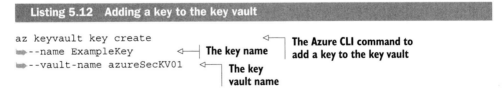

```
az keyvault key create
--name ExampleKey
--vault-name azureSecKV01
```

The Azure CLI command to add a key to the key vault

The key name

The key vault name

After this command runs, it adds the key to the key vault. The output should look similar to the following:

```
...
  "key": {
    "crv": null,
```

```
"d": null,
"dp": null,
"dq": null,
"e": "AQAB",
"k": null,
"keyOps": [
  "encrypt",
  "decrypt",
  "sign",
  "verify",
  "wrapKey",
  "unwrapKey"
],
"kid": "https://azureseckv01.vault.azure.net/keys/ExampleKey
➥/8c3ec318a0f6481c9cd380794f8a8431",
"kty": "RSA",
"n": "xIKX67lQ9N6hUb8culHtFOL2TNdSU05kAto28TCBfd6Arsmhw3IzDYEJO3i
  ➥YGuqfhu6mahNAZWrTgo+dfENQiKHkPNJahoB1bxRmeEhxn7TEqu4lTFdSZ3OJPgjDFU9
  ➥+1VI9IPEHr19M1/3b1jrPe7llcxx3ArJOEP/+FbT0q9h2hwJyAdAiMSmjuRWJhyt
  ➥+w0vSiD29oqFL2MM9d1wChuY8N50JlFNLQOYpVziLs5pAUfAOpE4EV1h5BXYOjrooZs
  ➥9QvPT0qPXmD/Eh1rq5v/OsR5Ac2z2vImjU9X6d8XlhvtKFbcn66kaYiTO9tgRH4feS
  ➥42w6nJCi+XOwVOE6DQ==",
"p": null,
"q": null,
"qi": null,
"t": null,
"x": null,
"y": null
},
...
```

For the storage account to access the key vault, you need to use a managed identity. As you recall from chapter 2, managed identity can either be user assigned or system assigned.

A user-assigned managed identity is a standalone Azure resource, whereas a system-assigned managed identity is tied to a specific Azure service (in this case, an Azure Storage account). To enable encryption with a customer-managed key for new storage accounts, you need a user-assigned managed identity, which you must create before you configure a customer-managed key. To enable encryption with a customer-managed key for existing storage accounts, you can use either a user-assigned or system-assigned managed identity.

Before you can use the system-assigned managed identity to authorize access to the key vault containing your customer-managed key, you need to assign it to the storage account. To assign a system-managed identity to the storage account you created at the beginning of the chapter, run the following command.

Listing 5.13 Assigning system-assigned managed identity (existing storage account)

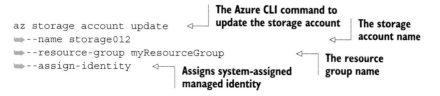

```
az storage account update
⮕--name storage012
⮕--resource-group myResourceGroup
⮕--assign-identity
```

The Azure CLI command to update the storage account

The storage account name

The resource group name

Assigns system-assigned managed identity

After this command runs, it assigns the system-assigned identity to the existing storage account. Your output should look similar to the following:

```
...
"extendedLocation": null,
  "failoverInProgress": null,
  "geoReplicationStats": null,
  "id": "/subscriptions/00000000-0000-0000-0000-000000000000
⮕/resourceGroups/chapter5/providers/Microsoft.Storage/storageAccounts/
⮕storage012",
  "identity": {
    "principalId": "b1c0fcde-adee-45f8-ad61-46dd299bb887",
    "tenantId": "00000000-0000-0000-0000-000000000000",
    "type": "SystemAssigned",
    "userAssignedIdentities": null
  },
  "immutableStorageWithVersioning": null,
  "isHnsEnabled": null,
  "isLocalUserEnabled": null,
  "isSftpEnabled": null,
  "keyCreationTime": {
    "key1": "2022-12-03T21:56:18.591285+00:00",
    "key2": "2022-12-03T21:56:18.591285+00:00"
  },": null
  },
...
```

The system-assigned managed identity must have permission to access the key in the key vault. You can assign the Key Vault Crypto Service Encryption User role to the system-assigned managed identity using the following command.

Listing 5.14 Assigning the required RBAC role to system-assigned managed identity

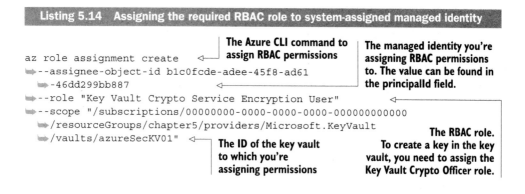

```
az role assignment create
⮕--assignee-object-id b1c0fcde-adee-45f8-ad61
  ⮕-46dd299bb887
⮕--role "Key Vault Crypto Service Encryption User"
⮕--scope "/subscriptions/00000000-0000-0000-0000-000000000000
  ⮕/resourceGroups/chapter5/providers/Microsoft.KeyVault
  ⮕/vaults/azureSecKV01"
```

The Azure CLI command to assign RBAC permissions

The managed identity you're assigning RBAC permissions to. The value can be found in the principalId field.

The ID of the key vault to which you're assigning permissions

The RBAC role. To create a key in the key vault, you need to assign the Key Vault Crypto Officer role.

After this command runs, it assigns the required RBAC role to the system-assigned identity. Your output should look similar to the following:

```
...
{
  "canDelegate": null,
  "condition": null,
  "conditionVersion": null,
  "description": null,
  "id": "/subscriptions/00000000-0000-0000-0000-000000000000/resourceGroups
➥/chapter5/providers/Microsoft.KeyVault/vaults/azureSecKV01/providers
➥/Microsoft.Authorization/roleAssignments/68c08d40-766a-4f48-b924
➥-09023e2d00f9",
  "name": "68c08d40-766a-4f48-b924-09023e2d00f9",
  "principalId": "b1c0fcde-adee-45f8-ad61-46dd299bb887",
  "principalType": "ServicePrincipal",
  "resourceGroup": "chapter5",
  "roleDefinitionId": "/subscriptions/00000000-0000-0000-0000-000000000000
➥/providers/Microsoft.Authorization/roleDefinitions
➥/e147488a-f6f5-4113-8e2d-b22465e65bf6",
  "scope": "/subscriptions/00000000-0000-0000-0000-000000000000
➥/resourceGroups/chapter5/providers/Microsoft.KeyVault/vaults/azureSecKV01",
  "type": "Microsoft.Authorization/roleAssignments"
}
...
```

To configure automatic updating of the key version when using a customer-managed key for an existing storage account, run the following command.

Listing 5.15 Configuring automatic updating of the key version

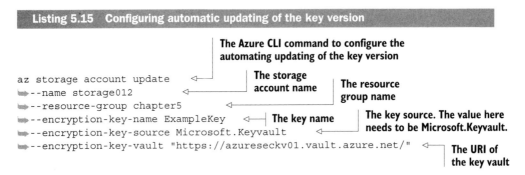

After this command runs, the new key version is automatically updated when a new version of the key becomes available in key vault. Your output should look similar to the following:

```
{
...
  "canDelegate": null,
  "condition": null,
  "conditionVersion": null,
  "description": null,
  "encryption": {
    "encryptionIdentity": null,
```

```
  "keySource": "Microsoft.Keyvault",
  "keyVaultProperties": {
    "currentVersionedKeyExpirationTimestamp": "1970-01-01T00:00:00+00:00",
    "currentVersionedKeyIdentifier": "https://azureseckv01.vault.azure.net
    ➥/keys/ExampleKey/8c3ec318a0f6481c9cd380794f8a8431",
    "keyName": "ExampleKey",
    "keyVaultUri": "https://azureseckv01.vault.azure.net/",
    "keyVersion": null,
    "lastKeyRotationTimestamp": "2022-12-05T01:47:16.548481+00:00"
  },
  "requireInfrastructureEncryption": true,
...
}
```

When encrypting a storage account with a key, the encryption is scoped (or applied) to the entire storage account. To apply encryption to a more granular level, you can use *encryption scopes*.

5.1.8 *Encryption scopes*

With encryption scopes, you can manage encryption with a key that is applied to a container or an individual blob rather than the entire storage account. Say you need to create boundaries between data from different customers inside the same storage account. With encryption scopes, you can do exactly that. Using encryption scopes allows you to specify whether you want to use Microsoft- or customer-managed keys.

ENCRYPTION SCOPES PROTECTED BY MICROSOFT-MANAGED KEYS

To create an encryption scope protected by Microsoft-managed keys on a container called ContosoScope, run the following command.

> Listing 5.16 Creating an encryption scope protected by Microsoft-managed key

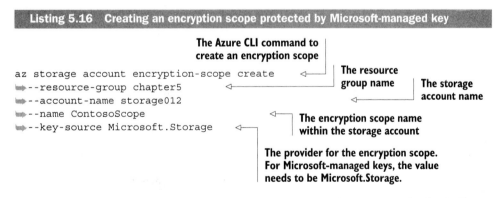

After this command runs, it creates the encryption scope. Your output looks similar to the following:

```
{
  "creationTime": "2022-12-09T00:48:37.530230+00:00",
  "id": "/subscriptions/00000000-0000-0000-0000-000000000000/resourceGroups
  ➥/chapter5/providers/Microsoft.Storage/storageAccounts/storage012
  ➥/encryptionScopes/ContosoScope",
```

```
"keyVaultProperties": {
  "currentVersionedKeyIdentifier": null,
  "keyUri": null,
  "lastKeyRotationTimestamp": null
},
"lastModifiedTime": "2022-12-09T00:48:37.530230+00:00",
"name": "ContosoScope",
"requireInfrastructureEncryption": true,
"resourceGroup": "chapter5",
"source": "Microsoft.Storage",
"state": "Enabled",
"type": "Microsoft.Storage/storageAccounts/encryptionScopes"
  "requireInfrastructureEncryption": true,
}
```

After you create the encryption scope, it's automatically enabled, and you can use it when creating blobs and containers. When you specify an encryption scope while creating a container, it will automatically apply to blobs inside of the specified container. As an alternative to Microsoft-managed keys, you can create encryption scopes protected by customer-managed keys.

ENCRYPTION SCOPES PROTECTED BY CUSTOMER-MANAGED KEYS

Creating an encryption scope using customer-managed keys implies you're using an Azure Key Vault or HSM to store the keys. You first need to assign a managed identity (either user or system assigned) to the storage account on which you'd like to create a new encryption scope. This managed identity needs permission to access the key vault (or HSM) where the keys are stored. Then, you can create the encryption scope by running the following command.

> **Listing 5.17** **Creating an encryption scope protected by a customer-managed key**

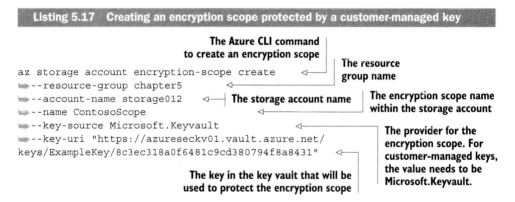

After this command runs, it creates the encryption scope. Your output looks similar to the following:

```
{
  "creationTime": "2022-12-09T00:48:37.530230+00:00",
  "id": "/subscriptions/00000000-0000-0000-0000-000000000000/resourceGroups
➥/chapter5/providers/Microsoft.Storage/storageAccounts/storage012
➥/encryptionScopes/ContosoScope",
```

```
"keyVaultProperties": {
  "currentVersionedKeyIdentifier": "https://azureseckv01.vault.azure.net/
  ➡keys/ExampleKey/8c3ec318a0f6481c9cd380794f8a8431",
  "keyUri": "https://azureseckv01.vault.azure.net/keys/ExampleKey
  ➡/8c3ec318a0f6481c9cd380794f8a8431",
  "lastKeyRotationTimestamp": null
},
"lastModifiedTime": "2022-12-09T01:26:29.646739+00:00",
"name": "ContosoScope",
"requireInfrastructureEncryption": true,
"resourceGroup": "chapter5",
"source": "Microsoft.Keyvault",
"state": "Enabled",
"type": "Microsoft.Storage/storageAccounts/encryptionScopes"
}
```

In addition to creating an encryption scope using customer-managed keys for organizations that have stringent security requirements, you can use *infrastructure encryption.*

5.1.9 Infrastructure encryption

Organizations that require data to be encrypted at the Azure Storage infrastructure level (for example, to be compliant with Federal Information Processing Standard 140-2) can use infrastructure encryption. When you enable infrastructure encryption, your data in Azure Storage is encrypted both at the service level and at the infrastructure level. That is, your data is effectively encrypted twice using 256-bit AES encryption with two different encryption algorithms and keys. Having data encrypted at the infrastructure level, in addition to having it encrypted at the service level, applies a defense-in-depth mindset. Should one of the encryption keys or algorithms be compromised, another is there as a backup. Whereas SSE supports a customer-managed key, infrastructure encryption uses a Microsoft-managed encryption key.

To enable infrastructure encryption for a storage account, the account needs to be of type general purpose v2 or premium block blob, and you need to enable infrastructure encryption at the time the storage account is created.

> **NOTE** You cannot enable infrastructure encryption after the storage account has been created. The same applies to disabling infrastructure encryption: it cannot be disabled after the storage account has been created.

To enable infrastructure encryption, add the `--require-infrastructure -encryption` parameter when creating the storage account, as in the following listing.

Listing 5.18 Creating a storage account with the infrastructure encryption enabled

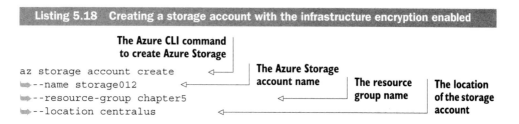

```
                    The Azure CLI command
                    to create Azure Storage

az storage account create          ◁─────┐   The Azure Storage
➡--name storage012          ◁────────────┘   account name        The resource    The location
➡--resource-group chapter5          ◁──────────────────────────  group name      of the storage
➡--location centralus          ◁──────────────────────────────────────────────   account
```

```
➡--sku Standard_RAGRS
➡--kind StorageV2
➡--require-infrastructure-encryption true
```

Enable infrastructure encryption

The type of storage account. The default value is StorageV2. Other accepted values are BlobStorage, BlockBlobStorage, FileStorage, and Storage.

The storage account SKU. The default value is Standard_RAGRS. Other accepted values are Premium_LRS, Premium_ZRS, Standard_GRS, Standard_GZRS, Standard_LRS, Standard_RAGRS, Standard_RAGZRS, and Standard_ZRS.

After this command runs, it creates the storage account with infrastructure encryption enabled, as you can see from the following output:

```
...
  "encryption": {
    "encryptionIdentity": null,
    "keySource": "Microsoft.Storage",
    "keyVaultProperties": null,
    "requireInfrastructureEncryption": true,
    "services": {
      "blob": {
        "enabled": true,
        "keyType": "Account",
        "lastEnabledTime": "2022-12-03T21:56:18.606901+00:00"
      },
...
```

To confirm whether infrastructure encryption is enabled for existing storage accounts, you can run the Azure CLI command `az storage account show` and check the `requireInfrastrucutreEncryption` field within the `encryption` property.

5.2   Securing Azure Key Vault

You will need a place to securely store keys, secrets, or certificates used by your Azure applications. Azure Key Vault provides a platform-as-a-service key management solution to store and tightly manage access to your secrets, keys, and certificates. Operations for Azure Key Vault resources are divided into two categories: control plane and data plane operations. For example, you can manage key vaults in your subscription, such as by creating, deleting, and updating access policies of key vault resources, using the control plane. On the other hand, you can use the data plane to work with the data stored in a key vault. For example, you can add, delete, and modify secrets, keys, and certificates stored in a key vault. An important aspect of securing your key vault resources is to provide authorization for both, starting with authorizing control plane operations.

5.2.1   Authorizing control plane operations

Azure Key Vault supports using Azure RBAC to authorize control plane operations. When you create a key vault resource in your environment, you can manage access to it with Microsoft Entra ID. To grant access to a user (like the fictional character Alice) to manage key vaults, you can use the Key Vault Contributor RBAC role. The Key Vault Contributor role allows you to manage key vault resources but doesn't allow you to assign roles in Azure RBAC. It also doesn't allow you to access secrets, keys, or certificates stored in a key vault.

You can assign the Azure RBAC role, as well as others, at various scopes. For control plane operations, you can assign a role at the management group, subscription, resource group, or storage account level. When determining the scope, as a best practice, you should adhere to the principle of least privilege (see chapter 2) and only grant the narrowest possible scope. The narrowest possible scope in the case of control plane operations for Azure Storage is at the key vault level.

Control plane operations on Azure Key Vault resources don't include permissions to access secrets, keys, or certificates stored in key vaults. However, if the user (like the fictional character Alice) is assigned the Key Vault Contributor role, they can set up a Key Vault access policy that allows them to grant themselves access to data plane operations in Azure Key Vault. Therefore, you should limit who has the Key Vault Contributor role assigned and carefully monitor it. The user with this role could grant themselves access to data plane operations through a Key Vault access policy.

To avoid this problem, it's recommended you use the RBAC permission model, which allows you to separate duties by limiting permission management to the Owner and User Access Administrator roles. To control who has access to secrets, keys, and certificates in your key vaults, you can authorize data plane operations.

5.2.2 *Authorizing data plane operations*

Azure Key Vault supports using Azure RBAC and Key Vault access policies to authorize data plane operations. Azure RBAC is an authorization system built on Azure Resource Manager (the management layer of Azure) that you can use to determine who should have what level of access to which key vault resources.

On the other hand, Key Vault access policies rely on an authorization system built into Key Vault itself. The advantage of using Azure RBAC to authorize data plane operations compared to using Key Vault access policies is that it provides administrators with a centralized way to manage access to resources across different types. Azure RBAC is also integrated with Privileged Identity Management (PIM; see chapter 2).

Azure RBAC

Similar to storage accounts, Azure RBAC has more than one built-in role that you can assign to your identities to authorize data plane operations. The built-in Azure RBAC roles specific to data plane operations in Azure Key Vault are the following:

- *Key Vault Administrator*—Can perform all data plane operations on a key vault, including on all the objects in the key vault (such as secrets, keys, and certificates)
- *Key Vault Reader*—Can read metadata on a key vault, including on all the objects in the key vault (such as secrets, keys, and certificates)
- *Key Vault Crypto Officer*—Can perform any actions on the keys of a key vault, except managing permissions
- *Key Vault Crypto User*—Can perform cryptographic operations using keys

- *Key Vault Certificates Officer*—Can perform any action on the certificate of a key vault, except managing permissions
- *Key Vault Crypto Service Encryption User*—Can read metadata of keys and perform wrap/unwrap operations
- *Key Vault Secrets Officer*—Can perform any action on the secrets of a key vault, except managing permissions
- *Key Vault Secrets User*—Can read secret contents of a key vault

These roles work only for key vaults that have the Azure RBAC permission model for data plane operations, which is also Microsoft's recommendation. Prior to Azure RBAC, organizations typically authorized data plane operations for key vault resources using a key vault access policy.

KEY VAULT ACCESS POLICY

A key vault access policy determines whether an identity can perform different data plane operations on secrets, keys, and certificates of your key vaults. Azure Key Vault supports up to 1,024 access policies, each of which can be used to give permissions to a particular identity (such as a user or application). Because of this limit, it's recommended that you assign access policies to groups rather than individual users. To assign an Azure Key Vault access policy, run the following CLI command.

Listing 5.19 Assigning an Azure Key Vault access policy

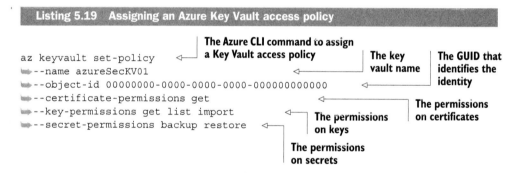

After this command runs, it assigns the Key Vault access policy. Your output should look similar to the following:

```
...
"properties": {
    "accessPolicies": [
        {
            "applicationId": null,
            "objectId": "00000000-0000-0000-0000-000000000000 ",
            "permissions": {
                "certificates": [
                    "get"
                ],
                "keys": [
                    "import",
                    "get",
```

```
        "list"
      ],
      "secrets": [
        "backup",
        "restore"
      ],
      "storage": null
    },
    "tenantId": "00000000-0000-0000-0000-000000000000 "
  }
],...
```

NOTE To view the list of available permissions for secrets, keys, and certificates, you can start at http://mng.bz/nWKV.

In addition to authorizing control and data plane operations, other important aspects when securing your key vaults are blocking and restricting network traffic using the *Azure Key Vault firewall.*

5.2.3   *Azure Key Vault firewall*

The Azure Key Vault firewall is disabled when you create a new key vault resource. Thus, by default, all Azure services and applications can send requests to the key vault resource you created. However, the ability to send requests to the key vault doesn't imply having access policy permissions. For this, you need to use Azure RBAC or an Azure Key Vault access policy. To make your key vault resource more secure, you can restrict access to one or more specified IP addresses, subnets, or trusted Azure services.

ALLOWING ACCESS FROM SPECIFIC VNETS

Imagine you wanted to restrict access to your key vault resources to specific VNets in your environment that contain VMs. To configure the Azure Key Vault firewall for this scenario, you need to specify the key vault resources and VNet.

Listing 5.20 Enabling a service endpoint for Azure Key Vault on a VNet and subnet

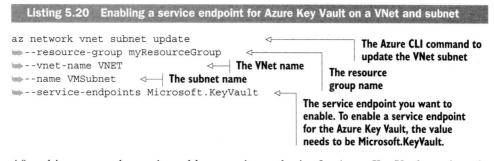

After this command runs, it enables a service endpoint for Azure Key Vault on the subnet you specify. Your output should look similar to the following:

```
...
  "serviceEndpoints": [
    {
```

```
        "locations": [
          "*"
        ],
        "provisioningState": "Succeeded",
        "service": "Microsoft.KeyVault"
      }
    ],
    "type": "Microsoft.Network/virtualNetworks/subnets"
}
...
```

Only after you enable a service endpoint for Azure Key Vault on the subnet can you add a network rule that restricts access to a VNet and subnet. To do this, run the following CLI command in Azure Cloud Shell.

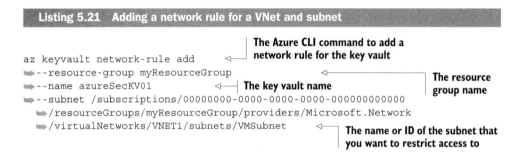

Listing 5.21   Adding a network rule for a VNet and subnet

After this command runs, it adds the network rule for the subnet you specify, as you can see from the following output:

```
...
"networkAcls": {
      "bypass": "AzureServices",
      "defaultAction": "Deny",
      "ipRules": [],
      "virtualNetworkRules": [
        {
          "id": "/subscriptions/00000000-0000-0000-0000-000000000000
          /resourcegroups/myResourceGroup/providers/microsoft.network/
          virtualnetworks/vnet1/subnets/vmsubnet",
          "ignoreMissingVnetServiceEndpoint": null,
          "resourceGroup": "myResourceGroup"
        }
      ]
    },
...
```

In addition to restricting access to the VNet and subnet (such as the one containing your VMs), you can also use a specific IPv4 address range.

ALLOWING ACCESS FROM SPECIFIC IPV4 ADDRESS RANGES

Imagine you want to restrict access to an IPv4 address range corresponding to your office location. You can do this by running the following CLI command.

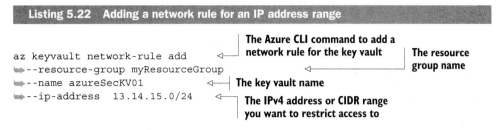

Listing 5.22 Adding a network rule for an IP address range

After this command runs, it adds the network rule for an IP address range. Your output should look similar to the following:

```
...
"networkAcls": {
      "bypass": "AzureServices",
      "defaultAction": "Deny",
      "ipRules": [
        {
          "value": "13.14.15.0/24"
        }
      ],
      "virtualNetworkRules": [
        {
"id": "/subscriptions/00000000-0000-0000-0000-000000000000/resourcegroups
➥/myResourceGroup/providers/microsoft.network/virtualnetworks/vnet1
➥/subnets/vmsubnet",
          "ignoreMissingVnetServiceEndpoint": null,
          "resourceGroup": " myResourceGroup "
        }
      ]
    },
...
```

In addition to restricting access to the VNet, subnet, and IP address range, you can configure trusted Microsoft Services to bypass the Azure Key Vault firewall.

ALLOWING ACCESS FROM TRUSTED SERVICES

Trusted services in the context of the Azure Key Vault firewall apply to a select set of Microsoft's services for which Microsoft controls all of the code that runs on the service.

> **NOTE** To determine whether a service you're interested in is on the list of trusted services, you can consult the latest list of services at http://mng.bz/vnVm.

This isn't to say that services not included on this list are untrustworthy or insecure. Some services allow customers to write their own custom code in them (such as Azure DevOps). Consequently, Microsoft will not provide a rubber stamp of approval for this service in the context of the Azure Key Vault firewall.

Imagine you wanted to allow Microsoft Purview to bypass the Azure Key Vault firewall. You can achieve this by running the following command in Azure Cloud Shell.

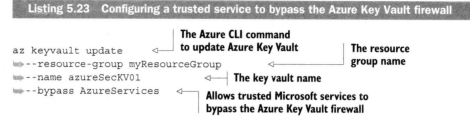

Listing 5.23   Configuring a trusted service to bypass the Azure Key Vault firewall

After this command runs, it allows trusted Microsoft services to bypass the Azure Key Vault firewall, as you can see from the following output:

```
...
"networkAcls": {
      "bypass": "AzureServices",
      "defaultAction": "Deny",
      "ipRules": [],
      "virtualNetworkRules": [
        {
          "id": "/subscriptions/00000000-0000-0000-0000-000000000000
            /resourcegroups/myResourceGroup/providers/microsoft.network
            /virtualnetworks/vnet1/subnets/vmsubnet",
          "ignoreMissingVnetServiceEndpoint": null,
          "resourceGroup": "myResourceGroup"
        }
      ]
    },
...
```

Based on your organization's requirements and needs, you can add different network rules to the Azure Key Vault firewall that restrict access to IP addresses and subnets, while allowing trusted Microsoft services to bypass the Azure Key Vault firewall. To enable the network rules you previously added, run the following CLI command.

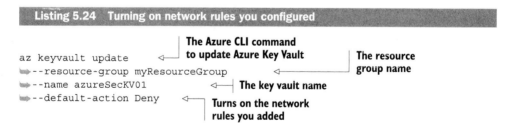

Listing 5.24   Turning on network rules you configured

After this command runs, it enables the rules you added, as you can see from the following output:

```
...
"networkAcls": {
      "bypass": "AzureServices",
      "defaultAction": "Deny",
      "ipRules": [],
      "virtualNetworkRules": [
        {
```

```
        "id": "/subscriptions/00000000-0000-0000-0000-000000000000
    ➥/resourcegroups/myResourceGroup/providers/microsoft.network
    ➥/virtualnetworks/vnet1/subnets/vmsubnet",
        "ignoreMissingVnetServiceEndpoint": null,
        "resourceGroup": "myResourceGroup"
      }
    ]
  },
... 
```

In addition to storage accounts and key vaults, another commonly used resource type in Azure in which data is stored is databases. I'll cover how you can secure your databases in Azure in the next two chapters.

Summary

- You can use Azure RBAC to authorize both data plane and control plane operations. In addition, data plane operations support authorizations using storage account keys and shared access signatures.
- Service-side encryption automatically encrypts all data that you persist to Azure Storage. It encrypts all Azure Storage data objects, such as blobs, disks, tables, queues, and files.
- Encryption using a customer-managed key implies using your own encryption key to control access to the key used to encrypt your data. This key can be stored in Azure Key Vault or Azure Key Vault Managed HSM. Using a Microsoft-managed key removes the need for Azure Key Vault or Azure Key Managed HSM.
- Encryption scopes empower you to create boundaries between data inside of the same storage account. This is done via encryption with a key applied to a container or an individual blob rather than to the entire storage account.
- Data in Azure Storage can be encrypted both at the service level and the infrastructure level using infrastructure encryption. You cannot enable infrastructure encryption after the storage account has been enabled. The same applies to disabling infrastructure encryption: it cannot be disabled after the storage account has been created.
- You can configure firewall rules on Azure Storage and Azure Key Vault to restrict access to your storage accounts and key vaults. This ensures that you control from which subnets and public IP addresses your storage accounts and key vaults allow incoming network traffic.

Implementing good security hygiene: Microsoft Defender for Cloud and Defender CSPM

This chapter covers

- Microsoft Defender for Cloud
- Cloud security posture management
- Cloud security graph
- Security governance
- Regulatory compliance

With cyberattacks increasing both in frequency and complexity (both of which are alarming trends), having good *cyber hygiene* has never been more important. Cyber hygiene is a set of practices aimed at ensuring the safety and security of your environment. Let's compare cyber hygiene and oral hygiene. As any parent knows, telling your kids to brush their teeth and floss daily is essential to keeping their teeth and gums healthy. It prevents oral health problems (such as cavities and gum disease) before they even start. Similarly, patching your software against common vulnerabilities and exposures prevents security problems before they arise. Unfortunately, many of the breaches you read about in the news are the result of poor cyber hygiene that opened the door to bad actors, like the fictional bad actor Eve used throughout this book.

A large number of cybercriminals still find success with their attack campaigns due to poor cyber hygiene, such as poor access controls or using software with well-known vulnerabilities. This challenge is shared by businesses across different sectors, sizes, and industries. Therefore, having good cyber hygiene is crucial to having any kind of security posture.

NOTE   To follow along with the exercises in this chapter, you can use the GitHub repository (https://github.com/bmagusic/azure-security).

The better the cyber hygiene of your environment, the lower the identified risk to your environment and the less the likelihood of bad actors succeeding in their attacks. Microsoft Defender for Cloud provides a set of capabilities to help ensure good cyber hygiene in your Azure environment.

6.1   *Microsoft Defender for Cloud*

Microsoft Defender for Cloud has a lot of capabilities that can help you implement good cyber hygiene. For simplicity's sake, most of Defender for Cloud's capabilities can be divided into the following three major cloud security pillars (figure 6.1):

- *Cloud security posture management (CSPM)*—Continuously assesses configurations of your cloud resources and detects misconfigurations or weaknesses. If it detects any misconfigurations or weaknesses, Defender for Cloud provides you with security best-practice guidance on how to fix those misconfigurations in the form of recommendations.

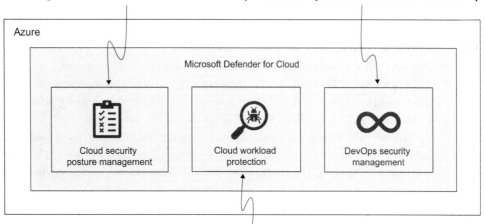

Figure 6.1   The three major cloud security pillars to which most of Microsoft Defender for Cloud's capabilities can be mapped back

- *Cloud workload protection*—Monitors your environment for suspicious activities and potential signs of compromise. If it detects activity at a level high enough to be indicative of a potential sign of compromise, Defender for Cloud generates a security alert.
- *DevOps security management*—Provides capabilities that allow developers to develop code more securely and security best-practice guidance for your source code repositories and scan templates used to deploy code into your Azure environment.

These three pillars of capabilities together play a key role in helping you determine, improve, and maintain the overall security posture of your Azure environment. They also help you implement good cyber hygiene for your Azure resources.

Support for AWS, Google Cloud Platform, and hybrid workloads

Microsoft Defender for Cloud is a multicloud security solution; in addition to Azure, its CSPM and cloud workload protection capabilities can be used to natively secure your AWS and Google Cloud Platform (GCP) workloads. Additionally, through integration with another Azure service, called Azure Arc, Defender for Cloud's capability can be extended to cover hybrid workloads too (for example, your on-premises VMs). This book is about Azure security, and in this chapter, I'll teach you how to use Defender for Cloud's capabilities for your Azure workloads only. However, many of the capabilities I discuss can also be used to secure your AWS, GCP, and hybrid workloads.

In this chapter, I focus on how to use Defender for Cloud's CSPM capabilities (I'll cover cloud workload protection and DevOps security in chapters 7 and 11, respectively).

6.2   *Cloud security posture management*

The first pillar of capabilities in Microsoft Defender for Cloud revolves around CSPM. At a high level, CSPM continuously assesses the security posture and configurations of your cloud workloads and provides you with security best-practice guidance on how to fix any misconfigurations or weaknesses.

This security best-practice guidance is aggregated for cloud workloads that already exist and have already been deployed in your Azure environment. Therefore, when remediating misconfigurations, you should incorporate this security best-practice guidance into how you deploy your Azure resource going forward (to prevent any future misconfigurations). Because you need to make a concerted effort to incorporate this security guidance into your organizational processes and deployment practices, CSPM can be considered a proactive approach to improving the security posture of your Azure environment. To use the CSPM capabilities, you need to onboard your subscriptions to Microsoft Defender for Cloud.

6.2.1 *Onboarding your subscriptions to Defender for Cloud*

To onboard your Azure subscriptions to Microsoft Defender for Cloud, you need to register your subscriptions with the `'Microsoft.Security'` provider.

Predeployment considerations

Before deploying Microsoft Defender for Cloud, you should consider certain best practices. Microsoft Defender for Cloud is an Azure service that is enabled on the subscription level. If possible, you should have a management group hierarchy in the Azure environment according to your organization's needs. This gives you an understanding of where Azure subscriptions are residing, and management groups help you more easily deploy and manage Microsoft Defender for Cloud at scale. You should also familiarize yourself with Azure role-based access control and different roles available in Microsoft Defender for Cloud. You can start at http://mng.bz/4DY5. Security Reader is the role with the least amount of privilege and can be used to view recommendations and security alerts in Microsoft Defender for Cloud. Security Admin is a role suited for users who work with Microsoft Defender for Cloud on a daily basis and need to perform certain tasks.

REGISTERING SUBSCRIPTIONS WITH THE RESOURCE PROVIDER

Run the following command in Azure Cloud Shell with the Contributor or Owner role on the subscription to register your subscription:

```
az provider register --namespace 'Microsoft.Security'
```

The command used to register the provider on your Azure subscription

This command registers your subscription with the `'Microsoft.Security'` provider and, in turn, onboards your subscription to Microsoft Defender for Cloud. In addition, you need to assign the Microsoft Cloud Security Benchmark (MCSB), which Defender for Cloud uses to provide recommendations and security suggestions on how to better secure your resources.

ASSIGNING THE MICROSOFT CLOUD SECURITY BENCHMARK

To assign the MCSB, run the following command using the same permissions as previously noted:

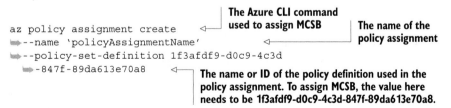

```
az policy assignment create
  --name 'policyAssignmentName'
  --policy-set-definition 1f3afdf9-d0c9-4c3d
    -847f-89da613e70a8
```

The Azure CLI command used to assign MCSB

The name of the policy assignment

The name or ID of the policy definition used in the policy assignment. To assign MCSB, the value here needs to be 1f3afdf9-d0c9-4c3d-847f-89da613e70a8.

After this command runs, it assigns the MCSB. Your output should look similar to the following:

```
{
  "description": null,
  "displayName": null,
  "enforcementMode": "Default",
  "id": "/subscriptions/00000000-0000-0000-0000-000000000000/providers
  ➥/Microsoft.Authorization/policyAssignments/'policyAssignmentName'",
  "identity": null,
  "location": null,
  "metadata": {
    "createdBy": "a2caa967-d1f6-4a9b-a246-dab5d8a93b91",
    "createdOn": "2022-12-21T21:46:39.5222617Z",
    "updatedBy": null,
    "updatedOn": null
  },
  "name": "'policyAssignmentName'",
  "nonComplianceMessages": null,
  "notScopes": null,
  "parameters": null,
  "policyDefinitionId": "/providers/Microsoft.Authorization
  ➥/policySetDefinitions/1f3afdf9-d0c9-4c3d-847f-89da613e70a8",
  "scope": "/subscriptions/00000000-0000-0000-0000-000000000000",
  "systemData": {
    "createdAt": "2022-12-21T21:46:38.563036+00:00",
    "createdBy": "bmagusic@gmail.com",
    "createdByType": "User",
    "lastModifiedAt": "2022-12-21T21:46:38.563036+00:00",
    "lastModifiedBy": "bmagusic@gmail.com",
    "lastModifiedByType": "User"
  },
  "type": "Microsoft.Authorization/policyAssignments"
}
```

After you register your Azure subscriptions with the `'Microsoft.Security'` provider and ensure that MCSB is assigned, you are able to see recommendations for your platform-as-a-service (PaaS) resources (such as storage accounts and Azure App Service) in the Microsoft Defender for Cloud dashboard. For PaaS resources, Defender for Cloud uses a backend integration to collect the required data to detect weaknesses and misconfigurations. However, for infrastructure-as-a-service (IaaS) resources (such as your virtual machines [VMs]), Defender for Cloud uses the Log Analytics (LA) agent to collect the required data.

Which agent should you use?

In Defender for Cloud, you can use one of two agents: the LA agent or the Azure Monitoring Agent (AMA). Microsoft is moving in the direction of AMA because it's the evolution of the LA agent. AMA is generally available; however, the integration between AMA and different Azure services might still be in public preview. An example of this is the integration between AMA and Microsoft Defender for Cloud: if you want to use AMA in combination with Defender for Cloud, you need to be aware that the integration between them is currently in public preview. Because many organizations reserve features that are generally available for production workloads, I'll only discuss using the integration that is generally available, meaning the integration between Microsoft Defender for Cloud and the LA agent.

The LA agent (previously known as the Microsoft Monitoring Agent) collects data from your VMs and sends it to a *Log Analytics workspace (LAW)*.

LAW SELECTION

The data the agents send to a LAW is used by Defender for Cloud to detect weaknesses and misconfigurations on your VMs. After you onboard your subscriptions, Defender for Cloud automatically creates one default LAW per region, depending on where your VMs are located. For example, if your Azure VMs are located in the United States or Brazil, then Defender for Cloud creates the default LAW with the location in the United States. For VMs in Europe, Defender for Cloud creates the default LAW with the location in Europe, etc. Thus, the location of the default LAW that Defender for Cloud creates depends on the Azure region where your VMs are deployed. Defender for Cloud can create the default LAW in the following regions:

- United States
- Canada
- Europe
- United Kingdom
- Asia
- Korea
- India
- Japan
- China
- Australia

After you onboard your subscriptions to Defender for Cloud, the name of the default LAW that Defender for Cloud creates is `DefaultWorkspace-<YourSubscriptionID>-<regionAbbreviation>`, where the LAW name contains the ID of your Azure subscription and the region in which it's located (e.g., `CUS` for central US).

Using a custom LAW with Defender for Cloud

Using a default LAW is convenient because it's automatically created by Defender for Cloud. However, imagine if, instead of having one LAW per region, you wanted to have a centralized LAW for easier management. Or maybe you want the LAW to adhere to your organization's naming convention. For this, instead of using the default LAW, you can use a custom one. To use a custom LAW with Defender for Cloud, the workspace needs to have the SecurityCenterFree solution enabled on it. After you enable this

(continued)

solution on the custom workspace, you can connect the LA agents to the workspace either manually or by using auto-provisioning, which is the recommended approach. Furthermore, if you're planning on using the same LAW for both Defender for Cloud and Microsoft Sentinel (I'll cover Sentinel in chapter 8), then you need to use a custom LAW. Microsoft Sentinel can't be used in combination with the default LAW created by Defender for Cloud because it lacks the necessary permissions.

To ensure that any new VMs that are deployed in the subscription you onboarded to Defender for Cloud send data directly to the LAW, you can use auto-provisioning.

AUTO-PROVISIONING

Auto-provisioning is a capability in Defender for Cloud that allows you to automatically deploy the required agents and extensions (I'll cover this in more detail in chapter 7) to your VMs. To monitor for security vulnerabilities and weaknesses on your VMs, Defender for Cloud uses the LA agent. The LA agent collects various security-related configuration data and event logs from your VMs. The data the LA agent collects from your VMs includes, among other things, operating system logs, running processes, IP addresses, and logged-in users.

> **NOTE** For a full list of security events collected by the LA agent on your VMs, you can start at http://mng.bz/QPz1.

The LA agent sends this data to LAW, which Defender for Cloud then uses for further analysis. To ensure all VMs in the subscription send data to the LAW you selected, you can configure auto-provisioning. To configure auto-provisioning on the subscription you onboarded to Defender for Cloud, perform the following actions:

1. Navigate to the Microsoft Defender for Cloud dashboard inside the Azure portal.
2. Select Environment Settings.
3. Click the subscription you onboarded to Defender for Cloud.
4. Select Settings and Monitoring in the upper taskbar of the blade that opens.
5. Enable the toggle next to Log Analytics Agent/Azure Monitor Agent.
6. Then, in the same row, click Edit Configuration.
7. Under agent type, choose Log Analytics Agent (Default), as in figure 6.2.
8. Under Workspace, either leave the Default Workspace(s) selected or select Custom Workspace and your custom LAW.
9. Select Apply, and then click Continue.
10. Click Save.

Defender for Cloud installs the LA agent side by side with existing agents, such as the System Center Operations Manager, on your VMs. Similarly, if the LA agent is already installed on your VMs, Defender for Cloud will upgrade the agent to the latest version

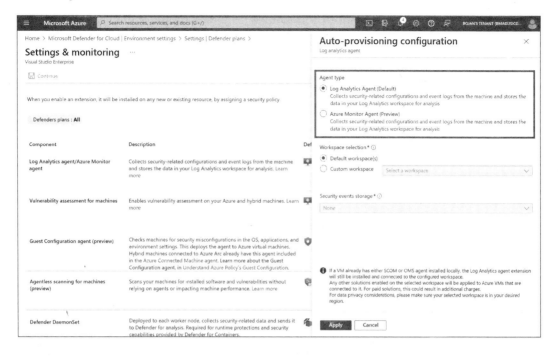

Figure 6.2 An overview of recommendations in the Microsoft Defender for Cloud dashboard

if necessary. After the LA agent is deployed on your VMs, it sends data to the LAW, which Defender for Cloud then uses to monitor and assess your VMs and IaaS resources. Defender for Cloud continuously assesses in near-real time your Azure resources, providing you with guidance and suggestions on how to best secure these resources. This guidance and suggestions come in the form of *recommendations*.

6.2.2 Recommendations

Recommendations are security best-practice guidance that Microsoft Defender for Cloud generates when it detects misconfigurations or weaknesses in resources in your environment. To provide this guidance, Microsoft Defender for Cloud uses MCSB under the hood. MCSB is a collection of security recommendations that are aligned with widely used security and compliance control frameworks such as the National Institute of Standards and Technology (NIST), the Center for Internet Security (CIS), and the Payment Card Industry Data Security Standard (PCI DSS), and provide you with clear and concise instruction on how to better secure your resources.

To view recommendations, after signing in to the Azure portal, type Microsoft Defender for Cloud in the search bar and navigate to the Defender for Cloud overview dashboard. Then select either Recommendations or Security Posture (and for the Azure subscription that you onboarded, click View Recommendations). You'll see a list of recommendations you can use to improve your overall security posture (figure 6.3).

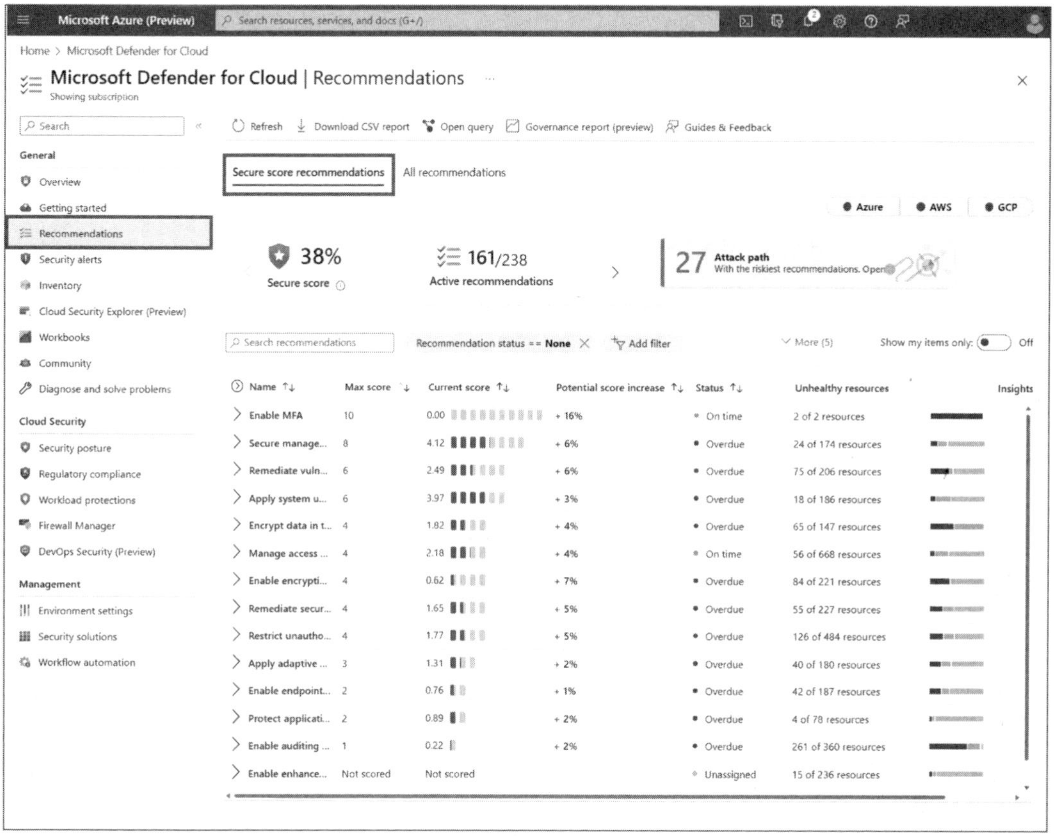

Figure 6.3   An overview of recommendations in the Microsoft Defender for Cloud dashboard

To get recommendations for your Azure resources, you need to onboard your Azure subscriptions to Microsoft Defender for Cloud and ensure the MCSB is assigned.

It can seem daunting to understand where to start and which recommendations to employ first. The Potential Score Increase column can help you identify which recommendations will contribute the most to increasing your *secure score*.

6.2.3   Secure score

A secure score provides you with a percentage ranging from 0% to 100%, which is an aggregation of all security findings for your environment (figure 6.4). At a high level, it tells you where your environment is currently from a CSPM perspective. The higher the score is, the greater the number of Azure resources that adhere to security best

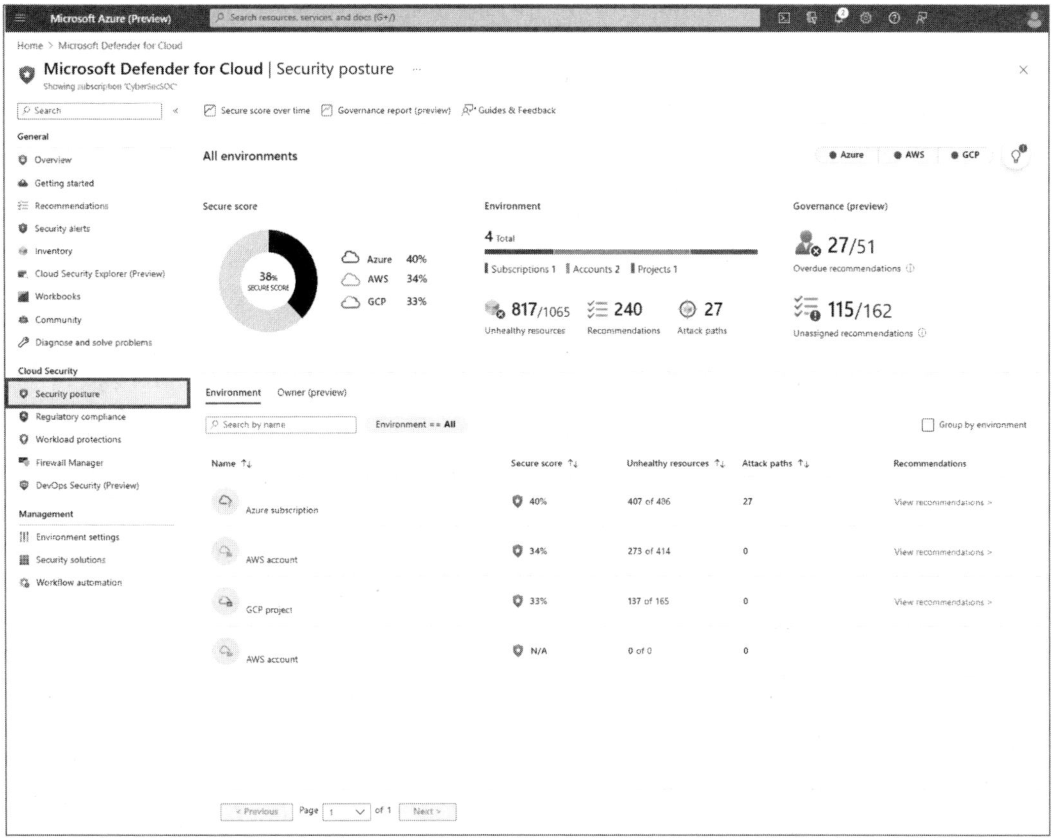

Figure 6.4   The security posture section with secure score in the Microsoft Defender for Cloud dashboard

practices and the lower the identified risk to your environment from the fictitious bad actor Eve.

NOTE   To get a maximum score for a particular security control, you must follow all recommendations (beneath that security control) for all resources. Recommendations flagged as Preview are not included in the secure score calculation. However, you should still follow those recommendations because when the preview ends, they'll be included in the calculation of your secure score.

You can even use the secure score as a singular security key performance indicator (KPI) that provides you with a numeric value you can use to determine the overall security posture of your cloud environment.

If you ever need to show the management of your organization why recommendations in your environment need to be addressed, this security KPI is a powerful tool because it allows you to track the security posture of your environment over time. You want to ensure that the secure score increases over time, especially after new resources are deployed in your Azure environment, because that suggests that the new resources are adhering to security best-practice guidance. Theoretically, the maximum secure score you can have is 100%. This would mean that you implemented all security suggestions and guidance and that all the workloads in your environment are properly configured and adhere to this guidance all the time. Reaching and maintaining a secure score of 100%, especially for large environments, is a difficult task to accomplish.

> ### What secure score should you strive for?
> I am often asked what secure score an organization should strive for. How high of a secure score is considered good enough? What secure score do other organizations have? In practice, you should strive for a consistent secure score of 85% and higher. This score suggests that the majority of your Azure workloads are properly configured and are adhering to security best-practice guidance, lowering the identified risk to your environment.

Implementing security best-practice guidance and suggestions that come in the form of recommendations in Defender for Cloud can help increase your secure score and correct misconfigurations. Recommendations provide you with guidance and suggestions on how to better secure your Azure resources.

NOTE Microsoft Defender for Cloud can generate more than 240 recommendations for different Azure resource types (across compute, App Services, container, data, networking, and identity and access). To consult the complete reference list of recommendations for Azure resources, you can start at http://mng.bz/XNEl.

To use this guidance, follow the Remediation Steps provided in the recommendations. Figure 6.5 shows an example of a recommendation that machines (such as your Azure VMs) should have a vulnerability assessment solution installed. To fulfill this (or any other) recommendation, perform the following actions:

1 Navigate to the Microsoft Defender for Cloud dashboard inside of the Azure portal.
2 Select Recommendations.
3 Using the Potential Score Increase column, expand the security control with the highest potential score increase.
4 In the list, click any recommendation that has unhealthy resources.
5 Expand the Remediation Steps section in the blade that opens.
6 Implement the remediation steps.
7 Based on the time indicated in the Freshness Interval, check back after the recommendation has been updated to ensure the guidance has been implemented and the security problem on the resource has been fixed.

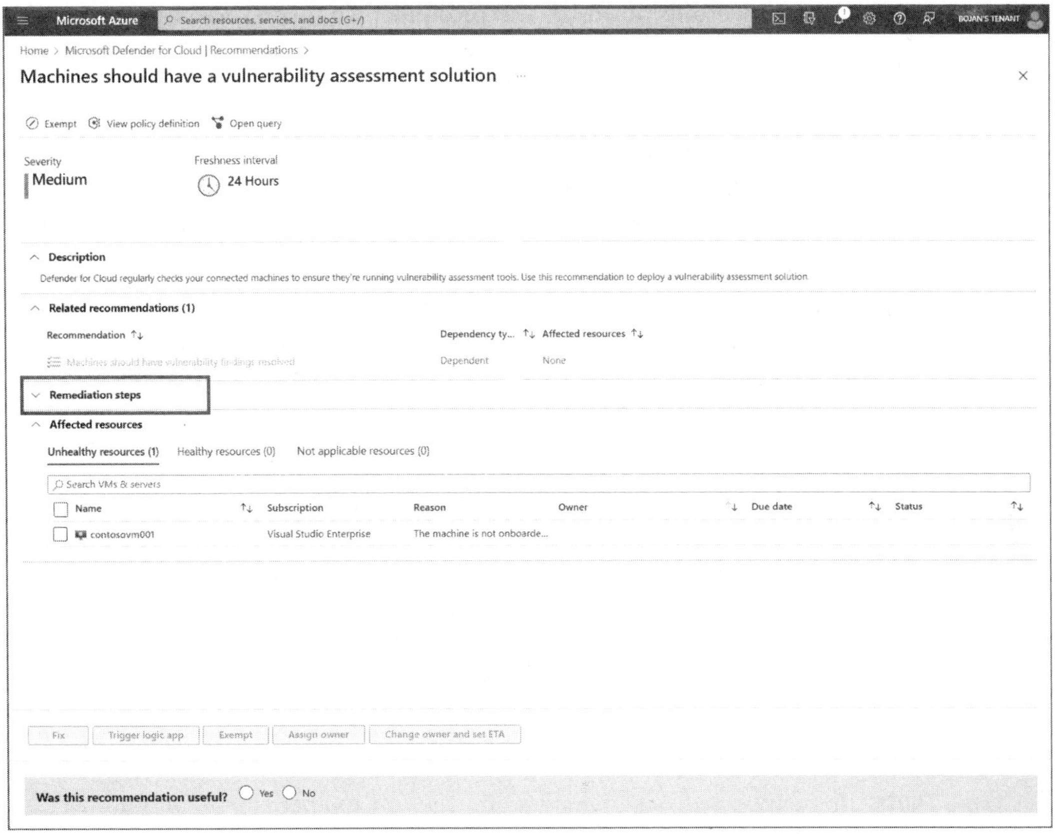

Figure 6.5 The recommendation Machines Should Have a Vulnerability Assessment Solution shown by Defender for Cloud for VMs

Each recommendation provides you with a short description of the problem, the remediation steps to follow to implement the recommendation, and the resources affected by this recommendation. In addition, other fields can be of real value as you go about implementing this recommendation:

- *Severity*—Defender for Cloud supports three severity categories: low, medium, and high.
- *Freshness interval*—How often the recommendation is refreshed (this interval varies between recommendations).
- *Related recommendations*—Where applicable, show recommendations that need to be implemented prior to this recommendation, an alternate recommendation that can be used to achieve the same goal, or another recommendation that is a prerequisite.
- *Exempt*—Where applicable, Microsoft Defender for Cloud shows the Exempt option. This feature allows you to exempt a resource or subscription (or

management group) to ensure this recommendation and resources don't affect your secure score. This is typically done when you find that a specific recommendation is not applicable to the resources of your environment, such as when you already have a third-party solution that is responsible for fixing the problems in the particular recommendation.

- *Mapping to MITRE ATT&CK® framework*—Where applicable, if a recommendation has defined tactics and techniques, Defender for Cloud shows a mapping to the MITRE ATT&CK® framework.

NOTE   MITRE ATT&CK® is a globally accessible knowledge base and model of adversary tactics and techniques based on real-world observations To learn more about MITRE ATT&CK®, you can start at https://attack.mitre.org/.

- *State of affected resources*—Affected resources are grouped and shown in one of three tabs. Unhealthy resources are resources for which the security problem identified in the recommendation has not been followed yet. Healthy resources are resources that you already implemented the remediation steps for (or that, to begin with, didn't have the security problem identified in the recommendation). Resources for which the recommendation is not able to provide a definite answer are shown under Not Applicable resources.

- *Fix*—Supported recommendations will include a Fix option. This feature allows you to correct the problem across your resources at scale using a built-in remediation logic in Defender for Cloud.

NOTE   For supported recommendations, the top toolbar shows the Enforce or Deny option. This feature can be used to either automatically fix noncompliant resources (Enforce) or stop unhealthy resources from being created (Deny). As Microsoft continues to add Enforce and Deny support for more recommendations, you can consult the most up-to-date list of supported recommendations at http://mng.bz/yQV7.

After you successfully follow the steps provided in the recommendation, you can consider the security problem and recommendation to be fulfilled. After you follow all the recommendations that are part of a particular security control and the time indicated in the freshness interval has passed, your secure score increases by the value indicated in the Potential Score Increase column.

Exercise 6.1

To help you internalize what you learn in this chapter, after you onboard your Azure subscription or subscriptions to Microsoft Defender for Cloud, using the recommendations section, identify three security controls whose remediation would contribute the most to an increase in your secure score. Expand each of these three security controls to view recommendations that have unhealthy resources. Click each recommendation and perform the suggested remediation steps. The outcome of this exercise should result in your secure score increasing and the identified risk in your environment decreasing. I'd love to hear how much your secure score increased after this exercise. Feel free to share the outcome of this exercise in the book forum.

6.2.4 *Free vs. paid security posture management capabilities in Microsoft Defender for Cloud*

Secure score and recommendations are available at no additional cost in Microsoft Defender for Cloud. That means you can onboard your Azure subscriptions to Defender for Cloud and, for free, get a secure score and recommendations on how to fix security problems for your resources. In addition to secure score and recommendations, Defender for Cloud offers advanced CSPM capabilities that are part of a plan called *Defender CSPM*. To use the advanced capabilities, you need to enable the Defender CSPM plan on your Azure subscriptions. To do so, run the following command with the Owner role on the subscription:

```
az security pricing create -n CloudPosture -tier 'standard'
```

A command used to enable Defender CSPM plan on your Azure subscription

After this command runs, it enables the Defender CSPM plan, and your output should look similar to the following:

```
{
  "freeTrialRemainingTime": "0:00:00",
  "id": "/subscriptions/00000000-0000-0000-0000-000000000000/providers
  ➥/Microsoft.Security/pricings/CloudPosture",
  "name": "CloudPosture",
  "pricingTier": "Standard",
  "type": "Microsoft.Security/pricings"
}
```

Enabling Defender CSPM allows you to use more advanced CSPM capabilities, such as the *cloud security graph*.

6.3 *Cloud security graph*

The bigger the environment is, the higher the probability you'll have a proportional number of security problems (and recommendations) to fix. What can help is prioritizing the remediation of security problems that represent the biggest risk to your environment. For this, you can use the cloud security graph. The cloud security graph is a capability in Defender CSPM that analyzes your environment and identifies risks to your environment based on what can be exploited and business effect. For example, exploitability can be VMs exposed to the internet with vulnerabilities on them (such as common vulnerabilities and exposures corresponding to a newly found weakness), whereas business effect can be those VMs having access to a storage account containing sensitive information (such as customer data).

The cloud security graph uses contextual information about your environment, such as connections between your resources, exposure to the internet, network connections, lateral movement possibilities, and vulnerabilities. This data is then used to build a graph representing your environment and identify the biggest risks to your environment. Defender for Cloud uses this graph to perform an analysis of your environment and find possible *attack paths*.

6.3.1 *Attack paths*

Attack paths are Defender for Cloud's way of analyzing your environment's contextual information and cloud security graph data to inform you of the highest risks that exist within your environment. This analysis exposes paths by which bad actors could breach your environment. For each attack path, Defender for Cloud provides recommendations for the best way to fix the security problem.

To investigate an attack path, perform the following actions:

1 Navigate to the Microsoft Defender for Cloud dashboard inside of the Azure portal.

2 Select Recommendations and then, in the blade that appears, click the Attack Path tile.

3 From the list of available Attack Paths, select one depending on your environment, such as Internet Exposed VM Has High Severity Vulnerabilities and Read Permission to a Key Vault.

4 Select the tab Attack Path, and then click a row to expand the graphical representation of the attack path (figure 6.6).

5 Interact with the different entities in the graphical representation by clicking them.

6 In the blade on the right, select the Insight tab to view the associated insights for that particular entity.

7 In the blade on the right, select the Recommendations tab to view the associated suggestions and recommendations for that particular entity.

8 Select the Recommendations tab to see all suggestions and recommendations for how to best fix the security problems shown in the Attack Path.

9 For each recommendation, follow the recommended steps to solve the security problem.

NOTE To get the most value out of the cloud security graph and attack paths, you should enable a Defender CSPM plan across your entire Azure environment (or, alternatively, across as many Azure subscriptions as possible). Oftentimes, when there are few or no attack paths shown, it's because Defender CSPM is enabled on one (or a couple of) Azure subscriptions that contain few resources.

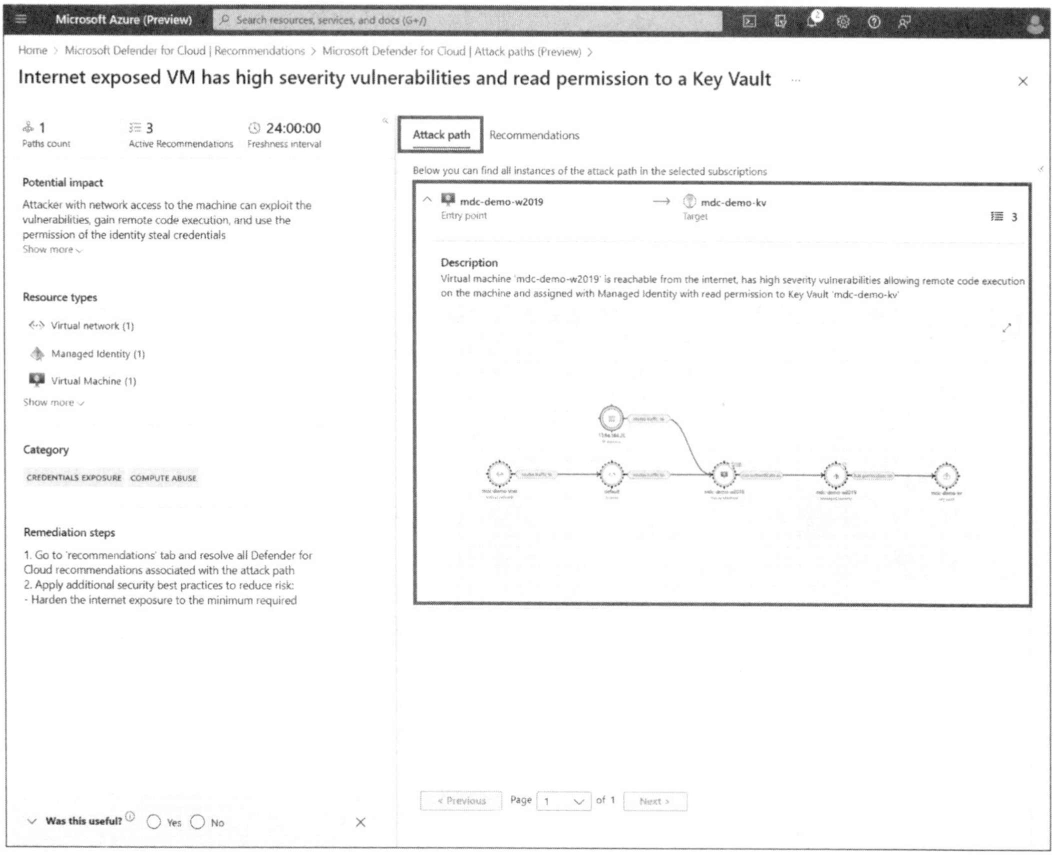

Figure 6.6   An attack path shown for an internet-exposed VM that has high-severity vulnerabilities and read permission to a key vault

Attack paths are a powerful feature because they provide a risk assessment of your environment and help identify the security problems that could be exploited by bad actors to cause a negative effect on business. While Microsoft keeps adding more attack paths, they will never know your Azure environment as intimately as you do. You know your environment best! Luckily, you can distill the knowledge of your environment into what you consider to be exploitable and to have business effects using the *cloud security explorer.*

6.3.2   Cloud security explorer

The cloud security explorer allows you to tap into the cloud security data and contextual security information of your environment and run graph-based queries against it to identify risks to your environment (figure 6.7). The queries return information about what can be exploited in your environment and its business effect, such as VMs with high-severity vulnerabilities that have access to storage accounts containing customer data.

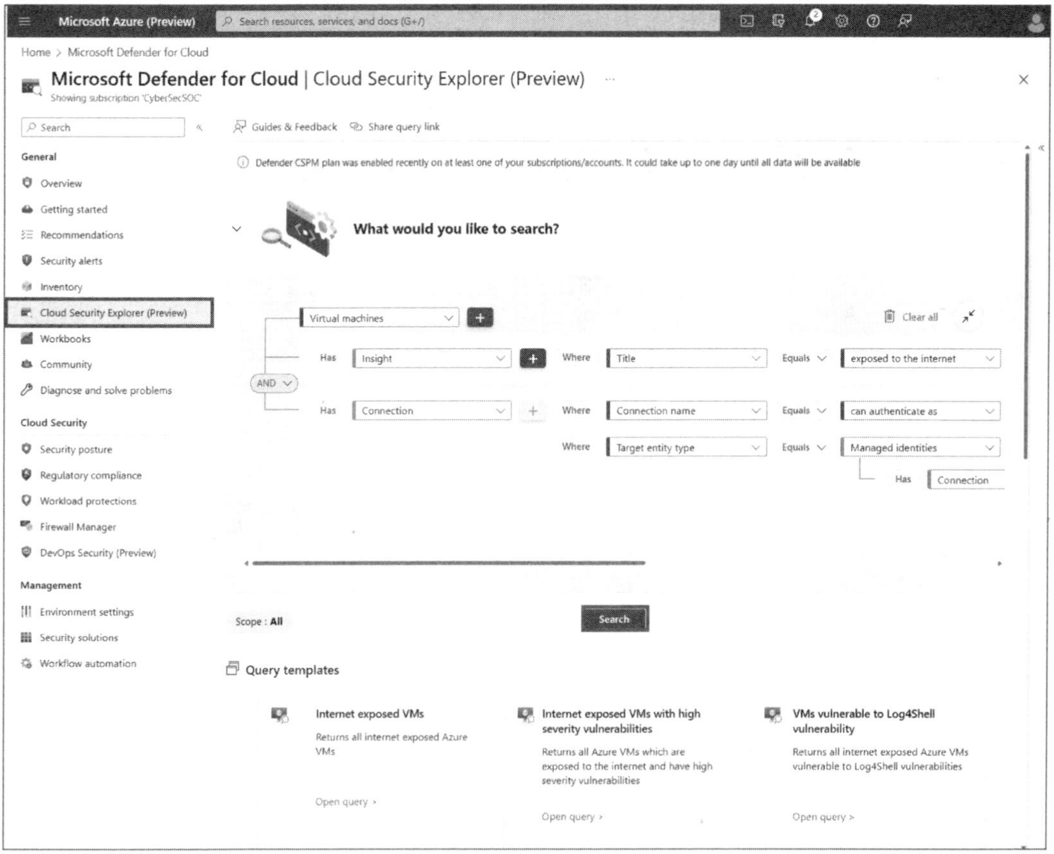

Figure 6.7   The cloud security explorer in Microsoft Defender for Cloud

When querying data using cloud security explorer, you can use the following information:

- *Recommendations*—All recommendations supported by Microsoft Defender for Cloud
- *Vulnerabilities*—All vulnerabilities found by Microsoft Defender for Cloud
- *Insights*—Contextual data about the resources in your environment
- *Connections*—Connections existing between different resources in your environment

Imagine you wanted to discover which compute resources that your application uses (such as Azure VMs) are exposed to the internet and have high-severity vulnerabilities on them. For this, you can use the cloud security explorer. To build a query that returns VMs exposed to the internet with high-severity vulnerabilities, perform the following actions:

1   Navigate to the Microsoft Defender for Cloud dashboard inside of the Azure portal.

2   On the left, select Cloud Security Explorer.

3   From the drop-down menu, select Virtual Machines.

4   Select + to add a filter.

5   From the drop-down menu, select Vulnerabilities, and then click + to add a sub-filter to your query.

6   Choose Where > Severity from the drop-down and then Equals > High.

7   Click + to add another filter to your query.

8   From the drop-down menu, select Insight, and then click + to add a sub-filter to your query.

9   Select Title from the drop-down menu, and then select Exposed to the Internet.

10 Click Search.

11 The results populate at the bottom of the page. Click any of the displayed results to see more insights about that particular resource.

Can you think of other use cases for the cloud security explorer in your environment? Imagine you want to discover whether data resources (such as databases) that your application uses are exposed to the internet and contain sensitive data (such as customer credit card information). To discover resources that fit this bill, use the cloud security explorer to perform the following actions:

1   Navigate to the Microsoft Defender for Cloud dashboard inside of the Azure portal.

2   On the left, select Cloud Security Explorer.

3   From the drop-down menu, choose Data. Click Databases, and then select Done.

4   Select + to add a filter.

5   From the drop-down menu, select Exposed to the Internet, and then click + to add a subfilter to your query.

6   Choose Where > Port from the drop-down menu, and then, after Equals, insert 1433 (the TCP port commonly used to perform brute-force attacks).

7   Click + to add another filter to your query.

8   From the drop-down menu, select Data, and then click on Contains Sensitive Data.

9   Click Search.

10 The results populate at the bottom of the page. Click any of the displayed results to see more insights about that particular resource.

You can use the cloud security explorer to proactively identify risks to your environment. To get started, you can use the existing query templates (such as to discover Azure Key Vault keys and secrets without any expiration period that your application uses) located at the bottom of the cloud security explorer blade. You can even use these queries as a starting point for building queries specific to your environment.

> ### Exercise 6.2
> For extra practice, use the cloud security explorer to discover which user accounts without multifactor authentication (MFA) have access to storage accounts. If you need help writing this query with the cloud security explorer, you can start at http://mng.bz/MBpE.

6.3.3   *Agentless scanning for machines*

To discover software installed on your resources and vulnerabilities in the installed software on your machines (such as VMs), cloud security graphs use an agentless scanning capability. The agentless scanning capability takes snapshots of your VMs and analyzes them using the Microsoft Defender Vulnerability engine to detect vulnerabilities installed in software without needing to deploy any agents or extensions to your VMs. The advantage of using an agentless approach is that there is zero effect on the OS of your VMs. In addition, after you enable the agentless scanning capability for your VMs, results are available within hours (which is less time compared with an agent-based approach of discovering installed software and vulnerabilities). Security governance can help drive the remediation process of vulnerabilities.

6.4   *Security governance*

When Defender for Cloud discovers security problems, such as misconfigurations or weaknesses in your Azure resources, the team responsible for operating Defender for Cloud often is not the same team inside of the organization that owns the Azure resources on which misconfigurations or weaknesses have been discovered. The role that owns Azure resources is commonly referred to as the *resource owner* (or, less frequently, *product owner*). Resource owners are usually tasked with performing the remediation steps outlined in recommendations, given that they're the ones who own the resources.

To complete the remediation process more effectively, you can use a set of capabilities in Microsoft Defender for Cloud called *security governance*. Security governance is not one but a set of capabilities that assign the following:

- *Owner*—A person or group of people who is responsible for driving the remediation process
- *Due date*—The timeframe by which the remediation steps need to be completed
- *Grace period*—An optional setting, which, when enabled, limits the effect of your unhealthy resources on your secure score until the due date is surpassed
- *Email notifications*—An optional setting, which, when enabled, sends emails weekly to owners with an overview of on-time and overdue tasks, as well as to their management (if an email for the owner's manager is found in the organizational Microsoft Entra ID)

6.4.1   *Manually assigning owners and due dates*

Say that Defender for Cloud identified VMs that have management ports open. For every resource affected by this recommendation, you can assign an owner who is going to be in charge of the remediation process, as well as a due date, by which time the remediation steps need to be completed (figure 6.8). You can also apply a grace period, which ensures that until the due date is reached, these resources don't negatively affect your secure score.

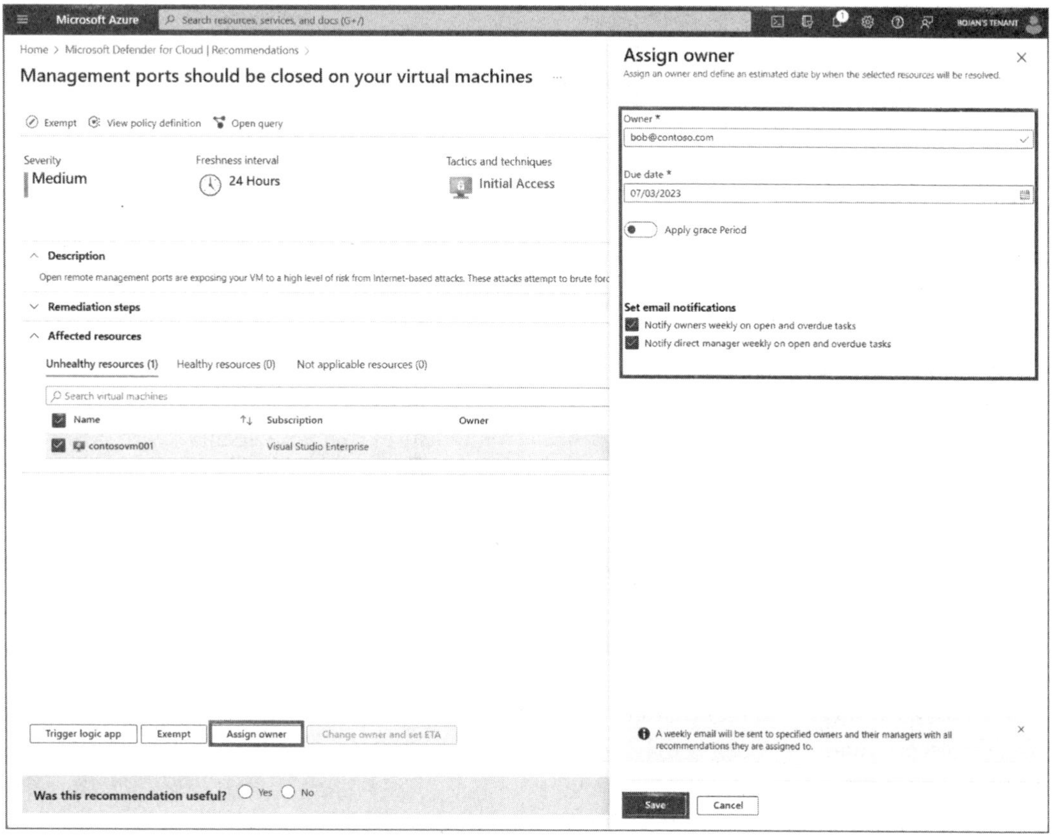

Figure 6.8   Using security governance to set an owner and due date of recommendations in Microsoft Defender for Cloud

You can manually assign owners and a due date for a particular recommendation by performing the following actions:

1 Navigate to the Microsoft Defender for Cloud dashboard inside of the Azure portal.
2 On the left, select Recommendations.

3   Choose a particular recommendation (such as one of the recommendations highlighted in the Attack Path).

4   Select a resource that does not have an owner or due date assigned and click Assign Owner.

5   In the blade that opens, under Owner, type the email address of the person responsible for performing the remediation steps for the resources in question.

6   Specify the date by which the remediation steps need to be performed.

7   Optionally, you can keep the grace period toggle enabled and email notifications selected.

8   Click Save.

6.4.2   *When should you use a grace period?*

Imagine that you have several hundred VMs running Windows in Azure that you regularly need to apply patches to when they become available. When new patches are released, until you patch your VMs, they will not be adhering to security best-practice guidance. For your secure score not to decrease, you need to patch your VMs as soon as new patches are made available, which, for large environments, is not feasible (most organizations apply patches to a smaller number of VMs first to test them).

So, after every Patch Tuesday (which is the common name for the monthly release of security updates for Windows OS), your secure score will drop until you apply the patches. Thus, you might feel you're playing catch-up with the secure score. To avoid this situation, you can apply a *grace period*, which ensures that your secure score is not negatively affected until the due date is surpassed. Although you can manually assign owners and due dates (as shown in figure 6.6), it's recommended you use *governance rules*.

6.4.3   *Programmatically assigning owners and due dates*

Governance rules allow you to programmatically set the owner and due date for recommendations. When using governance rules to assign owners and due dates, you can select a timeframe of 7, 14, 30, or 90 days from the time when the governance rule detects the recommendation. An advantage of using governance rules for assigning owners and due dates is that you can assign owners based on resource tags (which are what a lot of organizations use to drive the remediation process). Additionally, when using governance rules, you can specify different scopes on which the rule will apply (such as at the Azure management group level).

Say you want to drive system updates on your VMs by giving owners 14 days to follow the System Updates Should Be Installed on Your Machines recommendation. To create a governance rule for this recommendation, perform the following actions:

1   Navigate to the Microsoft Defender for Cloud dashboard inside of the Azure portal.

2   On the left, select Environment Settings, and then click Governance Rules.

3   Select + Create Governance Rule.

4   Enter a name for the rule (for example, OS updates campaign).

5   From the drop-down menu, select the scope to which the rule applies (such as the Tenant Root Group).

6   Enter a brief description that indicates the intended purpose of the governance rule.

7   Select the recommendation to which this rule applies by choosing By Specific Recommendations, and then select System Updates Should Be Installed on Your Machines.

8   Set the owner by selecting the By Resource Tag option and, under Specify Tag Key, select the Resource tag.

9   From the drop-down menu, select 14 Days as the remediation timeframe.

10 Leave the grace period toggle on, which will prevent this recommendation from affecting your secure score until it's overdue.

11 Optionally, deselect the email notification settings.

12 Click Create.

After you create the governance rule, you can use the Security Posture section to track how many recommendations are overdue and how many recommendations are unassigned. As a best practice, you should ensure that all recommendations have an owner and due date assigned to ensure accountability and that each recommendation is being addressed.

Workbooks can help track the status of recommendations (I'll cover workbooks in chapter 7). Although implementing recommendations can fix security problems and improve the overall security posture of an organization, many organizations require that their resources are assessed and mapped to specific compliance controls to meet regulatory compliance requirements. For this, you can use the *regulatory compliance dashboard*.

6.5   *Regulatory compliance*

Regulatory compliance is a dashboard in Defender for Cloud through which you can assess the compliance posture of your environment. Defender for Cloud continuously assesses the configuration of your resources and maps them to compliance controls and best practices in regulatory compliance standards. The regulatory compliance dashboard reflects your compliance with technical security controls from specific standards, such as built-in industry standards, regulatory standards, and benchmarks (figure 6.9).

As standards evolve and get updated over time, Microsoft keeps up with changes and improves its coverage over time. The regulatory compliance dashboard displays specific standards and benchmarks and maps the applicable assessments of your resources to the requirements of the standard. When you make changes to configurations of your resources over time, the results displayed in the regulatory compliance dashboard get updated to allow you to continuously assess the compliance posture of your Azure over time.

6.5.1 *Regulatory compliance in action*

Does your application handle customer credit card information? If so, you may like to know how the configurations of the resources for your applications running on Azure compare with the widely used PCI DSS. For this, you can use the regulatory compliance dashboard by performing the following actions (figure 6.9):

NOTE The permissions needed to access and manage the regulatory compliance dashboard differ from other parts of Defender for Cloud. To access the regulatory compliance dashboard and manage standards, you need to have at least the Resource Policy Contributor and Security Admin role.

1 Navigate to the Microsoft Defender for Cloud dashboard inside of the Azure portal.
2 On the left, select Regulatory Compliance.
3 Select the tab with PCI DSS 3.2.1 compliance standard.

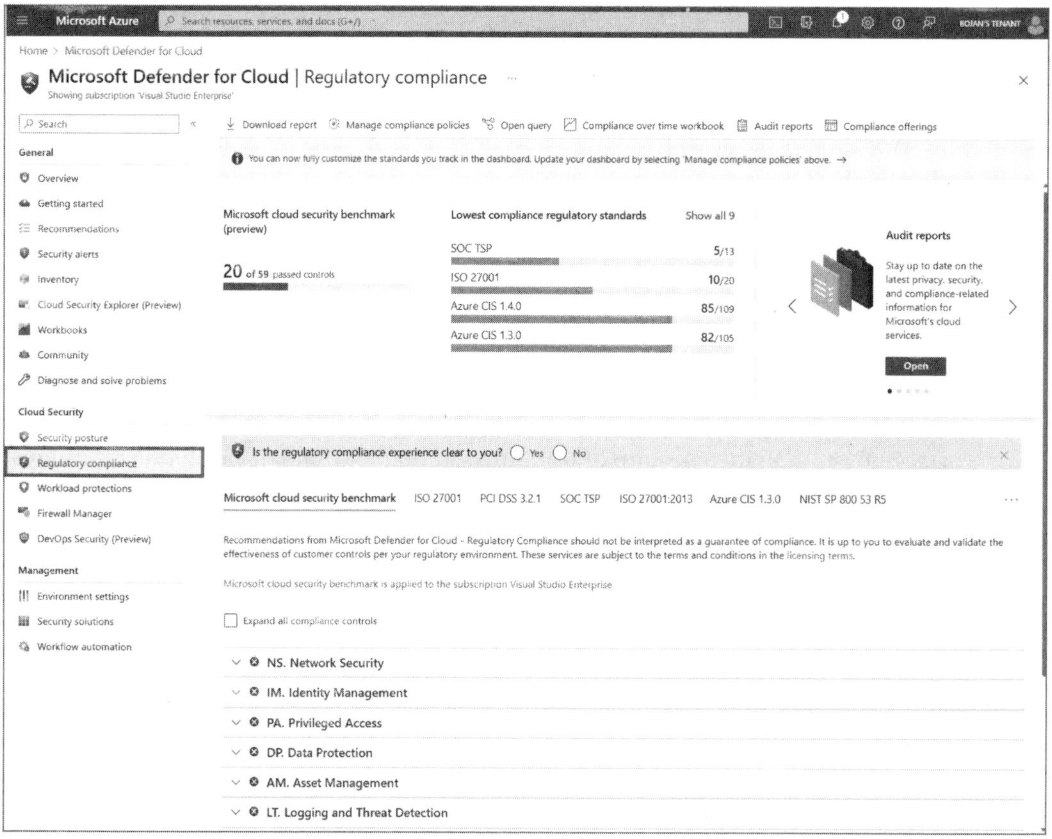

Figure 6.9 The regulatory compliance dashboard in Microsoft Defender for Cloud

4 Expand one of the failing controls highlighted in red by clicking it.

5 Select any of the recommendations with failed resources.

6 Follow the suggestions and guidance from the Recommendation Details page.

7 It can take up to 12 hours for the results in the regulatory compliance blade to update.

Why are some compliance controls grayed out?

Some compliance controls might appear grayed out because either there are no assessments mapped to them or because Defender for Cloud isn't able to automatically assess these compliance controls. For example, controls that are grayed out can be procedure or process related.

The regulatory compliance dashboard in Microsoft Defender for Cloud is powerful because it can aid you in improving the compliance posture of your resources (such as the resources used by your application). The default standard shown when you navigate to the regulatory compliance dashboard is MCSB. In addition to MCSB, the dashboard contains other built-in regulatory compliance and industry standards. Certain standards, such as ISO 27001, are visible as tabs next to MCSB (figure 6.9). Other built-in standards, such as Cybersecurity Maturity Model Certification (CMMC) Level 3 or HIPAA/HITRUST, need to be added to the dashboard before you can use them.

6.5.2 *Adding a built-in standard*

You can add more built-in standards beyond the ones displayed as tabs in the regulatory compliance dashboard. Among others, these include widely used standards such as Cybersecurity Maturity Model Certification (CMMC) Level 3 and NIST Special Publication 800-53 Revision 5.

> **NOTE** For a reference list of what regulatory compliance standards are available in the regulatory compliance dashboard, you can start at http://mng.bz/qrvK.

You can benchmark the configuration of your Azure resources against a built-in standard, such as CMMC level 3. To use this built-in standard (like any other of the built-in standards not displayed), you first need to add it to the regulatory compliance dashboard by performing the following actions:

1 Using a user with the Owner or Policy contributor role, navigate to the Microsoft Defender for Cloud dashboard inside of the Azure portal.

2 On the left, select Regulatory Compliance.

3 Select the tab Manage Compliance Policies.

4 Click the subscription or management group to which you want to assign the built-in standard. As a best practice, select the highest scope for which the built-in standard is applicable. This ensures that compliance data is aggregated.

5 On the left, select Security Policy.

6 Under Industry & Regulatory Standards, click Add More Standards.

7 Select the built-in standard you want to add (such as CMMC Level 3) by clicking Add.

8 Complete the click-through wizard to assign the initiative on the desired scope, and then click Create.

It can take up to a few hours for the built-in standard you added to appear in the regulatory compliance dashboard. After the standard you added appears in the regulatory compliance dashboard, you can use it to benchmark the configuration of your Azure resources against CMMC Level 3.

> **What about custom standards?**
>
> Say your organization wants to adhere to standards or has unique requirements that are not part of the built-in standards in the regulatory compliance dashboard in Microsoft Defender for Cloud. In addition to adding the built-in standards, you can also create custom standards based on your organization's requirements. I'll cover creating custom standards and adding them to the regulatory compliance dashboard in chapter 10.

Although it's important to adhere to compliance control frameworks and fix security problems found in recommendations, it's equally important to monitor the environment for potentially suspicious activities and signs of compromise after security problems have been solved. You can monitor your Azure resources with cloud workload protection, which is what the next chapter teaches you.

6.6 Answers to exercises

Exercise 6.1

1 Navigate to the Microsoft Defender for Cloud dashboard inside of the Azure portal.

2 Select Recommendations.

3 Expand the security control Enable MFA.

4 In the list, click any recommendation that has unhealthy resources.

5 Expand the Remediation Steps section in the blade that opens.

6 Implement the remediation steps.

7 Based on the time indicated in the Freshness Interval, check back after the recommendation has been updated to ensure the guidance has been implemented and the security problem on the resource has been resolved.

After you follow all recommendations for unhealthy resources that are part of the Enable MFA security control, repeat these steps for the Secure Management Ports and Remediate Vulnerabilities Security Controls.

Exercise 6.2

1 Navigate to the Microsoft Defender for Cloud dashboard inside of the Azure portal.

2 On the left, select Cloud Security Explorer.

3 From the drop-down menu, select Identity & Access, and then click User Accounts.

4 Select + to add a filter.

5 From the drop-down menu, select Security, and then click Doesn't Have MFA Enabled.

6 Click + to add another filter to your query.

7 From the drop-down menu, select Identity & Access, and then click Has Permissions To.

8 Choose Data > Object Storage > Azure Storage Accounts.

9 Click Search.

10 The results populate at the bottom of the page. Click any of the displayed results to see more information about that particular user account.

Summary

- Microsoft Defender for Cloud is a solution you can use to improve the security posture of your Azure environment. It provides you with a lot of capabilities, one of which is CSPM, which allows you to better secure your Azure resources.

- Defender for Cloud includes both free and paid cloud security posture capabilities. When you onboard your Azure subscriptions, you get a secure score and recommendations for your Azure resources for free.

- To use the advanced CSPM capabilities, such as the cloud security graph, you need to enable the Defender CSPM plan. The regulatory compliance dashboard, which allows you to benchmark the configurations of your resources against industry regulatory standards, also requires the Defender CSPM plan.

- The cloud security graph is a capability upon which attack paths and the cloud security explorer are built. The identified attack paths help you understand which security problems you need to fix first because they're the ones that bad actors can attempt to exploit to compromise your environment. With the cloud security explorer, you can translate the knowledge you have about your environment and create graph-based queries that run against the cloud security graph data.

- Security governance helps drive the remediations process of security problems in your organization by answering questions, such as who is responsible for remediating security problems and until when, and transparently tracking the progress of the remediation process.

Security monitoring for Azure resources: Microsoft Defender for Cloud plans

This chapter covers

- Cloud workload protection
- Microsoft Defender for Cloud plans
- Security alerts
- Workflow automation
- Exporting data
- Workbooks

As you learned in chapter 6, having good security hygiene by practicing and applying security best practices can help you avoid breaches and keep your Azure resources secured and protected. It's important to adhere to compliance control frameworks and fix security problems found in recommendations, but there is more to it than that. After security problems have been solved, it's equally important to monitor your Azure environment for potentially suspicious activities and signs of compromise. With the amount of Azure resources being deployed in your environment increasing both in numbers and resource types, it can be challenging to employ the right security monitoring capabilities for the right resource type. As you can imagine, monitoring virtual machines (VMs) differs from monitoring containerized applications (such as Kubernetes).

> **NOTE** To follow along with the exercises in this chapter, you can use the GitHub repository (https://github.com/bmagusic/azure-security).

Microsoft Defender for Cloud provides you with the ability to monitor your environment for potentially suspicious activities and signs of compromise. For this purpose, this chapter teaches you how to use Defender for Cloud's security monitoring capabilities to employ the right security monitoring for commonly used resource types in Azure (such as VMs, Kubernetes, databases, key vaults, and more). Another term commonly used when referring to these security monitoring capabilities is *cloud workload protection*.

7.1   Cloud workload protection

Another major pillar of capabilities in Microsoft Defender for Cloud that can help you improve your organization's security posture revolves around cloud workload protection. At a high level, cloud workload protection continuously monitors your environment for suspicious activities and signs of compromise. When Defender for Cloud detects an activity with a high level of suspicion, it triggers a security alert that notifies you about what happened and provides information to help you investigate this activity further.

The continuous security monitoring capabilities in Defender for Cloud are distributed across the various stages of the kill chain model (see chapter 1). Being distributed across the stages of the kill chain model means that Defender for Cloud is able to detect suspicious activities and potential signs of compromise whether a bad actor is in an initial stage of their attack (such as probing your Azure environment) or at a more advanced stage (such as moving laterally or looking to exfiltrate data from your Azure environment). These cloud workload-protection capabilities in Defender for Cloud support a variety of resource types and come in the form of *Defender for Cloud plans.*

7.2   Microsoft Defender for Cloud plans

Defender for Cloud plans are resource-specific and span across compute, data, and service layers in Azure. You enable Defender for Cloud on a subscription level, meaning it provides coverage and protection for all resources within your Azure subscription. Figure 7.1 shows the different Defender for Cloud plans that can be enabled on your Azure subscriptions, which are as follows:

- Defender CSPM
- Microsoft Defender for Servers
- Microsoft Defender for App Service
- Microsoft Defender for Azure SQL Databases

- Microsoft Defender for SQL Servers on Machines
- Microsoft Defender for Open-Source Relational Databases
- Microsoft Defender for Azure Cosmos DB
- Microsoft Defender for Storage
- Microsoft Defender for Containers
- Microsoft Defender for Key Vault
- Microsoft Defender for Resource Manager
- Microsoft Defender for DNS

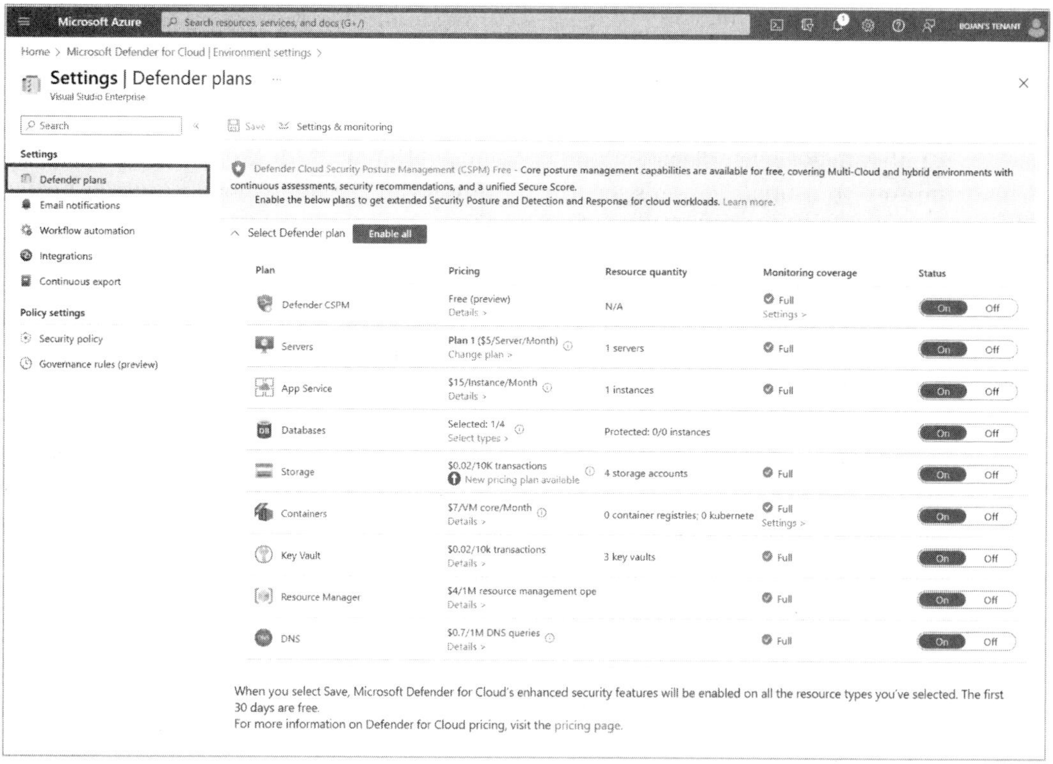

Figure 7.1   Microsoft Defender for Cloud plans that can be enabled on an Azure subscription

I covered Defender CSPM in chapter 6 in the context of cloud security posture management. Therefore, in this chapter, I'll focus on the remaining plans related to cloud workload protection, starting with *Microsoft Defender for Servers.*

7.2.1   *Microsoft Defender for Servers*

Microsoft Defender for Servers provides a comprehensive set of capabilities to protect your Azure VMs, including the following:

- Microsoft Defender for Endpoint (MDE)
- Vulnerability assessment
- Just-in-time (JIT) VM access
- Adaptive application control
- File integrity monitoring
- Adaptive network hardening

MICROSOFT DEFENDER FOR ENDPOINT

Microsoft Defender for Servers includes an integrated license for MDE. This means that you can use MDE's capabilities for your servers in Azure. These capabilities include, among others, endpoint detection and response, next-generation antivirus protection, attack surface reduction, threat and vulnerability management, auto-investigation, and auto-remediation.

VULNERABILITY ASSESSMENT

At a very high level, you can consider the vulnerability assessment capability as a scanner that performs a series of security checks on your servers to detect any weaknesses or vulnerabilities. Microsoft Defender for Servers provides you with the ability to choose between Qualys and Microsoft's threat and vulnerability assessment solution. They both continuously scan installed applications on your servers to find vulnerabilities.

JUST-IN-TIME VM ACCESS

JIT VM access allows you to lock down inbound traffic to your VMs. As you recall from chapter 3, leaving management ports exposed on VMs is a security risk. With JIT VM access, you can reduce exposure to attacks while providing access when needed.

ADAPTIVE APPLICATION CONTROL

The adaptive application control uses machine learning to determine what applications are being run on your machines. Based on this knowledge, it then establishes an allow list of safe applications that can be run on your machines.

FILE INTEGRITY MONITORING

File integrity monitoring enables you to select files and registries that you want to monitor. It supports monitoring of, among others, OS files, Windows registries, application software, and Linux system files because changes made to these files and registries can be indicative of an attack.

ADAPTIVE NETWORK HARDENING

Adaptive network hardening provides you with recommendations on how to further reduce the attack surface by hardening network security group rules. To provide you with recommendations, this capability uses machine learning that factors in actual traffic, threat intelligence information, and other indicators of compromise.

A Defender for Servers plan comes in two flavors: plan 1 and plan 2 (table 7.1). Plan 1 is better suited for organizations that want their VMs to be protected solely with MDE (such as on-premises VMs), whereas plan 2 is better suited for organizations that have requirements going beyond having only MDE on their VMs (such as using JIT

VM access or adaptive network hardening on Azure VMs). Some capabilities, such as JIT VM access and adaptive network hardening, are only available for cloud-based VMs (such as Azure VMs) and are not available for on-premises VMs. Because this book focuses on securing Azure resources, I'll only cover Defender for Servers plan 2 because it provides more capabilities to secure your VMs (applying a defense-in-depth mindset).

Table 7.1   Comparison of Defender for Servers plans

Defender for Servers plan 1	Defender for Servers plan 2
Microsoft Defender for Endpoint	Microsoft Defender for Endpoint
Microsoft Defender Vulnerability Management	Microsoft Defender Vulnerability Management
Auto-provisioning	Auto-provisioning
	Agentless vulnerability scanning for machines
	Just-in-time VM access for machine ports
	Adaptive application control
	File integrity monitoring
	Adaptive network hardening
	Network layer threat detections
	Integrated vulnerability assessment powered by Qualys
	Log Analytics 500 MB free data ingestion

To enable Microsoft Defender for Servers plan 2 on your subscription, run the following command with the Security Admin role on the subscription:

```
az security pricing create -n VirtualMachines
-tier 'standard'
```

The command used to enable the Microsoft Defender for Servers plan on your Azure subscription

After this command runs, it enables the Microsoft Defender for Servers plan. Your output should look similar to the following:

```
{
    "freeTrialRemainingTime": "0:00:00",
    "id": "/subscriptions/00000000-0000-0000-0000-000000000000/providers
    /Microsoft.Security/pricings/VirtualMachines",
    "name": "VirtualMachines",
    "pricingTier": "Standard",
    "type": "Microsoft.Security/pricings"
}
```

In addition to enabling the plan on the subscription, you need to ensure the Log Analytics agent (see chapter 6) and vulnerability assessment are deployed to your VMs. Certain capabilities in Microsoft Defender for Servers rely on the Log Analytics agent. These capabilities include, among others, integration with MDE, file integrity monitoring, and adaptive application control.

You can deploy both the Log Analytics agent and the vulnerability assessment for new and existing VMs with auto-provisioning by performing the following steps:

1 Navigate to the Microsoft Defender for Cloud dashboard inside of the Azure portal.
2 Select Environment Settings.
3 Click the subscription you onboarded to Defender for Cloud.
4 Select Settings & Monitoring in the upper taskbar of the blade that opens.
5 Enable the toggle next to Log Analytics Agent/Azure Monitor Agent.
6 Enable the toggle next to Vulnerability Assessment for Machines (as in figure 7.2).
7 Select Continue.
8 Click Save.

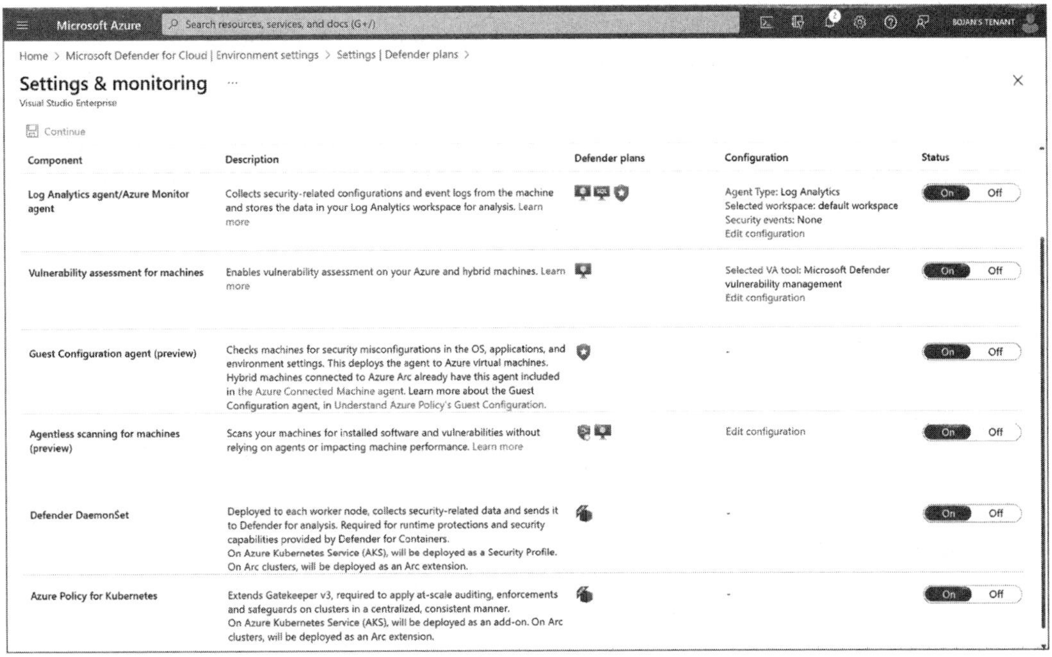

Figure 7.2 Configuring auto-provisioning for the Defender profile and Azure Policy for Kubernetes

Perform these steps again when you need to deploy other agents and extensions required by specific Defender for Cloud plans (like Defender for Containers and Defender for SQL Servers on Machines). For future reference, the requirements for Defender for Cloud plans that require agents and extensions are shown in table 7.2.

Table 7.2   Overview of Defender for Cloud plans that require agents

Defender for Servers	Defender for SQL Servers on Machines	Defender for Containers
Log Analytics agent Microsoft Defender for Endpoint Vulnerability assessment powered by Qualys (if using it)	Log Analytics agent Automatic SQL discovery and registration	Defender profile Azure Policy Add-On for Kubernetes

NOTE   Microsoft Defender for Cloud is a multicloud solution, which means you can apply Defender for Cloud's capabilities to other public clouds (like AWS and Google Cloud Platform) and even on-premises servers by integrating with Azure Arc. To apply Defender for Servers, Defender for SQL Servers on Machines, and Defender for Containers to multicloud and on-premises servers, in addition to the agents listed in table 7.2, you also need the Azure Arc agent.

> ### Exercise 7.1
> Defender for Cloud plans can be evaluated for free for the first 30 days on your Azure subscriptions. To solidify your knowledge of Defender for Servers, enable plan 2 for 30 days on subscriptions in your environment that contain VMs. If you don't want to keep using the plan after the first 30 days, make sure to disable it. Otherwise, you're going to be charged based on the number of resources that are covered by the plan.

Another compute resource type to which you can apply Defender for Cloud's cloud workload protection capabilities is containers. You can protect containers in your environment with *Microsoft Defender for Containers*.

7.2.2   *Microsoft Defender for Containers*

Microsoft Defender for Containers provides you with a unified plan for your container security. As mentioned in chapter 4, container security challenges differ compared with more traditional compute resources (such as VMs). Containers are usually short lived, and images are immutable. That, coupled with a variety of threats, such as exploiting vulnerable images, accessing exposed applications, and abusing overpermissioned roles, makes it important to have a solution in place that can detect these threats. To make container security challenges more palpable, I offer an example (figure 7.3).

Say your cluster exposes an interface, such as the Kubeflow dashboard, to the internet. Kubeflow is a framework used for running machine-learning tasks in Kubernetes. Exposing the Kubeflow dashboard to the internet allows unauthenticated access. Bad actors can exploit this weakness to gain access to your environment.

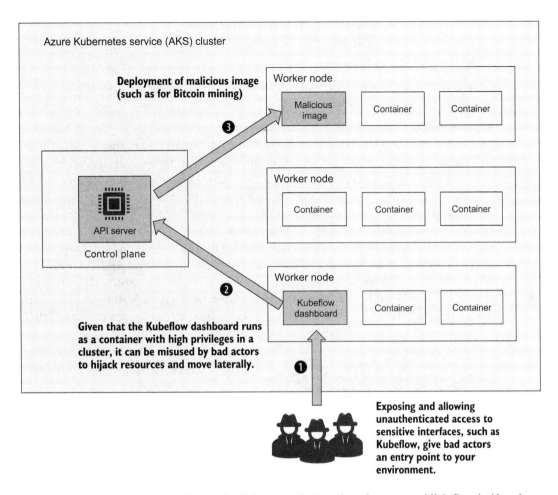

Figure 7.3 An example of an attack targeting Kubernetes clusters through an exposed Kubeflow dashboard

Furthermore, because the Kubeflow dashboard runs as a container with high privileges in the cluster, bad actors can misuse this vulnerability to escalate privileges and gain access to the control plane of the cluster.

After bad actors have access to the control plane, they can then deploy malicious container images in a cluster, such as images with crypto miners. After being deployed on worker nodes, these container images could be used to mine digital currency (such as Bitcoin), often incurring significant costs to your Azure consumption. This example highlights the different parts that need to be secured in container security, including the container registry used to deploy container images, the control plane of the cluster itself, and the worker nodes that run the containerized applications.

Microsoft Defender for Containers addresses container security challenges by providing you with a single plan that includes the following capabilities:

- Run-time threat detection for nodes and clusters
- Vulnerability assessment for container images
- Hardening and Kubernetes policy

I cover each one of these capabilities in more detail, starting with run-time threat detection for nodes and clusters.

RUN-TIME THREAT DETECTION FOR NODES AND CLUSTERS

An important aspect of container security is being able to detect threats. Due to the very nature of Kubernetes (and based on the example in figure 7.2), threat detection in Kubernetes clusters needs to happen at the control plane level as well as the worker (or host) node level. Microsoft Defender for Containers detects threats at both levels. It provides threat detection at the cluster level by collecting Kubernetes audit logs and security events from the API server in the control plane. The collection of these logs and events for Azure Kubernetes Services is done through a backend integration.

To provide run-time threat detection at the worker node level, Defender for Containers relies on a native Kubernetes agent called the Defender profile. The Defender profile was developed by Microsoft and is deployed on each node in your Kubernetes cluster (figure 7.4). The Defender profile collects signals from nodes and sends them

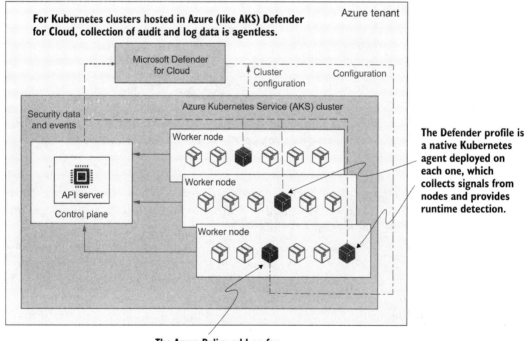

Figure 7.4   An architecture diagram of Defender for Containers for an Azure Kubernetes Service cluster

to Defender for Cloud for further analysis. You can automatically deploy the Defender profile to nodes in your Kubernetes cluster using auto-provisioning (similar to the Log Analytics agent in Defender for Servers). Using the Defender profile ensures Defender for Containers is able to detect suspicious activities and signs of compromise on your clusters (such as crypto-mining activity on your nodes).

In addition to providing threat detection for worker nodes and the control plane of your Kubernetes cluster, it's also important to scan container images stored in the container registry (such as Azure Container Registry) for vulnerabilities. For this purpose, you can use *vulnerability assessment for container images.*

VULNERABILITY ASSESSMENT FOR CONTAINER IMAGES

When you enable Microsoft Defender for Containers, it automatically discovers and onboards your Azure container registries. After onboarding your container registries, Defender for Containers then scans your container images for vulnerabilities on push, pull, and import. If your container images have any vulnerabilities, Defender for Containers surfaces these in the Microsoft Defender for Cloud dashboard.

Defender for Containers also performs continuous scanning of your running images and detects running images with known vulnerabilities. To detect these vulnerabilities, Defender for Containers pulls the container image from the container registry and runs it in an isolated sandbox. It then uses a scanner to detect known vulnerabilities in the container image.

> **NOTE** For a reference list of supported registries and images, you can start at http://mng.bz/7Dqx.

In addition to vulnerability assessment, it's also important to continuously monitor your cluster for misconfigurations.

HARDENING AND KUBERNETES POLICY

Microsoft Defender for Containers also provides recommendations for both the control plane and data plane of your Kubernetes clusters. Control plane recommendations offer suggestions and guidance on how to better secure your worker nodes, whereas data plane recommendations audit or enforce security best practices for Kubernetes workloads.

To audit or enforce your Kubernetes workloads, Defender for Containers relies on the Azure Policy add-on for Kubernetes. This add-on ensures that every request to the API server of your Kubernetes cluster is monitored against the predefined set of best practices before changes are made to your cluster. You can also use the add-on for such tasks as blocking the creation of privileged containers.

ENABLING MICROSOFT DEFENDER FOR CONTAINERS

To enable Microsoft Defender for Containers on your subscription, run the following command with the Security Admin role on the subscription:

```
az security pricing create -n Containers -tier 'standard'    ⟵
```
The command used to enable Microsoft Defender for Containers plan on your Azure subscription

After this command runs, it enables the Microsoft Defender for Containers plan. Your output should look similar to the following:

```
{
      "freeTrialRemainingTime": "0:00:00",
      "id": "/subscriptions/00000000-0000-0000-0000-000000000000/providers
      ➥/Microsoft.Security/pricings/Containers",
      "name": "Containers",
      "pricingTier": "Standard",
      "type": "Microsoft.Security/pricings"
}
```

In addition to enabling the Defender for Containers plan on your Azure subscription, you need to ensure that both the Defender profile and Azure Policy add-on for Kubernetes are deployed to your Kubernetes cluster. You can do so using auto-provisioning. Using auto-provisioning ensures that the Defender profile and Azure Policy add-on for Kubernetes are deployed to both existing and new clusters created in your subscription.

> **NOTE** Defender for Containers can be used both for managed and unmanaged Kubernetes. For a list of supported capabilities based on a particular Kubernetes distribution, you can start at http://mng.bz/7Dqx.

Defender for Cloud plans can be enabled independently on a subscription. That is, you can enable a plan, such as Defender for Containers on your subscription, regardless of other Defender for Cloud plans.

Another plan designed to protect compute resources types is *Microsoft Defender for App Service.*

7.2.3 Microsoft Defender for App Service

Microsoft Defender for App Service detects a multitude of threats to your Azure App Service resources. It can detect the execution of multiple types of scanners that bad actors frequently use to probe applications for weaknesses. It can also detect attempts to run high-privilege commands, connections from an anomalous IP address, fileless attack behavior, digital currency-mining tools, and many other suspicious and malicious code execution activities. Also, Microsoft Defender for App Service can detect any dangling DNS entries (see chapter 4).

To enable a Microsoft Defender for App Service plan on your subscriptions, run the following command with the Security Admin role on the subscription:

```
az security pricing create -n AppServices -tier 'standard'
```

The command used to enable the Microsoft Defender for App Service plan on your Azure subscription

After this command runs, it enables the Microsoft Defender for App Service plan. Your output should look similar to the following:

```
{
  "freeTrialRemainingTime": "0:00:00",
  "id": "/subscriptions/00000000-0000-0000-0000-000000000000/providers
  ➥/Microsoft.Security/pricings/AppServices",
  "name": "AppServices",
  "pricingTier": "Standard",
  "type": "Microsoft.Security/pricings"
}
```

In addition to protecting compute resources (such as Azure App Service, Azure Kubernetes Services, and VMs), Defender for Cloud plans can be used to protect data. There are various Defender for Cloud plans you can enable for this purpose. I'd like to start with storage accounts and *Microsoft Defender for Storage.*

7.2.4 Microsoft Defender for Storage

Microsoft Defender for Storage provides you with threat detection capabilities for your blob containers, file shares, and data lakes in Azure. It detects unusual and potentially harmful attempts to access or exploit weaknesses in storage accounts. For this purpose, after you enable Microsoft Defender for Storage, it continuously analyzes the transaction stream generated by Azure Blob Storage and Azure Files. Threats particularly relevant to storage accounts include, among others, malware upload, data exfiltration, scanning accounts/containers/blobs, credential theft, malicious insiders, and more. To detect these and other threats to your storage accounts, Defender for Cloud has a rich detection suite.

Defender for Storage is able to detect suspicious access patterns (such as accessing storage accounts from suspicious IPs or a Tor exit node), the uploading of malicious content (such as potential malware upload), suspicious behavior (such as an unusual amount of data extracted or deleted), and other threats to your storage accounts (such as scanning publicly accessible containers). To alert on potential malware uploads, Defender for Storage uses reputation hash analysis supported by Microsoft's Threat Intelligence data. Defender for Cloud compares the hash of the uploaded file with hashes of known viruses, trojans, and ransomware.

To enable the Microsoft Defender for Storage plan on your subscriptions, run the following command with the Security Admin role on the subscription:

```
az security pricing create -n StorageAccounts
-tier 'standard'
```

The command used to enable the Microsoft Defender for Storage plan on your Azure subscription

After this command runs, it enables the Microsoft Defender for Storage plan. Your output should look similar to the following:

```
{
  "freeTrialRemainingTime": "0:00:00",
  "id": "/subscriptions/00000000-0000-0000-0000-000000000000/providers
  ➥/Microsoft.Security/pricings/StorageAccounts",
  "name": "StorageAccounts",
  "pricingTier": "Standard",
```

```
    "type": "Microsoft.Security/pricings"
}
```

> ## Managing the cost of high-transaction accounts
>
> Cost is often a concern within an organization. Defender for Storage continuously analyses the transaction stream generated by the Azure Blob Storage and Azure Files services. Therefore, protecting a storage account with a high transaction rate can be costly.
>
> To estimate cost, you can use the price estimation workbook (discussed later in this chapter), which gives you an estimate of how much it would cost to enable Defender for Storage based on the telemetry of your storage accounts. If you decide to enable Defender for Storage, you can then specify a security budget and set multiple security alerts using Azure Monitor (see chapter 9) to be notified should the cost of Defender for Storage come close to the budget you specified.

In addition to protecting storage accounts, Defender for Cloud's cloud workload protection capabilities can be applied to various databases. For this, you can use *Microsoft Defender for Databases*.

7.2.5   *Microsoft Defender for Databases*

Microsoft Defender for Databases provides threat detection for your data regardless of where it resides. It does this through four different Defender for Cloud plans:

- *Microsoft Defender for Azure SQL databases*—Covers Azure SQL databases, Azure SQL Managed Instance, Azure SQL Elastic Pools, and the dedicated SQL pool in Azure Synapse
- *Microsoft Defender for SQL servers on machines*—Covers SQL Server on-premises and SQL Server on Azure Virtual Machines
- *Microsoft Defender for open-source relational databases*—Covers Azure Database for MariaDB, Azure Database for MySQL, and Azure Database for PostgreSQL
- *Microsoft Defender for Azure Cosmos DB*—Covers Azure Cosmos DB

These four plans provide dedicated threat detection for different resource types. They detect unusual and harmful attempts on your data, like potential brute-force attacks, data attacks, and data exfiltration, and can discover security misconfigurations.

AZURE SQL DATABASES

Table 7.3 provides an overview of threat detections relevant to SQL that Defender for SQL databases and SQL Servers on machines are able to detect, but is by no means meant to be an exhaustive list, as there are more. To enable Microsoft Defender for Azure SQL Databases plan on your subscriptions, run the following command with the Security Admin role on the subscription:

```
az security pricing create -n SqlServers -tier 'standard'   ◁
```

The command used to enable the Microsoft Defender for Azure SQL Databases plan on your Azure subscription

After this command runs, it enables the Microsoft Defender for Azure SQL Databases plan. Your output should look similar to the following:

```
{
  "freeTrialRemainingTime": "0:00:00",
  "id": "/subscriptions/00000000-0000-0000-0000-000000000000/providers
  /Microsoft.Security/pricings/SqlServers",
  "name": "SqlServers",
  "pricingTier": "Standard",
  "type": "Microsoft.Security/pricings"
}
```

SQL SERVERS ON MACHINES

To enable a Microsoft Defender for SQL servers on machines plan on your subscriptions, run the following command with the Security Admin role on the subscription:

```
az security pricing create -n SqlServerVirtualMachines
-tier 'standard'
```

The command used to enable the Microsoft Defender for SQL servers on machines plan on your Azure subscription

After this command runs, it enables the Microsoft Defender for SQL servers on machines plan. Your output should look similar to the following:

```
{
  "freeTrialRemainingTime": "0:00:00",
  "id": "/subscriptions/00000000-0000-0000-0000-000000000000/providers
  /Microsoft.Security/pricings/SqlServerVirtualMachines",
  "name": "SqlServerVirtualMachines",
  "pricingTier": "Standard",
  "type": "Microsoft.Security/pricings"
}
```

Table 7.3   Overview of threats Defender for SQL can detect

Query analysis	Threat intelligence	Brute-force attack
Potential SQL injection Vulnerability to SQL injection Query obfuscation Shell external source execution	Access from an unusual location Access from a suspicious IP Domain anomaly Principal anomaly	Potential brute-force attack Potential brute-force attack on a valid user Potential successful brute-force attack

OPEN SOURCE RELATIONAL DATABASES

To enable a Microsoft Defender for open source relational databases plan on your subscriptions, run the following command with the Security Admin role on the subscription:

```
az security pricing create -n
OpenSourceRelationalDatabases -tier 'standard'
```

A command used to enable Microsoft Defender for open source relational databases plan on your Azure subscription

After this command runs, it enables the Microsoft Defender for open-source relational databases plan. Your output should look similar to the following:

```
{
  "freeTrialRemainingTime": "0:00:00",
  "id": "/subscriptions/00000000-0000-0000-0000-000000000000/providers
➥/Microsoft.Security/pricings/OpenSourceRelationalDatabases",
  "name": "OpenSourceRelationalDatabases",
  "pricingTier": "Standard",
  "type": "Microsoft.Security/pricings"
}
```

AZURE COSMOS DB

Compared to other databases, Azure Cosmos DB is a different breed of database. It's a cloud-native database with low latency and high availability. It provides an extra layer of security to detect and mitigate threats against your Azure Cosmos DB resources by analyzing both the control plane and data plane traffic. The threats it can detect include anomalous connections, potential data exfiltration, and SQL injection.

To enable a Microsoft Defender for Azure Cosmos DB plan on your subscriptions, run the following command with the Security Admin role on the subscription:

```
az security pricing create -n CosmosDbs –tier 'standard'   ◄──────────┐
```
                              The command used to enable the Microsoft Defender
                              for Azure Cosmos DB plan on your Azure subscription

After this command runs, it enables the Microsoft Defender for Azure Cosmos DB plan. Your output should look similar to the following:

```
{
  "freeTrialRemainingTime": "0:00:00",
  "id": "/subscriptions/00000000-0000-0000-0000-000000000000/providers
➥/Microsoft.Security/pricings/CosmosDbs",
  "name": "CosmosDbs",
  "pricingTier": "Standard",
  "type": "Microsoft.Security/pricings"
}
```

Microsoft Defender for Cloud's capabilities can also be applied to Azure's service layer, which includes Azure Key Vault, Azure Resources Manager, and Azure DNS.

To protect your key vaults, you can use *Microsoft Defender for Key Vault.*

7.2.6   *Microsoft Defender for Key Vault*

Microsoft Defender for Key Vault detects unusual and potentially harmful attempts to access or compromise key vaults. When suspicious activity occurs for key vault resources, it generates a security alert containing details of the suspicious activity. Some of the threats it can detect are access from a TOR exit node to a key vault, unusual users accessing the key vault, users accessing the key vault a high number of times, suspicious policy changes, and a secret query in a key vault.

To enable the Microsoft Defender for Key Vault plan on your subscriptions, run the following command with the Security Admin role on the subscription:

```
az security pricing create -n KeyVaults -tier 'standard'
```

The command used to the enable Microsoft Defender for Key Vault plan on your Azure subscription

After this command runs, it enables the Microsoft Defender for Key Vault plan. Your output should look similar to the following:

```
{
  "freeTrialRemainingTime": "0:00:00",
  "id": "/subscriptions/00000000-0000-0000-0000-000000000000/providers
  ➥/Microsoft.Security/pricings/KeyVaults",
  "name": "KeyVaults",
  "pricingTier": "Standard",
  "type": "Microsoft.Security/pricings"
}
```

Another Defender for Cloud plan that you can use for Azure's service layer is *Microsoft Defender for Resource Manager.*

7.2.7 *Microsoft Defender for Resource Manager*

Microsoft Defender for Resource Manager provides threat detection of malicious usage of Azure Resource Manager, whether it comes through the Azure portal, REST APIs, or PowerShell. It can detect permissions abuse, malicious insiders, and credential theft. Some other threats Microsoft Defender for Resource Manager can detect are suspicious high-privilege activities (such as suspicious usage in VM extensions), suspicious user access (such as impossible travel), and malicious Azure pen-test toolkits usage (such as running the MicroBurst toolkit) (table 7.4).

Table 7.4 Examples of threats Defender for Resource Manager can detect

Suspicious high-privileged management activities	Usage of malicious Azure exploit toolkits	Suspicious user access to Azure
Suspicious invocation of high-risk operations based on MITRE tactics Suspicious usage in VM extensions Suspicious privileged role assignment	MicroBurst toolkit PowerZure toolkit Azurite toolkit	Management operations from suspicious IPS (like TOR exit nodes or botnets) Suspicious management sessions Impossible travel

To enable the Microsoft Defender for Resource Manager plan on your subscriptions, run the following command with the Security Admin role on the subscription:

```
az security pricing create -n Arm -tier 'standard'
```

The command used to enable the Microsoft Defender for Resource Manager plan on your Azure subscription

After this command runs, it enables the Microsoft Defender for Resource Manager plan. Your output should look similar to the following:

```
{
    "freeTrialRemainingTime": "0:00:00",
    "id": "/subscriptions/00000000-0000-0000-0000-000000000000/providers
➥/Microsoft.Security/pricings/Arm",
    "name": "Arm",
    "pricingTier": "Standard",
    "type": "Microsoft.Security/pricings"
}
```

The remaining Defender for Cloud plan you can use for Azure's service layer is *Microsoft Defender for DNS*.

7.2.8   *Microsoft Defender for DNS*

Microsoft Defender for DNS detects threats to Azure resources connected to Azure DNS. To make this more palpable, I provide the following example. Imagine the fictional bad actor Eve successfully compromised one of your Azure resources and is trying to access an external host (such as her command-and-control server). As part of this process, the domain name for the command-and-control server is translated to the IP address using Azure DNS. Microsoft Defender for DNS continuously monitors DNS queries and responses for your environment. Thus, it can detect your Azure resource communicating with the malicious domain (in this case, Eve's command-and-control server) and generate a security alert. Table 7.5 provides an overview of threats that Defender for DNS is able to detect.

> **NOTE**   Microsoft Defender for DNS supports Azure DNS only. It doesn't support on-premise DNS.

Table 7.5   Examples of threats Defender for DNS can detect

Communication with malicious domains	Exploitation of the Azure DNS layer
Communication with suspicious domains	DNS tunneling
Bitcoin mining activity	Sinkhole DNS
Phishing activity	DNS cache poisoning
Dark web	Network intrusion signature

To enable a Microsoft Defender for DNS plan on your subscriptions, run the following command with the Security Admin role on the subscription:

```
az security pricing create -n Dns –tier 'standard'
```

The command used to enable the Microsoft Defender for DNS plan on your Azure subscription

After this command runs, it enables the Microsoft Defender for DNS plan. Your output should look similar to the following:

```
{
  "freeTrialRemainingTime": "0:00:00",
  "id": "/subscriptions/00000000-0000-0000-0000-000000000000/providers
  ➥/Microsoft.Security/pricings/Dns",
  "name": "Dns",
  "pricingTier": "Standard",
  "type": "Microsoft.Security/pricings"
}
```

When responding to security alerts generated by Defender for Cloud plans, minutes matter, and it's paramount to react quickly. Later in this chapter, I'll discuss how you can automate a response (for example, blocking traffic to suspicious IPs) using workflow automation. By default, regardless of which Defender for Cloud plan you enable, whenever a high-severity security alert is generated, Defender for Cloud notifies subscription owners by sending them emails.

Sometimes, you need to notify other people in your organization in addition to the subscription owners. To do so, you can configure *email notifications*.

7.2.9 Email notifications

Email notifications allow you to enable Defender for Cloud to send emails to other people or groups in addition to the subscription owners. Configuring email notifications ensures the relevant people (called *security contacts*) and roles inside your organization are notified about security alerts that Defender for Cloud triggers in your environment. To configure email notifications for security alerts, run the following command with the Security Admin or Subscription Owner role.

Listing 7.1   Configuring email notifications for security alerts

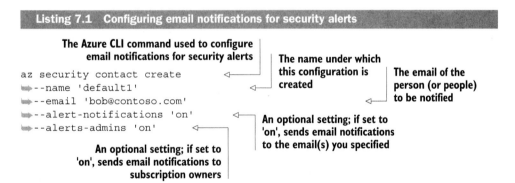

After this command runs, it configures Defender for Cloud to send email notifications to user Bob (in addition to sending them to subscription owners) whenever there is a high-severity security alert. Your output should look similar to the following:

```
[
  {
    "alertNotifications": "On",
    "alertsToAdmins": "On",
    "email": "bob@contoso.com",
    "etag": "\"02010000-0000-0d00-0000-0000b4c30000\"",
```

```
  "id": "/subscriptions/00000000-0000-0000-0000-000000000000/providers
  /Microsoft.Security/securityContacts/default1",
  "location": "West Europe",
  "name": "default1",
  "phone": "214000-0000",
  "type": "Microsoft.Security/securityContacts"
}
]
```

Some organizations may need more granularity when configuring email notifications for security alerts. Say that instead of high-severity alerts, you want to configure email notifications to be sent for security alerts with a medium-level severity or higher. You might also want to notify specific roles inside of your organization, such as users with the Contributor role on the subscription. If your organization has these requirements, you can further customize email notifications for security alerts using the Defender for Cloud dashboard (figure 7.5).

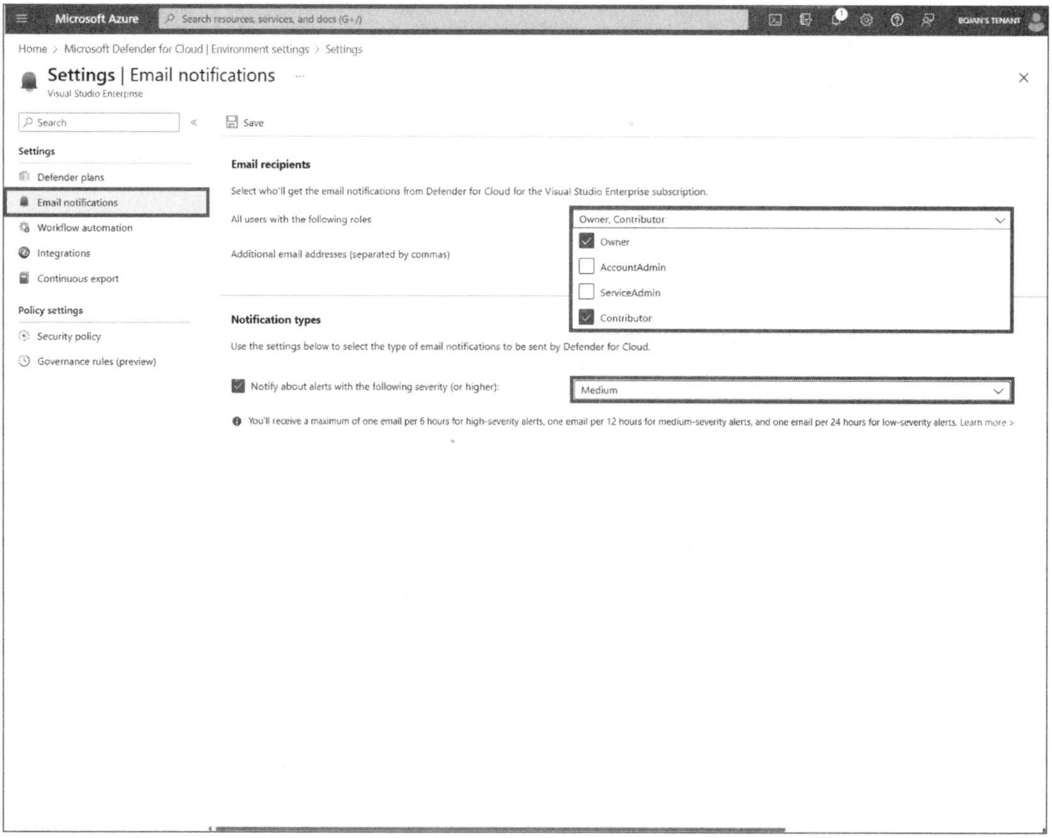

Figure 7.5   Customizing email notifications using the Microsoft Defender for Cloud dashboard

To configure this scenario with the Defender for Cloud dashboard, perform the following actions:

1 Navigate to the Microsoft Defender for Cloud dashboard inside of the Azure portal.

2 Select Environment Settings, and then click the Azure subscription for which you want to configure email notifications.

3 In the blade that opens on the left, select Email Notifications.

4 Choose the Contributor role to get email notifications using the drop-down menu. The available roles are Owner, AccountAdmin, ServiceAdmin, and Contributor; you can choose one or more roles.

5 Insert the email address of users or groups who'll get email notifications. You can insert more than one email address, separating them with commas.

6 Choose Medium for which severity (or higher) that Defender for Cloud should send email notifications for using the drop-down menu. The available options are High, Medium, or Low.

7 Click Save.

To alleviate alert fatigue, Defender for Cloud limits the volume of email notifications sent, depending on the severity of security alerts. You receive a maximum of one email every 6 hours for high-severity security alerts, one email every 12 hours for medium-severity, and one email every 24 hours for low-severity security alerts.

Using workflow automation for security alert notifications

Although being notified about security alerts via email is sufficient for some, many organizations require security alert notifications to be integrated with their collaboration tool or IT service management solution of choice. To achieve this, you can use *workflow automation* (covered later in this chapter). Workflow automation allows you to create customizable workflows, such as posting a message in a Teams chat and creating a ticket in ServiceNow when a high-severity security alert is triggered in Defender for Cloud.

After you configure email notifications, the relevant people (and roles) in your organizations are notified whenever Defender for Cloud triggers a *security alert*.

7.3 *Security alerts*

After you enable cloud workload protection capabilities using various Defender for Cloud plans, Defender for Cloud continuously monitors your environment for threats and potential signs of compromise. To detect threats to your environment, it correlates data from multiple sources. Among others, these data sources include Microsoft's own security researchers and security specialists and signal sharing between security teams across Microsoft's portfolio of business and consumer services.

Using the correlation of data among these data sources, Defender for Cloud employs various techniques (like behavioral analytics and anomaly detection) to detect threats to your environment and potential signs of compromise. When Defender for Cloud has a high-enough level of confidence that it has detected a threat to your environment, it triggers a security alert for your team to triage and investigate what happened further.

NOTE   Microsoft Defender for Cloud can generate a variety of security alerts for different OSs (Windows and Linux) and Azure resource types (across compute, container, data, networking, and service layers). To consult the complete reference list of security alerts for Azure resources, you can start at http://mng.bz/mV5n.

If there are several security alerts, Defender for Cloud can collect them into a collection of security alerts, called *security incidents*.

> **What about false positives?**
>
> Have you ever needed to perform a penetration testing exercise on your Azure resources covered by Defender for Cloud plans? Defender for Cloud triggers security alerts for this penetration testing activity because the activity might be indicative of a bad actor trying to probe and compromise your environment.
>
> To prevent alert fatigue, you can configure alert-suppression rules in Defender for Cloud to automatically dismiss alerts that you consider to be false positives or security alerts that are triggered too often to be useful. Although there are valid reasons for suppressing alerts (such as the penetration testing exercise), you should use suppression rules with caution and monitor them over time. To learn more about suppression rules in Defender for Cloud, you can start at http://mng.bz/5wJ4.

7.3.1   Security alerts in action

All security alerts that Defender for Cloud triggers are displayed in the Security alerts dashboard (figure 7.6), from where you can decide which security alert to investigate first. By default, Defender for Cloud prioritizes security alerts based on alert severity. Security alerts triggered in Defender for Cloud can have one of the following severities:

- *High*—Indicative that Defender for Cloud has high confidence that your resource is compromised and you should investigate it with the highest priority (such as detecting a known malicious tool typically used for credential theft).
- *Medium*—Indicative that your resource might be compromised due to a suspicious activity (such as a sign-in from an unusual location).
- *Low*—Indicative of a benign positive or a blocked attack (such as log clear, which, in many cases, is a routine task and not necessarily an attacker trying to hide their tracks).

- *Informational*—Security alerts that are part of a security incident might have this status, indicative that in the context of other security alerts, they might warrant further investigation.

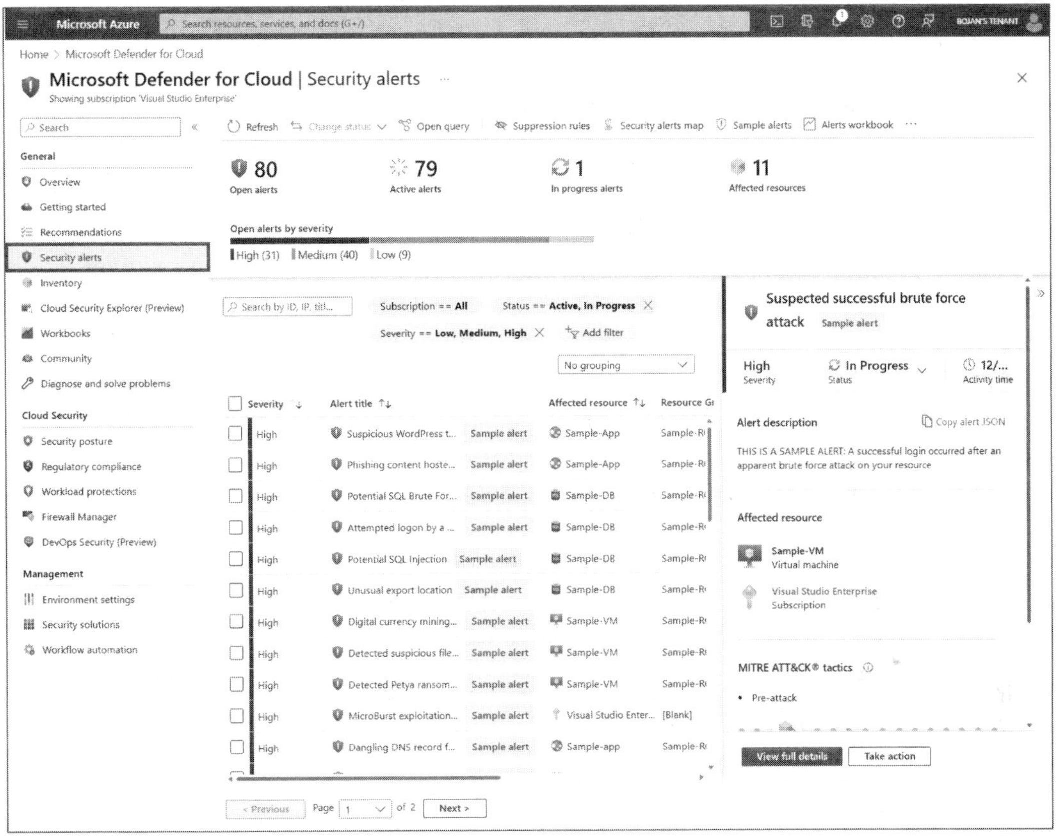

Figure 7.6   The Security Alerts dashboard in Microsoft Defender for Cloud

In addition to the severity of security alerts, the integration with the MITRE ATT&CK® framework can help you determine which security alert to investigate first. Where applicable, if a security alert (or recommendation) has defined tactics and techniques, Defender for Cloud shows a mapping to the MITRE ATT&CK® framework. This information can help you understand the intent of bad actors and prioritize the investigation of security alerts.

NOTE   Defender for Cloud's integration is based on version 9 of the MITRE ATT&CK® matrix. To understand which MITRE ATT&CK® tactics are supported in the scope of this integration, you can start at http://mng.bz/6D5G.

Exercise 7.2

After you enable Defender for Cloud plans, Defender for Cloud monitors your environment and triggers security alerts only when it detects a potential sign of comprise. Therefore, it might take some time for Defender for Cloud to trigger security alerts. For the next section, it's beneficial if you already have alerts in the Security Alerts dashboard.

If you don't have any security alerts triggered for your environment, you can generate sample security alerts. To follow along in the next section, generate sample alerts for VMs. If you need help with this exercise, you can start at http://mng.bz/o1BN.

7.3.2   *Investigating security alerts*

In addition to the categories of severity and tactic on the MITRE ATT&CK® matrix, each security alert provides you with a description and more insights about the detected activity, alert status, and activity time. Say Defender for Cloud triggers a security alert that is indicative of a successful brute-force attack in your environment. To investigate this security alert (or any other security alert, for that matter), perform the following actions:

1 Navigate to the Microsoft Defender for Cloud dashboard inside of the Azure portal.
2 Select Security Alerts, and then click the security alert that you want to investigate (such as the sample alert Suspected Successful Brute-Force Attack). Optionally, you can use the search bar to filter results (for example, to see security alerts for a particular resource, MITRE ATT&CK® tactic, or an attack occurring in the last 24 hours).
3 In the upper taskbar, select Change Status, and then choose In Progress. This changes the status of the security alert.
4 Select View Full Details to view more information about the security alert (figure 7.7).
5 Review the details shown on the right side, such as client IP address, location, and related entities.
6 Click either the button or tab Take Action to take further actions.
7 Click Mitigate the Threat to show remediation steps for this security alert.
8 Click Prevent Future Attacks to see top recommendations for preventing future attacks.
9 After you complete the investigation, click Status, and choose Resolve to change the status of this security alert.

An important part of investigating security alerts is responding to them. You can respond to security alerts by selecting Trigger Automated Response in the Take Action tab. This triggers a Logic App as a response to the particular security alert. Logic Apps

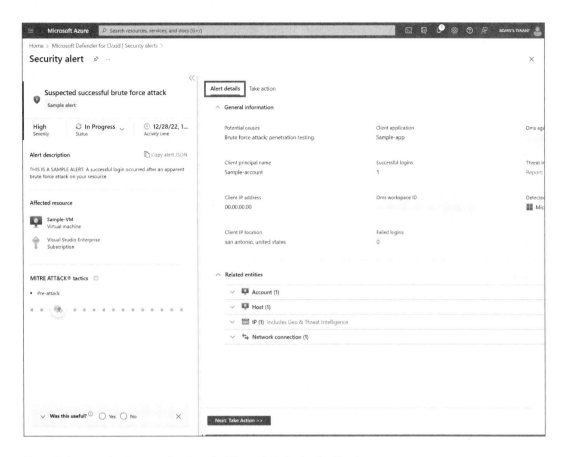

Figure 7.7 Investigating security alerts in Microsoft Defender for Cloud

are an Azure service that allows you to create customizable workflows that interact with a variety of systems (both Microsoft and non-Microsoft).

The integration in Defender for Cloud with Logic Apps allows you to run existing Logic Apps you built as a response to security alerts triggered by Defender for Cloud. Although you can run this Logic App workflow manually during the investigation process, minutes matter when it comes to detecting and responding to threats. You can programmatically configure and run Logic Apps as a response to security alerts using *workflow automation*.

7.4 Workflow automation

So far in this chapter, you've learned how you can use Defender for Cloud's cloud workload protection capabilities to detect threats to your Azure resources and be notified via security alerts. What is missing? In addition to monitoring the environment for potential signs of compromise and detecting threats, it's important to be able to respond to threats and suspicious activities. For this, you can use workflow automation.

Workflow automation is a capability in Defender for Cloud that allows you to automate responses not only to security alerts but also to recommendations and regulatory compliance standards. Workflow automation integrates with Logic Apps to automatically run customizable workflows (built with little code) as an automated response.

> **NOTE** A thriving Defender for Cloud community continuously creates Logic App workflows that solve a variety of use cases and pain points. These already-built Logic Apps are publicly accessible and available at http://mng.bz/nWlv. Although the Logic Apps in the official GitHub repository have been vetted by Microsoft, you should perform your own analysis and due diligence before using them in your environment. You can adopt these Logic Apps as they are and use them right away in your environment. Alternatively, you can customize them to better align to the needs and requirements of your organization.

7.4.1 Workflow automation in action

As a firm believer in learning by doing, I want to make workflow automation more tangible to you. I do this with an example. Let's say that whenever Defender for Cloud triggers a security alert about a suspected brute-force attack on your VMs, you want to respond by blocking IP addresses from which the brute-force attacks originated.

> **NOTE** For this scenario, you can use an already-built Logic App, available at http://mng.bz/vnQx.

To use workflow automation to achieve this objective, perform the following actions with the Security Admin or Contributor role on the resource group (to work with Logic App workflows, your user needs to have the Logic App Operator permissions to read or trigger access and Logic App Contributor to create or modify Logic Apps):

1 Navigate to the Microsoft Defender for Cloud dashboard inside of the Azure portal.
2 Select Workflow Automation.
3 In the upper taskbar, select +Add Workflow Automation.
4 In the new blade that opens (figure 7.8), enter a name for the workflow automation (like Block brute-force attacks on VMs), and then add a description.
5 From the drop-down menu, choose the Azure subscription for which you want to configure this workflow automation.
6 From the drop-down menu, choose the resource group in which this workflow automation will be stored.
7 Then, using the drop-down menu, choose Security Alert as the Defender for Cloud data type.
8 Insert Failed SSH Brute-Force Attack (alternatively, you can consult the reference list of security alerts to find the exact name of keywords that match the security alert).

9 Choose Select All for alert severity.

10 From the drop-down menu, choose the Azure subscription in which the Logic App resides, and then choose the Logic App in question.

11 Click Create.

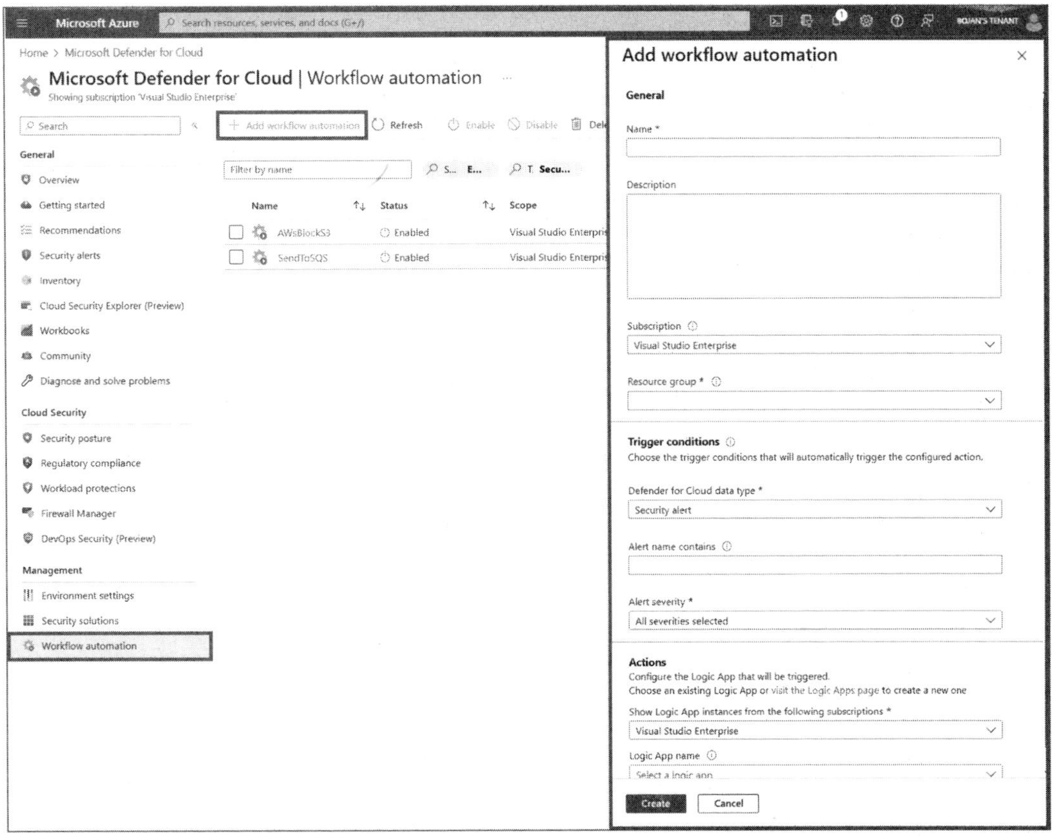

Figure 7.8 The Workflow Automation dashboard in Microsoft Defender for Cloud

---

What about recommendations and regulatory compliance standards?

In addition to using workflow automation for security alerts, you can also use it to generate an automated response for Defender for Cloud recommendations and regulatory compliance standards. In this context, you can run Logic Apps as a response for a specific recommendation name, severity, state, and specific regulatory compliance standard and control state. You can specify this data using trigger conditions when you create workflow automation by choosing either Recommendation or Regulatory Compliance Standards (instead of Security Alerts).

(continued)

The supported trigger types in Defender for Cloud for workflow automation are security alert, recommendation, and regulatory compliance standards. This means you can use workflow automation to automatically run a Logic App for any of these triggers.

After you create the workflow automation, Defender for Cloud automatically runs the Logic App as a security response whenever the security alert Failed SSH Brute-Force Attack is triggered. You can repeat these actions to automate responses to other security alerts (in addition to recommendations and regulatory compliance standards) in alignment with the needs and requirements of your organization.

Exercise 7.3

To solidify your knowledge of workflow automation, create a workflow automation rule that sends a notification whenever a resource exemption has been created in your subscriptions. If you need help with this exercise, you can start at http://mng.bz/ 4DVB.

In addition to using Defender for Cloud to solve security problems and detect threats, many organizations also use other systems, such as a Security Information and Event Management (SIEM) system that requires data from Defender for Cloud to be exported (see chapter 8).

7.5   *Exporting data*

Although extremely valuable, Defender for Cloud data only provides information for resources it covers (in this chapter, Azure resources). Many organizations use a central system to collect, analyze, and respond to security problems and findings across their entire environment (spanning Azure, on-premises, and other public cloud providers).

7.5.1   *Continuous export*

You can take data from Defender for Cloud and stream it to another system with a capability called *continuous export*. With continuous export, you can export the following Defender for Cloud data types:

- Recommendations
- Secure score data
- Security alerts
- Regulatory compliance data

Continuous export allows you to export these data types either to a Log Analytics workspace (LAW) or an Event Hub. This binary choice begs the question: Do you intend to keep this exported data inside of Azure or take it outside Azure? Exporting Defender for Cloud data to a LAW is suited for organizations that wish to keep this data inside Azure, whereas exporting to an Event Hub allows organizations to take this data outside Azure (such as by sending it to their on-premises SIEM).

> **NOTE** If your organization is using Microsoft Sentinel, you don't need to configure continuous export to send security alerts from Defender for Cloud to Sentinel. Instead, you use a native connector (see chapter 8).

At a high level, continuous export provides an answer to this question: What data should be sent to which destination with what frequency? The supported data types (such as security alerts) answer the question regarding what data you can send. LAW and Event Hub provide an answer to which destination this data can be sent. The only question remaining is with what frequency the supported data types can be exported. Continuous export supports the following frequencies:

- *Streaming updates*—Sends data whenever there is a change (such as when the resource's health state changes from healthy to unhealthy). If no changes or updates occur, no data is sent.
- *Snapshots*—Sends a snapshot of the current state of the supported data types you select once a week (per subscription).

These two frequencies are not mutually exclusive, as you can configure both frequencies to be used for the supported data types you wish to export. While it's tempting to think of continuous export as a data dump for the current states of all your Azure resources, that is not the case. Continuous export was built with the streaming of events in mind. Supported data types (such as security alerts) that are triggered by Defender for Cloud prior to configuring continuous export won't be exported.

> **WARNING** Although using continuous export to stream data from Defender for Cloud is free, if you selected a LAW as the destination, depending on your LAW configuration, you may incur costs for retention and ingestion of data (for example, retaining data for 120 days).

7.5.2 *Continuous export in action*

To see continuous export in action, I'd like to offer an example. Security alert data in Defender for Cloud is retained for 90 days. Say you want to export all security alerts and recommendations with a medium (or higher) severity to a LAW to retain them there for 180 days. To achieve this task and configure continuous export for your Azure subscription, perform the following actions with the Security Admin role or Owner on the resource group:

1 Navigate to the Microsoft Defender for Cloud dashboard inside of the Azure portal.
2 Select Environment Settings.
3 Click the Azure subscription for which you want to configure continuous export.

4 In the new blade that opens (figure 7.9) on the left, select Continuous Export.
5 Select the tab Log Analytics Workspace.

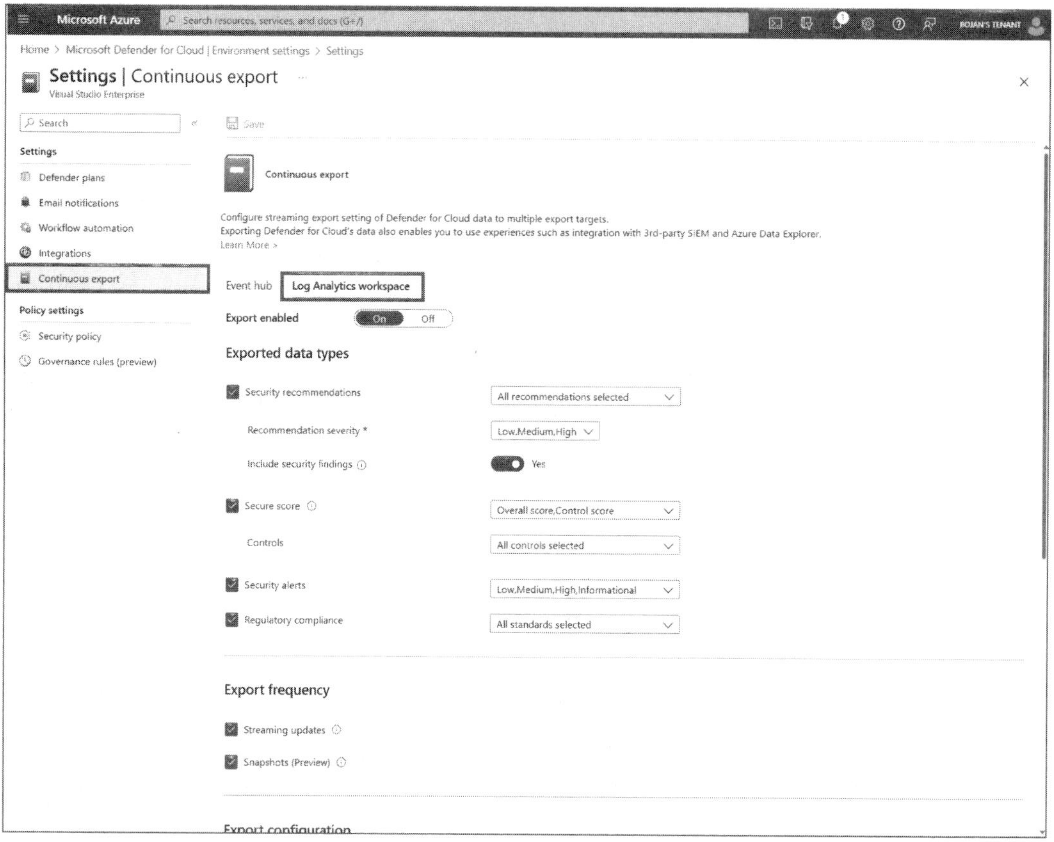

Figure 7.9 Configuring continuous export in Microsoft Defender for Cloud

NOTE To export data to a Log Analytics workspace, if the LAW has the SecurityCenterFree solution, you need read permissions for the workspace solution: Microsoft.OperationsManagement/solutions/read. Otherwise, you need to write permissions Microsoft.OperationsManagement/solutions/action. To export data to Event Hub, you need to write permission on the Event Hub policy.

1 Select the check box next to Security Recommendations and then, using the drop-down menu, choose Medium and High.
2 Enable Security Findings (if a recommendation has other recommendations beneath it, enabling Security Findings includes these recommendations).

3 Select the check box next to Security Alerts, and then, using the drop-down menu, choose Medium and High.

4 Select both export frequencies (Streaming Updates and Snapshots).

5 Choose the resource group in which this continuous export configuration is saved.

6 Choose the Azure subscription with the destination LAW, and then choose the LAW.

7 Click Save.

Based on the configuration you performed, after there has been a change (and once per week), security alerts and recommendations data are sent to the LAW, where you can analyze them. When using continuous export to export Defender for Cloud data to a LAW, security alerts are stored in the SecurityAlert table, whereas recommendations are stored in the SecurityRecommendation table.

Exporting data to a LAW is suited for organizations that want to use the Defender for Cloud data they exported to build rich data visualizations using *Azure Monitor workbooks*.

7.6 Workbooks

Azure Monitor workbooks, or just *workbooks*, as they're commonly referred to, can be used to build rich data visualizations using Defender for Cloud data (like the data types you configured to be exported to a LAW with continuous export). You can access workbooks through the Azure portal and Microsoft Defender for Cloud dashboard. Every user with access to Azure is a potential candidate to consume data visualized using workbooks.

7.6.1 Using workbooks

Using workbooks to visualize data is powerful because workbooks can be used to monitor various aspects of Defender for Cloud, giving you an end result, like in figure 7.10. In addition, using workbooks can help drive the adoption of Defender for Cloud inside your organization and help you operationalize Defender for Cloud.

There are several built-in workbooks available in the Defender for Cloud dashboard, including the following:

- *Secure Score Over Time*—An overview of your organization's secure score over time and recommended changes to your resources
- *Compliance Over Time*—An overview of your organization's compliance posture over time in alignment with the regulatory compliance standards you select
- *Vulnerability Assessment Findings*—An overview of vulnerability scans of your Azure resources
- *Active Alerts*—An overview of security alerts by severity, MITRE ATTA&CK® tactics, type, tag, and location
- *System Updates*—An overview of missing system updates by OS, severity, resources, and more

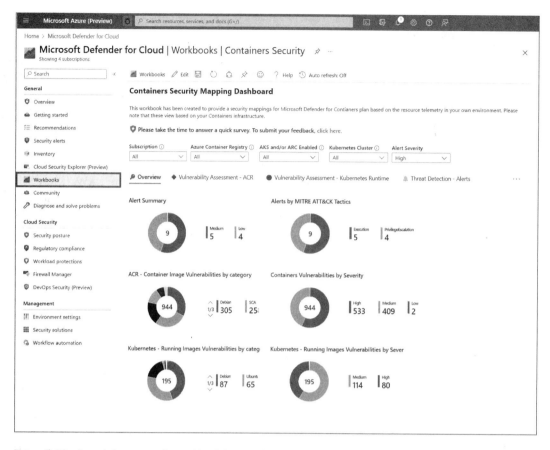

Figure 7.10   A containers security workbook in the Microsoft Defender for Cloud dashboard

- *Governance*—Tracks the progress of governance rules in your organization
- *Coverage*—Identifies gaps in Defender for Cloud plans coverage across your environment
- *Ransomware Dashboard*—Helps you prioritize recommendations that can reduce the likelihood of getting compromised by a ransomware attack
- *Cost Estimation*—Provides a price estimation for different Defender for Cloud plans specific to your environment (based on resource telemetry)
- *Containers Security*—Brings together vulnerability assessment scanning results, recommendations, security alerts by MITRE ATT&CK® tactic, and more for containers in your environment

Each one of these workbooks was created to address a specific need of organizations big and small—whether to track the security posture of your environment over time (using the Secure Score Over Time workbook) or help you discover any gaps in Defender for Cloud plans coverage across your environment (using the Coverage workbook).

> **Using workbooks built by the community**
>
> There is a thriving Defender for Cloud community that creates various artifacts (including workbooks) and contributes them to the official Defender for Cloud GitHub repository. The official repository contains even more workbooks than are available in the Defender for Cloud dashboard. These community-created workbooks are vetted by Microsoft, and you can import them from the GitHub repository. To import workbooks from the repository, you can start at http://mng.bz/QPlm.

The cost of security is an important matter. Logically, security teams need to plan and budget how much they spend. If you haven't enabled Defender for Cloud plans but need to provide your management with a price estimation for doing so in your environment, you can use the Cost Estimation built-in workbook to approximate the cost of enabling Defender for Cloud plans in your environment. You can then share this estimation with your management team.

7.6.2 Workbooks in action

To estimate the cost of enabling Defender for Cloud plans in your environment, with a user assigned at least a Reader role on the subscriptions you're interested in enabling Defender for Cloud plans on, perform the following actions:

1 Navigate to the Microsoft Defender for Cloud dashboard inside of the Azure portal.
2 On the left, select Workbooks.
3 In the blade that opens, select the built-in workbook Cost Estimation.
4 Select the subscriptions that you want to enable Defender for Cloud plans on.
5 Select the particular Defender for Cloud plans that you're interested in enabling.
6 Optionally, set the Additional Information toggle to On for more information about the workbook to be displayed.

The workbook displays costs for a particular Defender for Cloud plan. These are monthly estimates per subscription you selected. They're based on the list prices of Defender for Cloud plans and might differ from the actual costs you see in the invoice.

7.7 Answers to exercises

Exercise 7.1

Run the following command with the Security Admin role on the desired subscription:

```
az security pricing create -n VirtualMachines -tier 'standard'
```

Exercise 7.2

1 Navigate to the Microsoft Defender for Cloud dashboard inside of the Azure portal.
2 Select Security Alerts, and then click Sample Alerts.

3 Select the subscription and relevant Defender for Cloud plans for which you want to generate alerts. By default, all plans are selected.

4 Click Create Sample Alerts.

After a few minutes, the alerts should appear in the security alerts dashboard.

Exercise 7.3

Perform the actions available at http://mng.bz/4DVB.

Summary

- Defender for Cloud's cloud workload protection capabilities come in the form of different Microsoft Defender for Cloud plans. These plans are resource specific (like Microsoft Defender for Servers, Microsoft Defender for Containers, Microsoft Defender for SQL servers on machines, etc.). After you enable any of the plans, Defender for Cloud triggers security alerts for potential signs of compromise.

- You can configure email notifications for the relevant stakeholder(s) in your organization to be notified whenever Defender for Cloud triggers a security alert. In addition to configuring email notifications, you can use workflow automation to integrate with other systems your organization is using (like an IT service management or messaging platform).

- With workflow automation, you can automate a response and trigger a Logic App for security alerts, recommendations, and regulatory compliance standards. Logic Apps provide you with a fully customizable workflow, which you can modify to meet the requirements of your organization.

- To export data from Defender for Cloud to another system, you can use continuous export, which allows you to stream data to either an Event Hub or a LAW. The continuous export capability is free, but if you're exporting data to a LAW, you may incur charges depending on the workspace configuration (like retention).

- Integration with Azure Monitor workbooks in Defender for Cloud allows you to use rich data visualizations for Defender for Cloud data. Workbooks are great for monitoring various aspects and can help you operationalize Defender for Cloud.

Part 3

Going further

The last part of this book covers advanced concepts applicable to Azure security.

Chapter 8 teaches you how to build out next-generation security operations center capabilities with Microsoft Sentinel. This chapter also covers the importance of security orchestration, automation, and response and how to implement it using Sentinel to reduce the time it takes you to respond to suspicious activities and potential signs of compromise to your Azure environment.

In chapter 9, you'll learn about the different log types available in Azure and how to use them effectively with Azure Monitor. Chapter 10 covers how to ensure the configurations of your Azure resources are compliant and adhere to your organization's business rules with the help of Azure Policy. In chapter 11, I touch on a hot topic—DevSecOps. Here, I'll teach you about a new Azure security service called Microsoft Defender for DevOps and how it is applicable to implementing security early on in your software development lifecycle.

When you're finished with this part of the book, the journey that you're on with respect to Azure security shouldn't stop. I hope you're going to continue to learn more about Azure Security because the innovation in this space doesn't stop.

Security operations and response: Microsoft Sentinel

This chapter covers

- Security information and event management
- Microsoft Sentinel
- Data collection
- Analytics rules
- Incidents
- User entity behavior analytics
- Security orchestration, automation, and response
- Automation rules

As you learned in chapter 7, enabling threat detection for commonly used resource types in Azure (such as your virtual machines [VMs], containers, storage accounts, and others) notifies you about suspicious activities and potential signs of compromise in your Azure environment. Many organizations, in addition to infrastructure-as-a-service (IaaS) and platform-as-a-service (PaaS) resources, use software-as-a-service (SaaS) applications (such as Microsoft 365 or SAP). To complicate things further, large enterprises typically have many resources on-premises (and even in other public cloud providers such as AWS or Google Cloud Platform).

How do you detect threats across your entire digital estate (spanning IaaS, PaaS, SaaS, and on-premises)? Historically, organizations have relied on a system called Security Information and Event Management (SIEM), which provides them with the end-to-end visibility of their entire digital estate in a single dashboard.

NOTE You can see how Gartner defines SIEM at http://mng.bz/XN4Y.

8.1   Security Information and Event Management

SIEM systems are intended to support threat detection through the collection and analysis of security events, other contextual data sources, and management of security incidents.

NOTE To follow along with the exercises in this chapter, you can use the GitHub repository (https://github.com/bmagusic/azure-security).

Many organizations use a SIEM because it helps them connect the dots across a plethora of security events spanning many different data sources. A SIEM is often referred to as a *single pane of glass,* highlighting its ability to display security events and threats across your entire environment in a single dashboard. Because SIEM systems need to collect security events and contextual data from a variety of sources and piece that data together to provide you with security context, SIEM systems have been hard to maintain.

This complexity comes from traditional SIEMs requiring a lot of hardware to collect security events from different sources and processing power to piece together these events into security incidents to make sense of it all. As you can imagine, it takes time to size hardware, budget it, and get it through procurement—not to mention the effort and expertise that it takes to set everything up and troubleshoot potential problems (such as data from certain sources not being ingested into your SIEM). And you need to make all of that happen before you collect additional security events. Due to these constraints, some organizations even need to forgo collecting security events and data sources that otherwise would be of real value to their investigation. To address these (and other) challenges and to protect your entire environment, you can use *Microsoft Sentinel.*

8.2   Microsoft Sentinel

Microsoft Sentinel is a cloud-native SIEM solution built into Azure. Sentinel is built into Microsoft's public cloud platform, so you can to tap into Azure's scalable processing power to collect large volumes of data with ease. In addition, because Sentinel is an Azure service, you can apply machine learning algorithms across large datasets to detect attacks that otherwise might go unnoticed.

8.2.1 Microsoft Sentinel capabilities

Microsoft Sentinel has a lot of capabilities that can help you investigate incidents, detect threats, and respond to them accordingly. At a high level, you can use Microsoft Sentinel to achieve the following (figure 8.1):

- *Collect data*—Collect security events and contextual data at cloud scale from various data sources (including on-premise and the public cloud).
- *Detect threats*—Use Microsoft's analytics and threat intelligence to detect threats to your environment.
- *Investigate threats*—Understand the blast radius and potential root cause of security incidents.
- *Respond to threats*—Automate security orchestration and remediation using proven Azure services.

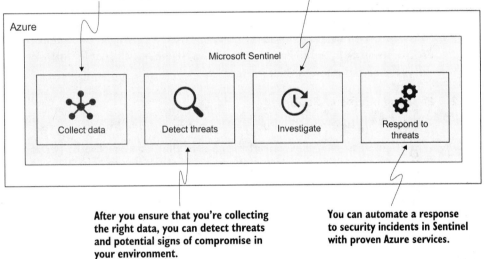

Figure 8.1   Understanding the high-level capabilities of Microsoft Sentinel

Before investigating threats and incidents, you sometimes need to ensure that you're collecting data and that it's available when you need it. In the context of Sentinel, the term *data collection* is often used interchangeably with *data ingestion*. Because Sentinel needs to collect (or ingest) data, it's only logical that this data needs to be stored someplace. To store the data that you collect, Microsoft Sentinel uses Log Analytics workspaces (LAWs), which you learned about in chapter 7.

Predeployment considerations

Before deploying Microsoft Sentinel, it's important to choose an appropriate LAW architecture based on your organization's needs. Generally, as a best practice, you should try to keep the number of LAWs to a minimum. However, depending on your organization's requirements (for example, data needing to reside inside a particular geographic region), you might need to have more than one LAW.

If you need help with designing your LAW architecture, you can start at http://mng.bz/yQMJ. You should also familiarize yourself with Azure role-based access control and different roles available in Microsoft Sentinel, which you can start learning about at https://learn.microsoft.com/en-us/azure/sentinel/roles.

Microsoft Sentinel Reader is the role with the least amount of privilege and can be used to view Microsoft Sentinel resources such as data, incidents, and workbooks (I cover workbooks in chapter 7). Another role that you should be aware of is the Microsoft Sentinel Contributor. This role is suited for users who, as part of their work, need to create and edit analytics rules, workbooks, and other Microsoft Sentinel resources.

After the data from your relevant data sources is stored in a LAW, Sentinel is able to consume this data and analyze it to detect threats to your environment. Therefore, to use Microsoft Sentinel in your organization, you need to enable it first on a LAW that stores data from relevant data sources.

8.2.2 *Enabling Microsoft Sentinel*

To enable Microsoft Sentinel on a LAW, perform the following actions:

1 Sign in to the Azure portal with a user that has contributor permissions on the subscription and resource group in which the LAW resides.
2 Navigate to Microsoft Sentinel.
3 Click +Create, and then choose the LAW on which you want to enable Sentinel.
4 Click Add.
5 If you receive a notification that the Microsoft Sentinel free trial has been activated, click OK.

After you enable Microsoft Sentinel on your LAW, you can start collecting data.

8.3 *Data collection*

As with any SIEM, ingesting data from relevant data sources is key in having end-to-end visibility of your environment and being able to detect threats to it. For on-premise SIEM solutions, you need to first add new hardware before being able to ingest more data. One of the advantages of using Sentinel as a SIEM is that it's cloud native and able to ingest large amounts of data without resizing hardware or open support tickets for Microsoft to increase the capacity. Ingesting large amounts of data (and even increasing the ingestion amount over time) happens seamlessly using the scalability and elasticity of the Azure cloud.

Sentinel can scale and ingest large amounts of data—even terabytes per day—with ease. This capability makes it tempting to consider Sentinel as the destination for all of your data sources, but I encourage you to consider the data that should go into your SIEM.

8.3.1 What data should go in a SIEM?

The data you send to your SIEM needs to be based on the use cases that you want to cover with Sentinel. Hoarding data in Sentinel is unwise unless this data provides you with security value. Sending data to your SIEM without it aligning to your use cases often leads to inefficiency and unnecessary charges. Ask yourself this: Do you have the right data to investigate threats in your environment, and do you have enough data sources?

What data do other organizations send to their SIEM? Typical data sources sent to SIEMs are alerts from Microsoft security solutions (such as Microsoft Defender for Cloud or Microsoft Defender 365). Other data sources include alerts and logs from network security solutions, servers, endpoints, identity and access management, SaaS solutions, threat intelligence feeds, and custom logs.

After you define your use cases and identify what data should go into your SIEM, you can start collecting data. There are different ways to collect data ingested into Sentinel. The main three options for collecting data are the following:

- *Data connectors*—Allows you to integrate data from various services (such as Microsoft Entra ID, Azure Activity Log, third-party applications, and others)
- *REST API integrations*—Allows you to use APIs integrations that connect with the provider data source either by using the providers' API or through Azure Functions
- *Agent-based integration*—Allows you to use agent-based mechanisms to stream logs from, for example, your on-premises data sources to Sentinel

These three options provide you with flexibility in collecting data from the right data sources to use with Sentinel. However, organizations typically appreciate the most straightforward way to ingest data into Sentinel, which is through *data connectors*.

8.3.2 Data connectors

A challenge that many organizations face is the wide variety of data sources they have and want to ingest into Sentinel. Suppose that your organization, in addition to Azure IaaS and PaaS resources, is using SaaS applications for collaboration (such as email, chat, file hosting, and others). The identity an employee uses to access Azure IaaS and PaaS resources is the same identity they use to access their collaboration apps (such as a email). If the identity used to access email or chat is compromised (for example, through phishing attacks), bad actors, like the fictional character Eve, can use the compromised identity to access your Azure environment.

Therefore, in addition to having visibility of your Azure IaaS and PaaS resources, it's important to get data from other data sources that your organization uses to connect the dots. You can ingest data into Microsoft Sentinel from relevant data sources with data connectors. Sentinel has more than 100 out-of-the-box data connectors you can use to ingest data from commonly used applications and data sources.

Data connectors provide a convenient way to ingest data from both Microsoft and third-party sources. After you've identified data sources from which you want to collect data, you can navigate to the Sentinel dashboard to confirm whether a relevant data connector already exists. To check whether a connector exists for the data source you want to collect data from, perform the following actions:

1 Navigate to the Microsoft Sentinel dashboard.
2 Select Data Connectors.
3 In the list of connectors, find the appropriate data source.

What about creating your own data connector?

Imagine you provide a security service to your customers and would like to make data for that service available through a data connector in Sentinel. You can create your own data connector using the Codeless Connector Platform (CCP). The CCP allows organizations, such as managed security service providers and independent software vendors, to expose data for their services or applications over a public REST API endpoint, which you can then use to ingest data into Sentinel. To learn more about how to build your own data connector using the CCP, you can start at http://mng.bz/ MB82.

After you identify the relevant data sources, you need to configure data collection for these data sources. To teach you how to configure data collection in Sentinel, I'll use a data source that you're familiar with. In chapter 7, you learned about Microsoft Defender for Cloud and how it can generate security alerts whenever it detects suspicious activities and threats to your environment, such as threats to your applications running in Azure. To analyze these suspicious activities further and correlate them with other relevant data sources, you can use an out-of-the-box data connector.

8.3.3 Data connectors in action

In the real world, security operations teams are swamped with the sheer volume of alerts that are generated daily from the workloads they're tasked with protecting. You would like to avoid your security operations team needing to close the same security alerts in two different dashboards: in both Sentinel and Defender for Cloud. Enabling bidirectional sync saves your team from a lot of manual work. Suppose you close an incident containing a security alert in Sentinel. With bidirectional sync enabled, the corresponding security alerts that are part of the incident you closed are also closed in Defender for Cloud.

As I previously mentioned, data connectors can solve a lot of problems. The following process solves the requirement for ingesting data into Sentinel from one data source, but it can be applied to other situations/data sources. To ingest security alerts from Microsoft Defender for Cloud into Sentinel through a data connector, perform the following actions:

1 As a user that has read and write permissions to the LAW, navigate to the Microsoft Sentinel dashboard.

2 Select Data Connectors and, from the list of the connectors, choose the solution from which you want to collect data (in this case, Microsoft Defender for Cloud).

3 In the blade that opens on the right, select Open Connector Page. Follow the instructions to configure data collection.

4 Under Configuration, select the subscription on which you enabled Defender for Cloud, and enable the Status toggle. By default, bidirectional sync of security alerts is enabled.

5 Scroll down, and below Create Incidents, click Enable. This step ensures that Microsoft Sentinel creates incidents for security alerts coming from the security solution you're collecting data from (in this case, Microsoft Defender for Cloud).

6 Close the Data Connector blade.

NOTE Sentinel is a paid service. Storing data in LAW and ingesting data into Sentinel incur charges. Certain data types are free to ingest into Sentinel. Security alerts from Microsoft Defender for Cloud are one of the free data types. For more information about other free data types, you can start at http://mng.bz/a1OJ.

After some time, the status of the connector switches to Connected (figure 8.2), and data from the data source you connected is ingested into Sentinel.

Exercise 8.1

To solidify your knowledge of the data connectors, configure a data collection from another data source relevant to your investigation. I know there are many data connectors to choose from. If you're lacking inspiration as to what data source to connect, select Office 365. Office 365 Audit Logs are one of the free data types and provide you with insights into Teams, SharePoint, and Exchange admin activity. If your organization isn't using Office 365, you can pick a substitute data source.

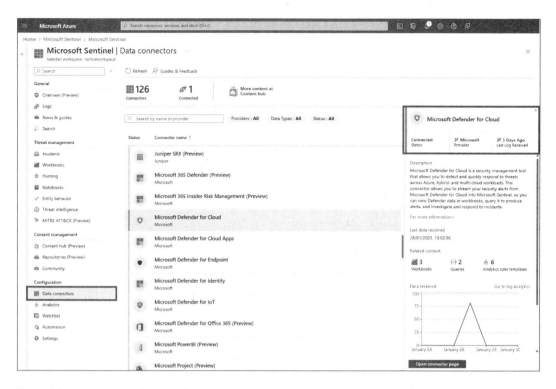

Figure 8.2   The Microsoft Defender for Cloud data connector in Microsoft Sentinel

Say the status of the data connector states Connected, but you want to confirm that data is actually being ingested into Sentinel. To confirm that data from Microsoft Defender for Cloud is actually being ingested into the LAW in which Sentinel stores the data, perform the following steps:

1 Navigate to the Microsoft Sentinel dashboard.
2 Select Logs.
3 Choose SecurityAlerts, and then click Run.
4 The output should return results confirming data is being received from Defender for Cloud.

These steps can also be applied to other data sources.

What about data coming from other Microsoft security solutions?

Microsoft Defender for Cloud is only one of many security solutions in Microsoft's security portfolio. For example, Microsoft Defender for Endpoint, Microsoft Defender for Office 365, Microsoft Defender for Cloud Apps, and Microsoft Defender for Identity are on the SaaS side. Separate data connectors are available for each of these security solutions. However, you should use the Microsoft 365 Defender data con-nector, which unifies data collection across the different Microsoft Defender SaaS-security solutions.

Data connectors provide you with a straightforward way to connect your data sources and start ingesting data into Sentinel (in many cases, with only a few clicks). But recent zero-day vulnerabilities have demonstrated that organizations require not only data to be ingested but also additional content, such as analytics rules, workbooks, and playbooks, which can detect and respond to threats. To address these requirements, Microsoft has *Content hub*.

8.3.4 Content hub

Say a new zero-day vulnerability is discovered. In addition to ingesting data from rele-vant data sources, you must detect whether the vulnerability is present in your envi-ronment and what you need to do to respond to it. Content hub in Sentinel (figure 8.3) was created to address end-to-end product and industry vertical scenarios. It allows you to deploy all the content that you need (such as data connectors, work-books, analytics, and automations) for a new zero-day vulnerability in a single step.

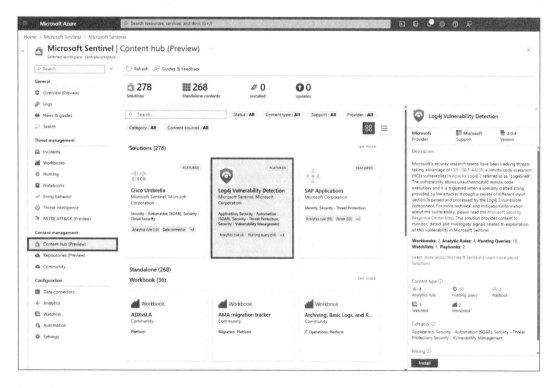

Figure 8.3   An overview of Content hub in the Microsoft Sentinel dashboard

> ### Data connectors vs. Content hub
>
> Content hub allows you to deploy data connectors. What should you use to collect data to Sentinel—data connectors or Content hub? Microsoft is moving in the direction of Content hub. The majority of data sources displayed in the Data Connectors blade can be found in Content hub. However, Content hub is currently in public preview, so you can continue to use data connectors until Content hub becomes generally available.

After you connect the relevant data sources to ensure you're ingesting the right data in Sentinel, you can use *analytics rules* to detect threats to your environment.

8.4   *Analytics rules*

Imagine that you have resources in your organization that are critical to your business (such as a revenue-generating application). You monitor and detect threats to these resources by creating threat-detection rules—called *analytics rules*—which allow you to detect suspicious activities and signs of compromise in your environment. Analytics rules are a core functionality in Microsoft Sentinel. Depending on your use cases, you can use different types of analytics rules. Microsoft Sentinel supports the following threat-analytics rules:

- *Microsoft security*—Allows you to create incidents automatically in Sentinel for alerts generated by Microsoft security solutions (such as Microsoft Defender for Cloud, Microsoft Defender for Endpoint, and others).
- *Fusion*—Uses a correlation engine based on scalable machine learning algorithms that correlates multiple signals from various Microsoft security products to detect advanced multistage attacks automatically by identifying combinations of suspicious activities and anomalous behavior observed at various stages of the kill chain model.
- *Machine learning behavioral analytics*—Allows you to create threat-detection rules using machine learning behavioral analytics templates based on Microsoft's proprietary machine learning algorithms. Because these templates are based on Microsoft's proprietary machine learning algorithms, you're unable to see their internal logic or modify them.
- *Anomaly*—Allows you to use templates to create threat-detection rules, which use machine learning to detect specific types of anomalous behavior.
- *Threat intelligence*—Allows you to generate an alert whenever an indicator from Microsoft's threat intelligence feeds matches data in your event logs (such as Syslog data, IPs, and URLs).
- *Scheduled*—Allows you to create threat-detection rules either by using built-in queries written by Microsoft's security experts or by writing your own queries.
- *Near-real time (NRT)*—Functions similarly to scheduled rules but is designed to run once every minute.

The rule for the Fusion correlation engine is enabled by default. Depending on your use cases, you can enable different types of analytics rules in Sentinel. Many organizations already use Microsoft security solutions, which generate security alerts for suspicious activities that might indicate the environment is compromised. Therefore, a logical step is to generate incidents in Sentinel based on security alerts coming from Microsoft's security solutions. You can automatically create incidents in Microsoft Sentinel for alerts generated by different Microsoft security solutions; this step is one of the first taken by many organizations when starting with analytics rules.

8.4.1 *Microsoft security rules*

Microsoft security rules allow you to use built-in templates to automatically create incidents for alerts generated by the following Microsoft security solutions:

- Microsoft Defender for Cloud
- Microsoft Defender for Endpoint
- Microsoft Defender for Cloud Apps
- Microsoft Defender for Identity
- Microsoft Defender for Office 365
- Microsoft 365 Insider Risk Management
- Microsoft Defender for IoT
- Microsoft Entra ID Protection

I cover Microsoft Entra ID protection in chapter 2 and security alerts generated by Microsoft Defender for Cloud in chapter 7. To generate incidents from relevant sources, such as alerts and entities from Defender for Endpoint, Defender for Cloud Apps, Defender for Identity, Defender for Office 365, and Microsoft Entra ID Protection, you can use the Microsoft 365 Defender connector. Microsoft Defender products other than Defender for Cloud and Microsoft Entra ID Protection are not covered in this book because the majority of them are aimed at protecting SaaS resources.

> **NOTE** To learn more about the other Microsoft Defender products, you can start at http://mng.bz/gB9R.

The prerequisite for creating rules based on any of these security solutions is that you have connected the relevant security solutions to Microsoft Sentinel using either the data connectors or Content hub.

8.4.2 *Microsoft security rules in action*

To create incidents in Microsoft Sentinel automatically for all alerts generated by Microsoft Entra ID Protection, complete the following steps, giving you an end result as shown in figure 8.4. These steps also can be applied to other Microsoft security solutions:

1 Navigate to the Microsoft Sentinel dashboard.
2 Select Analytics, and then click the tab Rule Templates.

3 Click the Add Filter Option, and then choose Rule Type. In the drop-down menu, choose Microsoft Security Only, and click Apply.

4 In the list of displayed templates (figure 8.4), click the row where the Data Sources column shows the relevant Microsoft security solution (in this case, Microsoft Entra ID Protection).

5 In the blade that appears, click Create Rule.

6 Enter the name for the rule and description. Both come prepopulated, and you can leave them as they are.

7 You can leave the remaining options as they are by default and click Next.

8 Leave Automation Rules blank (I cover automation rules later in this chapter), and click Next.

9 You should see a message appear at the top of the blade stating validation passed.

10 Click Create.

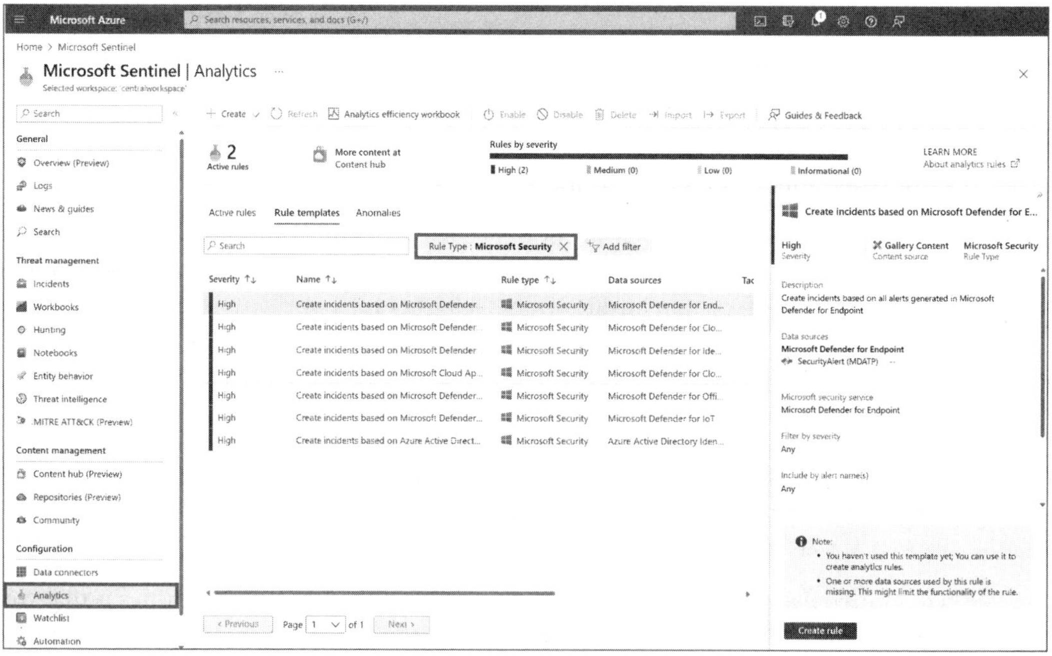

Figure 8.4 An overview of Microsoft security rule templates in Microsoft Sentinel

After you perform these actions, you can see the Microsoft security rule under Active Rules. To create other analytics rules, such as machine learning behavioral analytics or threat intelligence rules, repeat similar actions to those in steps 1 through 3.

Although being able to create incidents based on alerts from different Microsoft security solutions such as Microsoft Entra ID Protection or Microsoft Defender for

Cloud is of value, you can also implement custom logic for detecting threats based on your own use cases. For this, you can use *scheduled rules*.

8.4.3 Scheduled rules

With scheduled rules, you can determine whether certain activities have taken place in your environment that you consider potentially malicious. Scheduled rules in Microsoft Sentinel allow you to run your own threat-detection logic every specific number of days, hours, or minutes. The threat-detection logic used in scheduled rules can be based on either templates containing built-in queries written by Microsoft's security experts or your own use cases. When you're first starting out with scheduled rules, it's worthwhile to go over the built-in queries written by Microsoft's security experts. Some of your use cases can likely be covered with the built-in queries, without the need to create queries from scratch. To check the available built-in queries, complete the following actions:

1. Navigate to the Microsoft Sentinel dashboard.
2. Select Analytics, and then click the tab Rule Templates.
3. Click the Add Filter Option, and then choose Rule Type. In the drop-down menu, choose Scheduled Only, and click Apply.

This process displays the built-in queries you can use to detect threats in your environment. You can customize them to meet the needs of your specific use cases or create a new scheduled rule from scratch.

8.4.4 Scheduled rules in action

Suppose you want to be notified whenever a user tries and fails to log in 10 times inside of 5 minutes. This is a common use case for many organizations, as it might indicate that a bad actor is trying to compromise a user account. The fictional bad actor Eve might have discovered a username of a particular user and may be trying to guess their password over and over again inside of a short period of time. Do you remember what this type of attack is called?

To detect this attack, you can create a scheduled rule that notifies you whenever a user exceeds 10 failed logins in 5 minutes. To create a scheduled rule, you need to configure the following:

- General
- Rule logic
- Incident settings
- Automated response

Whenever you create a scheduled rule in Sentinel, you need to go through a wizard and sequentially configure all four parts, starting with general.

GENERAL

To begin creating a scheduled rule in Sentinel, perform the following actions:

1 Navigate to the Microsoft Sentinel dashboard.

2 Select Analytics.

3 Click +Create, and then choose Scheduled Query Rule.

4 Enter the name for the rule, such as User Login Failed 10 Times Within 5 Minutes.

5 Enter a brief description for the rule.

6 In the drop-down menu, choose the tactic and techniques. For this particular rule, you can select Credential Access and T1110 – Brute Force.

7 Choose Severity. For this rule, you should select High because 10 failed logins inside of a short timeframe could be indicative of a brute-force attack in progress.

8 The status is enabled by default. Leave it enabled, and then click Next.

After you're finished configuring your general rule, you can proceed with configuring the logic of your scheduled rule.

RULE LOGIC

You can run a simulation, and the result will be displayed in the form of a two-dimensional chart that shows you how many results per day would be generated for the rule logic you specified. In addition to the two-dimensional chart, the simulation also displays a red line representing the alert threshold. Whenever the value in the two-dimensional chart is above the red line, an incident is created. To help you visualize the results of the scheduled rule, you can test the rule logic with current data from your environment, giving you an end result as shown in figure 8.5.

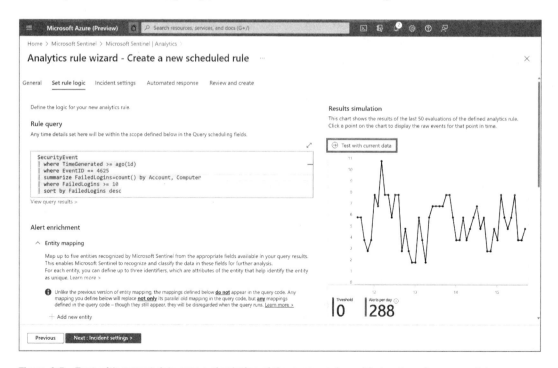

Figure 8.5   Test with current data runs a simulation of the query you're writing on top of your own data

The following steps fulfill the requirement for detecting failed logins:

1 In the Rule Query field, enter the rule logic used to detect threats. The Rule Query field validates your query in real time as you're writing it. To detect users with failed logins, use the following query:

```
SecurityEvent
| where TimeGenerated >= ago(1d)
| where EventID == 4625
| summarize FailedLogins=count() by Account, Computer
| sort by FailedLogins desc
```

2 Entity mapping allows you to take the results of your query and map them to entities recognized by Microsoft Sentinel, which you can use later when you investigate incidents (I'll cover investigating incidents in chapter 8).

You can map up to five entities recognized by Microsoft Sentinel. Suppose you want to determine which account and endpoint are used in the failed logins. For entity type, using the drop-down menu, choose Account; for Identifier, choose Name; and for Value, choose Account. Click Add Identifier, and choose Host. Then, for Identifier, choose HostName, and for Value, choose Computer. This ensures that both the user and endpoint/computer used in the failed login attempt are mapped to Sentinel entities, helping discern which account and computer are involved in the failed login attempts.

3 Leave Custom Details and Alert Details blank. Custom Details allow you to surface particular event data as part of the alert properties. Alert Details allow you to specify particular event data that can be surfaced in the name or description of each instance of an alert.

4 Query Scheduling allows you to specify how often your scheduled query runs and how far back it looks up data when it runs. The values in Run Query Every and Lookup Data from the Last must be between 5 minutes and 14 days. To look up logins every 5 minutes for Run Query Every, choose 5 minutes, and for Lookup Data from the Last, choose 5 minutes. This ensures that your query runs every 5 minutes and that Sentinel runs your query against the last 5 minutes of data collected (figure 8.6).

5 Alert Threshold allows you to specify a threshold value used to generate an incident. For example, if you want to generate an incident whenever your query returns a match, choose Is Greater Than, and for the value, press 0.

6 Event grouping allows you to specify whether you want to group all events into a single alert or trigger an alert for each event. By default, it's set to Group All Events into a Single Event.

7 Suppression allows you to specify whether you want to stop running the query for a specific amount of time. The value must be between 5 minutes and 24 hours. Leave the Suppression toggle set to Off and click Next.

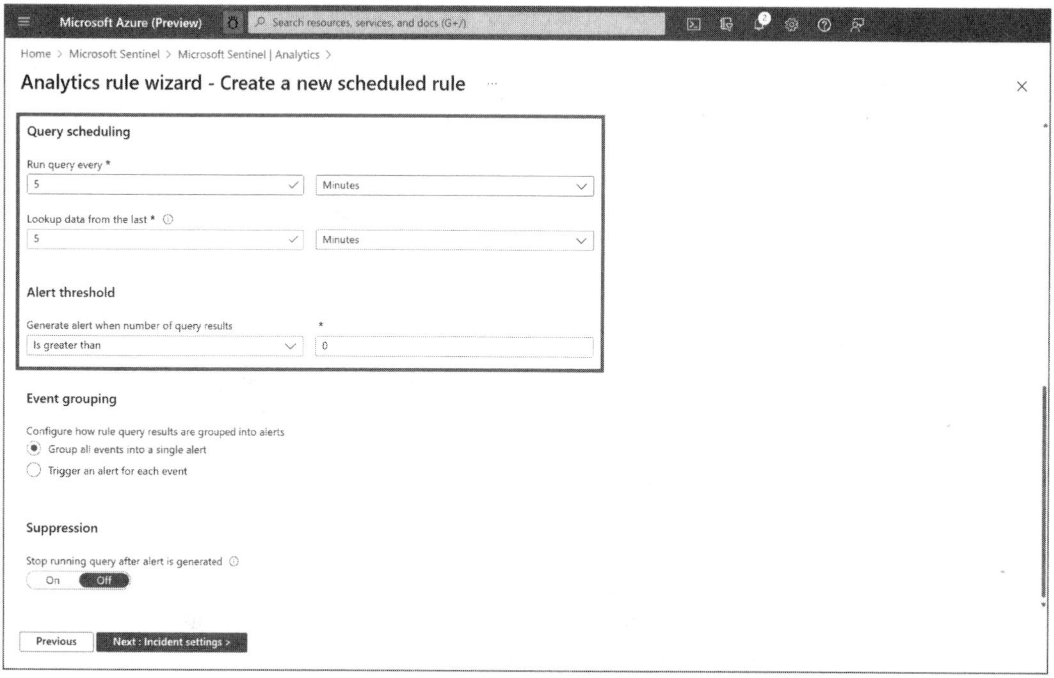

Figure 8.6 Configuring query scheduling and alert threshold as part of the scheduled rule configuration

> ### Near-real-time rules
>
> The minimum amount of time you can specify in scheduled query rules is 5 minutes to account for ingestion time lag. If you need to run detection even faster, you can use NRT rules. NRT rules are similar to scheduled rules but run every minute to provide you with the most up-to-date information possible. While NRT rules are in preview, you should be aware of the limitations listed at http://mng.bz/e10J.

These steps fulfill the requirement for detecting failed logins, but they can also be applied to other use cases. After you're finished with the rule logic, you can proceed with configuring the incident settings for your scheduled rule.

INCIDENT SETTINGS

Incident settings allow you to specify whether the alerts created by your rule logic should generate Sentinel incidents. By default, when creating scheduled rules, this configuration is set to Enabled. Another configuration setting you need to be familiar with is alert grouping. It allows you to specify how alerts triggered by your rule logic are grouped into incidents. You can leave the alert grouping setting as is and click Next.

AUTOMATED RESPONSE

Automated response allows you to programmatically trigger a response to alerts or incidents. You can do this by using automation rules and playbooks. I cover automation rules and playbooks in more detail later in this chapter. You can leave this setting as is and click Next. After you click Review, your scheduled rule is created.

Exercise 8.2

To solidify your knowledge of analytics rules in Sentinel, create another scheduled rule that generates an incident whenever an Azure VM is deleted from your environment. If you're up for an even bigger challenge, create an additional scheduled rule that creates an incident in Sentinel whenever there is an anomalous number of resources created in your environment.

The scheduled rule you create is displayed in the Active Rules tab. Whenever there is a match based on the rule logic you defined, Sentinel generates an incident, which you can investigate further.

8.5 Incidents

The analytics rules you create allow you to detect threats on top of the data ingested into Sentinel from relevant data sources. To investigate potentially suspicious activities and signs of compromise across all of these data sources, you can use the Incidents dashboard (figure 8.7) in Sentinel.

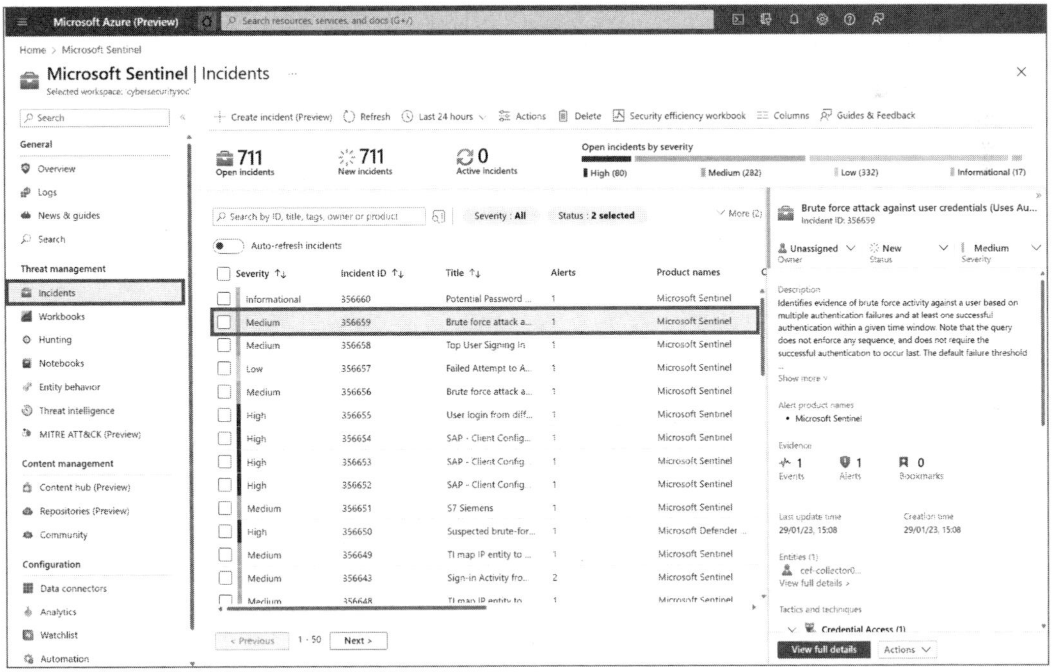

Figure 8.7   Incidents dashboard in Microsoft Sentinel

Sentinel correlates different security events—such as security alerts—into an *incident*. Incidents provide you with more information and context about what happened so you can investigate it further. Because you may end up with many incidents inside of your Sentinel dashboard, filters help you determine which incidents to triage first (for example, based on an incident severity of High).

After you click a particular incident, on the right, a blade appears containing an overview with more information about that particular incident, including evidence that contains information about events, alerts, and bookmarks. To view more details, click View Full Details, which opens up a new blade that contains the following information (figure 8.8):

- *Timeline*—Shows a chronological order of suspicious activities that happened in your environment. Suppose that a user clicked on a suspicious URL, and as a result, the identity they use to log in to the Azure environment was compromised. Timeline displays this information together with other suspicious activities in chronological order. You can click any activity in the timeline to view more details. When you select a particular activity, a new blade opens containing information about what happened. You can use the Add Filter option to filter activities based on severity or tactic.

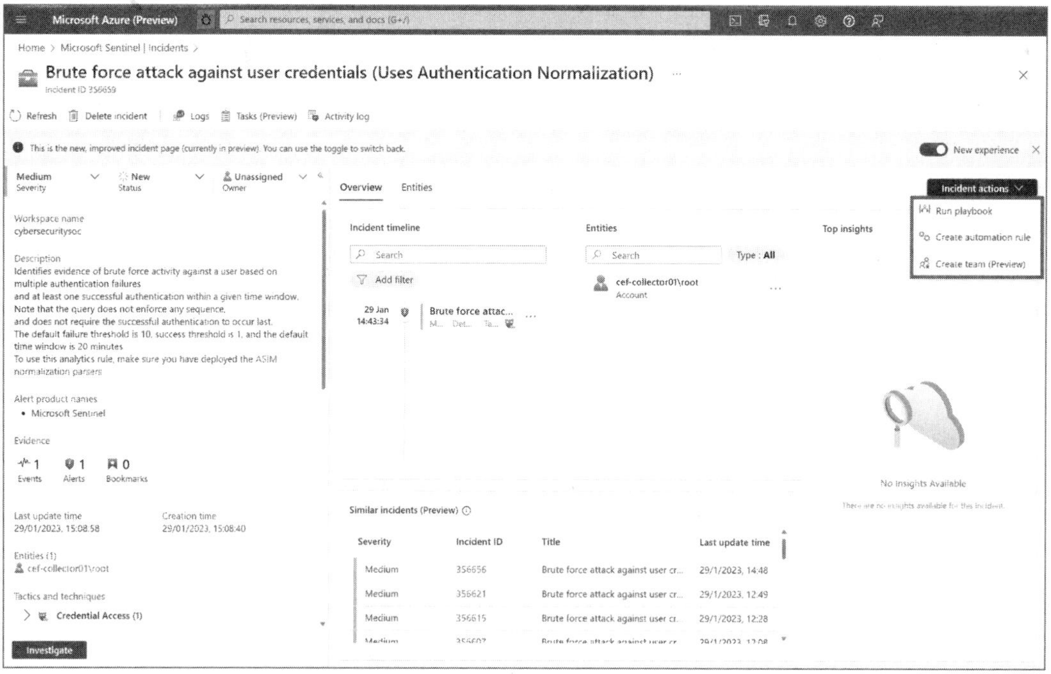

Figure 8.8   The Full Details dashboard of an incident in Microsoft Sentinel

- *Top Insights*—This section provides you with immediate insights that are chosen by Microsoft's security experts. The purpose of displaying top insights is to help you determine whether the incident that you're investigating is a false positive. In addition, it can display other insights that might be of real value in your investigation, such as user activity.
- *Entities*—Provides you with an overview of all entities involved in the incident you're investigating, such as user accounts that are part of a security alert.
- *Similar Incidents*—This section uses machine learning to display the 20 most-similar incidents over the past 14 days compared to the incident you're currently investigating. Incidents displayed in this section might be connected to the incident you're investigating or, alternatively, be false positives.

This blade also contains hidden gems located in the toolbar. The Activity Log captures everything that you can do with that particular incident, such as activities performed during the lifecycle of the incident. Suppose you wanted to capture a series of steps that whoever is investigating this incident needs to go through. You can create tasks to ensure a specific sequence is followed when investigating a particular incident. A task might include validating an IP address because it appears suspicious. The preferred way to add tasks is from the automation rule. Alternatively, you can use the incident response option to run a playbook (I cover automation rules and playbooks shortly) that adds tasks.

The incidents blade allows you to investigate suspicious activities and threats to your environment. However, the challenge that many organizations face is determining what constitutes a suspicious activity. There is a large gray area between benign user activities and malicious activities performed by bad actors (like the fictional character Eve used throughout this book). To further complicate things, sophisticated bad actors do their best to fly under the radar and make their activities tough to discern compared to daily activities performed by your user population. Some bad actors might even be malicious insiders. How do you detect anomalous activities in your environment such as malicious insiders? You can use a capability in Sentinel called *user and entity behavior analytics (UEBA)*.

8.6   *User and entity behavior analytics*

UEBA in Sentinel uses machine learning to analyze the logs and alerts to build a behavioral baseline over a period of time. This baseline helps to discern between legitimate activities and potentially suspicious ones. By comparing activities against the baseline that represents legitimate activities, any activity that falls outside of the baseline is considered suspicious. Each entity (for example, a user) has their own baseline. The benefit of using UEBA in Sentinel is that it's multidimensional. By analyzing different aspects of data sources you ingest in Sentinel, UEBA looks for indicators of suspicious behavior across any behavior type. A behavior type can be, for example, a particular user, geolocation, device, or activity performed.

8.6.1   *When to use UEBA*

Why should you use UEBA if you're already using analytics rules? Analytics rules focus on detecting specific threat scenarios or known patterns that might be indicative of your environment being compromised (for example, a certain number of failed log-ins over a short period of time). UEBA, on the other hand, is able to detect suspicious activities and attacks that aren't known yet (such as zero-day vulnerabilities).

> **NOTE**   For a full list of anomalies detected by UEBA in Sentinel, you can start at http://mng.bz/pP5P.

An additional advantage of using UEBA is that each entity's baseline is determined by their past activities and the past activities of their peers and entire organization. To make this more palpable, I'll rely on the help of Bob, one of the fictional characters used throughout this book. Bob is an application developer in his organization. Suppose he signs in from a new location (such as Beijing, China) and accesses the file customerDataCSV. If this is the first time that Bob signs in from Beijing and no other user from his organization signs in from Beijing, this action is anomalous. Furthermore, UEBA is able to detect whether anyone else in the organization accessed the same file as Bob. The unusual file access from an unusual geographic location is considered anomalous.

8.6.2   *User and entity behavior analytics in action*

To configure UEBA in Sentinel, giving you an end result similar to figure 8.9, complete the following steps:

1 Navigate to the Microsoft Sentinel dashboard.
2 Select Entity Behavior.
3 Select Entity Behavior Settings.
4 Mark the checkbox next to Microsoft Entra ID.
5 Mark the checkboxes next to relevant data sources. You can mark all of them.
6 Click Apply.

These actions enable UEBA, and Sentinel starts to analyze different aspects of data sources you selected, looking for indicators of suspicious behavior across any behavior type.

When responding to security incidents and threats to your environment, minutes matter. Thus, decreasing the time it takes to respond to a security incident is important. Bad actors don't play by anyone's rules. They can even launch their attacks in the middle of the night when most people are sleeping. To respond to incidents and security alerts (even if they happen in the middle of the night), you can use a capability called *security orchestration, automation, and response (SOAR)*.

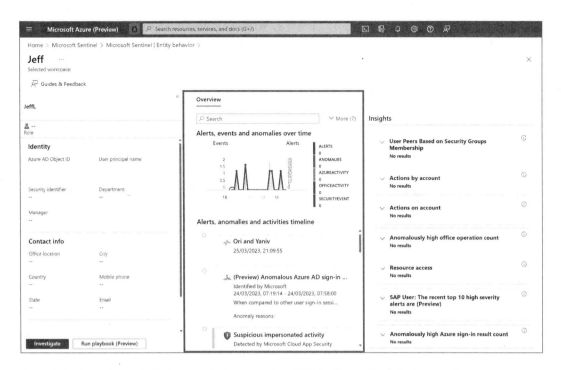

Figure 8.9 Anomalous activity for a particular user using UEBA in Microsoft Sentinel

8.7 Security orchestration, automation, and response

SOAR combines incident response, threat-intelligence, platform-management capabilities, and automation into a single solution.

NOTE To see how Gartner defines SOAR, you can start at http://mng.bz/ OxNP.

SOAR is important because it allows you to automate specific activities. The activities you can automate in Sentinel using SOAR include remediation tasks, enrichment of incidents, and security response. Automating these activities decreases the time it takes to resolve incidents. You can use SOAR to automate low-severity security alerts generated by Microsoft security solutions to free up time for you to focus on more important tasks and activities, such as high-severity incidents. SOAR in Sentinel integrates with Azure Logic Apps, similar to workflow automation in Microsoft Defender for Cloud (discussed in chapter 7).

SOAR allows you to centrally manage tasks related to automation in Microsoft Sentinel. However, as you learned in chapter 7, workflow automation in Defender for Cloud can also be used to automate tasks and respond to security alerts generated by Defender for Cloud. If you're sending security alerts from Defender for Cloud to Sentinel, where do you automate tasks related to remediation and response? Do you automate them in Defender for Cloud or in Sentinel?

Organizations typically use SOAR in Sentinel to centrally manage all response and remediation activities across the entire organization. At the same time, there are certain scenarios that can add a lot of value if they're automated in Defender for Cloud. For example, if Defender for Cloud detects a remote desktop protocol (RDP) brute-force attack, you can use workflow automation to add the IP address from where the attack generated to your network security group and block traffic from that IP address to prevent further RDP brute-force attacks. SOAR capabilities in Defender for Cloud are referred to as *workflow automation*; in Sentinel, they are referred to as playbooks and *automation rules.*

8.8   *Automation rules*

Automation rules allow you to centrally manage activities and tasks related to automation in Microsoft Sentinel. These rules can range from assigning owners and changing the status of new incidents to inspecting the content of an incident and calling a playbook. A playbook in Sentinel is a customizable workflow that allows you to define a specific set of remediation actions using Azure Logic Apps.

8.8.1   *Automation elements and trigger events*

Automation rules consist of the following three elements:

- *Triggers*—Defines what causes the automation rule to run
- *Conditions*—Defines under what circumstances the automation rule runs
- *Actions*—Defines what activities are performed when the automation rule runs

Automation rules can be triggered by the following events:

- When an incident is created (for example, when a new incident is created by a scheduled rule or when a security alert is generated by Defender for Cloud)
- When an incident is updated (for example, when an incident's status or severity changes)
- When an alert is created (for example, when an alert is created by a scheduled rule)

These three trigger types allow you to control what causes your automation rule to run. To control when and under what circumstances your automation rule runs, you can use conditions.

Conditions can include the event that triggered the automation rule to run the states of rules, values of the incident's and entity's properties, and even the analytics rule or rules that generated the incident or alert. After you define under what circumstances your automation rule runs, you can control what activities are performed using actions. Actions range from running a playbook to defining many actions in the rule (such as adding a task to an incident, changing the severity of an incident, and others).

8.8.2   *Automation rules in action*

Earlier in this chapter, you created a scheduled rule that creates an incident in Sentinel whenever there are 10 failed login attempts within 5 minutes for any of your users. How can you automatically block the user in Microsoft Entra ID when this incident is created? You can use automation rules to run a playbook in Sentinel that blocks the user.

NOTE For this scenario, you can use an already-built playbook, available at http://mng.bz/Y1m7.

As I previously mentioned, automation rules and SOAR can solve a lot of problems. The following steps solve the requirement for running a playbook that blocks a user in Microsoft Entra ID, but it can also be applied to other use cases:

1 Navigate to the Microsoft Sentinel dashboard inside of the Azure portal.
2 Select Automation, and then click +Create.
3 In the new blade that appears (figure 8.10), enter a name for the automation rule, such as Run Playbook on 10 Failed Login Attempts.
4 From the drop-down menu, choose When Incident Is Created.
5 For Analytics Rule Name, choose Contains, and then select the scheduled rule you created earlier in this chapter.

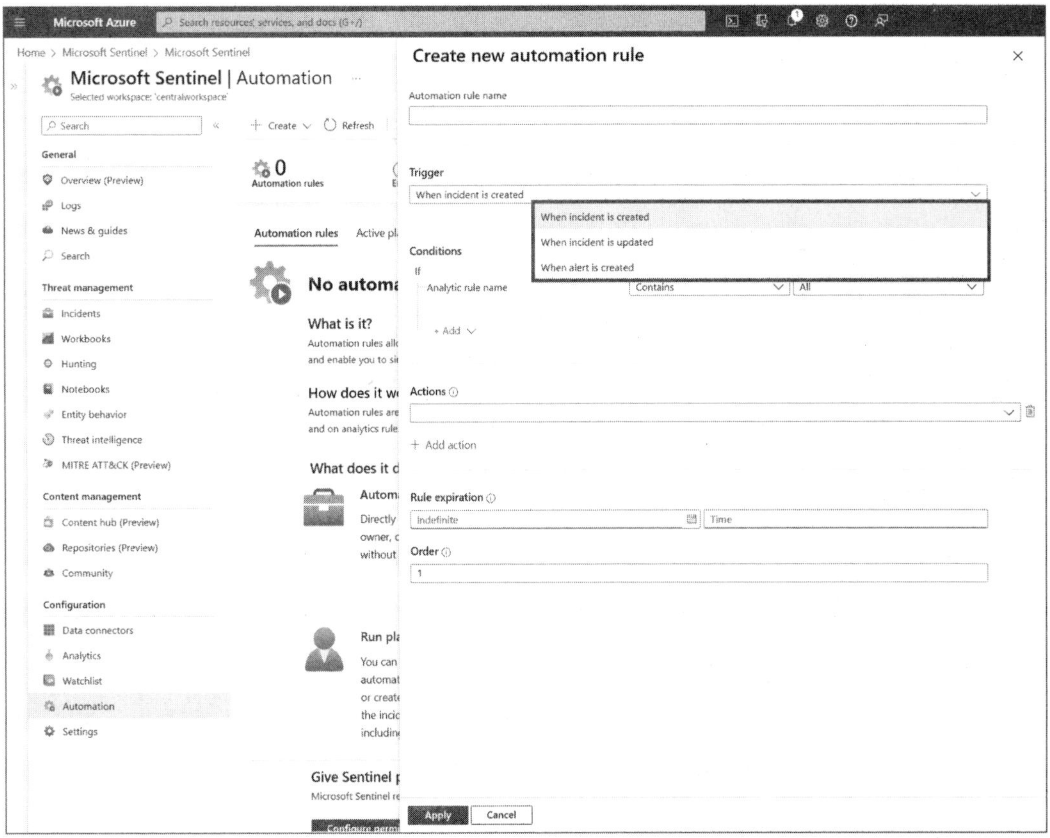

Figure 8.10   Automation rules in Microsoft Sentinel

6 In actions, select Run Playbook, and then choose the playbook you want to run.

7 Leave Rule Expiration and Order as they are.

8 Click Apply.

Rule expiration allows you to define an end date for your automation rule. Suppose you're doing a penetration testing exercise. You can use a rule expiration to align the expiration date to the timeline of the penetration testing exercise.

You can also configure the order in which automation rules run. This capability is useful because automation rules with a higher order evaluate the conditions of incidents according to their state after previous automation rules run. Suppose the first automation rule changes the incident severity from medium to high. If the second automation rule is configured to run on medium incidents only, it won't run because the previous automation rule changed the severity of the incident to high.

> ### Exercise 8.3
> For extra practice, create an automation rule that sends an email whenever Sentinel receives a security alert generated by Defender for Cloud. If you need help with the playbook for this automation rule, you can start at http://mng.bz/Y1m7.

8.9   Answers to Exercises

Exercise 8.1

With a user who has read and write permissions on the Sentinel LAW and Security Administrator assigned on the LAW's tenant, perform the following actions:

1 Sign in to the Azure portal, and navigate to Sentinel.

2 Select the LAW on which you enabled Sentinel.

3 Data Connectors > Office 365 > Open Connector Page.

4 Under Configuration, select All That Apply.

5 Click Apply Changes.

Exercise 8.2

1 Navigate to the Microsoft Sentinel dashboard.

2 Analytics > +Create > Scheduled Query Rule.

3 Click Name for Rule, such as VMs Deleted in Production, and provide a brief description.

4 Under Tactics and Techniques, select Impact and T0828 – Loss of Productivity and Revenue.

5 Severity > Medium.

6 Status > Enabled.

7 Click Next: Set Rule Logic.

8 Use the following query:

```
AzureActivity
| where OperationName == 'Delete Virtual Machine'
| where ActivityStatus == 'Succeded'
```

9 Click Next: Incident Settings.
10 Click Next: Automated Response.
11 Click Next: Review.
12 Click Create.

The query for detecting an anomalous number of resources is available at http://mng.bz/GyzN.

Exercise 8.3

The playbook for this scenario is available at http://mng.bz/zXaZ:

1 Navigate to the Microsoft Sentinel dashboard.
2 Automation > +Create.
3 Click Send Email for Defender for Cloud Alerts.
4 Under Trigger, select When Incident Is Created.
5 Under Analytic Rule Name, select Contains and Create Incidents Based on Microsoft Defender for Cloud.
6 Under Actions, select Run Playbook, and then choose Incident Email Notification.
7 Click Apply.

Summary

- Microsoft Sentinel is a cloud-native SIEM solution that allows you to collect data from relevant data sources to detect threats, investigate them, and automate remediation tasks and response.
- When collecting data, you should ensure that you're collecting the right data for your investigation and that you have sufficient data sources to provide you with the necessary visibility. The simplest way to collect data from relevant data sources is through the data connectors. However, as a best practice, I encourage you to use Content hub instead because with a single click, it provides you with data connectors as well as everything else you might need, such as analytics rules and playbooks.
- After you ingest data from relevant data sources, you can start detecting threats using the built-in templates and creating scheduled query rules. Scheduled query rules allow you to define the detection logic based on your organization's use cases and requirements. As you create the rule, you can even simulate results on top of your own data to ensure you're getting the results that you need.

- When Sentinel detects a threat or potential sign of compromise, you can use the Incidents dashboard to investigate this further. The Incidents dashboard provides you with a lot of powerful capabilities that can supercharge your investigation and help reduce the time it takes to resolve the incident.

- Minutes matter when resolving incidents. You can use automation rules to centrally manage remediation tasks and activities that help you decrease the time it takes to resolve incidents. They can also run playbooks, which integrate with Azure Logic Apps and provide you with a customizable workflow that you can modify to suit the requirements of your organization.

Audit and log data:
Azure Monitor

This chapter covers

- Understanding different log types in Azure
- Azure Monitor
- Diagnostic settings
- Data collection rules
- Alert rules

As you learned in chapter 8, it's important to have relevant data sources when detecting threats and investigating incidents. Relevant data sources provide the breadth and depth of data needed to detect potentially malicious activities and signs of compromise. However, relevant data sources can contain data that is both useful and, well, not really useful for your security operations.

To ensure you have the right data from the relevant data sources, it's important to understand the different log types that are available in Azure. These log types help you determine what data you need to collect and how long you need to keep it. The same goes for performance metrics.

In addition to collecting log data, you can collect specific performance metrics such as CPU usage of Azure virtual machines (VMs), which can be useful in investigating suspicious activities. These performance metrics can be used to create alerts that inform you when a specific threshold is breached, which might be indicative of a suspicious activity.

Imagine that Eve, the fictional bad actor, has compromised the environment and is looking to run crypto miners on compute resources in Azure, such as VMs or Azure Kubernetes Service (AKS) clusters, to elicit financial gain. In addition to collecting relevant data sources that can help detect suspicious activities in the environment, monitoring specific performance metrics can be indicative of anomalous usage that requires further investigation.

> **NOTE** To follow along with the exercises in this chapter, you can use the GitHub repository (https://github.com/bmagusic/azure-security).

Because Azure is one of the three biggest public cloud platforms, it contains many different Azure services. To determine what data is useful in security operations, we need to know the different *log types* that are available in Azure.

9.1   *Understanding different log types in Azure*

Suppose you have an application running in Azure. For this scenario, I rely on the help of the three fictional characters used throughout this book—namely, Alice, Bob, and Eve. Alice is tasked with ensuring that the application built by Bob and running on Azure is secure using several Azure security services I cover in this book and applying a defense-in-depth mindset.

Eve, the bad actor, is trying to spoil Alice's plans and compromise the application. What are some data types in Azure that you, like Alice, can collect to detect Eve's intentions and suspicious activities? First, you can collect data about the application itself, like the one Bob built. In addition to collecting information about the application, you can collect data about the underlying OS on top of which the application runs (assuming it's running on top of an OS). If you're using containers like AKS to run your application, you can also collect data about containers where the application is running.

The application (and OS) is running on top of compute resources (such as VMs) in Azure, from which you can also collect data, but data collection doesn't end with the application, OS, and compute resources. Because the application is running on Azure, you can collect data about the Azure platform itself. The data relating to Azure as a platform is multifaceted. You can collect data about the operations within Azure resources, as well as data about management operations, such as in an Azure subscription pertaining to Azure resources. Because Azure subscriptions reside inside an Azure tenant, you can also collect data about operations at the tenant level of Azure services, such as Microsoft Entra ID (figure 9.1).

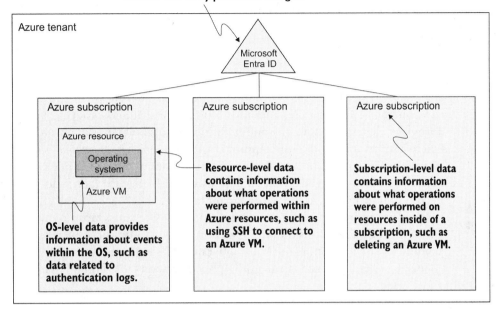

Figure 9.1   Understanding different log types in Azure

What about custom log sources?

You can also collect information from custom sources. Custom sources are typically used in situations when your organization has a requirement to monitor specific resources whose data can't be collected using other data sources. More information about collecting information from custom sources using an API is available at http://mng.bz/o1jr.

You can think of log types as being similar to stacking dolls: an application runs on Azure on top of an OS, followed by the underlying compute resources, and then the Azure platform itself. A set of wooden dolls of decreasing size are placed one inside another, where the application corresponds to the smallest doll and the Azure platform to the largest doll, which holds all the other dolls inside of it. As you may realize, there are various log types in Azure that you can collect. We will start with logs relating to the *Azure tenant* itself.

9.1.1   Azure tenant logs

When you're first starting out with Azure, an Azure tenant is one of the first concepts you learn about. An Azure tenant represents your organization and helps you manage the many different Azure services that you can use. In this chapter, I focus on specific Azure tenant-level services that you can collect data from—namely, Microsoft Entra ID (discussed in chapter 2). The most relevant data sources in Microsoft Entra ID that you need to be aware of for the purposes of this chapter are Microsoft Entra ID audit logs and sign-in logs.

MICROSOFT ENTRA ID AUDIT LOGS

Imagine that the fictional bad actor Eve, despite all of Alice's efforts, manages to somehow compromise the environment and gain unauthorized access. As with most bad actors, Eve likely wants to move laterally and escalate privileges she has in the environment—for example, adding her user to the admin group to be able to perform specific tasks. Where do you find information about lateral movement in Azure? Microsoft Entra ID audit logs capture information such as password resets and users in your tenant being added to an admin group. Because they include comprehensive reports on every logged event in Microsoft Entra ID, they provide an important record of information at the Azure tenant level.

As you can imagine, there can be many of these events. Most events in Microsoft Entra ID audit logs, however, are related to users, groups, or applications, which are commonly used identities in Microsoft Entra ID and, therefore, in Azure environments in general. These log categories provide answers to common questions, such as those listed in table 9.1.

Table 9.1   Questions that can be answered by each log category in Microsoft Entra ID audit logs

Events relating to users	Events relating to groups	Events related to applications
What operations did an administrator perform in the directory?	What changes were made to group ownership?	What applications have been added or changed?
Which type of operation was performed on users? Who are these users?	What changes were made to group membership?	Who gave consent to an application?
How many passwords have been changed?	What groups (if any) have been added?	What changes (if any) were made to a service principal for an application?

Say, for example, you want to find out which users had their password reset and who performed this operation. You can use the information available in Microsoft Entra ID audit log records. Changing a password can be a legitimate activity performed by either the users themselves (for organizations that allow self-service password reset) or by users with higher privilege permissions, such as user administrators. However, password changes can also be indicative of potentially suspicious activities.

MICROSOFT ENTRA ID AUDIT LOGS IN ACTION

Suppose Eve performs a password reset to be able to sign into the Azure environment using a compromised user identity. Information about Eve performing a password user reset is contained in the Microsoft Entra ID audit logs. To access Microsoft Entra ID audit logs, perform the following actions using one of the Reader roles (such as Security Reader or Reports Reader):

1   Sign in to the Azure portal.
2   Navigate to the Microsoft Entra ID dashboard.
3   Select Audit Logs (figure 9.2).

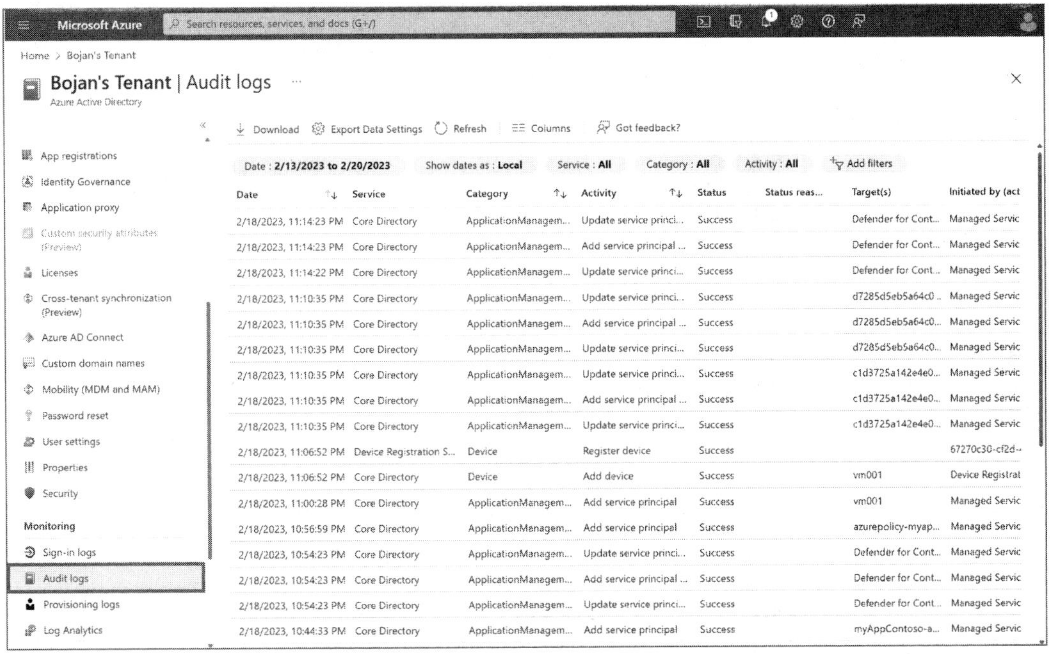

Figure 9.2   Microsoft Entra ID audit logs in the Azure portal

4   Click the Date filter, and choose 7 Days.
5   Click the Activity filter. In the search box, click Password, and then choose Reset User Password.
6   Click one of the results displayed on the screen.
7   In the blade that opens, the Activity tab contains information about who performed the operation in question (in this case, the user password reset).
8   Click the Target(s) tab. This blade contains information about the user on which the password reset was performed.
9   Perform steps 7 and 8 for the remaining rows displayed in the output.

Together, this information gives you the answer to the question of which users had their password reset and who performed this operation.

Because Azure AD audit logs contain Azure tenant-level information about various directory-related activities, typically, they contain plenty (if not a plethora) of data. This amount of information is further exacerbated in large environments that have a large user base. Therefore, knowing what information to look for is half the job. You can use the filters to refine your search to a subset of relevant results.

> ### Exercise 9.1
>
> For extra practice and to solidify your knowledge of Microsoft Entra ID audit logs, use the information in the audit logs to answer this question: What operations did an administrator perform in your directory? This exercise is also an opportunity to familiarize yourself with the different filters that can be used in Microsoft Entra ID audit logs.

To complement the information available in Microsoft Entra ID audit logs, you can use Microsoft Entra ID *sign-in logs*.

MICROSOFT ENTRA ID SIGN-IN LOGS

Whereas Microsoft Entra ID audit logs provide you with information about every task performed in your tenant, Microsoft Entra ID sign-in logs help you determine who has performed the tasks specified in the audit logs. Sign-in logs provide valuable insights into how identities access resources in your Azure environment. Similar to Microsoft Entra ID audit logs, sign-in logs can contain many events. Most are related to users, applications, or managed identities, which are commonly used identities in Microsoft Entra ID. They are further grouped into the categories listed in table 9.2.

Table 9.2 Categorization of different sign-in types in Microsoft Entra ID sign-in logs

Interactive user sign-ins	Noninteractive user sign-ins	Service principal sign-ins	Managed identity sign-ins
Where a user signs in with an authentication factor, such as a password or multifactor authentication challenge	Where a client signs in on behalf of a user and the user isn't required to enter credentials	Where an application or service principal signs in without any user involvement	Where Azure services sign in and have secrets managed by Azure

Imagine you created a conditional access policy (discussed in chapter 2) that applies to the user, Bob. Bob's sign-in activity is logged in Microsoft Entra ID sign-in logs. To be more precise, when you enter Bob's credentials, this information is logged in the interactive user sign-ins.

MICROSOFT ENTRA ID SIGN-IN LOGS IN ACTION

How do you determine the sign-in location for Bob and whether or not the conditional access policy you created is applied to Bob's identity? To achieve this, you can use the information stored in the interactive user sign-in portion of the Microsoft Entra ID sign-in logs. To access Microsoft Entra ID sign-in logs, using one of the Reader roles (such as Security Reader or Reports Reader), complete the following actions:

1 Sign in to the Azure portal.
2 Navigate to the Microsoft Entra ID dashboard.
3 Select Sign-In Logs (figure 9.3).

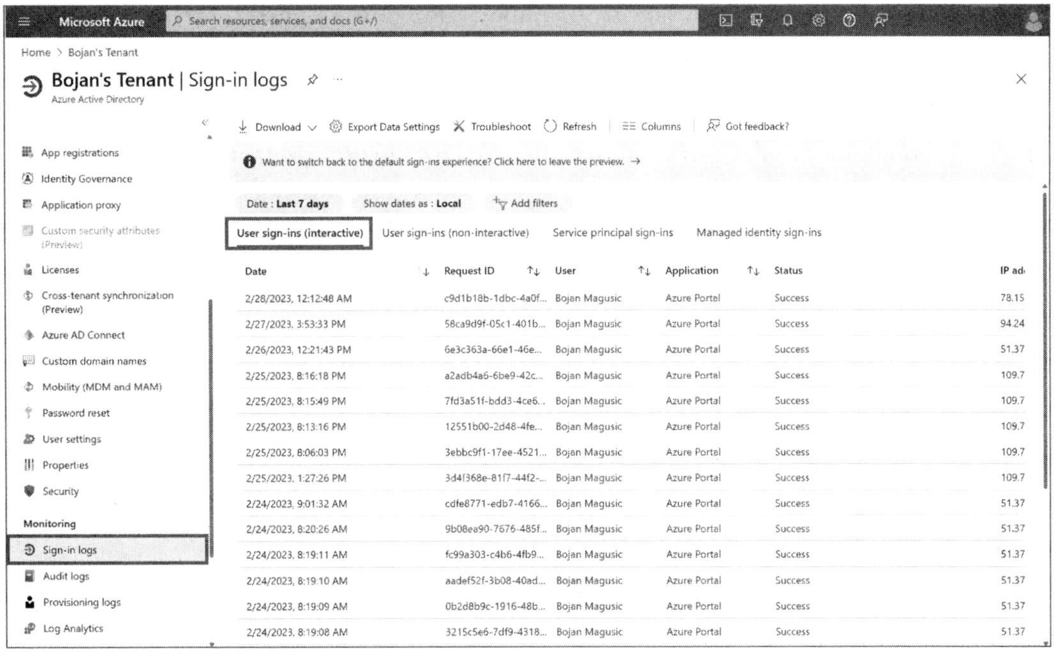

Figure 9.3 Microsoft Entra ID sign-in logs in the Azure portal

4 Click the Date filter, and then choose 7 Days. If you have an Microsoft Entra ID Premium license, choose 30 Days instead.

5 Click the Add filter. Choose User, and then click Apply.

6 Click the name of the user, such as Bob, and click Apply.

7 The list of results updates automatically based on the filter selection. Click one of the results displayed on the screen.

8 In the blade that opens, the Basic Info tab contains information about the sign-in.

9 Click the Location tab. This blade contains the IP address and location from where the sign-in was performed.

10 Select the Conditional Access tab. This blade shows the conditional access policy applicable to the sign-in.

This process provides you with the location of Bob's sign-in and whether the conditional access policy you created applied to the sign-in.

In chapter 2, I discussed the relationship between Microsoft Entra ID and Azure subscriptions, noting that more than one Azure subscription in your environment can be associated with the same Microsoft Entra ID tenant. This capability is beneficial because it allows you to use the same set of identities (such as for your users and applications) across all the Azure subscriptions in your tenant. These identities, in turn, can be used to perform specific operations on Azure resources, such as creating or deleting an Azure VM, in your Azure subscriptions.

9.1.2 *Azure subscriptions*

Among other things, Azure subscriptions act as a logical container for resources that you provision in Azure, such as VMs, databases, AKS clusters, storage accounts, and others. Data related to the health and operation of your Azure subscriptions contains information, including configuration changes made to your Azure resources, the health of the Azure services in your subscription, and insights into changes to your Azure application.

Information about the health of Azure services in your subscription is provided in the Azure Service Health portal. Insights about changes to your Azure applications are stored in Azure Change Analysis. Both provide valuable information.

> **NOTE** To learn more about Azure Service Health, you can start at http:// mng.bz/nW9g, and for Change Analysis, at http://mng.bz/vnBJ.

In this chapter, I focus on information about operations performed on your Azure resources provided in the *Azure activity log*.

AZURE ACTIVITY LOG

Suppose that you discover that a production VM in your Azure subscription has been deleted. To find information about what happened to it, you can use the Azure activity log. The Azure activity log contains information about operations performed on your Azure resources tracked by Azure Resource Manager (such as deleting an Azure VM). Information provided in the Azure activity log helps answers questions about, for example, who did what when and on which Azure resources.

> **NOTE** Events in the Azure activity log are deleted after 90 days. If your organization requires events in the Azure activity log to be retained for longer than 90 days, you can configure diagnostic settings to stream these events to another location (I'll cover diagnostic settings in chapter 9).

Going back to the example I gave, suppose you wanted to determine who deleted a VM in a specific Azure subscription. You can find this information in the Azure activity log.

AZURE ACTIVITY LOGIN ACTION

To access the Microsoft Entra ID activity log at the Azure subscription level, using one of the Reader roles (such as Security Reader), complete the following steps:

1 Sign in to the Azure portal.
2 Navigate to the Monitor dashboard.
3 Click Activity Log.
4 Click the Timespan filter, and then choose the desired duration (for example, Last 24 Hours).

5 Select Add Filter, and then choose Resource Type. In the drop-down menu that appears, choose Virtual Machines (Microsoft.Compute/VirtualMachines).

6 The list of results updates automatically based on the filter selection. Click one of the Deallocate Virtual Machine results displayed on the screen.

7 In the blade that opens, the Summary tab contains information about the operation name. Click the Change History tab. This blade contains information about the changes made to the Azure resources—in this case, about the Azure VM that got deleted (figure 9.4).

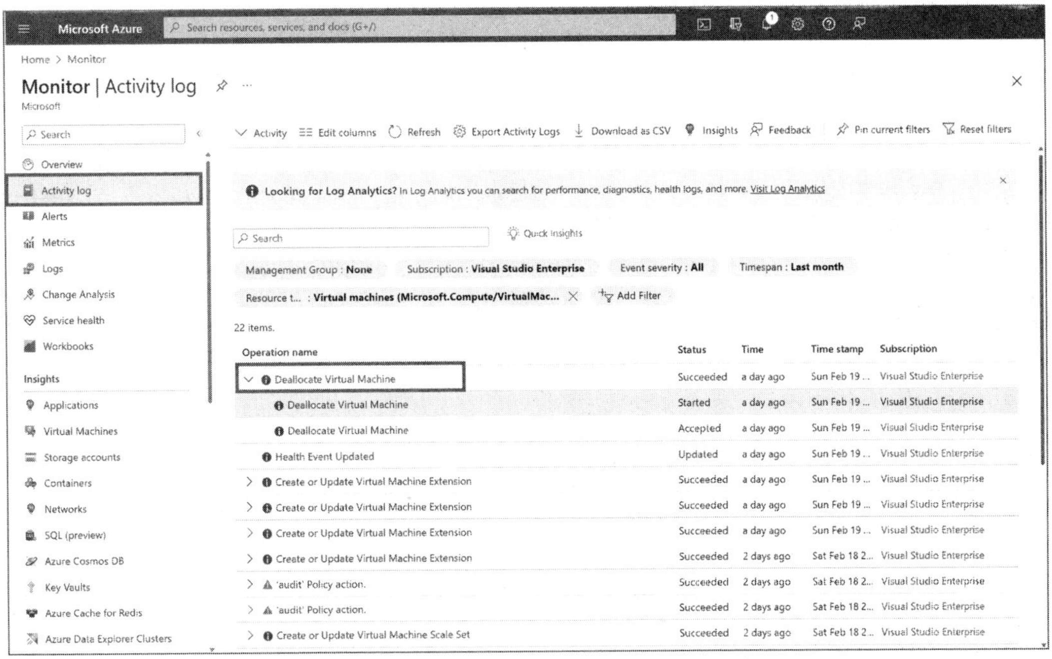

Figure 9.4   The Azure login activity the Azure portal

You can access the Azure activity log from most menus in the Azure portal. When accessing it through the Monitor dashboard, the filter is set on the subscription. In contrast, when you access the Azure activity log from the menu of a particular Azure resource, the filter is set to that resource.

Exercise 9.2

To help internalize what you've learned about Azure activity logs and the information they contain, use the Azure activity log to determine who listed account keys for storage accounts in your Azure environment over the last two weeks.

The Azure activity log provides information related to control plane operations in Azure. For information related to the data plane, you can use the resource logs.

Control plane vs. data plane in Azure

Operations performed on your Azure resources can be divided into the control plane and the data plane. The control plane (or *management plane*, as it's often referred to) is used to manage Azure resources in your subscription (for example, creating an Azure VM in your subscription). The data plane, on the other hand, is used to manage the capabilities of your Azure resources (such as using a remote desktop protocol to connect to the Azure VM you created using the control plane).

To help you differentiate the control plan from the data plane, I offer the following example. Imagine the application that Bob is building in Azure needs to store and access blob data. You create a storage account through the control plane. After you create the storage account, the application reads the data from the storage account through the data plane. Information related to control plane operations in your Azure subscriptions is stored in the Azure activity log. The information related to data plane operations in your Azure subscriptions is stored in the resource logs.

9.1.3   *Azure resources*

When it comes to Azure resources in your subscription, you need to be aware of both *platform metrics* and *resource logs*.

PLATFORM METRICS

Platform metrics represent numeric data collected from Azure resources in your environment. They're useful in describing a particular aspect of your Azure resources at a point in time, particularly when it comes to the health and performance of your resources—for example, CPU usage of your VMs or the number of transactions for your storage accounts.

> **NOTE**   Because Azure has so many services, it can be challenging to understand what platform metrics are available. For a full list of supported platform metrics, you can start at http://mng.bz/5oYD.

Platform metrics are collected automatically from your Azure resources every minute (by default) and at no additional cost. In addition, you can collect custom metrics from different data sources (such as your applications or VMs).

RESOURCE LOGS

Whereas platform metrics provide you with numeric values, resource logs in Azure provide you with information about operations performed within an Azure resource in your subscription. Similar to platform metrics, resource logs are created automatically. However, unlike platform metrics, resource logs aren't collected by default. To collect resource logs, you need to create diagnostic settings (I'll cover diagnostic settings in section 9.3).

> **NOTE** For a full list of supported Azure services for resource logs, you can start at http://mng.bz/XNBG.

Because resource logs are generated by Azure services, they describe the operations within resources, and the content of resource logs depends on the particular Azure service and resource type in question.

Say you have VMs running in your Azure environment. Platform metrics are collected automatically, but you need to configure resource logs to be collected. One of the most commonly used resource types in Azure is VMs. VMs generate similar data to that generated by other Azure resources. However, VMs have a guest *operating system*, from which you can collect data.

9.1.4 Operating system

To collect data from the OS, you need an agent. Currently, there are two Microsoft agents you can use to collect data from the OS: the Log Analytics (LA) agent and the Azure Monitoring agent (AMA).

AMA VS. LA AGENT

AMA is the evolution of the LA agent (also referred to by its predecessor, the Microsoft Monitoring agent [MMA] and, at times, the Operations Management Suite [OMS] agent). OMS is an agent you might recall if you've been working with Azure for a while; then came MMA and, later on, the LA agent. They empowered organizations to collect data and monitor their Azure VMs.

One of the challenges that companies faced, however, was wanting to send performance- and security-related events they were collecting from their VMs to different LA workspaces (LAWs). Why would they do that, you ask? Suppose you have Microsoft Sentinel enabled on the top of the LAW to which you're sending both performance- and security-related events. Because you're charged for data ingested in the LAW on top of which you enabled Sentinel, you may be paying for performance-related data that doesn't provide you with a lot of security value.

Consequently, many organizations send performance-related data they collect on VMs to one LAW and send security-related events to another LAW (also known as *multihoming*). AMA supports multihoming scenarios through data collection rules (DCRs; discussed in section 9.4). However, you should be aware that although AMA is generally available, the integration between AMA and different Azure services might still be in public preview. An example is the integration between AMA and Microsoft Defender for Cloud: if you want to enable auto-provisioning of AMA in Defender for Cloud (see chapter 7), you need to be aware that the integration between AMA and Defender for Cloud is currently in public preview. However, the integration between the LA agent and Microsoft Defender for Cloud is generally available. Because Microsoft is moving in the direction of AMA, I'll cover collecting data from the OS using AMA.

THE AZURE MONITOR AGENT

AMA offers comprehensive monitoring capabilities for VMs running either Windows or Linux. AMA replaces two other agents that were previously used for monitoring purposes—the LA agent and the Azure diagnostic extension. You can configure AMA to collect both logs and performance counters from your VMs using one agent.

To install AMA on your VMs, you need to meet certain prerequisites. The prerequisites for installing AMA on Azure VMs are aggregated in table 9.3.

Table 9.3 Prerequisites for installing AMA on your Azure VMs

Permissions	Networking	Authentication
The Virtual Machine Contributor role on VMs The Azure Connected Machine Resource Administrator role on VMs The Log Analytics Contributor role on your VMs (or any other role that includes the action Microsoft .Resources/deployments/*)	The VMs must have access to the following HTTPS endpoints: • global.handler.control.moni-tor.azure.com • \<your-VMs-region-name>.han-dler.control.monitor.azure.com • \<log-analytics-workspace-id>.ods.opinsights.azure.com	Managed identities must be enabled on your VMs. You can use either a user- or system-assigned managed identity.

In addition, if you use network firewalls, the virtual network service tag for Azure Resource Manager needs to be enabled on the virtual network for your VMs. To install AMA on an Azure VM running Windows, run the following command in Azure Cloud Shell. This code installs AMA using a user-assigned managed identity. To install AMA using a system-assigned managed identity, remove the line with `settings`.

Listing 9.1   Installing AMA on Azure VM

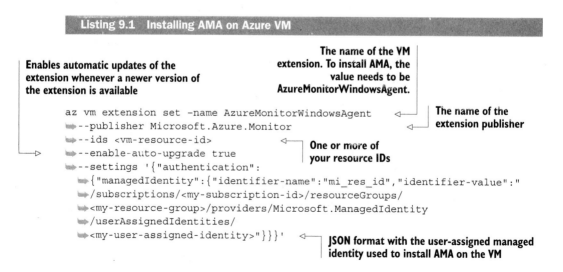

Enables automatic updates of the extension whenever a newer version of the extension is available

The name of the VM extension. To install AMA, the value needs to be AzureMonitorWindowsAgent.

```
az vm extension set –name AzureMonitorWindowsAgent
--publisher Microsoft.Azure.Monitor
--ids <vm-resource-id>
--enable-auto-upgrade true
--settings '{"authentication":
{"managedIdentity":{"identifier-name":"mi_res_id","identifier-value":"
/subscriptions/<my-subscription-id>/resourceGroups/
<my-resource-group>/providers/Microsoft.ManagedIdentity
/userAssignedIdentities/
<my-user-assigned-identity>"}}}'
```

The name of the extension publisher

One or more of your resource IDs

JSON format with the user-assigned managed identity used to install AMA on the VM

To install AMA on VMs running Linux, replace the `-name` parameter with `Azure-MonitorLinuxAgent`.

> **NOTE** For guidance on how to install AMA on Windows 10 or 11 desktops and workstations, you can start at http://mng.bz/yQPG.

When installing AMA on your VMs for large-scale deployments, using a user-assigned managed identity rather than a system-assigned managed identity is recommended. By their very nature, user-assigned managed identities can be used by multiple VMs, whereas system-assigned managed identities are tied to the resources in question (in this case, to each one of your VMs). Imagine you want to install AMA on 100 Azure VMs. Using system-assigned managed identities implies that 100 managed identities are created—one managed identity for each of your 100 VMs on which you're installing AMA. To avoid having a substantial number of identities created in your Microsoft Entra ID, you can opt to use user-assigned managed identities.

9.2   Azure Monitor

Azure Monitor is a comprehensive solution in Azure that you can use to collect, analyze, visualize, and respond to data from your Azure resources. With the proliferation of different Azure services, it would be cumbersome for each Azure service to have its own way of exposing security- and performance-related data. Azure Monitor simplifies data collection across many Azure resources in a uniform and standardized way.

In chapter 7, I touched on workbooks, one of the Azure Monitor capabilities. The focus of this book is on native Azure security services. Although Azure Monitor might not necessarily come to mind when you think of security, the data collected by Azure Monitor can be useful when investigating suspicious activities and potential signs of compromise. You can use Azure Monitor to collect and analyze the different log types discussed in this chapter. However, this discussion doesn't do Azure Monitor justice because it covers only a small portion of its functionalities.

> **NOTE** To learn more about other Azure Monitor functionalities not covered in this chapter, you can start at http://mng.bz/MBz7.

The purpose of this section is to cover aspects of Azure Monitor that can be of real value from a security point of view. Azure Monitor allows you to collect data from your applications, OS, the underlying Azure services on top of which they're built, and Azure as a platform.

Data related to Azure as a platform is sent automatically to Azure; you don't need to configure anything. This data includes platform metrics. However, platform logs (such as resource or activity logs) are not collected automatically. Resources deployed in your Azure environment automatically generate resource logs that contain information about the operations performed within the resource, but you need to configure resource logs to collect them. To do that, you can create *diagnostic settings*.

9.3   Diagnostic settings

Diagnostic settings allow you to collect resource activity logs and metrics by specifying from which resources you want to collect this data and where you want to send it. You can send data to one of the following destinations:

- *A LAW*—A suitable option when you want to use this data for queries, alerts, and visualizations, alongside other data
- *An Azure Storage account*—A cost-effective option for archiving logs and metrics
- *An Azure Event Hub*—A suitable option for taking data outside of Azure, for exaple, by sending it to an external Security Information and Event Management system
- *Azure Monitor partner integrations*—A suitable option when you're already using one of the specialized non-Microsoft monitoring platforms.

NOTE   To learn more about the Azure Monitor partner integrations, you can start at http://mng.bz/a1Xz.

If you want to send data to more than one destination (say, to two different LAWs or to a LAW and a storage account), you need to create two diagnostic settings. Each diagnostic setting can define one destination only. Another caveat is that each Azure resource can only have up to five diagnostic settings. When creating diagnostic settings, you can create them for an individual Azure resource, a group of resources, and the activity log. Creating diagnostic settings for more than one Azure resource is done through the Azure Monitor dashboard, whereas creating diagnostic settings for an individual resource is done in the resource's menu.

9.3.1   Diagnostic settings in action

Imagine you want to collect resource logs generated by an Azure Key Vault instance. You can do so by completing the following actions:

1 Navigate to the Azure Monitor dashboard inside of the Azure portal.
2 On the left, select Diagnostic Settings.
3 Using the filter, choose the subscription and resource group of the key vault instance.
4 The list of results updates automatically based on the filter selection. Then click the key vault instance.
5 In the new blade that opens, click Add Diagnostic Setting.
6 Enter a name for the diagnostic setting, such as Audit (figure 9.5).
7 Select the platform logs and metrics you want to collect, such as allLogs.
8 Select the desired destination, such as a LAW. Then select the subscription and LAW using the drop-down menus.

NOTE   Depending on the destination you select, the options displayed may differ.

9 Click Save.

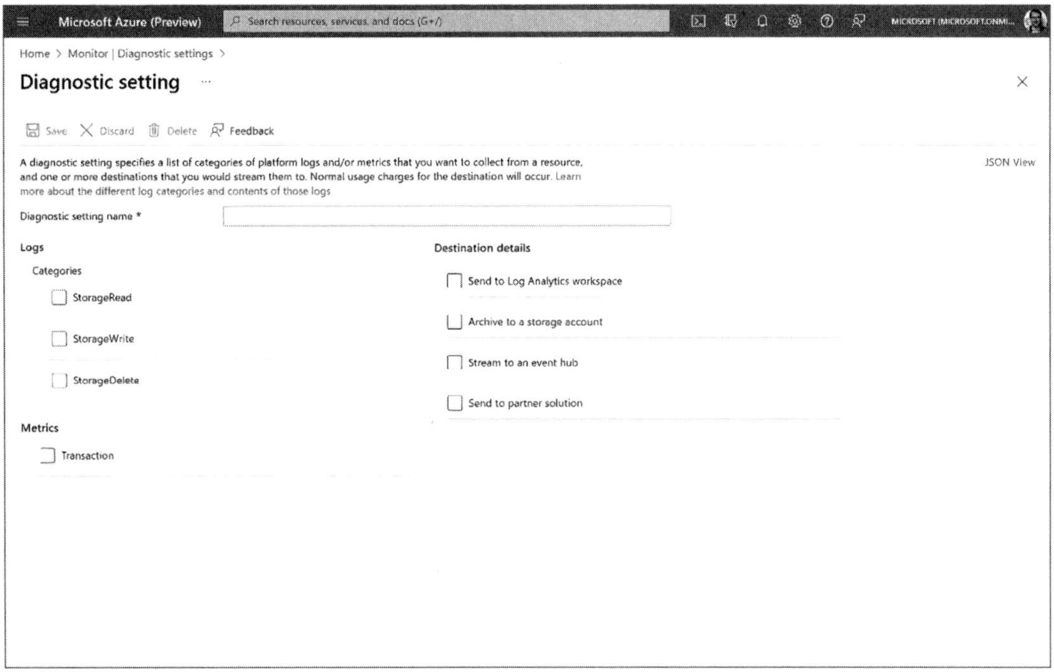

Figure 9.5   Configuring diagnostic settings in Azure Monitor

After you create the diagnostic setting, you should see data in the destination you selected within 90 minutes.

> **NOTE**   When you delete and recreate an Azure resource, the previous diagnostic setting could be combined with the current diagnostic setting and resume sending logs to the previously defined destination. Therefore, as a best practice, when deleting an Azure resource, make sure to delete any diagnostic settings first.

VMs generate similar data to that generated by other Azure resources. However, because VMs have a guest OS, to collect data from the OS, you need an agent. To collect data from a guest OS on your VMs, you can use AMA with *data collection rules*.

9.4   Data collection rules

DCRs specify what data is collected from the guest OS of your Azure VMs, where it's sent, and how it's transformed. The option to transform data you're collecting is especially valuable in scenarios where you need to manipulate incoming data (figure 9.6).

To highlight the value of transforming data, I offer the following example. Suppose incoming data contains sensitive information, such as customer credit card information. If you don't want this data stored, either due to privacy or compliance

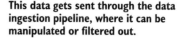

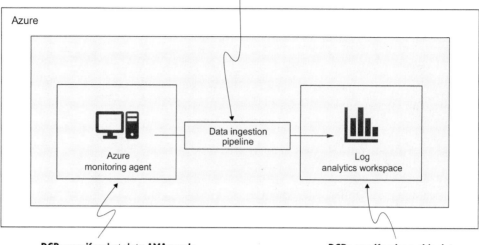

Figure 9.6   Collecting data from the guest OS using AMA and DCRs

reasons, you can filter sensitive information using transformations. Say you also have data that isn't sensitive and isn't required for your scenario. Because you pay ingestion costs for any data sent to a LAW, you can also use transformations to filter data that you don't need, in turn reducing your data costs.

> **NOTE**   To learn more about how transformations work in Azure Monitor, you can start at http://mng.bz/gBpl.

You can use AMA to create DCRs that collect events and performance-related data from your Azure VMs (see figure 9.6). However, before you start, you need to fulfill certain prerequisites. The necessary prerequisites in terms of permissions are aggregated in table 9.4.

Table 9.4   Permissions required to create DCRs using AMA

Monitoring Contributor	Virtual Machine Contributor Azure Connected Machine Resource Administrator	Any role that includes the action Microsoft.Resources/ deployments/*
To create or edit DCRs, you need to have this role assigned on the Azure subscription, resource group, and/or any existing DCR.	To assign DCRs to a VM, for example, you need to have this role assigned on the VM or Virtual Machine Scale Sets.	To deploy Azure Resource Manager templates, you need to have a role with these permissions assigned on the Azure subscription, resource group, and/or an existing DCR.

DCRs allow you to collect data from your VMs and send it to a LAW. Now, say you need to collect authentication logs from your VMs in Azure running Linux to track and analyze authentication-related data. You can collect authentication-related data using AMA and DCRs.

9.4.1   Data collection rules in action

To create a DCR to collect authentication-related data, complete the following steps:

1   Navigate to the Azure Monitor dashboard inside the Azure portal.
2   On the left, select Data Collection Rules.
3   Click Create to create a new DCR.

NOTE   Although your screen displays all DCRs (including those for AMA and other workflows), this page allows you to create and edit DCRs for AMA only. If you need to create and update DCRs for other workflows, you can start at http://mng.bz/e1gz.

4   Enter the rule name, and then select the Azure subscription and resource group where the DCR is created.
5   Choose the platform type. For the purposes of this example, choose Linux. Other available options are Windows and Custom. Custom allows both Windows and Linux.
6   Click Next: Resources.
7   Select +Add Resource, and select the resources from which you want to collect data, such as your VMs running Linux (figure 9.7).

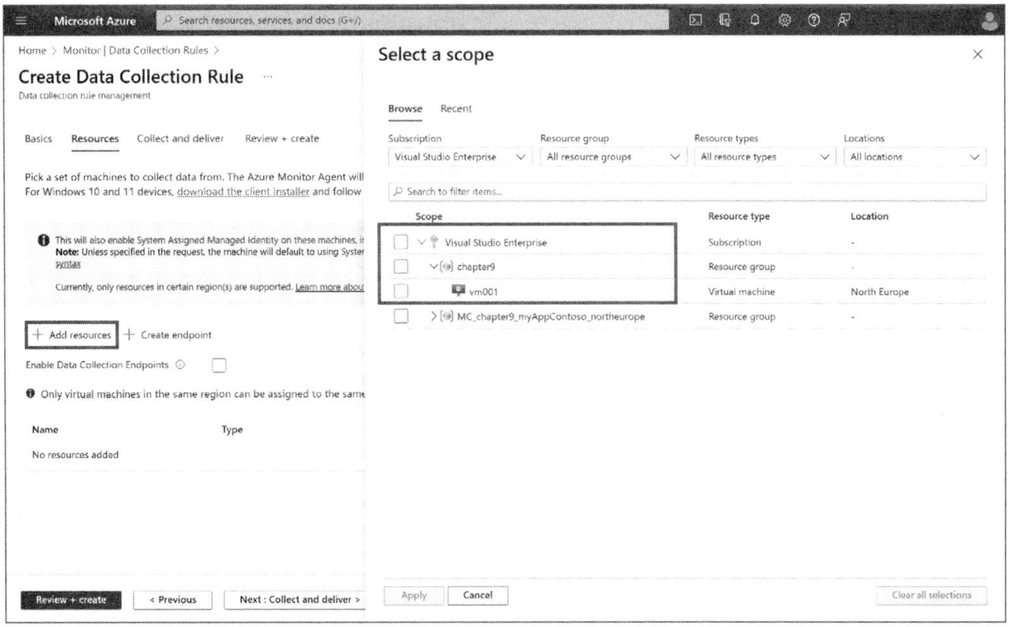

Figure 9.7   Creating DCRs in Azure Monitor to collect data from VM with AMA

NOTE   AMA is automatically installed on the Azure VMs you select to collect data from. If you select Windows 10 or 11 devices, you will need to install AMA. To install AMA on Windows 10 and 11 devices, you can start at http://mng.bz/ yQPG.

NOTE   By default, the Azure portal enables a system-assigned managed identity on the selected resources, along with any existing user-assigned identities. While a system-assigned managed identity is suitable for testing purposes, for large-scale deployments, the best practice is to use user-assigned managed identities.

8   If you don't have a data collection endpoint in the same Azure region as your Azure VMs, select +Create Endpoint. AMA can connect to and retrieve the associated DCRs from the data collection endpoint.

9   Enter the data collection endpoint, and then select the Azure subscription and resource group where the data collection endpoint is created. The Azure region needs to be the same as the AMAs connected to it. If you have AMAs in different Azure regions, you will need to create one data collection endpoint for each region.

10   For each of the resources you selected, in the drop-down menu, select the data collection endpoint (as shown in figure 9.8), and then click Next: Collect and Deliver.

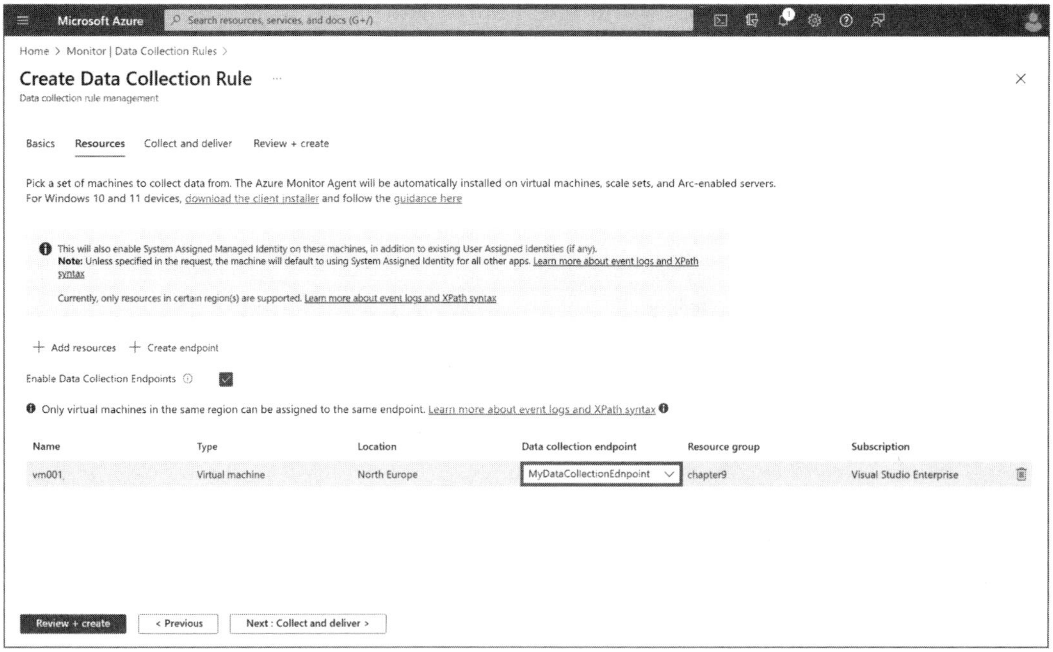

Figure 9.8   Selecting a data collection endpoint while creating DCRs

11   Click +Add Data Sources to specify the data you want to collect and the destination to which the data will be sent.

12   In the drop-down menu, select the data you want to collect. For example, to collect authentication logs from your VMs running Linux, select Linux Syslog. Then, for LOG_AUTH and LOG_AUTHPRIV, select LOG_DEBUG (figure 9.9), and for others, select None (this action helps reduce data ingestion costs).

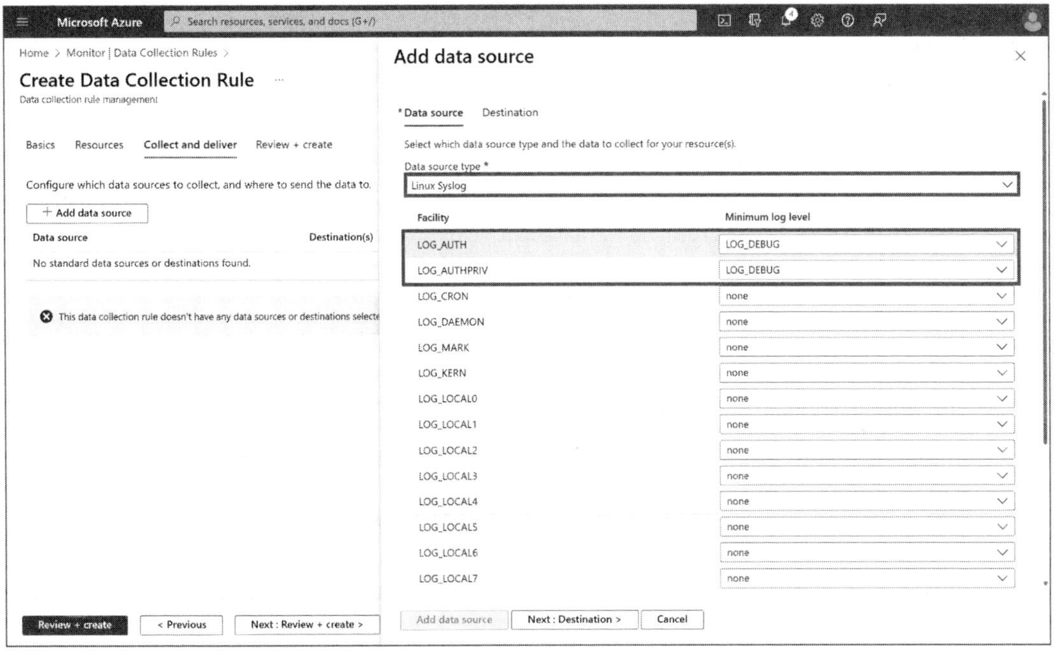

Figure 9.9   Adding data sources when creating DCRs

13   Select the destination, and then click the +Add Destination tab to specify the locations you want to send data to. You can send different data types to multiple destinations (multihoming).

NOTE   Windows and Syslog data sources can be sent to Azure Monitor logs only. In contrast, you can send performance counters to Azure Monitor logs and Azure Monitor Metrics.

14   After you finish adding destinations, select Add Data Source.

15   Select Review + Create, and then click Create to create the DCR.

> **Exercise 9.3**
>
> To solidify your knowledge of DCRs and AMA, create a DCR that collects security and system event logs from all VMs inside a particular Azure subscription and sends them to a LAW of your choice.

After you configure data collection rules, you can use the data that AMA collects, as well as other data (such as performance metrics), to monitor for anomalous usage using *alert rules.*

9.5 Alert rules

Alert rules in Azure Monitor allow you to monitor resources and specify conditions to define the processing logic of alert rules. When the condition(s) you specified are met, Azure Monitor generates an alert. As part of this process, you can also integrate alerts that generate notifications (such as email or SMS) with proven Azure services (such as Azure Logic Apps or Azure Functions).

9.5.1 Types of alerts

Azure Monitor supports different types of alerts, including metrics, activity logs, and log alerts. To create an alert rule, you must have the necessary permissions, as shown in table 9.5.

Table 9.5   Permissions required to create alert rules in Azure Monitor

Target resource for which the alert rule is created	Resource group in which the alert rule is created	Action group associated with alert rule (if applicable)
Read permission	Write permission	Read permission

Alternatively, you can use the built-in Azure role-based access control role, called *Monitoring Contributor,* to create alert rules.

9.5.2 Alert rules in action

Suppose you want to receive an alert when the CPU of your VM surpasses 80%. You can do so with alert rules in Azure Monitor by completing the following steps:

1 Navigate to the Azure Monitor dashboard inside the Azure portal.
2 On the left, select Alerts.
3 Choose Select + Create, and then click Alert Rule.
4 In the blade that opens, select the resource(s) you want to create an alert rule for. You can choose all resources inside an Azure subscription, resource group, or a particular resource (such as a VM). After you select the desired scope, click Apply (figure 9.10).

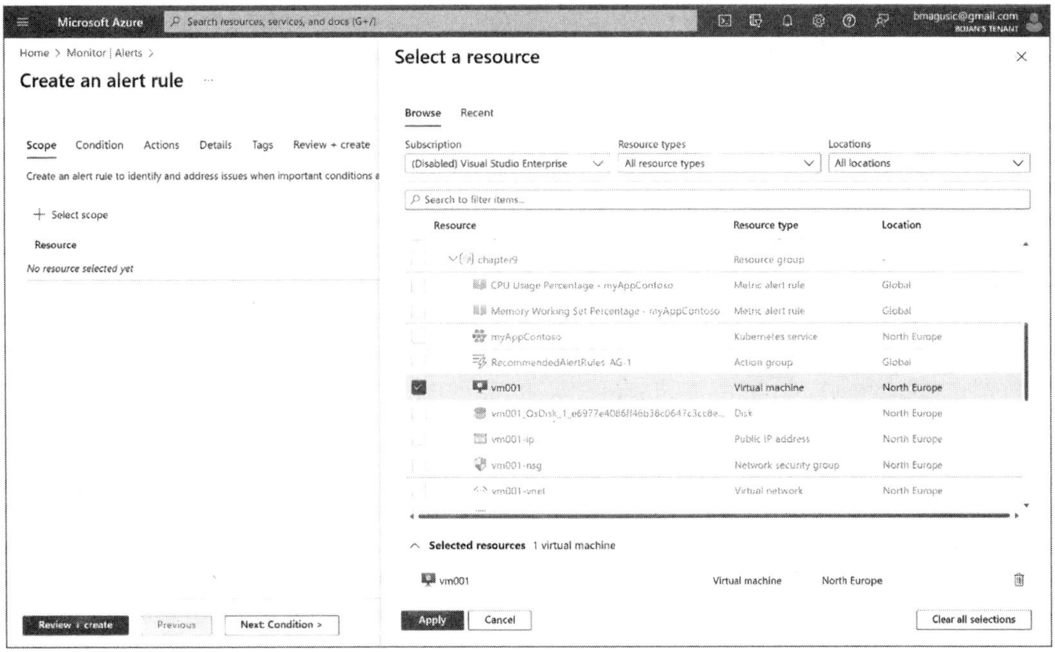

Figure 9.10   Selecting a resource to be monitored when creating alert rules

5   Click Next: Condition.

6   Add the name of the desired metric or log, such as CPU Usage Percentage, and then click it.

7   Leave the threshold as Static. This option uses a static value you define, whereas Dynamic uses machine learning to calculate the threshold automatically.

8   For Aggregation Type, leave Average selected.

9   Select Greater Than as an operator.

10   Insert 80 for the threshold value.

11   Select 5 Minutes for Check Every and 5 Minutes for Lookback Period.

12   Click Next: Actions. An action group is a set of actions that can apply to the alert rule.

13   Select Next: Details.

14   Select the subscription and resource group in which you want to save the alert rule.

15   For severity, choose 2-Warning.

16   Enter the name and a description for the alert rule.

17   Click Next: Tags. This part is optional.

18   Click Next: Review + Create and then click Create.

This procedure creates an alert rule so that whenever the CPU of the VM you selected surpasses 80%, you receive an alert.

9.6   Answers to exercises

Exercise 9.1

1. Sign in to the Azure portal.
2. Navigate to the Microsoft Entra ID dashboard, and select Audit Logs.
3. Click the Date filter, and then choose 7 Days.
4. Click the Activity filter. In the search box, click Admin, and then choose a particular activity, such as Reset Password (By Admin).
5. Click one of the results displayed on the screen.
6. In the blade that opens, the Activity tab contains information about who performed the operation in question (in this case, the password reset).
7. Click the Target(s) tab. This blade contains information about the user on which the password reset was performed.
8. Perform steps 4 through 8 to perform more operations for an additional two activities of your choice. This activity helps familiarize you with the different filters that can be used in audit logs.

Exercise 9.2

1. Navigate to the Monitor dashboard and select Activity Log.
2. Click the Timespan filter, and then choose the desired duration (for example, Last 2 Weeks).
3. Select the Add filter, and then choose Operation. In the drop-down menu that appears, choose List Storage Account Keys (Microsoft.Storage/storageAccounts/listkeys/action).
4. The list of results updates automatically based on the filter selection. Click one of the List Storage Account Keys results displayed on the screen.
5. In the blade that opens, the Summary tab contains information about the operation name as well as who initiated the operation.

Exercise 9.3

1. Navigate to the Azure Monitor dashboard.
2. On the left, select Data Collection Rules.
3. Click Create to create a new DCR.
4. Enter the rule name, such as DCR_Security_System, and then select the Azure subscription and resource group where the DCR is created.
5. Choose Windows as the Platform type, and then click Next: Resources.
6. Select +Add Resource, and select all the VMs inside of the desired subscription that are running Windows.
7. Click Next: Collect and Deliver.

8 Click +Add Data source, and then, under Data Source Type, select Windows Event Logs.

9 Set the toggle to Basic, and select everything under Security and System.

10 Select the destination, and then click +Add Destination.

11 Add the location you want to send security and system event logs to. After you finish adding the desired destination, select Add Data Source.

12 Select Review + Create, and then click Create to create the DCR.

Summary

- In Azure, you can collect data about an application, guest OS, and underlying compute resources (such as VMs), as well as data about the Azure platform itself.

- Azure Monitor is a comprehensive solution in Azure that you can use to collect, analyze, visualize, and respond to data from your applications and OS, the underlying Azure services on top of which they're built, and Azure as a platform. Data collected by Azure Monitor can potentially be useful when investigating suspicious activities and potential signs of compromise.

- To collect logs from the guest OS on your VMS, you need an agent. Microsoft is moving in the direction of AMA, which you can use to collect data from the host OS of your Azure VMs. To collect data using AMA, you need to create a DCR, which specifies what data AMA collects and the destination it's sent to.

- Whereas data related to Azure as a platform is collected automatically without any configuration necessary, the logs generated by Azure resources are not collected automatically. To collect logs generated by Azure resources, such as resource logs or activity logs, you need to create diagnostic settings. Diagnostic settings allow you to send this data to one of the supported destinations, such as a LAW or an Azure Storage account.

- You can create alert rules to be automatically notified if a specific performance metric (for example, CPU usage on compute resources such as your VMs) surpasses a defined threshold. Alert rules can help you detect suspicious activities in your Azure environment that may be indicative of anomalous usage and warrant further investigation.

Importance of governance: Azure Policy and Azure Blueprints

This chapter covers
- Understanding Azure Policy
- Getting started with Azure Policy
- Custom policies
- Centralized security policy management
- Azure Blueprints

Governance in Azure can be seen as a combination of different Azure services you can use to manage your resources and ensure they meet your organization's guidelines. What does governance have to do with Azure security? I'd like to offer a perspective. In chapter 6, you learned about cloud security posture management and how you can use Microsoft Defender for Cloud to continuously assess the configurations of resources in your environment and detect misconfigurations. New resources can be deployed daily (as can subscriptions).

If new resources that are deployed to your Azure environment do not adhere to security best practices, potential misconfigurations or vulnerabilities can have a negative effect on your organization's overall security posture. This chapter teaches you how you can use Azure Policy to prevent this vulnerability, ensuring that resources that are deployed to your environment adhere to security best practices. That way, Defender for Cloud doesn't flag these resources as having misconfigurations or vulnerabilities, ensuring a baseline of security is met in your environment. Thus, you can use Azure Policy to apply guardrails that prevent your resources from being deployed in a way that doesn't align with security best practices, allowing you to better govern the resources in your Azure environment by identifying resources that don't adhere to security best practices and that don't align with your organization's business rules.

Say you need to prevent people in your organization from deploying Azure resources to certain Azure regions. Many organizations have business rules that dictate that resources can only be deployed in a subset of Azure regions, for example, due to regulatory requirements. Suppose you have most of your resources deployed in the East US and want to prevent people in your organization from deploying resources to a region where your organization doesn't have any resources, such as Germany. You can enforce these business rules and requirements by using Azure Policy.

10.1   What is Azure Policy?

Azure Policy is an Azure service that allows you to control the configurations of your resources and assess their compliance evaluations, giving you an end result like that in figure 10.1. Azure Policy can be used to apply guardrails that prevent resources from being deployed if they aren't configured to align with your business rules. You can even auto-remediate resources whose configurations aren't compliant with your organization's business rules.

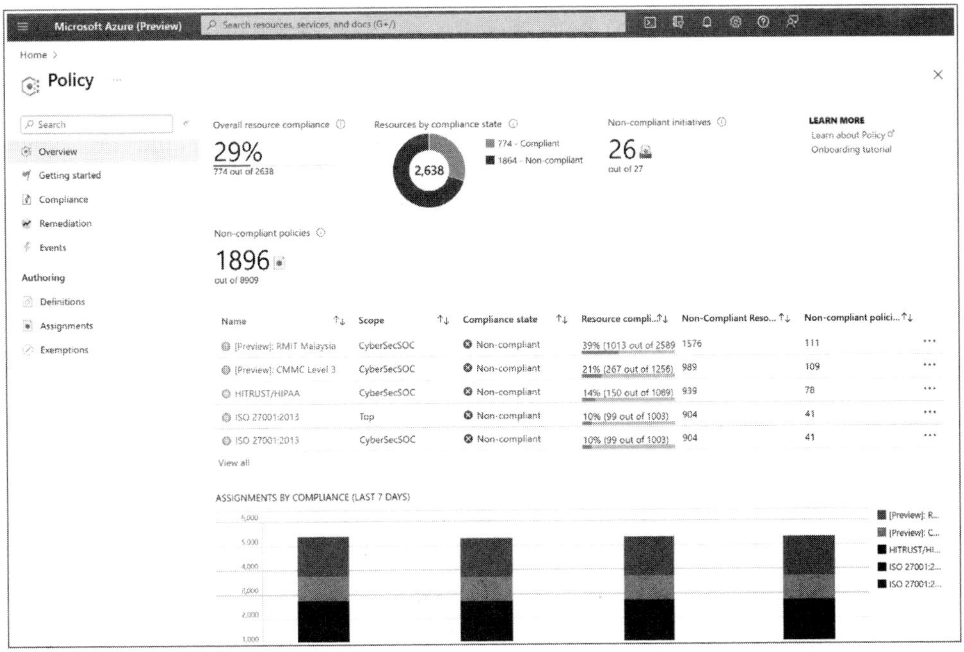

Figure 10.1   Using Azure Policy to assess the compliance evaluations of your resources

Azure Policy is powerful because you can use it to check at scale, even across many thousands of resources, whether the configurations of those resources are compliant with your organization's business rules. An example of a business rule is to only use specific SKUs for virtual machines (VMs) to better manage Azure costs.

10.2 Getting started with Azure Policy

When you're first starting to explore Azure Policy, beginning with the built-in policies is recommended. You don't need to start from scratch because Microsoft has already created policies you can explore to determine whether they meet the business rules that you want to evaluate or enforce in your Azure environment. These built-in policies from common use cases are available in the Azure portal. Some examples are as follows:

- Enabling monitoring agents across your VMs
- Controlling which VM SKUs can be used in your environment
- Controlling to which Azure regions your resources can be deployed
- Ensuring that resources that get deployed have tags applied to them
- Preventing VMs from having a public endpoint
- Applying tags to resources automatically

Azure Policy evaluates resources in Azure by comparing the resources' properties to your business rules. These business rules, which are described in a JSON format, are known as *policy definitions*.

10.2.1 Azure Policy in action

Say your management team asks you to allow deployment of only specific types of compute resource SKUs to better manage costs in your environment. You can do that with Azure Policy. The best way to get started with Azure Policy is to explore built-in policy definitions in the Azure portal. To do that for this scenario, complete the following steps:

1 Sign in to the Azure portal.
2 Navigate to Policy.
3 Select Definitions.
4 Definition Type > Policy.
5 Look for policy definitions with BuiltIn in the Type column. These are built-in policies provided by Microsoft.
6 In the Search box, click SKU.
7 In the list of results that appear, click Allowed Virtual Machine Size SKUs.

These steps help identify the built-in policy definition you can use to allow deployment of specific SKUs only, but they can be applied to other business rules or policy definitions. You can even pick one of the built-in policies, modify it to suit your needs, and then save it under a new name. Azure Policy definitions are described in JSON format, and the output on your screen should look similar to the following:

```
{
  "properties": {
    "displayName": "Allowed virtual machine size SKUs",
    "policyType": "BuiltIn",
    "mode": "Indexed",
    "description": "This policy enables you to specify a set of virtual
    ➥machine size SKUs that your organization can deploy.",
    "metadata": {
      "version": "1.0.1",
      "category": "Compute"
    },
    "parameters": {
      "listOfAllowedSKUs": {
        "type": "Array",
        "metadata": {
          "description": "The list of size SKUs that can be specified for
          ➥virtual machines.",
          "displayName": "Allowed Size SKUs",
          "strongType": "VMSKUs"
        }
      }
    },
    "policyRule": {
...
```

A policy definition controls a specific configuration on any given resource. Individual policy definitions map back to your business rules. You can have one policy definition for each business rule. To simplify management, you can group several policy definitions together to form a *policy initiative* (figure 10.2). An initiative is a grouping of different Azure Policy definitions that support an overarching objective.

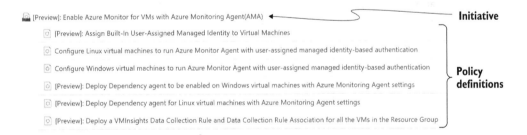

Figure 10.2 The difference between a policy definition and a policy initiative in Azure Policy

Suppose you want to ensure that your VMs have monitoring agents deployed on them (as discussed in chapter 9). In this case, the overarching objective is to ensure the monitoring agents are deployed on all VMs in your Azure environment. To accomplish this objective, you can have one policy that ensures you have the monitoring agents, such as the Azure Monitor Agent, deployed on your Windows VMs. Another policy might ensure that you have the Azure Monitor Agent deployed on your Linux

VMs. Then, you can have additional policies to ensure the Azure Monitor agent is deployed, such as assigning a built-in user-assigned managed identity to your VMs (figure 10.3).

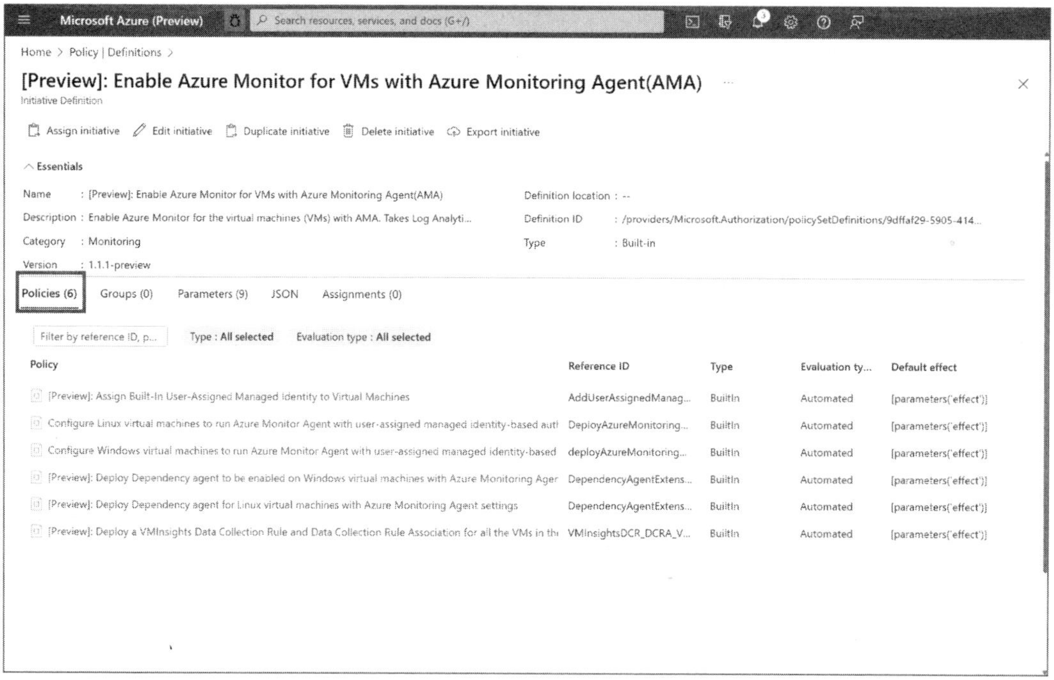

Figure 10.3 **An example of a policy initiative in the Azure Policy dashboard**

> **NOTE** I would be remiss if I didn't mention an initiative at the center of Azure security—namely, the Microsoft Cloud Security Benchmark. This initiative covers all the different security-related policy definitions. You can learn more about the Microsoft Cloud Security Benchmark at http://mng.bz/OxKn.

To apply the policy initiative or definition to desired Azure resources, you need to determine the *scope* at which it gets applied.

10.2.2 Scope

Azure Policy works with the following scopes:

- *Management group*—`/providers/Microsoft.Management/managementGroups/{mgName}`
- *Subscription*—`/subscriptions/{subID}`
- *Resource group*—`/subscriptions/{subID}/resourceGroups/{rgName}`

- *Resource*—/subscriptions/{subID}/resourceGroups/{rgName}/providers/ {rType}/{rName}

As a best practice, you should apply Azure Policy to a scope as high as applicable for your organization. When you assign the initiative or policy definition at a scope, Azure Policy scans all existing resources, evaluates their compliance based on the policy initiative or definition, and then generates a report. Then, for any future deployments, Azure Policy evaluates the resources that are being deployed and their compliance. For example, you can assign Azure Policy at the management group level (figure 10.4).

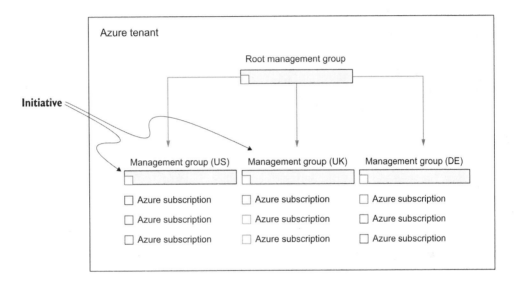

Figure 10.4   Assigning Azure Policy definition/initiative at the management group level

Suppose that to manage costs better, you want only certain VM SKUs to be deployed in your subscription. Expensive VM SKUs come to mind here. As I mentioned, Azure Policy can solve this requirement. The following commands solve the requirement for deployment of only certain VM SKUs by applying an Azure Policy definition on a subscription, but the commands can also be applied to other scopes and initiatives.

To apply the policy definition `Allowed virtual machine size SKUs` that you used previously, use the following command:

```
az policy definition list --query "[?displayName== Allowed virtual machine
➥size SKUs ']".
```

You can use the ID displayed on your screen with `--policy` when running the following commands in Azure Cloud Shell

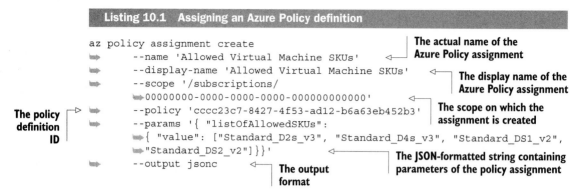

Listing 10.1 Assigning an Azure Policy definition

After this command runs, the output contains information about the Azure Policy definition that you assigned, including parameters, scope, and name. Your output should look similar to the following:

```
{
  "description": null,
  "displayName": "Allowed Virtual Machine SKUs",
  "enforcementMode": "Default",
  "id": "/subscriptions/00000000-0000-0000-0000-000000000000/providers
 ➡/Microsoft.Authorization/policyAssignments/Allowed Virtual Machine SKUs",
  "identity": null,
  "location": null,
  "metadata": {
    "createdBy": "bfa3a967-d1f6-4a9b-a246-dac2a8a93b91",
    "createdOn": "2023-03-29T18:50:32.196179Z",
    "updatedBy": null,
    "updatedOn": null
  },
  "name": "Allowed Virtual Machine SKUs",
  "nonComplianceMessages": null,
  "notScopes": null,
  "parameters": {
    "listOfAllowedSKUs": {
      "value": [
        "Standard_D2s_v3",
        "Standard_D4s_v3",
        "Standard_DS1_v2",
        "Standard_DS2_v2"
      ]
    }
  },
  "policyDefinitionId": "/providers/Microsoft.Authorization/policyDefinitions/
 ➡cccc23c7-8427-4f53-ad12-b6a63eb452b3",
  "scope": "/subscriptions/00000000-0000-0000-0000-000000000000",
  "systemData": {
    "createdAt": "2023-03-29T18:50:32.174809+00:00",
    "createdBy": "alice@contoso.com",
    "createdByType": "User",
    "lastModifiedAt": "2023-03-29T18:50:32.174809+00:00",
    "lastModifiedBy": "alice@contoso.com",
    "lastModifiedByType": "User"
```

```
    },
    "type": "Microsoft.Authorization/policyAssignments"
}
```

Exercise 10.1

To strengthen your knowledge of Azure Policy, I have a fun exercise for you that combines what you learned in this chapter about Azure Policy and what you learned in chapter 5 about storage account shared key access. Using Azure Policy, evaluate which storage accounts in your environment allow shared key access. For the purposes of this exercise, you can assign the relevant policy definition at the management group or subscription scope.

Now, what happens if you assign a policy at the management group scope and find there are resources at a lower-level scope that are not applicable? An example might be a particular subscription (such as test or dev) or resource group to which the policy you assigned shouldn't apply. In this case, you can use exemptions to define which set of subscriptions or resources are not applicable for the scope on which the policy is assigned.

Suppose you wanted to apply a policy to ensure all outbound ports are blocked in your nonproduction environment. You can assign the Azure Policy at the management group level for your nonproduction environment. If some resources are not applicable, such as VMs running an application you built, you can create an exemption at the scope for those resources.

When creating a policy exemption, you can choose between two exemption categories: mitigated or waiver. Mitigated implies that the business rule for which you use the policy is achieved using other means, such as through the use of a third-party solution. Waiver, on the other hand, implies that the business rule for which you use the policy is not achieved but that this result is acceptable for the resources to which the policy exemption applies.

To teach you how to use policy exemptions, I offer the following example. Imagine that after you assigned the policy definition `Allowed virtual machine size SKUs`, you'd like to exclude VMs from resource group `testVMsRG`. To do so, run the following commands in Azure Cloud Shell.

Listing 10.2 Creating an Azure policy exemption

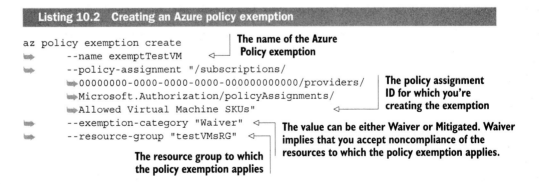

```
az policy exemption create
        --name exemptTestVM                         ◁──┐  The name of the Azure
                                                         Policy exemption
        --policy-assignment "/subscriptions/
        00000000-0000-0000-0000-000000000000/providers/
        Microsoft.Authorization/policyAssignments/            The policy assignment
        Allowed Virtual Machine SKUs"           ◁────────     ID for which you're
                                                              creating the exemption
        --exemption-category "Waiver"    ◁──┐
        --resource-group "testVMsRG"     ◁──┤  The value can be either Waiver or Mitigated. Waiver
                                            │  implies that you accept noncompliance of the
    The resource group to which            │  resources to which the policy exemption applies.
    the policy exemption applies
```

After this command runs, the output contains information about the Azure policy exemption that you created, including the exemption category, name, and resource group to which the exemption applies. Your output should look similar to the following:

```
{
  "description": null,
  "displayName": null,
  "exemptionCategory": "Waiver",
  "expiresOn": null,
  "id": "/subscriptions/00000000-0000-0000-0000-000000000000
➥/resourceGroups/testVMsRG/providers/Microsoft.Authorization
➥/policyExemptions/exemptTestVM",
  "metadata": null,
  "name": "exemptTestVM",
  "policyAssignmentId": "/subscriptions/00000000-0000-0000-0000-000000000000
➥/providers/Microsoft.Authorization/policyAssignments
➥/Allowed Virtual Machine SKUs",
  "policyDefinitionReferenceIds": null,
  "resourceGroup": "testVMsRG",
  "systemData": {
    "createdAt": "2023-04-05T19:43:42.509856+00:00",
    "createdBy": "alice@contoso.com",
    "createdByType": "User",
    "lastModifiedAt": "2023-04-05T19:43:42.509856+00:00",
    "lastModifiedBy": "alice@contoso.com",
    "lastModifiedByType": "User"
  },
  "type": "Microsoft.Authorization/policyExemptions"
}
```

After you create an exemption, exempted resources are not evaluated, but they still count toward your overall compliance.

> **Creating an exemption while lacking the necessary permissions**
>
> Imagine you assigned a policy at the management group level. Someone who has access on the resource group, such as a workload owner, isn't able to create an exemption on the resource group. Azure Policy doesn't check to ensure whoever is creating exemptions has the permissions on the assignment too, which, in this case, is at the management group level. Many organizations in these situations use an IT service management or ticketing tool that can be used to inform the team with the necessary permissions at the management group level that the exemption need to be created.

When assigning a policy, you can control what actions happen whenever there is a match with the policy rule. These actions are often referred to as *effects*.

10.2.3 *Policy effects*

The effect in Azure Policy determines what happens when the policy rule in the policy definition is evaluated. Each policy definition in Azure Policy has a single effect.

What takes precedence between Azure Policy and Azure Resource Manager? Requests to create or update a resource through Azure Resource Manager are evaluated by Azure Policy first. Azure Policy creates a list of all assignments that apply to the resource and then evaluates the resource against each definition. Azure Policy processes several of the effects *before* handing the request to the appropriate resource provider.

There are several effects in Azure Policy. The most commonly used include the following:

- *Audit*—Allows resources to be created, but Azure Policy still assesses them and flags them either as compliant or noncompliant.
- *Deny*—Allows you to prevent a resource from being created if it isn't compliant with your policies. You should be careful when using Deny to prevent it from having any unintended consequences to your environment. As a best practice, before you set the enforcement type to Deny, have it as Audit for a while to get a better understanding of what you're going to be blocking. Switch over to Deny only after you're confident about the evaluation results while in Audit. Taking the earlier example, suppose you have a user trying to deploy VM SKUs that are not allowed in your environment. With Deny, you can prevent the user from deploying VM SKUs, which helps you manage costs. However, users might be puzzled about what's preventing them from deploying certain resources. You can use the noncompliance reasons message to let them know why their actions were blocked.
- *Modify*—Allows you to implement an auto-remediation capability using Azure Policy. Using auto-remediation, you can enforce configurations by default without any action required by users. Suppose a user tries to deploy a resource missing a configuration, such as tags from the relevant resource group. With auto-remediation, you can apply the missing configuration to the request and deploy the resource in such a way that it aligns with your organization's business rules.

Suppose you decide to set the action to Audit. As mentioned, Audit allows the resource to be deployed. Information about the resource being deployed is captured in the Azure activity log (discussed in chapter 9). In addition to the information captured in the Azure activity log about the resource, Azure Policy produces a compliance statement about the action, such as a resource being noncompliant with your business rules.

The many effects of Azure Policy

In addition to those mentioned, Azure Policy supports other effects that solve a wide range of problems. Say you need to evaluate a configuration setting on Azure resources and, if it isn't enabled, ensure that it gets enabled. In particular, suppose you want to evaluate your SQL Server databases to determine whether `transparent-DataEncryption` is enabled and, if not, enable it. You can solve this requirement with the `DeployIfNotExists` effect. To learn more about `DeployIfNotExists` and other effects in Azure Policy beyond the ones already mentioned, you can start at http://mng.bz/Y1dN.

What happens to your existing resources when you apply a policy on their scope with a Deny effect? Azure Policy evaluates and enforces the effect the next time the resource is updated, such as the next time you modify a setting on a storage account. With `DeployIfNotExists`, you can configure a remediation on existing resources. As a best practice, you should do a gradual rollout of remediations for existing resources.

As I mentioned, a policy definition controls a specific configuration on any given resource, and individual policy definitions map back to your business rules. However, each organization is unique and can have custom requirements and business rules. If you can't find a built-in policy definition for certain business rules mandated by your organization, you can create a *custom policy definition or initiative*.

10.3   *Custom policies*

Suppose your organization mandates that VMs must be deployed in the East US region only. After exploring the built-in policies, you realize that none of the policies provided by Microsoft fit your scenario. To address this and other custom business rules your organization might have, you can create a custom policy definition and assign the policy definition directly on a particular scope.

Alternatively, you can group several custom policy definitions into a policy initiative and apply the initiative at the desired scope. The commands in listing 10.2 solve the requirement for allowing deployment of VMs only to certain locations—in this case, the East US region. However, you can apply the following commands to other custom business rules your organization might have.

Listing 10.3   Creating a custom policy definition

```
az policy definition create                    The actual name of the
    --name allowedLocationsOnly    ◁─┘         custom policy definition
    --display-name 'Allowed Virtual Machine Locations Only'    ◁───────
    --rules "{ \            ◁──  The rule of the custom        The display name of the
            \"if\": \          policy definition              custom policy definition
            { \"not\": { \
                \"field\":
    \"Microsoft.Compute/virtualMachines/Locations[*].locationName\", \
                \"in\": [ \
                    \"East US\", \
                    \"East US 2\" \
                ] \
            } \
        }, \
        \"then\": { \
            \"effect\": \"deny\" \
        } \
    }"
```

After these commands run, they create the custom policy definition. Your output should look similar to the following:

```
{
  "description": null,
```

```
  "displayName": "Allowed Virtual Machine Locations Only",
  "id": "/subscriptions/00000000-0000-0000-0000-000000000000/providers
➥/Microsoft.Authorization/policyDefinitions/allowedLocationsOnly",
  "metadata": {
    "createdBy": "bca3a967-d1f6-4a9b-a246-dab5d8a93b91",
    "createdOn": "2023-03-29T19:26:06.1436779Z",
    "updatedBy": null,
    "updatedOn": null
  },
  "mode": "Indexed",
  "name": "allowedLocationsOnly",
  "parameters": null,
  "policyRule": {
    "if": {
      "not": {
        "field": "Microsoft.Compute/virtualMachines
        ➥/Locations[*].locationName",
        "in": [
          "East US",
          "East US 2"
        ]
      }
    },
    "then": {
      "effect": "deny"
    }
  },
  "policyType": "Custom",
...
  "type": "Microsoft.Authorization/policyDefinitions"
}
```

Exercise 10.2

As a firm believer in learning by doing, I have another exercise for you. To solidify your knowledge of creating custom policies, create a custom policy definition that allows deployment of storage accounts to only the two Azure regions used when you created the previous custom policy definition for VMs. After you create the policy definition, group the two custom policy definitions you created into a policy initiative.

To evaluate the compliance of resources based on the built-in and custom policies you assigned, you can use the Azure Policy UI. To evaluate the compliance state with the Azure Policy UI, complete the following steps:

1 Sign in to the Azure portal.
2 Navigate to Azure Policy.
3 On the left, ensure Overview is selected.
4 In the list of Azure Policy assignments, click a particular assignment.

The page that opens displays the evaluation results for the particular assignment you selected. They can help you identify which resources are not compliant with the policy and business rules of your organization.

Built-in and custom policies allow you to evaluate and configure the resources in your environment at scale to ensure that your resources adhere to security best practices when they are deployed. In turn, they allow you to implement a baseline of security in your environment that aligns with your organization's requirements and business rules. As an alternative to the Azure Policy UI, you can add custom initiatives to the regulatory compliance dashboard in Microsoft Defender for Cloud (discussed in chapter 6).

10.4 *Centralized security policy management*

The Regulatory Compliance dashboard in Defender for Cloud allows you to benchmark your resources' configurations to commonly used regulatory compliance standards such as the Center for Internet Security (CIS) or the National Institute of Standards and Technology (NIST). When you onboard your Azure subscriptions to Defender for Cloud, the Microsoft Cloud Security Benchmark is assigned to your Azure subscriptions. Defender for Cloud uses the Microsoft Security Benchmark as a security baseline to continuously assess the resources in your environment. Based on the evaluation of that assessment, Defender for Cloud is able to detect misconfigurations and generate recommendations for your resources.

To centrally display all the security-related policies in your environment, you can use the Microsoft Regulatory Compliance dashboard in Microsoft Defender for Cloud. In addition to this and other regulatory standards (such as CIS or NIST), you can add a custom policy initiative to the Microsoft Regulatory Compliance dashboard in Defender for Cloud, giving you a result like that shown in figure 10.5.

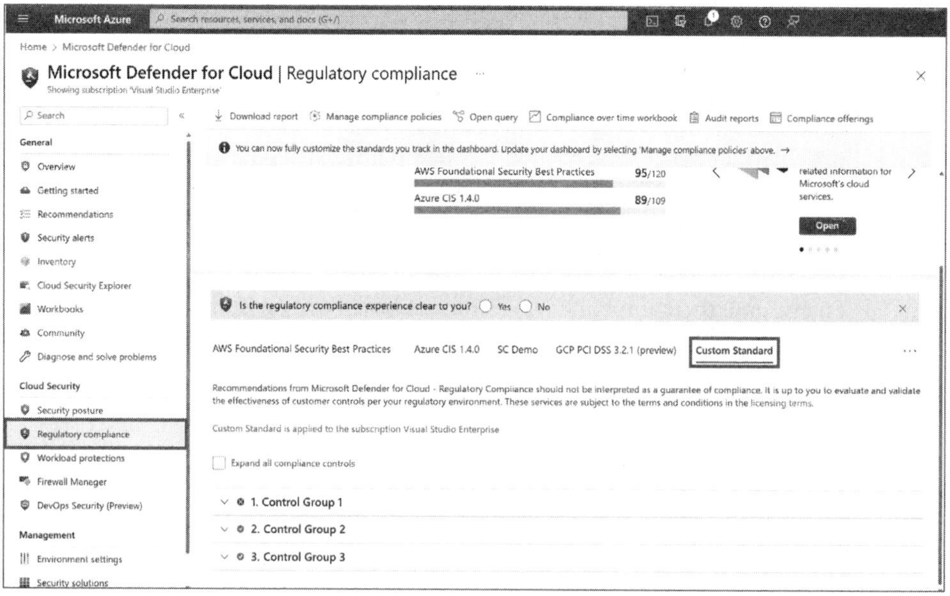

Figure 10.5   A custom policy initiative displayed in the Regulatory Compliance dashboard in Microsoft Defender for Cloud

Suppose you want to determine for your environment which key vaults in Azure Key Vault have secrets without an expiry date, which, as you learned in chapter 5, can be considered a security liability. To help you identify such key vaults, you can create a custom policy definition that audits Azure Key Vault secrets. The evaluation of this custom policy definition provides results that help you identify which key vaults are not compliant with the custom policy definition you created. As mentioned, you can view these results in the Azure Policy UI.

Which policy takes precedence if several policies apply and there is an overlap between them? As a best practice, you should assign policies at the highest scope possible to avoid overlapping multiple policies. However, as a rule of thumb, the most restrictive policy takes precedence.

Given that Defender for Cloud's dashboard displays security-related configurations for your resources, you can see custom security checks in Defender for Cloud instead of switching over to the Azure Policy UI. You can add custom security checks in the form of an initiative that contains custom policy definitions, such as the policy that audits which key vaults have secrets without an expiry date. You can add the initiative to the Regulatory Compliance dashboard in Defender for Cloud by completing the following steps:

1 Navigate to the Microsoft Defender for Cloud dashboard inside the Azure portal.
2 Select Regulatory Compliance.
3 At the top, select Manage Compliance Policies.
4 Select the scope at which you want to assign the initiative, such as a management group.
5 On the page that opens, click Add a Custom Initiative (figure 10.6).
6 Click Add next to the initiative you want to add.

After you add the initiative, a couple of hours may pass before it appears in the regulatory compliance dashboard in Defender for Cloud. In addition to appearing in the Regulatory Compliance dashboard, the custom policies you added appear in the Recommendations blade. The Defender for Cloud dashboard provides you with a centralized view of security policies in your environment without needing to constantly switch between the Defender for Cloud dashboard and Azure Policy UI. Centralizing security policies in the Defender for Cloud dashboard can both save time and simplify the management of security policies.

As I previously mentioned, Azure Policy can solve a lot of problems. Policies provide an allow-or-deny mechanism you can use to ensure that resource configurations and properties align with your organization's business rules. In the real world, organizations require that resources adhering to business rules cannot be tampered with, which you can achieve with *Azure Blueprints.*

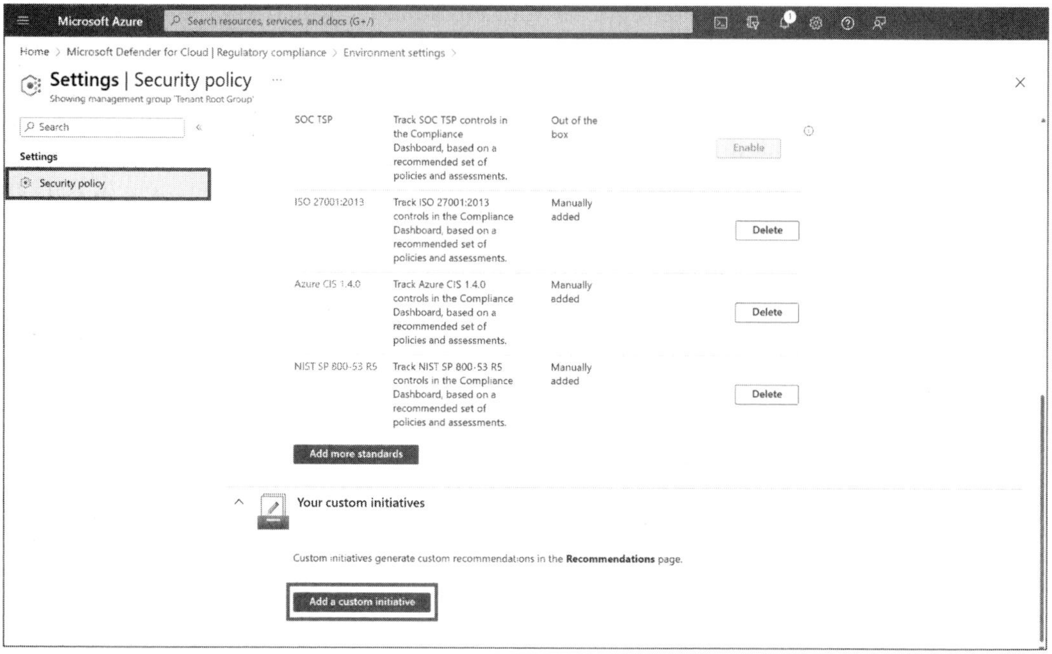

Figure 10.6   Adding a custom policy initiative on the Regulatory Compliance dashboard in Defender for Cloud

10.5   *Azure Blueprints*

Azure Blueprints allows organizations to further solidify the way they govern resources in Azure by providing the ability to assign Azure policies and other blueprint *artifacts*. Artifacts answer this question: What can you deploy to your Azure environment to help you better govern your resources in Azure? Blueprint artifacts include the following:

- Azure Policy assignments
- Azure resource groups
- Role assignments
- Azure Resource Manager (ARM) templates

The intention behind using Azure Blueprints is to orchestrate the deployment of blueprint artifacts to streamline consistency across your environment and ensure it aligns with your organizations' business rules. Say you need to prepare an environment for your application's developers. Specifically, you want to ensure that the environment the developers are going to use is configured to adhere to security best practices while, at the same time, adhering to the business rules of your organization. You can use Azure Blueprints to orchestrate the creation of resource groups, deployment of necessary Azure resources using ARM templates, and assignment of Azure Policy initiatives and least-privileged roles to be sure the developers have the right amount of access to the right resources. You can also use the Azure Blueprints service in combination with continuous integration/continuous delivery, which I'll cover in the next chapter.

> **NOTE** Azure Blueprints is currently in public preview. To learn more about how to create and assign an Azure blueprint to your environment, you can start at http://mng.bz/Gygq.

10.6 Answers to exercises

Exercise 10.1

Run the following command in Azure Cloud Shell with the Azure Policy Contributor role assigned:

```
az policy assignment create
    --name 'Storage accounts should prevent shared key access'
    --display-name 'Storage accounts should prevent shared key access'
    --scope '/subscriptions/00000000-0000-0000-0000-000000000000'
    --policy '8c6a50c6-9ffd-4ae7-986f-5fa6111f9a54'
```

After this command runs, perform the following actions:

1 In the Azure portal, navigate to Policy.
2 Select Assignments.
3 Click View Compliance.
4 Analyze the list of storage accounts that appear under Resource Compliance.

Exercise 10.2

Run the following command in Azure Cloud Shell with the Azure Policy Contributor role assigned:

```
az policy definition create
    --name allowedStorageAccountsLocationsOnly
    --display-name 'Allowed Storage Accounts Locations Only'
    --rules "{ \
            \"if\": \
            { \"not\": { \y
                \"field\": 
    \"Microsoft.Storage/storageAccounts/sku.locations[*]\", \
                \"in\": [ \
                    \"East US\", \
                    \"East US 2\" \
                    ] \
                } \
            }, \
            \"then\": { \
                \"effect\": \"deny\" \
            } \
        }"
```

Summary

- Azure Policy can be used to apply guardrails that prevent resources from being deployed in a way that doesn't align with your business rules; it can also auto-remediate resources that are not compliant with business rules. Azure Policy is powerful because you can use it to assess at scale whether your resources are compliant with your organization's business rules.

- Business rules can be mapped back to individual policy definitions. A policy definition controls a specific configuration on any given resource. You can have one policy definition for each business rule. To simplify management, you can group several policy definitions to form a policy initiative.

- As a best practice, you should apply Azure Policy to the highest applicable scope. When you assign the initiative or policy definition at a scope, Azure Policy scans all existing resources and evaluates their compliance state based on the policy initiative or definition.

- To streamline the management of security-related policies in your environment, you can add custom initiatives to Microsoft Defender for Cloud. When you add custom initiatives, your customer policies appear in the Regulatory Compliance dashboard and the Recommendations blade.

- Azure Blueprints is a service that allows you to apply Azure Policy assignments and orchestrate the creation of resource groups, deployment of Azure resources, and assignment of roles to users to ensure your environment setup is secure and adheres to your organization's business rules.

11
DevSecOps: Microsoft Defender for DevOps

This chapter covers

- Shifting security left
- Infrastructure as code
- Microsoft Defender for DevOps
- Cybersecurity as an infinite game

You could argue that a big part of cybersecurity is dealing with bugs found in code—both bugs known and unknown at a given point in time. These bugs could present vulnerabilities and eventually increase the risk of bad actors (like the fictional bad actor Eve) exploiting the vulnerabilities in code to compromise applications running in your environment. What we're also seeing is that it's taking less and less time for bad actors to weaponize vulnerabilities in code, which is an alarming trend.

If you need a prime example of why this topic matters, you need look no further than the SolarWinds attack. SolarWinds was breached, and software used by their customers was compromised by a nation-state bad actor. This kind of attack is commonly referred to as a *supply chain attack*. In a supply chain attack, bad actors look

277

to compromise an environment through less-secure elements in the supply chain (for example, a software vendor whose software is used).

> **NOTE**   To learn more about the SolarWinds attack, you can start at http://mng.bz/zXPa.

A relationship between a software vendor and their customers is built on trust. Bad actors misused this trust to launch their attacks against SolarWinds's customers. Thus, it's very important to develop code securely and embed security directly into all phases of the software development lifecycle when you're developing your applications.

11.1   *Developing code more securely*

To help your organization develop code more securely, this chapter teaches you about the tools you can add to your software development lifecycle, including Microsoft Defender for DevOps (figure 11.1). Microsoft Defender for DevOps helps you get better visibility of security across the different phases of the software development lifecycle.

> **NOTE**   To learn more about security considerations and guidelines that Microsoft uses internally to build more secure products and services, you can start at https://www.microsoft.com/en-us/securityengineering/sdl/.

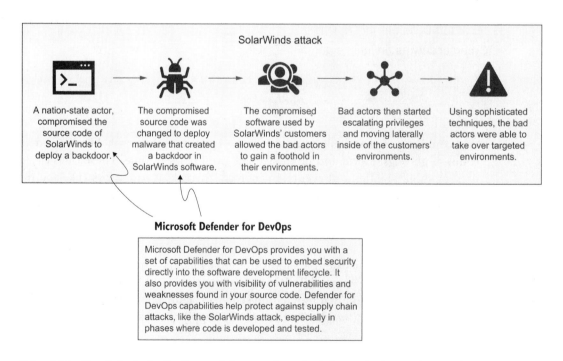

Figure 11.1   How Defender for DevOps can help prevent supply chain attacks like the SolarWinds attack

Defender for DevOps is quite new, and you likely haven't heard about it yet, which is that much more of a reason to read this chapter. In addition, this chapter teaches you how you can streamline deploying and managing security in your environment using infrastructure as code (IaC).

> **NOTE** To follow along with the exercises in this chapter, you can use the GitHub repository (https://github.com/bmagusic/azure-security).

The SolarWinds attack highlights the need to embed security directly into the software development lifecycle—much sooner than the deployment stage. This is commonly referred to as *shifting security left.*

11.2   *What is shifting security left?*

Shifting security left brings advantages to your organization's security posture. It allows you to embed security in all phases of the software development lifecycle. By shifting security left, you can do the following:

- Build more secure applications
- Create awareness about security across stakeholders in your organization
- Apply secure coding practices
- Analyze code during development
- Implement Open Worldwide Application Security Project (OWASP) security knowledge
- Perform threat modeling

Embedding security in all phases of the software development lifecycle helps you develop more secure applications and decreases the likelihood of bad actors discovering vulnerabilities in your applications. Fewer vulnerabilities being discovered in your code also translates into a financial benefit. Suppose your application isn't operational because you needed to take it down to fix a vulnerability or misconfiguration. What if that application was generating revenue for your organization? As you can see, cost savings are associated with detecting bugs and weaknesses in code early on in the software development lifecycle.

Unfortunately, many organizations have challenges with embedding security into all phases of their software development lifecycle and combining it with other Azure security services to shift security left. IaC can help streamline the configuration and management of security in your environment.

11.3   *Infrastructure as code*

IaC allows you to describe the desired state of your public cloud infrastructure using code or templates that can be written in a variety of languages, such as ARM, Bicep, Terraform, CloudFormation, and others. You can use IaC to programmatically deploy resources to your environment and manage various aspects of it. For example, you can configure resources to be deployed while adhering to security best practices by default.

Suppose one of your developers is developing an application that you're planning to run in Azure. While they're developing this application and making changes to the source code of the application, they check the code into a source code management system such as GitHub or Bitbucket. You can use IaC to deploy the source code of your application to your Azure environment.

In addition to security considerations, IaC offers other advantages. It can help with business continuity and disaster recovery and prevent configuration drift. Configuration drift occurs when configurations of your environment gradually change over time and are no longer consistent with your organization's requirements, including with the security best practices mandated by your organization. This chapter teaches you how using IaC together with Microsoft Defender for DevOps can help you develop more secure applications (figure 11.2).

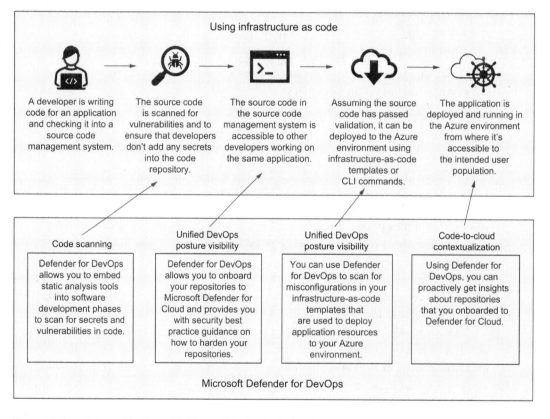

Figure 11.2   IaC in combination with Microsoft Defender for DevOps

To deploy the newest version of your application to Azure after a developer has made changes to the source code, you can combine IaC with a version control such as Git to track changes made to your IaC templates or code over time. Suppose a vulnerability was discovered in the code of an application already running in Azure. To fix the discovered vulnerability, you can programmatically deploy these changes to your public cloud environment using continuous integration and continuous delivery (CI/CD) platforms, such as GitHub Actions or Azure DevOps (ADO) Pipelines.

CI/CD platforms allow you create workflows that perform a series of configurable steps. These steps can include building and testing every pull request in your repository before deploying merged pull requests to your production environment.

11.3.1 Infrastructure as code in action

As I previously mentioned, IaC can help you streamline security best practice configuration in your environment. In this chapter, I'll use GitHub as a source code management system and GitHub Actions as a CI/CD platform. Choosing GitHub seems logical considering that throughout this book, you relied on examples provided in the GitHub repository (available at https://github.com/bmagusic/azure-security). If you're not familiar with GitHub or are using a different source code repository system and CI/CD platform, don't worry. Many of the concepts that I teach in this chapter can be applied to source code repository systems and CI/CD platforms other than GitHub.

To make IaC more real to you, I'll rely on the help of three fictional characters used throughout this book—Alice, Bob, and Eve. Imagine that Bob is writing code for an application that gets deployed on Azure. Eve is trying to disrupt his plans by looking for ways to compromise the application (and the environment in which the application runs). Like most developers, Bob uses a source code repository such as GitHub to commit the code for his application. He'd like to ensure that when he makes changes to his code, these changes are programmatically deployed to the Azure environment in which the application is running. He did so using IaC. Alice is helping Bob by securing the Azure environment.

Alice can also use IaC to ensure consistency of security configurations and streamline them across the environment in which Bob's application is running. Suppose Alice wants to ensure that Microsoft Defender for Cloud plans (discussed in chapters 6 and 7) are automatically enabled on every Azure subscription that holds resources for Bob's application. As you recall, Defender for Cloud plans offer additional protection against bad actors, such as the fictional bad actor Eve. Alice can create a workflow in a CI/CD platform, such as GitHub Actions, that enables Defender for Cloud plans via Azure CLI on every Azure subscription that holds resources for Bob's application.

To accomplish this scenario end to end, Alice needs to perform the following steps in order:

1 Create a service principal.
2 Configure the CI/CD platform to use the service principal.
3 Deploy changes to the Azure environment with the CI/CD platform.

Prior to using a CI/CD platform to enable Defender for Cloud plans across the environment, Alice needs to ensure that the CI/CD platform has the necessary permissions to make changes in the Azure environment. She can do so by creating an identity the CI/CD platform can use in the form of a *service principal.*

> **NOTE** As an alternative to creating a service principal, you can configure OpenID Connect in Azure. To learn more about configuring OpenID Connect for GitHub Actions, you can start at http://mng.bz/0Kxx. The advantage of configuring OpenID Connect in Azure over using a service principal is that you don't need to store secrets in the CI/CD platform.

CREATING A SERVICE PRINCIPAL

To create a service principal in Microsoft Entra ID, run the following command in Azure Cloud Shell.

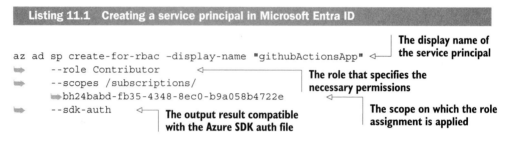

Listing 11.1 Creating a service principal in Microsoft Entra ID

```
az ad sp create-for-rbac –display-name "githubActionsApp"    ◁───  The display name of
                                                                   the service principal
    --role Contributor       ◁─────────────────────  The role that specifies the
    --scopes /subscriptions/                          necessary permissions
        bh24babd-fb35-4348-8ec0-b9a058b4722e  ◁───
    --sdk-auth   ◁────  The output result compatible        The scope on which the role
                        with the Azure SDK auth file        assignment is applied
```

After this command runs, it creates the identity for an application called `github-ActionsApp`. Your output should look similar to the following:

```
{
  "clientId": "e9ia691f-7a62-4624-9b25-c66c7cecf3b2",
  "clientSecret": "9708Q~p9u6ZKQpnzAFCJTVVTpciTKgYx9LrQ7anA",
  "subscriptionId": "bh24babd-fb35-4348-8ec0-b9a058b4722e",
  "tenantId": "85f141e1-6ec9-4967-98ab-d097f9128929",
  "activeDirectoryEndpointUrl": "https://login.microsoftonline.com",
  "resourceManagerEndpointUrl": "https://management.azure.com/",
  "activeDirectoryGraphResourceId": "https://graph.windows.net/",
  "sqlManagementEndpointUrl": "https://management.core.windows.net:8443/",
  "galleryEndpointUrl": "https://gallery.azure.com/",
  "managementEndpointUrl": "https://management.core.windows.net/"
}
```

> **WARNING** In the output, you see the credentials that can be used to authenticate to your environment. Make sure to keep these credentials away from prying eyes because anyone who has these credentials could impersonate the identity of the service principal you created.

Collect the output of the service principal you created. You need to store this output in the CI/CD platform to allow it to deploy changes to your Azure environment.

CONFIGURING THE CI/CD PLATFORM TO USE THE SERVICE PRINCIPAL

The following example fulfills the requirement for configuring GitHub Actions to use the service principal to make changes to your Azure environment, but it can be applied to other CI/CD platforms. To store the credentials of the service principal you created in GitHub, complete the following actions:

1 Sign in to GitHub.
2 Navigate to the repository used to deploy code in your environment.
3 Select Settings.
4 On the left, select Secrets and Variables, and then click Actions.
5 Select New Repository Secret.
6 Enter a name for the repository secret. For the purposes of this example, you can use something like Azure_Credentials. Paste the credentials you copied from the output after you created the service principal.
7 Select Add Secret.

After performing these actions, the output on your screen should look similar to figure 11.3.

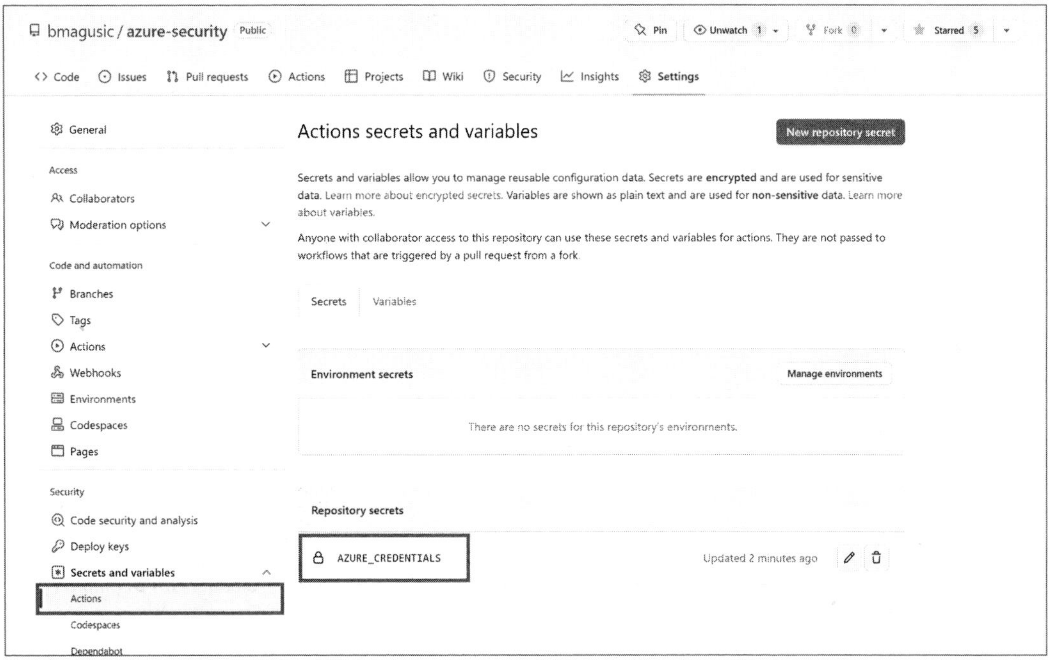

Figure 11.3   Creating a new repository secret in GitHub

These actions ensure that the service principal you created can be used by the CI/CD platform (in this case, GitHub Actions) to perform changes in your Azure environment. After creating the service principal and storing its credentials as a repository secret in GitHub, you can proceed with configuring the CI/CD platform to deploy changes to your Azure environment.

DEPLOYING CHANGES TO YOUR AZURE ENVIRONMENT WITH THE CI/CD PLATFORM

Just to remind you, GitHub Actions is a CI/CD platform that allows you to create customizable workflows, build pull requests to your repository, or deploy merged pull requests to your environment. The workflow in GitHub Actions performs the series of steps you'd like to run in your Azure environment, such as using Azure CLI to enable Defender for Cloud plans on all Azure subscriptions and giving you an end result like in figure 11.4. For the purpose of this example, you use an already-built workflow that is available at https://github.com/bmagusic/azure-security/tree/main/ch11. This workflow enables Defender CSPM, which is a Defender for Cloud plan that provides you with advanced cloud security posture management capabilities (discussed in chapter 6).

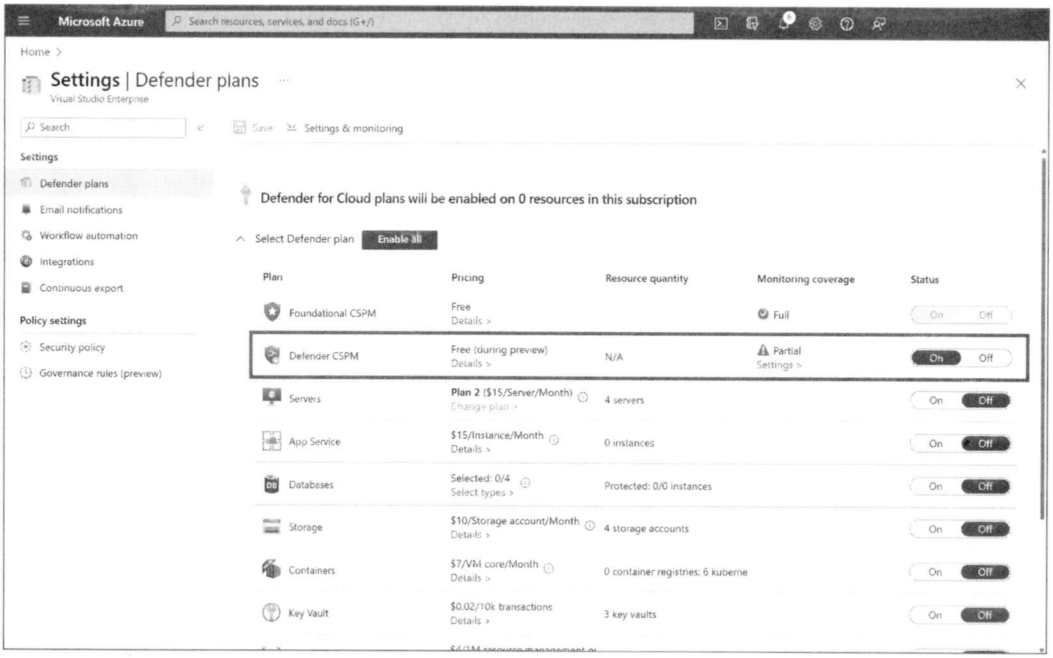

Figure 11.4   The GitHub Actions workflow can be used to programmatically enable Defender CSPM plan on your Azure subscriptions.

Although the following example fulfills the requirement for configuring GitHub Actions to enable Defender for Cloud plans across subscriptions in your Azure environment, it can be applied to achieve other use cases. To configure a workflow in GitHub actions that enables Defender for Cloud plans on your Azure subscriptions, complete the following steps:

1   Sign in to GitHub.
2   Navigate to the repository used to deploy code in your environment.

3 Select Actions.

4 On the left, select New Workflow > Configure > Simple Workflow.

5 Enter a name for the workflow, such as enablePlans.yml.

6 In Edit New File, define the steps performed as part of the workflow (figure 11.5). You can copy and paste the workflow available at https://github.com/ bmagusic/azure-security/tree/main/ch11.

7 Select Start Commit, and then click Commit New File.

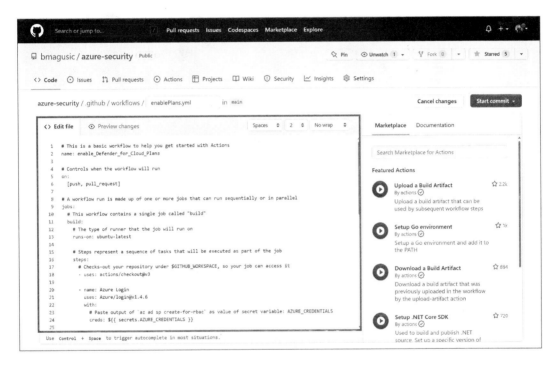

Figure 11.5   Creating a new workflow in GitHub Actions

After the workflow runs, you can see the results by selecting Actions, then clicking Update enablePlans.yml, and then selecting Build. These actions will show the log files of the workflow, like in figure 11.6.

As a result, you can see the Defender CSPM plan enabled on the Azure subscription in your environment.

Although using IaC can help streamline how you describe, deploy, and manage your public cloud infrastructure, new vulnerabilities are discovered daily. What happens when a new vulnerability is discovered in the library or binary that Bob uses in his application? What about existing vulnerabilities? As previously mentioned, there is a significant cost reduction if Bob is able to discover vulnerabilities in code early,

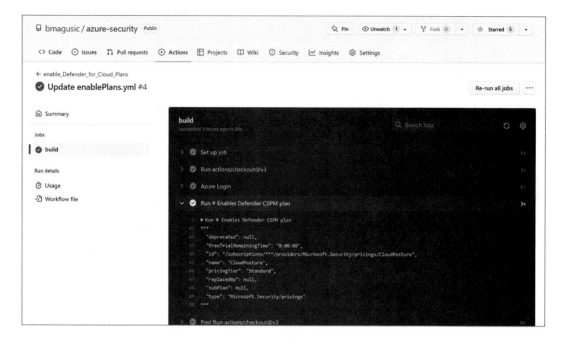

Figure 11.6   Log file output after running the workflow in GitHub Actions

before the code gets deployed in the Azure environment. In addition, developing an early defense against vulnerabilities is a much more secure approach.

Whose is responsible for fixing vulnerabilities in code that have already been discovered? Should it be whoever created the code in the first place, such as the application development team or a particular person on that team? Although whoever developed the code is best positioned to fix vulnerabilities after they've been discovered, they're not the only ones who bear the burden of responsibility.

11.3.2   Who is responsible for fixing vulnerabilities in code?

I'd like to offer a perspective that fixing security vulnerabilities in code is a shared responsibility between the developers who write code and the security teams that discover vulnerabilities in code. Having these two teams work side by side to fix these vulnerabilities is key. But at times, it's challenging to get these two teams on the same page because developers typically have a different viewpoint than security teams.

Security teams tend to view vulnerabilities from their Security Information and Event Management system of choice, such as Microsoft Sentinel (discussed in chapter 8). This perspective can reveal vulnerabilities across many applications. In contrast, developers don't typically have this end-to-end visibility and are focused mostly on the applications they develop. What can help is getting both teams on the same page by providing them with the same visibility from the same viewpoint. To achieve this, you can use *Microsoft Defender for DevOps.*

11.4   *Microsoft Defender for DevOps*

Microsoft Defender for DevOps is the newest addition to Microsoft Defender for Cloud (discussed in chapters 6 and 7). It adds to Microsoft Defender for Cloud's capabilities (figure 11.7) by allowing organizations to shift security left and providing them with centralized security management. Microsoft Defender for DevOps is not a single feature but rather a set of capabilities that come in the form of a single plan and are aimed at helping you shift security left and embed security in the software development lifecycle. For simplicity's sake, most of Defender for DevOps's capabilities can be divided into the following groupings:

- *Unified DevOps posture visibility*—Provides security insights about code, dependencies, secrets, and container images in source code repository systems
- *IaC security*—Minimizes the risk of cloud misconfigurations being deployed to production by securing IaC templates and container images
- *Code-to-cloud contextualization*—Helps you prioritize misconfigurations detected for your DevOps resources
- *Pull request annotations*—Provides visibility to developers about unresolved security findings

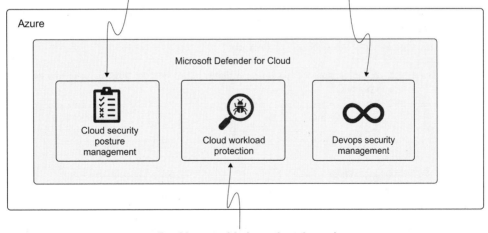

Figure 11.7   Understanding where Defender for DevOps fits among Microsoft Defender for Cloud's capabilities

Code security is not new, and existing security tools such as GitHub Advanced Security (GHAS) can help you discover vulnerabilities, secrets, and other security misconfigurations in your source code management systems. If you're already using security tools like GHAS, why do you also need Defender for DevOps? Isn't security already embedded into the development lifecycle if you're using tools like GHAS? I'd like to offer a perspective that goes back to the shared security responsibility for fixing vulnerabilities in code.

Security tools like GHAS are built primarily for developers, whereas Defender for DevOps is built to address the gap between security teams and developers. Security teams are often tasked with detecting vulnerabilities running in production environments. The value that Defender for DevOps adds is that it's able to integrate with GHAS and provide security teams with visibility of security vulnerabilities, secrets, and misconfigurations in source code management systems inside of the Defender for Cloud dashboard.

To provide security teams with this visibility, Defender for DevOps requires you to onboard your source code management systems to Defender for Cloud and install an application to your repositories called Microsoft Security DevOps. It's through this application that Defender for DevOps is able to detect secrets, vulnerabilities, and misconfigurations in your code. Therefore, to realize the full value of the capabilities in Defender for DevOps, you need to do both of the following actions:

- Onboard your source code management systems
- Install the Microsoft Security DevOps application to your repositories

While Defender for DevOps is in public preview, it supports two source code management systems—namely, GitHub and Azure DevOps. You can see the capabilities available to each of these source code management systems in table 11.1. As time passes, you can expect Microsoft to add more capabilities and support for other source code management systems, such as GitLab.

Table 11.1   A comparison of capabilities available in Defender for DevOps for source code management systems

GitHub	Azure DevOps
Security recommendations	Security recommendations
Exposed secrets	Exposed secrets
Code scanning findings	Pull request annotation status
Open source scanning vulnerabilities	

Before the Defender for DevOps plan becomes generally available, it's in public preview and available for free. So, you can validate Defender for DevOps capabilities for free before it becomes generally available, at which point it is a paid plan and you are charged according to its pricing model. While in public preview, Defender for DevOps doesn't yet support all Azure regions.

NOTE For a list of supported regions while Defender for DevOps is in public preview, you can start at http://mng.bz/KeYK.

The first pillar of capabilities in Microsoft Defender for Cloud revolves around cloud security posture management for your source code management systems, providing you with *unified DevOps posture visibility*.

11.4.1 Unified DevOps posture visibility

Cloud security posture management assesses the security posture and configurations of your cloud workloads and provides you with security best practice guidance on how to fix any misconfigurations or weaknesses. Suppose you're not adhering to the principle of least privilege or not using multifactor authentication for your repositories. Defender for DevOps assesses the security posture of your repositories and can detect misconfigurations. This capability provides you with security best practice guidance on how to harden your repositories. To assess your repositories, you need to onboard your source code management systems to Defender for Cloud.

ONBOARDING YOUR SOURCE MANAGEMENT SYSTEM

You can onboard your Azure DevOps and GitHub repositories to Defender for Cloud through a click-through wizard in the Defender for Cloud dashboard. The result of that onboarding process is the creation of a security connector. The security connector is used by Defender for Cloud to store the configuration preferences you selected during the onboarding process. It's through the security connector that Defender for Cloud is able to connect to your source code management systems and provide you with unified DevOps posture visibility for your repositories.

ONBOARDING GITHUB REPOSITORIES TO DEFENDER FOR CLOUD

To onboard your GitHub repositories to Defender for Cloud, with a user assigned a Contributor role on the Azure subscription and a Security Admin role in Defender for Cloud, complete the following steps:

1 Sign in to the Azure portal.
2 Navigate to the Microsoft Defender for Cloud dashboard.
3 Select Environment Settings.
4 Select +Add Environment, and then click GitHub.
5 Enter a name for the security connector, such as ContosoGitHub.
6 Select the Azure subscription and resource group in which the security connector is created.
7 Select the Azure region, and then click Next.

NOTE Currently, Defender for DevOps supports the following Azure regions: Central US, West Europe, and Australia East. Support for more regions is planned soon. To learn more about important upcoming changes to Defender for DevOps, you can start at http://mng.bz/9D2l.

8 Security Posture Management is enabled by default and can't be deselected. You can enable (done by default) or disable the plan that provides you with cloud workload protection capabilities for your GitHub resources.

9 Click Next: Authorize Connection.

10 Select Authorize, and then, in the pop-up that appears, click Authorize Microsoft Security DevOps. After the connection has been authorized, a green check mark is displayed with Authorized.

11 Select Install to install the Defender for DevOps app on your repositories. If you want to install the app on existing GitHub repositories and any that you create going forward, select All Repositories (figure 11.8). Alternatively, you can choose Only Selected Repositories and then select the desired repositories from the drop-down menu. Click Install. After the app has been installed, a green check mark is displayed with Installed.

12 Select Next: Review and Create.

13 Click Create.

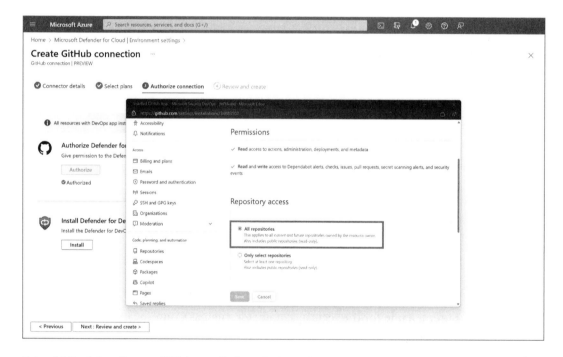

Figure 11.8   Onboarding your GitHub repositories to Defender for DevOps using the Defender for Cloud dashboard.

If you select All Repositories, it may take up to 4 hours for your GitHub repositories to appear in Environment Settings. If your organization is also using Azure DevOps as an alternative to GitHub, you can also onboard your Azure DevOps repositories to Defender for Cloud.

ONBOARDING AZURE DEVOPS REPOSITORIES TO DEFENDER FOR DEVOPS

The onboarding process for your Azure DevOps repositories is similar to the onboarding process for GitHub. The main difference is that you need to have third-party application access enabled via OAuth in your Azure DevOps. Once you've enabled third-party application access, with a user assigned a Contributor role on the Azure subscription in which the security connector is created and a Security Admin role in Defender for Cloud, complete the following steps:

1 Sign in to the Azure portal.
2 Navigate to the Microsoft Defender for Cloud dashboard.
3 Select Environment Settings.
4 Select +Add Environment, and then click Azure DevOps.
5 Enter a name for the security connector, such as ContosoADO.
6 Select the Azure subscription and resource group in which the security connector is created.
7 Select the Azure region, and then click Next: Select Plans.
8 Security Posture Management is enabled by default and can't be deselected. You can enable (done by default) or disable the plan that provides you with cloud workload protection capabilities for your ADO resources.
9 Click Next: Authorize Connection.
10 Select Authorize and then, in the pop-up menu that appears, after reading the list of required permissions, click Accept (figure 11.9).

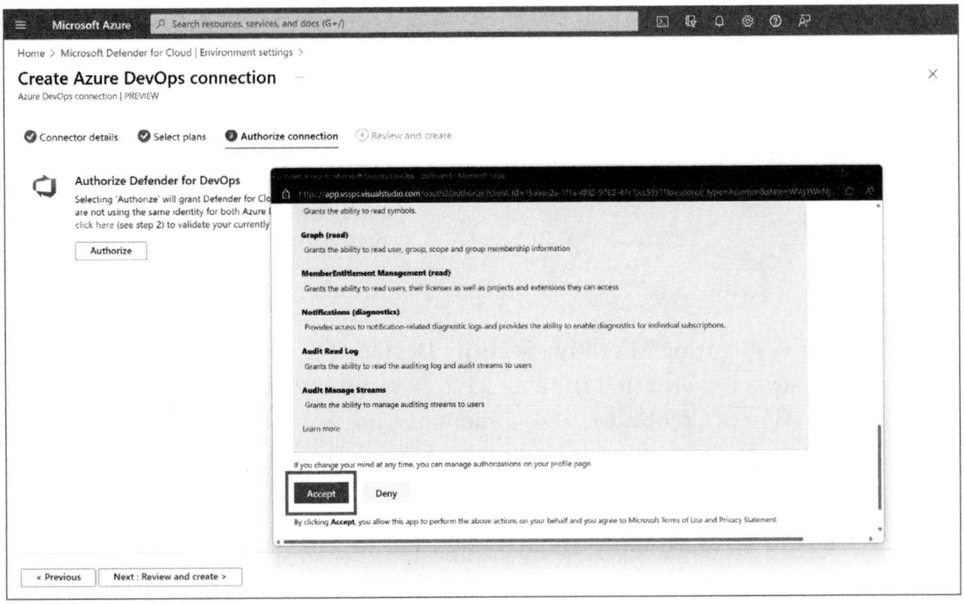

Figure 11.9 Onboarding your ADO repositories to Defender for DevOps using the Defender for Cloud dashboard

11   From the drop-down menu, select the ADO organizations to onboard.

12   If you want to discover existing ADO projects as well as any new ones you create, select Auto Discover Project. Alternatively, you can choose Selected Projects and then select the desired projects from the drop-down menu.

13   Select: Next: Review and Create.

14   Click Create.

If you selected Auto Discover Project, it may take up to 4 hours for your ADO repositories to appear in Environment Settings.

After you onboard your repositories to Defender for Cloud, you can embed security in your pipelines and deployments with the help of the *Microsoft Security DevOps* application that you installed during the onboarding process.

11.4.2 *Microsoft Security DevOps application*

Defender for DevOps provides you with an application that you can use to install, configure, and run the latest versions of static analysis tools. This application is called Microsoft Security DevOps, and it allows you to embed static analysis tools into the software development lifecycle and shift security left. Microsoft Security DevOps provides static code analysis, widely understood as static application security testing, using the open source tools listed in table 11.2. If you're using GHAS, these open source tools are provided on top of the tools GHAS uses.

Table 11.2   Open source tools used by the Microsoft Security DevOps application

Open source tool	Provides analysis of
Bandit	Python language
BinSkim	Binary—Windows, ELF
Eslint	JavaScript
Template Analyzer	ARM template, Bicep file
Terrascan	Terraform (HCL2) and Cloud Formation template, Kubernetes (JSON/YAML), Helm v3, Dockerfiles, Kustomize
Trivy	Container images, Git repositories, and file systems

When configuring Microsoft Security DevOps for Azure DevOps, in addition to the open source tools listed in table 11.2, you can also use a credential scanner (widely referred to as CredScan). The credential scanner for Azure DevOps is developed and maintained by Microsoft to prevent credentials such as passwords, SQL connection strings, and others from being leaked in source code and configuration files.

NOTE   To learn more about supported file types for credential scanning in Defender for DevOps, you can start at http://mng.bz/Wzl0.

When configuring Microsoft Security DevOps for GitHub Actions, the credential scanner you use is provided by GHAS.

11.4.3 *GitHub Advanced Security*

GHAS is a security tool with many features that can help embed security into the software development lifecycle. For simplicity's sake, most of the GHAS capabilities can be divided into the following groups:

- *Secret scanning*—Detects secrets in your repositories (such as keys or tokens)
- *Code scanning*—Scans your code for potential security vulnerabilities
- *Dependency review*—Helps you identify vulnerable versions of dependencies

These capabilities can be used to ensure that security is embedded into the software development lifecycle. As a prerequisite, you need to set up GHAS first to use Microsoft Security DevOps for GitHub.

NOTE To set up GitHub Advance Security, you can start at http://mng.bz/8rxP.

After you set up GHAS, you can proceed with configuring the Microsoft Security DevOps application for GitHub Actions.

11.4.4 *Microsoft Security DevOps for GitHub in action*

To configure the Microsoft Security DevOps application for GitHub Actions, complete the following steps:

1 Sign in to GitHub.
2 Navigate to the repository you want to configure GitHub Actions on.
3 Select Actions.
4 On the left, select New Workflow > Configure > Simple Workflow.
5 Enter a name for the workflow (such as msdevops.yml).
6 In the Edit New File, insert the following code:

```
name: MSDO windows-latest
    on:
    push:
    branches: [ main ]
    pull_request:
    branches: [ main ]
    workflow_dispatch:

    jobs:
    sample:

    # MSDO runs on windows-latest and ubuntu-latest.
    # macos-latest supporting coming soon
    runs-on: windows-latest

        steps:
        - uses: actions/checkout@v3
```

```
    - uses: actions/setup-dotnet@v3
      with:
        dotnet-version: |
          5.0.x
          6.0.x

      # Run analyzers
    - name: Run Microsoft Security DevOps Analysis
      uses: microsoft/security-devops-action@preview
      id: msdo

      # Upload alerts to the Security tab
    - name: Upload alerts to Security tab
      uses: github/codeql-action/upload-sarif@v2
      with:
        sarif_file: ${{ steps.msdo.outputs.sarifFile }}
```

7 Select Start Commit, and then click Commit New File.

After the workflow runs, the scan results are visible in GitHub. Prior to Microsoft introducing Defender for DevOps, these scan results were visible in GitHub only. With Defender for DevOps, after you onboard your GitHub repositories to Defender for DevOps, the scan results are also visible in the Defender for Cloud dashboard.

Remember the shared security responsibility model for fixing vulnerabilities in code? Defender for DevOps ensures that security teams have the same visibility in Defender for Cloud as the developers have in GitHub so that both teams can work together to fix vulnerabilities found in source code management systems.

In addition to vulnerabilities, you can use the Microsoft Security DevOps application to scan IaC templates in GitHub.

11.4.5 *IaC scanning in GitHub*

To scan IaC templates for misconfigurations, Microsoft Security DevOps uses Template Analyzer and Terrascan. Template Analyzer is used to scan and detect misconfigurations in ARM and Bicep templates. Terrascan, on the other hand, can scan and detect misconfigurations in Terraform, CloudFormation, Kubernetes, Helm, Dockerfiles, and Kustomize templates (used in Flux or ArgoCD, for those of you who are familiar with GitOps).

> **NOTE** To learn more about the Template Analyzer's built-in rules, you can start at http://mng.bz/EQmJ. To learn more about Terrascan's built-in rules, you can start at https://runterrascan.io/docs/policies/.

To configure the Microsoft Security DevOps application to discover misconfigurations in IaC templates in your GitHub repositories, complete the following steps:

1 Sign in to GitHub.

2 Navigate to the repository on which you configured the Microsoft Security DevOps.

3 Select Code, and then click github/workflows.

4 Click the msdefdevops.yml file.

5 On the left, select New Workflow, and then click Configure in Simple Workflow.

6 Enter a name for the workflow, such as msdevops.yml.

7 Select Edit File.

8 Ensure that the YAML file contains the following code:

```
name: Run Microsoft Security DevOps
uses: microsoft/security-devops-action@preview
continue-on-error: false
id: msdo
with:
    categories: 'IaC'
```

9 Select Start Commit, and then click Commit New File.

These actions ensure that you can scan IaC in GitHub with the help of the Microsoft Security DevOps application.

> **Exercise 11.1**
>
> To become more familiar with IaC scanning in Defender for DevOps, add an IaC template to your repository and use the Microsoft Security DevOps application to scan the IaC template. For the purposes of this exercise, you can use any repository that you already onboarded to Defender for DevOps.

In addition to configuring Microsoft Security DevOps for GitHub, you can also configure it for Azure DevOps.

11.4.6 *Microsoft Security DevOps for Azure DevOps in action*

To configure Microsoft Security DevOps for your ADO, using admin privileges to the ADO organization, complete the following steps:

1 Sign in to the Azure DevOps portal.

2 In the upper right corner, select Manage Extensions.

3 Using the search bar, find Microsoft Security DevOps, and then select it.

4 Select Get It Free (figure 11.10).

5 Select Install, and then, using the drop-down menu, choose the ADO organization on which you want to install the Microsoft Security DevOps application.

6 Click Install.

7 Select Proceed to Organization.

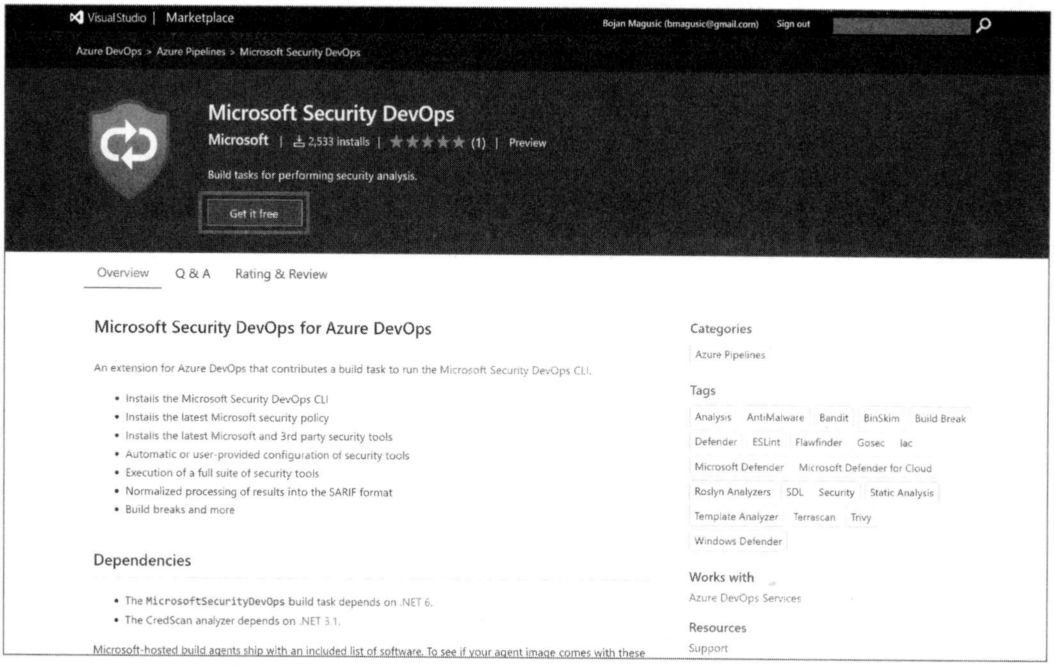

Figure 11.10   Microsoft Security DevOps extension for Azure DevOps

After you add the Microsoft Security DevOps Azure DevOps extension, you can proceed with configuring your pipelines and adding Defender for DevOps tools to provide protection for your CI/CD builds and deployments. To configure your pipelines in Azure DevOps, complete the following steps:

1 Sign in to the Azure DevOps portal.
2 Click the project you want to configure your pipelines for.
3 Select Pipeline.
4 Click New Pipeline.
5 Select Azure Repos Git, and then click the repository you want.
6 Of the available options, select Starter Pipeline, and then copy and paste the following code:

```
# Starter pipeline
    # Start with a minimal pipeline that you can customize to build
    and deploy your code.
    # Add steps that build, run tests, deploy, and more:
    # https://aka.ms/yaml
    trigger: none
    pool:
      vmImage: 'windows-latest'
    steps:
    - task: UseDotNet@2
```

```
     displayName: 'Use dotnet'
     inputs:
       version: 3.1.x
   - task: UseDotNet@2
     displayName: 'Use dotnet'
     inputs:
       version: 5.0.x
   - task: UseDotNet@2
     displayName: 'Use dotnet'
     inputs:
       version: 6.0.x
   - task: MicrosoftSecurityDevOps@1
     displayName: 'Microsoft Security DevOps'
```

7 Select Save and run.

After you configure the Microsoft Security DevOps application for Azure DevOps, you can use it to discover misconfigurations in IaC templates.

11.4.7 IaC scanning in ADO

To scan IaC templates for misconfigurations in your ADO with the Microsoft Security DevOps application, complete the following steps:

1 Sign in to Azure DevOps.
2 Click the project you want to configure IaC scanning on.
3 Select Pipeline.
4 Click the pipeline you configured the Microsoft Security DevOps application on.
5 Edit the pipeline YAML file, and ensure it contains the following code:

```
tasks: MicrosoftSecurityDevOps@1
displayName: 'Micrsooft Security DevOps'
inputs:
    categories: 'IaC'
```

6 Select Save, and then click Save again to commit the change to your main branch.

In addition to discovering misconfigurations in IaC templates, you can configure the Microsoft Security DevOps application for ADO to detect credentials and secrets.

11.4.8 Secrets scanning

Detecting secrets and misconfigurations is important because it allows you to discover vulnerabilities early on in the development lifecycle and fix them prior to these vulnerabilities getting deployed into production. To prevent secrets and credentials (such as passwords or connection strings) from being exposed, you can configure the Microsoft Security DevOps application to scan for secrets by completing the following steps:

1 Sign in to Azure DevOps.
2 Click the project you want to configure IaC scanning on.
3 Select Pipeline.

4 Click the pipeline you configured the Microsoft Security DevOps application on.

5 Edit the pipeline YAML file, and ensure it contains the following code:

```
tasks: MicrosoftSecurityDevOps@1
displayName: 'Microsoft Security DevOps'
inputs:
    categories: 'secrets'
```

6 Select Save, and then click Save again to commit the change to your main branch.

As you can see, both secrets and IaC are categories for which you can configure the Microsoft Security DevOps application.

NOTE To learn more about available categories in the Microsoft DevOps Security application, you can start at http://mng.bz/N20D.

What happens if a new zero-day vulnerability is discovered in your source code management systems or IaC templates? By their very nature, zero-day vulnerabilities are not known before they get deployed to production. This is where code-to-cloud contextualization can help.

11.4.9 Code-to-cloud contextualization

Code-to-cloud contextualization is a term used by Microsoft to refer to the integration between Defender for DevOps and Defender cloud security posture management (CSPM; discussed in chapter 6). After you onboard your repositories to Defender for DevOps, you can get insights about the repositories in other parts of Defender for Cloud, such as in the Cloud Security Explorer.

Cloud Security Explorer allows you to translate the knowledge you have of your environment into graph-based queries that you can run to determine what resources in your environment are exploitable and their business effect (figure 11.11).

Exercise 11.2

For extra practice, use the Cloud Security Explorer in Defender for Cloud to write a graph-based query that determines whether any repositories in your environment are accessible to the internet.

11.5 Cybersecurity as an infinite game

Congratulation on reaching the last chapter of this book. Writing this book has been a personally rewarding and exciting time. I feel privileged to have accumulated knowledge around Azure Security, and when I asked myself what I wanted to do with it, the timing seemed right to share this knowledge even more broadly in the form of the chapters you've read in this book. I hope you enjoyed reading this book as much (or more) as I've enjoyed writing it.

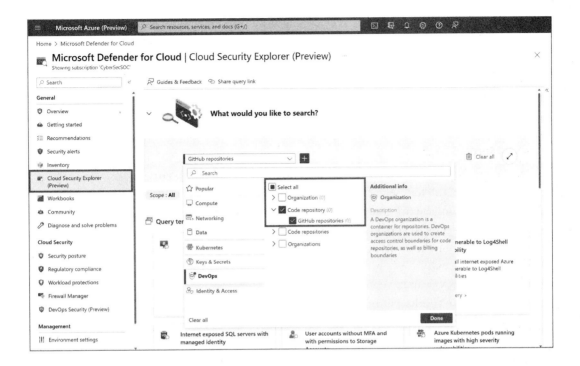

Figure 11.11 Defender for DevOps integration with Cloud Security Explorer

However, the journey that you're on with respect to Azure security shouldn't stop here. I caution you against thinking with a finite game mindset (discussed in chapter 1), where it's a winner-takes-all game. Cybersecurity is, in the end, an infinite game. So I encourage you to think differently, especially when it comes to Azure security, where the pace of innovation, agility, and complexity continues to be breathtaking. In this constantly changing game, I believe the future of Azure (and cloud) security is going to be shaped with an infinite mindset. We have to turn this game in our favor. There are many local user groups where you can get involved and interact with peers from the cybersecurity field. If you're looking to enhance your Azure security career, Microsoft's portfolio of security certifications might be of real value.

> **NOTE**   To learn more about Microsoft's security certifications, you can start at http://mng.bz/D4yE.

I hope you'll continue to learn more about Azure security. Microsoft keeps innovating, and new Azure security services are already being developed and existing ones improved based on what's working well (and less well) for organizations.

> **NOTE**   To learn more about the latest and greatest in Azure security, you can start at http://mng.bz/lW0y.

I encourage you to approach every day as an opportunity to learn, test new technologies, and challenge your assumptions about where Azure security will take you next.

11.6   Answers to exercises

Exercise 11.1

An example template for this exercise is available at http://mng.bz/BmQJ.

Exercise 11.2

1 Navigate to the Microsoft Defender for Cloud dashboard.
2 On the left, select Cloud Security Explorer.
3 From the drop-down menu, select DevOps, and then click Code Repositories.
4 Select + to add a filter.
5 From the drop-down menu, select Identity & Access and then Allows Public Access.
6 Click Search.
7 The results will populate at the bottom of the page. Click any of the displayed results to see more insights about that particular code repository.

Summary

- Shifting security further left implies embedding security and making it part of the software development lifecycle. By detecting security vulnerabilities early on—ideally, in the development stage (and much sooner than in the deployment stage)—you are able to decrease costs and avoid making resources unavailable to your users while you fix security vulnerabilities in production.
- To streamline the deployment, configuration, and management of security in your Azure environment, you can use IaC. IaC allows you to describe the desired state of your public cloud infrastructure. You can combine IaC with version control (such as Git) to track changes made to your IaC templates or code over time.
- Fixing vulnerabilities in code functions works best when the security teams tasked with detecting vulnerabilities and the developers tasked with fixing vulnerabilities in code have the same visibility of security vulnerabilities found in code.
- You can provide security teams with unified DevOps visibility of security findings across their source code management systems with the help of Microsoft Defender for DevOps. While Defender for DevOps is in public preview, you can validate its capabilities for free, but there are some limitations (for example, region support) that you need to be aware of.
- Defender for DevOps is a set of capabilities in Defender for Cloud that allows you to use parts of Defender for Cloud that you might already be familiar with (such as the Recommendations dashboard). You can combine Defender for DevOps and Defender CSPM to establish visibility of misconfigurations on your source code repository systems that you should focus on fixing first.

appendix
Setting up Azure CLI
on your machine

This appendix covers setting up Azure CLI locally on your machine, which allows you to connect to Azure and run commands on Azure resources without needing to use the Azure portal and Azure Cloud Shell. How you use Azure CLI locally on your machine is similar to how you use Azure Cloud Shell in that you run CLI commands or scripts using a terminal. Azure CLI is a cross-platform tool that you can install on Windows, Linux, and macOS.

> **NOTE** To determine which version is installed locally on your machine and if you need to update Azure CLI, run the `az --version` command.

A.1 *Setting up Azure CLI on Windows*

To install Azure CLI on Windows, it's recommended that you use an MSI, a distributable that allows you to use Azure CLI locally on your Windows machine. The MSI can be downloaded and installed, after replacing <version> with the current version of Azure CLI, from https://azcliprod.blob.core.windows.net/msi/azure -cli-<version>.msi. For example, to download the MSI distributable for Azure CLI current version 2.43.0, copy and paste https://azcliprod.blob.core.windows.net/ msi/azure-cli-2.43.0.msi in your browser.

After the MSI installer has finished downloading, you need to run it; if the installer asks whether it can make changes to your machine, click Yes. After the installer finishes, it gives you access to Azure CLI through PowerShell or Windows Command Prompt. You can run Azure CLI with the `az` command either in PowerShell or at the Windows Command Prompt (figure A.1).

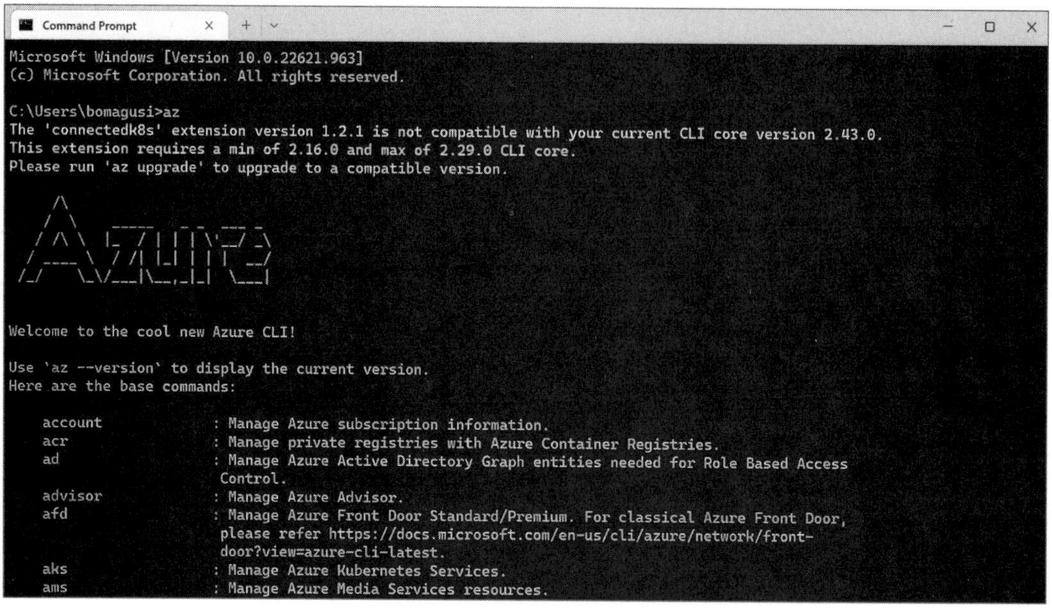

Figure A.1 Running Azure CLI from the Windows Command Prompt

After the installation process finishes, you should restart any active terminal windows for Azure CLI to work.

> **NOTE** If you encounter a problem during the installation process on Windows, you can consult some common troubleshooting tips at http://mng.bz/rWEX.

A.2 Setting up Azure CLI on Linux

When installing Azure CLI on Linux, it's recommended that you use a package manager. Using a package manager to install Azure CLI ensures you get the latest updates and guarantees the stability of CLI components. Before installing Azure CLI, confirm that there is a package for the distribution of Linux that you're using. Azure CLI has a dependency on Python (3.6.x, 3.7.x, or 3.8.x), libffi library, and OpenSSL 1.0.2.

> **NOTE** For detailed instructions on how to install Azure CLI using `apt`, `dnf`, `tdnf`, and `zypper` installation methods, you can start at http://mng.bz/V1D5.

To install the CLI on Linux, you can use `curl` and run the following command:

```
curl -L https://aka.ms/InstallAzureCli | bash
```

After the installation of CLI finishes, you should restart your shell before using Azure CLI.

> **NOTE**   If you encounter a problem during the installation process on Linux, you can consult some common troubleshooting tips at http://mng.bz/V1D5.

A.3   *Setting up Azure CLI on macOS*

When installing Azure CLI on macOS, you should use the Homebrew package manager. Using Homebrew to install Azure CLI makes it easy to keep the installation of the CLI up to date.

> **NOTE**   If you don't have Homebrew installed on you macOS, you can install it by following the instructions at https://docs.brew.sh/Installation.html.

Azure CLI has a dependency on the Homebrew Python@3.10 package and will install it. To install CLI on macOS, you can use `install` and update your Homebrew repository information by running the following command:

```
brew update && brew install azure-cli
```

> **NOTE**   If you encounter a problem during the installation process on macOS, you can consult some common troubleshooting tips at http://mng.bz/x4oB.

Getting started with Azure CLI

To help you get started with Azure CLI and complete common tasks, such as signing in and using common Azure CLI commands, you can start at http://mng.bz/AoMW.

index